CHINESE
RELIGIONS

Beliefs and Practices

The Sussex Library of Religious Beliefs and Practices

This series is intended for students of religion, social sciences and history, and for the interested layperson. It is concerned with the beliefs and practices of religions in their social, cultural and historical setting. These books will be of particular interest to Religious Studies teachers and students at universities, colleges, and high schools. Inspection copies available on request.

Published

The Ancient Egyptians   Rosalie David
Buddhism   Merv Fowler
Chinese Religions   Jeaneane Fowler and Merv Fowler
Christian Theology: The Spiritual Tradition   John Glyndwr Harris
Gnosticism   John Glyndwr Harris
Hinduism   Jeaneane Fowler
Humanism   Jeaneane Fowler
Islam   David Norcliffe
The Jews   Alan Unterman
The Protestant Reformation: Tradition and Practice   Madeleine Gray
Sikhism   W. Owen Cole and Piara Singh Sambhi
T'ai Chi Ch'üan   Jeaneane Fowler and Shifu Keith Ewers
Zen Buddhism   Merv Fowler
Zoroastrianism   Peter Clark

In preparation

The Bhagavad Gita: A text and commentary for students
   Jeaneane Fowler
Chanting in the Hillsides: Nichiren Daishonin Buddhism in Wales and the Borders   Jeaneane Fowler and Merv Fowler

Forthcoming

Hindu Goddesses   Lynn Foulston
You Reap What You Sow: Causality in the religions of the world
   Jeaneane Fowler and Merv Fowler

CHINESE RELIGIONS

Beliefs and Practices

JEANEANE AND MERV FOWLER

sussex
ACADEMIC
PRESS

BRIGHTON • *PORTLAND*

2 4 6 8 10 9 7 5 3 1

First published 2008 in Great Britain by
SUSSEX ACADEMIC PRESS
PO Box 139
Eastbourne BN24 9BP

and in the United States of America by
SUSSEX ACADEMIC PRESS
920 NE 58th Ave Suite 300
Portland, Oregon 97213–3786

British Library Cataloguing in Publication Data
A CIP catalogue record for this book is available from the British Library.

Library of Congress Cataloging-in-Publication Data

Fowler, Jeaneane D.
  Chinese religions : beliefs & practices / Jeaneane Fowler
  and Merv Fowler.
  p. cm.
  Includes bibliographical references and index.
  ISBN 978-1-84519-172-6 (pbk. : alk. paper)
  1. China—Religion. I. Fowler, Merv. II. Title.

BL1802.F69 2008
299.5′1—dc22
                                                            2007021156

Typeset by SAP, Brighton & Eastbourne.
Printed by TJ International, Padstow, Cornwall.
This book is printed on acid-free paper.

目 录

Contents

前言

Preface and Acknowledgements

Interest in the East has been considerable since the closing decades of the twentieth century. Today, in the early third millennium, we are no longer ignorant of cultures outside our western environment. Travel is so much more readily available to exotic places in the world and to far-away lands that were once only visible in textbooks. Students and the general public have also acquired a greater interest in religious cultures – perhaps because social and religious facets of life are so enmeshed that it is impossible to encounter the former without the latter. While some religious cultures of the East such as Hinduism and Buddhism are now widely studied in schools, colleges and universities as part of Religious Studies curricula, studies of Chinese religions have not featured prominently. Nevertheless, the sight of students practising T'ai Chi on the campus lawns is not so unusual, and even the BBC in Britain used a brief display of T'ai Chi as an interlude between its programmes. The practice is now very popular in leisure centres. Many home improvers and gardening enthusiasts today know a good deal about the art of arrangement according to the energies of the room, home, or grounds, or *feng-shui*, as it is known. Most individuals will be familiar with the concept of *yin* and *yang*, along with its appropriate symbol of a circle with dark and light entwined parts. These are all aspects of Chinese culture that have found their way into the West.

We were delighted to have the opportunity to extend our previous studies into the broader remit of *Chinese Religions*, having recently published works on Taoism and Buddhism. *Pathways to Immortality: An introduction to the philosophy and religion of Taoism* by Jeaneane Fowler examined, as the title suggests, Taoism as one of the religions of China. Merv Fowler's recent publication of *Zen Buddhism: Beliefs and practices* explored the origins of Japanese Zen Buddhism in the Ch'an Buddhism of China. Thus, we are extending our fields of study into this new publication, combining respective interests and writing expertise. The present book is written as an introduction to Chinese religions so that the reader requires no previous knowledge of China.

The authors would like to thank their colleagues at the Library and Learning Resources Centre of the University of Wales, Newport, especially Louise Williams and Nigel Twomey, who have been so helpful in procuring texts from inter-library loans. We would also like to thank Sarah Norman and Jamie Creswell at the Institute of Oriental Philosophy European Centre at Taplow Court, near Maidenhead, Berkshire for their support from the excellent library there. Dr Yanxia Zhao at the University of Wales, Lampeter, kindly provided the Chinese translations and characters for the chapter headings. Finally, we thank our publishers, Anthony and Anita Grahame and the team at Sussex Academic Press, for the opportunity to write this book, and for their enthusiastic support and friendly accessibility.

Perhaps the most fascinating aspect of Chinese religions is the point that they encompass almost every possible facet of spiritual experience: from the deeply meditative to the most colourful and flamboyant, from quiet serenity to loud cacophonies of music, from stillness to shamanic dance, and to the multitude of expressions between these extremes. But the one denominator that unites all is the search for harmony in life – harmony in one's own body, in family relationships, in society, between Heaven and Earth, between the living and the dead, and in the interrelated environment and wider cosmos. It is a foundation that lies in one way or another at the root of most individuals' enquiries into life.

Jeaneane and Merv Fowler
Spring 2007

Only persons possessed of humanity can truly like other people
or truly dislike them.

Honourable persons seek things within themselves.
Small-minded people, on the other hand, seek things from others.

If you rectify your own self, then even if you give no orders they
will still be carried out. If you don't rectify yourself, then even
if you do give orders they will still not be followed.

Confucius, translator Deborah Sommer

All things are complete within ourselves. There is no greater
happiness than daily to reflect within ourselves and be
sincere. Nothing comes closer to seeking humanity
than to be genuinely considerate in one's conduct.

Mencius, translator Deborah Sommer

The Tao is something miraculous. Spiritual, it has an essence;
empty, it has no form. It is unfathomable whether we
follow after it or go forth to meet it. It cannot be
found in shadow or echo. No one knows why
it is as it is. Supreme sages attained it in
antiquity; it has been transmitted to
the present by subtle means.

Chang San-feng, translator Thomas Cleary

If all things do not have emptiness in the centre, if they do not
have form as substance, if *yin* does not have *yang*, how can
they come into being? Know the light and hang on to
the dark. This is the secret of existence. Those who
know this intuitively know the wondrous
way of *Tao*.
Kuo-p'u

The Buddha appears everywhere in the ten directions,
And in the countless lands of every speck of dust
Wherein are infinite realism
The Buddha abides in all, infinitely unbounded.
The Buddha in the past cultivated an ocean
Of unbounded compassion for sentient beings,
Whom he instructed and purified
As they entered life and death.
The Buddha lives in the *dharma* realm of complex truth
Free of forms, signs, and all defilements.
When people contemplate and see his many different bodies,
All their troubles and sufferings disappear.
From the *Huayan jing*, translator George Tanabe

I delight in the Way of everyday life,
Here among the mist-veiled vines and caves of stone.
In the wilds I am footloose and free,
Lounging with my old friends the white clouds.
There's a road, but it doesn't lead to the world;
I have "no-mind", so who could bother me?
On a bed of stone, I sit through the night alone
As a full moon ascends Cold Mountain.
Han-shan, translator Deborah Sommer

Introduction

In the realm of Religious Studies in schools, colleges and universities, the exploration of Chinese Religions as a valid part of the curriculum has not been taken up as readily as it might have been, leaving the subject as a specialist discipline in certain universities. Part of the purpose of this present text is to open up the field for more general study, in the hope of encouraging interest in what is such a fascinating subject. While teaching at the University of Wales, we made it a policy to introduce students to a wide range of religious cultures during their early years of study, only selecting and deepening knowledge in the middle and later years. Of the religions of China, Ch'an Buddhism was taught as an integral facet of the study of Mahayana Buddhism. Taoism was taught as an independent course in its own right, and proved to be one of the most popular. We think that the interest generated had something to do with the attraction of the goals of harmony and balance in life, not least because the students were able to enjoy the theoretical exploration of harmony in the delightful texts of the *Tao Te Ching/ Daodejing* and the *Chuang-tzu/Zhuangzi* and the practical exploration of harmony through working with a visiting T'ai Chi Master. In the library, we found myths and legends about Chinese gods to be well-used books by those students training for teaching; these students also explored Chinese popular festivals, especially New Year, in their placements in local schools. In short, the interest in Chinese religions is already in place and the purpose of this text is to provide a broader framework for that interest.

In writing this book, however, we have not only students in colleges and undergraduates in universities in mind. So often these days, we have met people who have been to China, who are intending to go, or who have visited the many places where Chinese culture is influential, like Hong Kong. People have Chinese acquaintances and Chinese friends, are interested in Chinese food or join T'ai Chi/Taiji classes for health and relaxation. China is no longer remote, and the varied cultures of China are being displayed in a new genre of films, documentaries and articles. Our book is also written for the general reader who might be interested in deepening his or her knowledge of Chinese cultures, though the more academically minded will find it well referenced for further information and sources on many points. Nevertheless, as an introduction to Chinese religions, we have assumed no prior knowledge of our readers.

While Chinese religions are generally considered to be Confucianism, Taoism, Buddhism and popular religion, there has always been much overlap and influence from one to another of these, and there are many concepts that are common to all. Chapter 1 deals with the common origins of these overlapping cultures in what is called the *"Three Dynasties"*, the very early period that mainly predates the major religions. Chapter 2, *Rhythms of the Universe*, examines the well-known concept of *yin* and *yang*, along with the famous divination text, the *I Ching/Yijing* and the perhaps less well-known Five Agents. Chapters 1 and 2 are condensed from a more focused text on Taoism, *Pathways to Immortality: An introduction to the philosophy and religion of Taoism*, written by Jeaneane Fowler, published by Sussex Academic Press in 2005. Chapter 3 concentrates on *Confucianism*, which was to be the main state doctrine during the long years of Chinese history. The nebulous phenomenon of Classical Taoism is the subject of chapter 4, and Buddhism, which arrived in China at the dawn of the first millennium, is dealt with in chapter 5. Chapter 6 focuses on the religious and institutional aspects of Taoism. Again, more expansive focus on Taoism in both its classical and institutional expressions can be found in Jeaneane Fowler's *Pathways to Immortality*. In chapter 7, the evolution of Confucianism is taken up in its forms of Neo-Confucianism. Chapter 8 is devoted to *Ch'an Buddhism*, the precursor of Japanese Zen Buddhism. The kernel of the chapters on Buddhism is taken from two earlier works of Merv Fowler published by Sussex Academic Press, *Buddhism: Beliefs and practices* (1999) and *Zen Buddhism: Beliefs and practices* (2005) – here revised and amended for the present chapters. In chapter 9 we take up the colourful world of *Popular Religion*, while the final chapter examines the fate of religion in China and elsewhere today, and some of its influences on the West.

A few words on the romanization of Chinese characters are essential here. The Chinese language consists of a large number of pictorial symbols. The characters that compose these can be rendered into western vocalization by two methods. One is called the Wade–Giles method, and the other Pinyin. The former is the older of the two systems and has been popular in the West for many years. Hence, we are used to spellings like Taoism and, for those who have some knowledge of Taoism, Lao-tzu and Chuang-tzu, the great sages of classical Taoism. But Pinyin is becoming very popular, and is the method of romanization that is used officially in China: many writers today use this system. So Taoism becomes Daoism, Tao becomes Dao, and the sages Lao-tzu and Chuang-tzu, Laozi and Zhuangzi respectively. Sometimes, the difference is minimal or even non-existent, but on other occasions the difference is so radical that the names bear little similarity. We have debated at length about the use of one or the other or both in the text that follows.

As experienced teachers, we are aware of the difficulties for a teacher or student new to Chinese romanization. In our experience, because we taught with Wade–Giles romanization, students were unable to recognize the same name in Pinyin. Therefore, we have decided to use both forms throughout, the Wade–Giles form first, followed by Pinyin, thus Lao-tzu/Laozi. The reader who is used to one form rather than the other is then able to ignore the less familiar form. However, since texts often use one or the other and rarely both, it is critically important that the student will not be bewildered by an unfamiliar form when reading a quotation, or another book, and would not have to go through the tedious process of checking each unfamiliar name in the *Glossary* or *Index* at the end of the book. Despite the decision to use both Wade–Giles and Pinyin romanization throughout, the text would become very cumbersome should every Chinese word be written in both methods. We have therefore decided to leave some words in Wade–Giles alone, for example Taoism, and also Tao. The reader should note, however, that *Daoism* and *Dao* are the correct pronunciations. Similarly, Ch'an Buddhism in Wade–Giles becomes the very similar Chan in Pinyin, and since a whole chapter is devoted to Ch'an Buddhism, we have decided to drop the Pinyin for Ch'an here, also. Romanization throughout follows the table in the *Peoples Republic of China: Administrative Atlas*.[1]

Important here is a historical background to the religions dealt with in the book. This history is summarized in the table of dates below. It provides a backdrop for the chapters that follow, and inevitably it will be necessary for the reader to refer to it from time to time, as the dynasties, developments and characters of Chinese religious history are sometimes complex. Importantly, early dates are widely at variance, but begin to stabilize as time proceeds and records are more faithfully reliable. So we begin with the very earliest stages of Chinese prehistory and history. What seems to have occurred was the natural progression from segregated to integrated village cultures, which eventually developed into wider, more complex state cultures.

Hsia/Xia dynasty

Somewhere between 22nd–20th down to the 18th–16th centuries BCE
Legendary Yellow Emperor (traditionally 2500 BCE)

Shang (Yin) dynasty

17th–11th centuries BCE probably 1600–1027 BCE (traditionally 1766–1123 BCE)
Confirmed by archaeological findings
Religion characterized by ritual, divination and sacrifice, including human sacrifice
Ancestor veneration evident
Worship of nature via spirits
Ideas of immortality

Chou/Zhou dynasty

11th–3rd centuries BCE (c. 1027–256 BCE)
Beginnings of feudalism in China

Western Chou/Zhou

11th–8th centuries BCE probably c. 1027–771 BCE (traditionally 1122–771 BCE)
Founder King Wu
The *Chou I/Zhouyi*, the early *I Ching/Yijing*
Duke of Chou/Zhou's regency
Doctrine of the Mandate of Heaven
Beginnings of the *Five Classics*

Eastern Chou/Zhou

8th–3rd centuries BCE (c. 771–256 BCE)
Chou/Zhou King becomes central power (722–481 BCE, the "Spring and Autumn" period)
6th–5th centuries BCE: Confucius (c. 551–479 BCE)
Important intellectual and philosophical developments (6th century on)
5th–3rd centuries BCE: Warring States period

(*c.* 403–221 BCE)
Annals of Spring and Autumn
Yin–Yang and Five Agents schools
4th–3rd centuries BCE: Confucian Meng-tzu/Mengzi (371–289 BCE?)
The Yellow Emperor's Classic of Internal Medicine
Ideas of immortality widespread
Lao-tzu/Laozi and the *Tao Te Ching/Daodejing* (probably before 300 BCE)
The *Chuang-tzu/Zhuangzi* (traditionally 369–286 BCE)
Confucian Hsün-tzu/Xunzi (313–238)
The *Lie-tzu/Liezi*

During the demise of the Chou/Zhou, one state, the Ch'in/Qin, extended its power until, a few decades after the end of the Chou/Zhou, it was powerful enough to conquer all other states, so beginning the long centuries of imperial China.

Imperial China: Early Period

Ch'in/Qin dynasty
3rd century BCE (221–206 BCE)
China's first Emperor Ch'in Shih Huang-ti/Qinshi Huangdi (221–210 BCE)
Centralized, bureaucratic government based on the precepts of Legalism as the imperial doctrine
Building of the Great Wall of China
Unified system of writing introduced
Burning of books (213 BCE) and killing of Confucian scholars

Han dynasty
3rd century BCE–3rd century CE (206 BCE–220 CE)

Former (Western) Han
3rd century BCE–1st century CE (206 BCE–9 CE)
3rd century BCE: Beginnings of *fang-shih/fangshi* influence
2nd century BCE: Emperor offers sacrifices to

Confucius (195 BCE)

Introduction of competitive examinations for government posts in 165 under Emperor Wen (r. 180–157 BCE)

Confucian Tung Chung-shu/Dong Zhongshu (176–104 BCE)

Emperor Wu (140–86 BCE)

Tsou Yen/Zou Yan's coalescing of the Yin–Yang and Five Agents schools

Confucianism became the orthodox state doctrine (136 BCE)

Study of the Confucian *Classics* became compulsory (125 BCE)

Huang-Lao school of Taoism

The *Huai-nan-tzu/Huainanzi* text

Ssu-ma Ch'ien/Sima Qian's *Book of Documents*, the *Shih Chi/Shiji*

1ˢᵗ century BCE: Rise of Confucian apocryphal literature

Confucianism entered Korea, Japan and Vietnam

Confucian Yang Hsiung/Yang Xiong (53 BCE–18 CE)

Hsin/Xin dynasty   **1ˢᵗ century CE (9–23)**

Later (Eastern) Han   **1ˢᵗ–3ʳᵈ centuries CE (25–220)**

1ˢᵗ century: Buddhism introduced to China and Central Asia

Lao-tzu/Laozi deified

Sacrifices offered to Confucius by imperial decree (59)

2ⁿᵈ century: Beginnings of religious, institutional Taoism

Scripture of Great Peace text

Chang Tao-Ling/Zhang Daoling and Five Bushels of Rice Taoism

Sacrifices offered to Lao-tzu/Laozi

The Chang/Zhang brothers and Way of Great Peace Taoism

The Yellow Turbans rebellion

Kao-tsung/Gaozong the first government official to offer sacrifices to Confucius (195)
Early 3rd century: First Chinese translation of an Amitabha myth

Then followed a period of division and disunity with the:

Three Kingdoms   **3rd century (220–280)**
Wei (220–64) Shu (Han) (221–63) and Wu (222–80) kingdoms
Celestial Masters school of Taoism
Rise of Neo-Taoism
First Chinese translation of the *Lotus Sutra* (255)

The period of the Three Kingdoms was followed by a short dynasty:

Chin/Jin dynasty   **3rd–4th centuries (280–316)**

In 316, the Chin/Jin dynasty survived only in the South, while the North came under the power of non-Chinese invaders. A series of dynasties arose in the succeeding years, generally known as the Six Dynasties period:

The Six Dynasties   **4th–6th centuries (316–581)**
Separation of Chinese states
Taoism and Buddhism flourish
Decline in popularity of Confucianism
Rise of Devotional Buddhism

Southern dynasties (Chinese)   **Western Chin/Jin (265–317)**
Ko Hung/Ge Hong's *Pao-p'u-tzu/Baopuzi*
Eastern Chin/Jin 317–420
Shang-ch'ing/Shangqing Taoism
Ling-pao/Lingbao Taoism
Buddhism entered Korea (372)
Indian Buddhist Kumarajiva (344–413) translated texts, including the *Lotus Sutra* in 406, into Chinese
Buddhist texts translated into Chinese by Hui-yüan (334–416) and others

Chinese Buddhist pilgrim Fa-hien visited India (399–414)
Liu Sung/Liu Song 420–79
Lu Hsiu-ching/Lu Xiujing's first collection of Taoist scriptures
Southern Ch'i/Qi 479–502
Liang 502–57
Emperor Wu (502–50)
Buddhism entered Japan (538)
Ch'en/Chen 557–87
Growth of Buddhism
Growth of Taoism

Northern dynasties (non-Chinese)

Northern Wei 386–534
K'ou Ch'ien-chih/Kou Qianzhi began new, reformed Celestial Masters Taoism, later was invested as Celestial Master by the emperor
Taoism spread in the North
Emperor became Taoist (442)
Suppression of Buddhism (446)
T'an-luan/Tanluan (476–542) and the founding of Pure Land Buddhism
Buddhist Bodhidharma, founder of Ch'an Buddhism, arrived in China (520)
Death of Bodhidharma (532)
Eastern Wei 534–43
Western Wei 535–54
Northern Ch'i/Qi 550–77
Taoists defeated in debate by Buddhists and ordered to become Buddhists (555)
Emperor favoured Confucianism first, Taoism second and Buddhism last (569)
Suppression of Taoism (574) followed by restoration (580)
Northern Chou/Zhou 577–81
Tao-ch'o/Daochuo (562–645) developed Pure Land Buddhism
6ᵗʰ *century*: Widespread persecution of Buddhism under the Northern Chou/Zhou

Thus, from 534 a number of states existed in the North. In 577 one of these states, the Northern Chou/Zhou, succeeded in unifying the whole of the North and set up a new Sui dynasty. In 581 the whole of the South was also brought under Sui power, creating once more, an imperial China. At this point, we begin the Middle Period of imperial China that stretched from 581 to 907. A chronological outline of these years is as follows:

Imperial China: Middle Period

Sui dynasty

6th–7th centuries (581–617)
China is reunited
Beginning of golden age of Chinese Buddhism in the Sui
6th century: Buddhist T'ien-t'ai/Tiantai school founded by Hui-ssu/Huisi (515–76)
Chih-i/Zhiyi (538–97) gave the philosophy of the T'ien-t'ai/Tiantai school its definitive form
Fourth Ch'an Buddhist patriarch Tao-hsin/Daoxin (580–651)

T'ang/Tang dynasty

7th–10th centuries (617–907)
7th century: Development of Chinese Buddhist schools
Fifth Ch'an Buddhist patriarch Hung-jen/Hongren (602–75)
Lao-tzu/Laozi temple erected (620) and emperor worshipped there (624)
Taoists more influential than Buddhists (637)
Emperor T'ai-tsung/Taizong (r. 627–49) favoured Taoism
Chinese Buddhist pilgrim Hsüan-tsang/Xuanzang visited India (629–45)
Setting up of Confucian temples ordered by Emperor T'ai-tsung/Taizong (630)
Zen Buddhism first attested in Japanese chronicles (654)
Emperor K'ao-tsung/Kaozong (r. 650–83) and imperial court favoured Taoism, *Tao-Te-Ching/Daodejing* became the main text for examinations, and Taoist monasteries were built

Empress Wu Tse-t'ien/Wu Cetian (r. 684–704) favoured Buddhism over Taoism and withdrew the *Tao-Te-Ching/Daodejing* from examinations

Fa-tsang/Fazang (643–712) and the Flower Garland school of Hua-yen/Huayan. Fa-tsang/Fazang was summoned to the court of Empress Wu to explain the school's teachings (704)

Emperor Chung-tsung/Zhongzong (r. 705–9) reinstated the *Tao-Te-Ching/Daodejing* for examinations and built a Buddhist and Taoist temple in every district

Emperor Hsüan-tsung/Xuanzong favoured Taoism, elevated the *Tao-Te-Ching/Daodejing* and other Taoist material for study and bestowed honorary titles on Taoist figures of the past

Sixth Ch'an Buddhist patriarch Hui-neng (638–713) questioned the necessity for having a Buddhist master

7th–8th centuries: Buddhism at its height

8th century: Clearly defined Ch'an schools appear for the first time

Ch'an master (patriarch?) Ma-tsu/Mazu (709–788)

Emergence of Northern and Southern schools of Buddhism (732)

Fourth Hua-yen/Huayan patriarch Ch'eng-kuan/Chengkuan (738–839)

Ch'an master Pai-chang/Baizhang (749–814)

Ch'an master Kei-shan Ling-yu/Geishan Lingyou (771–853)

Beginning of Three Teachings debates (796)

Ch'an master Te-shan/Deshan (780–865)

8th–9th centuries: Great period of poetry

9th century: Persecutions of Buddhism by Emperor Wu-tsung/Wuzong (845). End of Pure Land Buddhism as a formal school in China; only Ch'an remained

Ch'an Buddhists Huang-po Hsi-yün/

Huangbo Xiyun (d. 850) and Lin-chi I-
hsüan/Linji Yixuan (d. 866)

In accordance with the pattern of previous dynasties, the greatness of
the T'ang/Tang declined. Political machinations eventually destroyed it
in the same way that they had destroyed earlier dynasties. The central
bureaucracy broke down, allowing the rise of separate states that virtually became autonomous. In 906, the T'ang/Tang dynasty finally came
to an end. In the ensuing hiatus in imperial history, disunion occurred
for almost half a century until reunification brought about the Late
Period of imperial China. Some important dates and a list of the dynasties succeeding the T'ang/Tang are as follows:

Five Dynasties

10th century (907–960)
Period of disunion
Five Northern Dynasties – Later Liang; Later
T'ang/Tang; Later Chin/Qin; Later Han; Later
Chou/Zhou
Ten Southern Kingdoms
Printing introduced
Rise of outstanding groups of Ch'an masters
continued from 9th century
Ch'an master Fa-yen/Fayan (885–958)
Ch'an master Yun-men (d. 949)
Imperial China: Late Period

Sung/Song dynasty

10th–13th centuries (960–1279)
Period of division with separate dynasties, the
Northern Sung/Song (960–1127); Southern
Sung/Song (1127–79); Chin/Qin (1115–1234);
and Liao (907–1119)
Rise of Neo-Confucianism
Decline of Buddhism

Northern Sung/Song

10th–12th centuries (960–1127)
Beginning of the cult of Ma-tsu/Mazu
First complete printing of Buddhist Canon,
known as Szcechuan edition (983)
Introduction of new Taoist rituals
Taoist inner alchemy
11th century: Revival of Confucianism

First Confucian temple built in Hanoi (1070)
Neo-Confucian master Chou Tun-i/Zhou Dunyi (1017–73)
Neo-Confucian master Shao Yung/Shao Yong (1011–77)
Neo-Confucian master Chang Tsai/Zhang Zai (1020–77)
Neo-Confucian masters Ch'eng Hao/Cheng Hao (1032–85) and Ch'eng I/Cheng Yi (1033–1107) and foundations of Orthodox Unity Taoism
Rise of Taoism under Emperor Hui-tsung/Huizong (r. 1101–25)
12th century: Northern China came under Jurchen rule (1115–1234) and fell to the Mongols in 1234

Southern Sung/Song

12th–13th centuries (1127–1279)
Neo-Confucian master Chu Hsi/Zhu Xi (1130–1200)
Neo-Confucian Practical Learning school of Ch'en Liang/Chen Liang (1143–94) and I Shi/Yi Shi (1150–1223)
13th century: Southern Sung Dynasty falls to Khubilai Khan (1279)

Yüan/Yuan dynasty

13th–14th centuries (1279–1367)
The first period of foreign, Mongol, rule. Khubilai Khan was Emperor of China (1279–1294)
Neo-Confucian Chu Hsi/Zhu Xi's notes and commentaries on the *Four Books* became the basis of the state examination system and his Neo-Confucianism became orthodox doctrine

Ming dynasty

14th–17th centuries (1368–1644)
Restoration of Chinese rule
Neo-Confucian Wang Yangming (Wang Shouren 1472–1528)
Korean Neo-Confucianists T'oegye (Yi Hwang) (1501–70) and Yulgok (Yi I 1536–84)

Neo-Confucian Lin Zhao'en (1517–98)
17th century: Fujiwara Seika (1561–1619) became the first Neo-Confucian master of the Tokugawa shogunate in Japan
Confucianism becomes prominent in Japan
Kang Hang (1567–1618) took Neo-Confucianism to Japan via Korea

Ch'ing/Qing dynasty **17th–20th centuries (1644–1911)**
Second period of rule by foreigners, the Manchus
Eastern Learning school of Neo-Confucianism founded in Korea by Choi Je-wu (1824–64)
Meiji period in Japan (1868–1912)
Prominent Confucian scholars in Japan
Decline of Confucianism (1911)

Republican China **20th century (1911–late 20th century)**
End of Imperial China and the beginning of Republican China with Sun Yat-sen's Nationalist Party
Taisho Shinshu Daizokyo edition of Chinese Buddhist Canon printed in Tokyo (1924–9)
Formation of the Communist Party (1921)
War with Japan (1937–45)
Communist Revolution of Mao Tse-tung/Mao Zedong and the People's Republic of China (1949)
Confucianism discredited and atheism became the state doctrine
1966–76 Great Proletarian Cultural Revolution
Anti-Confucius Campaign (1973–4)
Death of Chairman Mao (1976): China opened to western influence and limited expression of religion
Rise of Modern New Idealists and Modern New Rationalists Confucian schools

古代中国：三代

1 Ancient China

The Three Dynasties

The earliest strata of human existence in China are diffuse. Like those of the beginnings of many cultures, they are disguised amongst later mythological ideas with a little archaeological evidence here and there to supply some semblances of fact. The latter, for example, is evidenced by the discovery of the famous "Peking Man", a being that is dated back to the Pleistocene era, about 400,000 or 500,000 BCE. Earlier are the remains of some kind of humanoid found in China, dated to approximately a million years ago judging by fossil teeth unearthed in 1965.[1] Archaeology also supplies some facts about Stone Age and subsequent Neolithic cultures. Early Neolithic sites have been dated to around 7000–8000 BCE. Importantly, many different, regional, Neolithic sites have been found in China, illustrating very well the varied strands of culture that make up Chinese pre-history and later history. As we shall see, on these often sketchy factual strata of the past is imposed a mythological fibre: both provided the warp and weft of later Chinese beliefs and praxis.

The Chinese themselves believed their beginnings sprang from "Three Dynasties" – the Hsia/Xia, Shang and Chou/Zhou. Ancient China is normally agreed to have ended with the demise of the Chou/Zhou dynasty when feudalism gave way to imperialism. While many consider the first of the three dynasties to be mythical, the other two are certainly verifiable as we shall see below. However, it is not inconceivable that a political group known as the Hsia/Xia really existed. But the term "dynasty" is a misleading one, conjuring in the mind pictures of great palaces, considerable political and economic power, and extensive territorial control. This was certainly not the case of the earliest of the three, though we see an emerging concentration of power as time proceeded. So let us look now at each of these three dynasties in turn and, in particular, the blend of fact and myth that informs the religion of the respective periods.

The Hsia/Xia dynasty

The dates of the Hsia/Xia dynasty traditionally range from beginnings in the twenty-second to twentieth centuries BCE to its demise in the eighteenth to sixteenth centuries BCE, when it was replaced by the Shang. Chang Kwang-chih is one writer who thinks that the Hsia/Xia was a political group, and that it was parallel in time, or at least overlapping with, the Shang.[2] He identifies the Hsia/Xia with the Erh-li-t'ou/Erlitou culture of north-west Honan.[3] So while not a real "dynasty", Hsia/Xia times reflected the Neolithic village stage of existence when farming was the main occupation and dependency on agriculture was prolific. With such a dependency on the land, it was inevitable that the hostile and benign forces of nature were of great importance. From the earliest times, the forces of Earth and Heaven are likely to have been given animated powers. Archaeological discoveries from the fourth millennium BCE have found inscribed pottery, evidence of divination with animal bones, early altars and clay phallic objects, these last suggesting the possibility of worship of male ancestors.[4] If the Hsia/Xia "dynasty" existed, the same belief in animated forces within inanimate forces of nature, the use of divination to appease and work with those forces, and the ongoing life and role of the dead, are likely to have obtained in its culture. All that can be said is that they are beliefs and practices thoroughly entrenched in the better-known Shang dynasty that followed.

While there is sound evidence of Stone Age and Neolithic cultures, however, traditional Chinese prehistory is mostly legendary, full of mythical heroes and legendary emperors and sages. Of the legendary rulers of ancient China, most arising from Shang myths, the most celebrated is the figure known as the Yellow Emperor, Huang-ti/Huangdi, whom legend dates at around 2500 BCE. He is said to have had secret and divine knowledge. Although the famous sage Chuang-tzu/Zhuangzi frequently mentions the Yellow Emperor, real evidence to suggest his existence outside myth is impossible to find. But what is important about the Yellow Emperor is that traditionally he is said to have been the founder of Taoism. Although it was Lao-tzu/Laozi who gave Taoism its metaphysical and mystical emphasis, the Chinese themselves see the Yellow Emperor as beginning it all. He was one of the great sages of a Golden Age and was believed to have given the gifts of fire, ploughs and silk-looms to the Chinese. He was also reputed to hold the secrets of processes for immortality.

While the Yellow Emperor was the most important of the legendary emperors, he was preceded by Three August Ones. One of these, Fu Hsi/Fu Xi, was the founder of animal husbandry and hunting, as well as the calendar, marriage, civil administration and, some claimed, the eight trigrams that we shall meet in chapter 2. Another was the ox-headed Shen-nung/Shennong, who founded agriculture and medicine. Yü/Yu is said to have founded the Hsia/Xia dynasty and was the founder of engineering and of the essential irrigation systems for agriculture. These were characteristics cast retrospectively on mythical Hsia/Xia times from much later periods. The time of these legendary characters was known traditionally as a Golden Age when people lived in harmony with nature and with each other in a life of tranquillity and peace. Since each person's consciousness was harmonized with all other aspects of life, society needed no rules for living; these were introduced only when the Golden Age declined and the consciousness of human beings deteriorated.

Such legendary sage-rulers, then, belong to the Hsia/Xia dynasty of China, the first and partially mythical dynasty. The key to understanding its importance to the Chinese lies in the custom of veneration of ancestors. Ancestor reverence has been of crucial importance to the way in which the Chinese have ordered their lives, and this was no less the case for the great emperors as the poorest peasants. Aristocratic positions in society were hereditary, and to have an ancient lineage was essential, especially for an emperor. Thus, it was to this mythical Hsia/Xia dynasty that the great families projected legendary founders – founders that varied from a great emperor to a hero or deity. And just as immediate ancestors were felt to grant prosperity in wealth, peace and war to their descendants, so the powerful mythical founders were believed to grant even greater favours. Dynastic families or leading aristocratic families adopted or created founders and legends to support their ancestral line. The Chou/Zhou dynasty, for example, took as its ancestor Hou-chi/Huji the founder and King of Millet. Sometimes, such originating ancestors were non-human – a bird with a human voice, a fish, a bear, a mastiff. As far as we know then, the Hsia/Xia dynasty was partially legendary or semi-mythical. The third dynasty, the Chou/Zhou dynasty, justified its overthrow of the previous Shang dynasty by the point that the Shang itself had overthrown the Hsia/Xia dynasty. It was such propaganda that entrenched in the Chinese mind the existence of a first Hsia/Xia dynasty that archaeology has never positively verified.

Over time, a natural progression from segregated to integrated village cultures occurred, and these eventually developed into wider, more complex state cultures. It was the Shang dynasty that began Chinese civilization, revealing many of the basic ingredients that were to inform Chinese religions. The Chou/Zhou dynasty is even more important, for it included the age of classical China and produced some of its greatest thinkers – Confucius, Lao-tzu/Laozi and Chuang-tzu/Zhuangzi. Ancient China, then, refers to these two dynasties of the Shang and the Chou/Zhou.

The Shang dynasty

The Shang dynasty was an advanced Bronze Age culture. Traditionally, it is dated from the seventeenth to the eleventh centuries BCE, but it is more accurately dated from about 1600–1027 BCE. Its existence is well confirmed by archaeology. Despite being a literate culture, few documents survived, so that the second to first century BCE court historian, Ssu-ma Ch'ien/Sima Qian, had little to utilize in his survey of Shang history.[5] Thus, it is mainly through inscriptions, rather than texts, that knowledge about the Shang dynasty is gleaned. It was informed by the interaction of different locational cultural characteristics – what Needham called "culture-complexes".[6] These "culture-complexes" served to make the overall Shang culture multifarious. China is a vast country and the differences between North and South alone are considerable. The North, with its notable Yellow River, is temperate with warm summers, cold winters and little rainfall. The South, on the other hand, is subtropical and the rainfall heavy. It is easy to see how the different geographical circumstances might produce variants in religious beliefs and practices that were felt to be essential for the healthy agriculture of each locality. But the Shang and Chou/Zhou were mainly concentrated around the Yellow River valley, with not too extensive expanding geographical power.

It is with the Shang dynasty that we have the dawn of Chinese history. According to tradition, the last of the princes of the Hsia/Xia dynasty was a tyrant and was overthrown by one of his vassals, the Prince of Shang. This began the Shang dynasty, later to be known as the Yin dynasty, from the name of its last capital. It is likely that the people of the early Shang period also gained their living through agriculture. Needham noted that milk has been absent from the Chinese diet from ancient times, and a pastoral life is therefore unlikely even at this early period.[7] Apart from rice and millet, wheat also seems to have been cultivated. Cowrie shells were used as a means of exchange. While no books survive from the period, short inscriptions on stone or bone bear testimony to the ability to record important events, particularly religious ones. There seems to have been continuity of religious practices with pre-Shang times – a belief in ancestors, divination, and a developed sacrificial ritual – but an advance that makes the Shang dynasty the first real Chinese civilization. Archaeology has gleaned much about the period from oracle inscriptions, particularly from later Shang times. It is the later period of the Shang dynasty that has revealed an advanced Bronze Age culture, particularly through excavations at the earlier Shang capital at Anyang in the Honan valley. This mature culture had large buildings in its cities, and produced some beautifully and expertly crafted bronze utensils for religious ritual, for war, and as luxury items. It is from the decorative representations on some of these bronzes that we are able to glean something of life of the time. Indeed, the bronze work and woven silks are indicative of sensitivity to art and culture, and increased specialization.

Divination, which was focused around the king and the court diviners, was an important part of the religious cult, and the practice of it in different ways both preceded the Shang dynasty and stretched down the centuries after it. In Shang times, the undershells of tortoises and turtles or shoulder-blades of animals were heated so that the cracks could be "read" by trained priests, who would then relay the decision of the gods. We know that in early Shang times questions would be asked about the weather, the beginning of a campaign of war, setting out on a journey, the sex of an unborn child, an illness, interpretation of the king's dreams,[8] for example. However, in Sarah Allan's view, Shang divination was not so much a desire to know the outcome of a future event as an attempt to control it.[9]

In fact, there was more to Shang divinatory praxis than a first glance reveals. Keightley makes the point that Shang divination is set against a view of reality that was orderly. The hollows bored in the shell or bone were done in such a way that the diviner knew exactly where the cracks would occur.[10] The ancestors/deities to whom divination was made were part of the same rational order as humanity and, therefore, *could* be divined.[11] Smith considers that divination specialists were an occupational group in Neolithic northern China in the third millennium BCE. So by Shang times, divination had developed to a fine art.[12]

The divinatory question or statement could be made both positively and negatively on the same shell or bone. In late Shang times, statements were paired in very positive and mildly negative terms, for example, "Help will be received" (positive), and "Perhaps help will not be received" (mildly negative). The nature of the words as statements not requests is important. An increasing number of scholars are maintaining that divinations were *not* questions but statements of intent. The divination removed doubts by "posing two complementary, alternative charges in the indicative mood".[13] Thus, the statements may have been made in order to authenticate decisions already made.

By late Shang times, the king himself interpreted the cracks as a demonstration of his power and, thus, by these times inscriptions certainly show statements of the king's intent – not a wish to know what would happen in the future, but an action to ensure something would take place. According to Keightley: "Divination was not just a matter of determining what the spirits wanted; it was a way of telling the spirits what man wanted, and of seeking reassurance from the fact that the spirits had been informed."[14] Thus, the mild negativity of paired statements was abandoned, and the divining act became more of a "magical charm" against disaster.[15] Needless to say, the results of the divination always proved the king to be right. So whereas early Shang divination was concerned with disease, the harvest, dreams, hostile attack and the like, by late Shang times it was concerned mainly with statements of ritual sacrifices to be performed, or announcements of royal hunts. So as the Shang dynasty unfolded, divination inscriptions became less elaborate, more formalized, and with auspicious rather than inauspicious content. The emphasis on correct ritual sacrifice suggests that control of the future – the rains, the harvest and malign influences – must have been paramount. Ancestors and gods satisfied by sacrificial offerings would be supportive to the best kind of outcome. All these divination inscriptions are important since they were the beginnings of writing for China and East Asia, and divination, as we shall see, became a persistent characteristic of Chinese religious praxis right up to the present.

The kings of the Shang dynasty were numerous. Ssu-ma Ch'ien/Sima Qian listed thirty of them, who centred their rule in as many as seven towns at various times. Yin, near today's Anyang, was its last capital. It is with the developing Shang dynasty that we begin to see the patriarchal role of the ruler in relation to his subjects and a primitive feudalism that was to be developed in Chou/Zhou times. Like the father of a small family the king had complete control over his subjects as the wider family of his state. A hierarchized bevy of officials assisted the king, and formed the nobility, the aristocracy. Important diviners also assisted him. The role of the king was paramount in religious ritual, which took the form of leading the people in appeasing, and requesting the assistance of, the many spirits, deities and ancestors. It was critical that the sanction of these spirits and deities was obtained before any venture, and that they were appropriately thanked on its successful completion, or placated if it were to go wrong. The divinatory inquiries by the king, along with his ritual sacrifices, ceremonies and respect to ancestors, were conceived of as the most powerful form of contact with Heaven and the spirits of the other world.

Important to note is the meticulous sense of order and correctness in conducting ritual before the arrival on the historical scene of Confucius and the emphasis on moral and social order and etiquette that marked his beliefs. Such meticulous praxis in Shang times is described by Allan. She writes: "Not only did the ancestor have to be worshipped on the proper day, but the ceremony, animal or combination of animals (including humans), their preparation, number, sex, color were all suitable subjects of divination."[16] Gradually, as Allan goes on to say, ritual became increasingly ordered and codified. It is clear, too, that such prescribed order needed a large number of officials. These were aristocrats, who lived in cities and contrasted considerably with the rural peasants. They were frequently engaged in warfare, hunted, and supported the king not only in life but also in death, for they were immolated with the king when he died. Clearly life was thought to continue much the same after death as it had before for the Shang ruler and his nobility.

From what has been mentioned briefly concerning religious belief and practice, it is clear that Shang religion was pluralistic and polytheistic. It was, after all, the many nature deities and ancestral spirits that were felt to be closest to the needs of the people, and it was the forces of nature, both benign and malevolent, that were so critical to daily existence. While archaeological discoveries cannot project a philosophy of life onto physical artefacts, Donald Bishop has the following to say about the early Chinese direct experience with nature:

> Each day, as the farmer plants his fields and tills the land, he is directly aware of and apprehends the working of nature. But, and very important, intuitive insight is present also. Closely identifying himself with her, the farmer unconsciously knows or is aware of the nuances of nature. He is sensitive to her inner forces. Knowing what the day would bring weatherwise, when the right time to plant the seed is, whether the coming winter

will be harsh or mild was a skill so highly developed, among some, that it seemed as if they had an almost miraculous insight into the ways of nature or mother earth.[17]

The harmony between the human and spirit world was as essential for effective agriculture, for health, longevity and success, as the harmony between the farmer and the soil. Indeed both were part of the interrelated cosmic pattern. It was in the person of the king that harmony between Heaven and Earth was centred, and his earthly abode was the fulcrum for the important rites that linked the two: the king was the Son of Heaven and prime mediator.

To turn now to an analysis of more specific religious beliefs and practices, we need to look first at the supreme divine being that emerged during this time. He was Ti/Di, "Lord" or Shang-ti/Shangdi, "Lord-on-High". All ancestors were known as *ti/di*, but Shang-ti/Shangdi became the supreme *Ti/Di*. He was believed by the Shang to be their founder ancestor, the first and primeval ancestor spirit of the Shang aristocracy. While Shang-ti/Shangdi was the supreme god, he was not directly consulted through divination or ritual. Instead, intermediary spirits and lesser deities were summoned by the king to act as intercedents. As the supreme deity, Shang-ti/Shangdi presided over these ancestor spirits, as well as over a host of other deities of the natural world. He had the power to grant favours, but he could also bring disease. He controlled nature – the wind, rain, thunder and drought, and the king was sufficiently linked to him to be dethroned should he not rule well – so the following Chou/Zhou conquerors claimed. Every king, therefore, came to rule by the Mandate of Heaven. Since he could both reward and punish it was essential that sacrificial ritual associated with him, and with the ancestral spirits who interceded with him, was carried out meticulously. As the king presided over a hierarchized officialdom, just so Shang-ti/Shangdi presided over an equally hierarchized spiritual world: the microcosm on Earth reflected the macrocosm of Heaven.

Below Shang-ti/Shangdi, then, were the many ancestral spirits, in addition to nature deities, ghosts and even mythical monsters. Anything that went wrong in the natural order, anything that seemed strange, was seen as an omen that all was not well in the spirit world. It was here that diviners could help to ascertain the wishes of the spirits and restore balance and harmony in daily events. But it was only the ancestral spirits of the aristocracy that became divine or semi-divine beings worthy of worship. For the poorer rural peasant of the time we know little, but their ancestors, or *kuei/gui*, were probably thought of as more mundane ghosts who, nevertheless, could affect the family fortunes adversely without appropriate respect and ritual. The more remote in time ancestors became, the more they lost individual identity and blended in with the mass of others.

Then, too, there were many nature deities, gods of the sun and moon, of the rain, the wind, lakes and of clouds. But earthly gods were also very important, not only of rivers, mountains and such natural phenomena, but also of the earth itself, for gods of the soil and of the grain were more immediately effective in daily existence. Earth gods came to be distinctly parochial – a deity for the ground inhabited by each different group of people. Again, these would have been hierarchized in terms of their degree of territorial space and the prestige of the people who inhabited it. So each *home* would have its earth deity, its god of the soil. Each family *group* would have a higher-status earth god. Each community *area* would have a god; each geographical *country*; and so on until we have, at the top of the pyramid, the Earth God of the ruler himself, the ultimate Earth God. It is interesting that the ancient Chinese did not feminize their earth deities; they were clearly male, despite the emphasis on agriculture and fertility. Such a concept is perhaps indicative that the patriarchal, hierarchized life of the early Chinese people dominated societal interchange and thought at very radical levels. This is not to say that female deities were entirely absent, but they do not seem to have featured widely at this early period.

Ancient Chinese religion lacks the development of a rich mythical pantheon of deities for their role was more pragmatic.[18] At the level of the ordinary peasant it would have been the household gods and local earth gods that would have been all important, as well as the immediate ancestors. Although we have no real written evidence of the popular religion during the Shang we know that the later customs found in Chou/Zhou times obtained also in the Shang. Each household would have had a number of gods of its own, a major earth god, gods of the entrances and of the well. There would also be gods of the village and local fields. Such gods were probably more "forces" than anthropomorphized characters – another interesting feature of early Chinese religion. Perhaps the *territorial* nature of such gods rendered such amorphous characters a necessity, for once a home was destroyed, so too were its gods. Similarly, should a territory be conquered, its gods usually disappeared. Such temporality was enhanced by the fact that earth gods had their homes on the land, or in a forest, marked only by a rather temporary mound. Thus, it was difficult to anthropomorphize them in legend and myth. Then, too, while it is true to say that deities were thought of as anthropomorphized beings, there were too many of them for the characters to be really clear. Some were animals or part human, part animal. For the ordinary peasant earth gods and immediate ancestral spirits would have been seen as essential to the ongoing work in the fields. The rain was needed at the right time, and the forces of winter and summer were treated respectfully. But it would have to be claimed that we know little of the ordinary peasant in ancient China, for the information we have of the Shang and Chou/Zhou dynasties refers only to the higher class. What we do know is that the family was and always remained extremely important – what Maspero termed "the fundamental cell of ancient Chinese society".[19]

The necessary harmony between Heaven, Earth and humankind was effectuated through royal ritual. Such ritual ensured the success of the harvest, the rhythm of the seasons and of reproductive life. Ritual surrounding death was especially important. The spirit was believed to hang around the deceased until the body disintegrated. Given the importance of ancestors, the spirit was essential for the welfare of the remaining descendants, so it was prudent to keep the body as well preserved as possible so that the spirit would remain with it. The spirit, ghost or *kuei/gui*, of the deceased was offered food and drink to keep it happy in case it disturbed and harmed its living descendants. But the eventual fate of the souls of lower mortals was the earth. For aristocratic souls, Heaven and the company of Shang-ti/Shangdi were the ultimate fate. Either way, we see ideas of preservation of life energies as an important belief emerging from this era.

Since the souls of noble ancestors became *ti/di*, their tombs were filled with necessities for their lives with Shang-ti/Shangdi after death – lives very much like their earthly ones. These necessities even amounted to weapons of war and chariots, though ritual objects were also included. Human sacrifice was also practised, for wives, servants, slaves were certainly immolated with kings, as well as horses. Jade – the Chinese symbol of immortality – was also to be found in the tombs, again, to promote preservation and eternal life in Heaven. Some captives taken in war were certainly sacrificed to ancestors, and some were beheaded so that they could not rise to fight again in the world beyond death. But sacrifice was also a part of the general religious cult. Maspero called such sacrifices "marking-posts at particularly critical moments of the periodic cycle".[20] That is to say, they supported the rhythms of agricultural life as much as ancestor observance. Animal sacrifice was abundant. For the aristocracy at least all such ritual was meticulous, carried out with elaborate correctness – *li* as it came to be known.

The medium for dialogue with gods, spirits and ancestors were the shaman-diviners. The shaman-diviners had various other functions – rainmaking, exorcism, dream interpretation, fortune-telling, healing and prophesying. Then there were masters of ceremonies, or ceremonial officiants, *chu/zhu*, who made certain that proceedings and sacrifices were carried out correctly. Sorceresses were particularly employed for rain-making. The great centre of the state was the temple, and it was there that ceremonial feasts were held to which gods and ancestors were invited and entertained with meticulous ritual and correctness of ceremony. All important state events centred round the temple. Many ceremonies were connected with the agricultural year, others with the seasons, equinoxes and solstices, others, again, with ancestors. Campaigns of war, the illness of the king, strange events, all had their appropriate ceremonies.

Shamanism was probably the foundation of many religions. Palmer, for example, considers it to have been the world's first major religion,[21] beginning about eight thousand years ago in Siberia, where the term *shaman* originated, and spreading from there into many parts of Asia and to North and Central America. Such is its influence that it is not too difficult to see the traces of shamanism in many religions, for it really epitomizes humankind's deep-rooted subconscious beliefs and fears about the world in which we live.[22] Shamanism views the universe as an interconnectedness of spirit and matter. Humans live in the world of matter, along with the phenomena of that world – mountains, trees, the sun, moon, plants, rocks, animals, and so forth. It is the interconnected nature of, and interaction between, the two worlds of spirit and matter that are at the root of shamanist belief and practice. Every entity in existence is affected by the spiritual forces on the "other side". Thus, sickness, health, natural disasters, good harvests and the whole welfare of human and agricultural life are dependent on the benevolent or malevolent forces of the spirit world.

So far, this would make life a very arbitrary existence: it would be difficult to know how, when, and which spirits had been offended in order to produce bad luck, or for what reasons life was going well. It was in situations such as these that the role of shamans became crucial as mediums of contact between the physical and spiritual worlds. Through entering into a trance, they were able to come into contact with the spirits, talk to them, and mediate with them for other mortals. Or, a spirit could enter a shaman's body in order to communicate more directly to people. Shamans could ascertain why spirits were offended and, more importantly, what could be done to put things right. Indeed, it was believed that shamans could contact the spirits *before* something was undertaken so that people could proceed with their plans with confidence. Shamanism, therefore, revealed more than divination. Awareness of the fact that life and nature can so easily be hostile, and the need to tread respectfully so as not to offend the spirits of the other world, made shamans a necessary force in society.

Shamanism also involved the everyday life of the people, their ups and downs, their need to make sense of their environment, and their need to be assured that there was something they could *do* in order to make sense of life. We shall also see much later the influence of shamanism in many practices – the retained beliefs in a hierarchized pantheon of gods and spirits; in the use of magical practices, talismans and the like; in modern festivals such as Chinese New Year; and in deities such as the "Kitchen God", for example. At heart, shamanism is an attempt to gain some harmony with, and some control over, the natural forces of the world around, but "control" in the sense of being able to work *with* nature by assisting the physical and spirit worlds to return to harmony. There is an element of control over spirits by the shaman, because he or she is able to communicate with a spirit *at will*. And that interaction with a spirit is a very *ecstatic* one, not one in which the shaman is passive. For this reason shamans were often referred to as sorcerers and sorceresses, perhaps because their collective skills were multiple.[23] They were often believed to fly through the sky, visit the gods or the underworld, bring rain, exorcise demons, cure diseases and expel evil. Female shamans, especially, became associated with rain-making. Julia Ching crystallizes the meaning behind such early ritual when she says that it "pointed symbolically, and sometimes also actually to a primeval union between the human being and the gods, a union that was shamanic and ecstatic".[24]

Festivals were centred round the agricultural year, the year being divided up into unequal periods. Maspero depicted this well:

> There was the time of nature's great labour, which it was the aim of religion to help and sustain, and there was the time of her great repose, when – work in the fields ended and agricultural life suspended – nothing remained but to give thanks for harvests past and to pray for harvests to come. The festivals were linked once and for all to the proper season. Displacing them would have meant disordering the whole universe, thus bringing about unprecedented cataclysms.[25]

As Maspero pointed out, ritual was not for the benefit of individuals but to create order and harmony in the world.[26] Such ritual was undertaken by the aristocracy and local lords on behalf of all the people. Of importance to the whole population were the festivals that marked the end of winter and the beginning of spring, that came to mark the New Year – a highly auspicious occasion. It was marked with exact ritual, sacrifices, music and dancing and involved a whole series of ceremonies. Importantly, the gods of the earth had to be notified of all events. Winter forces that were antagonistic to spring and summer activity were ritualistically driven out, and the home fires ritually extinguished and taken outside, before the people left their homes to dwell in huts in their working fields. The springtime was the time for marriages. At the autumn, similar festivals and rituals marked the close of the hard work in the fields; a new fire was kindled in the homes to which the people returned and *everyone* was sealed in his or her home for the winter weeks, the doors of the houses being sealed with clay. The whole of nature was allowed to rest, to return to its natural state, free from the exactitudes of the human race. Interspersed with the many festivals and ceremonies related to agriculture were the ongoing rituals for ancestor worship, which served to reunite the deceased with their descendants. Marriages had to have the sanction of ancestors, baby sons presented to them, and initiation into manhood had to take place before them.

Archaeological discovery is continuing to build on our present information about the Shang. To date, excavations have revealed new Shang cities like that called Huanbei near modern Anyang, where a wall has been traced surrounding a city of two square miles. Huanbei dates to about the fourteenth century BCE.[27] What is interesting is that excavations in the last two decades suggest that the Shang "dynasty" consisted of many cultural centres. It may, in fact, have been small in geographical terms, though much larger culturally, the outreaches importing and exchanging both materials and ideas. Lady Hao, who features in late Shang divination inscriptions, was the wife of King Wu-ting/Wuding. Her tomb was excavated in the 1970s and was the first major tomb not to have been previously looted. The tomb revealed "195 bronze vessels, of which over a hundred were marked with Lady Hao's name. There were also 271 weapons, tools, and small bronzes, as well as 755 jade objects – the most jades ever found in a Shang tomb. The pit contained 16 human skeletons, along with six dogs. Lady Hao's bronze collection weighed over 3,500 pounds."[28] We know a good deal about Lady Hao from the divinatory inscriptions that mention her.[29]

Thus we have the Shang dynasty. Many of its customs were continued in the ensuing Chou/Zhou dynasty, which itself allows us to project back some ceremony into Shang times. Of the Shang customs and beliefs that emerge as important for future Chinese centuries, we need to single out the emphases on balance and harmony with nature, ancestor worship, harmony of heavenly spirits and earthly beings, a sense of order, divination, and magic. The belief seems to have emerged, too, that rulership was divinely permitted, provided it were morally effected. It is Keightley's view that Shang traditions and culture were still influential a millennium after the end of the dynasty. "Every idea, every pattern of thought, has its genealogy, and many of the mental habits central to Chou and Han culture can be traced back . . . to the ideas and thought of the Shang."[30] The Shang dynasty was overthrown by King Wu and broken up in parts to be given to loyal vassals. According to Chou/Zhou tradition, Heaven had withdrawn its Mandate from the tyrannical Shang kings and transferred it to the Chou/Zhou, a tributary state of the Shang.

The Chou/Zhou dynasty

The new ruler of the Chou/Zhou dynasty died shortly after the conquest of the Shang, and the state was ruled by the Duke of Chou/Zhou. He is an important figure because his rule was seen in subsequent centuries as a model one. The Chinese regarded him highly and in many ways he came to be thought of as an ideal sage-ruler. He predates Confucius by several centuries, though some Confucian ideas seem to have been pre-empted by him. The king (*wang*) was the "Son of Heaven", ruling by the Mandate of Heaven and, therefore, was mediator between Heaven and his subjects. He must rule well, lest the Mandate would be withdrawn. The conquest of the Shang had been justified by a prudent statement that the supreme Lord of Heaven had commanded the Chou/Zhou to overthrow the last, allegedly corrupt, ruler of the Shang and end his dynastic line. Bearing in mind the prevalent necessity to rule with the sanction of the supreme God and high ancestral spirits, this was a necessary tactical step to gain authenticity for the change in dynastic rule. We know little about the origins of the Chou/Zhou, but they seem to have come from the north-western part of China, to which they retired after their conquest of the Shang and other areas, ruling the country from there. In fact, things went on much as before their conquest, and areas were allowed to continue their normal existence without too much interference. The important corollary of such a policy was a good deal of continuity in religious ideas and practices. By about the eighth century BCE, a good many small states existed, each with its major walled city outside of which the peasants lived on the surrounding land.

Our knowledge of the Chou/Zhou is much more detailed than that of the Shang because they left us literary sources. Indeed in the later years of the Chou/Zhou dynasty we have the great age of classical literature. One source that tells us a good deal about everyday life is the *Book of Poetry* or *Songs*, the *Shih Ching/Shijing*, which is a record of popular songs sung in the court, as well as by ordinary folk, and also contains ceremonial hymns for special occasions. There is a *Book of Documents*, the *Shu Ching/Shujing* (or *Shang shu*), which is concerned with history, government and royal power, and is the earliest extant Chinese text. Then there is the famous *Book of Changes* the *I Ching/Yijing*; the *Book of Rites* or *Rituals*, the *Li Chi/Liji*, which gives details of ceremonies; and the *Annals of Spring and Autumn*, the *Lü-shih Ch'un-ch'iu/ Lüshih Chunqiu*, which contains a chronicle of events of the principality of Lü. Collectively, these are known as the *Five Classics*, and all pre-date Confucius. Several other historical texts, as well as the works of the philosophers of the age, contribute to our knowledge of this dynasty.

Non-textual sources are also important for our knowledge of the Chou/Zhou. Towards the end of the Shang dynasty it became fashionable to make inscriptions on bronze vessels, a fashion that reached its peak in the Western Chou/Zhou. Such inscriptions were cast in order to celebrate the appointment of, or royal favour granted to, noblemen. When the Chou/Zhou court disintegrated, the noblemen fled, leaving their inscribed vessels in underground vaults for the future; but they never returned.[31] It is interesting that Eastern Chou/Zhou bronze inscriptions celebrate personal triumphs, not royal favour, and secular rather than religious occasions.[32] Noblemen came to cast their own bronze vessels and inscribed them with their own merits for the benefit of both their ancestors and their descendants.[33]

With the consolidation of the Chou/Zhou dynasty a semi-feudal state was set up. While not a fully feudal state, the Chou/Zhou developed the proto-feudalism of the Shang considerably. The Chou/Zhou rulers had to divide the state into manageable principalities under the rulership of favoured aristocratic vassals. What prevents the Chou/Zhou dynasty from being fully feudal is the fact that these vassals did not then enfeoff their own vassals, and so on. The old Shang emphasis on ancestral lineage was never broken, and each clan felt the ties of familial and societal obligations through its own clan, and its religious obligations were to the ancestors of that clan. Inevitably, as time went on, some of the vassals became strong and others weak, and there was much annexing of the weaker territories by the stronger ones. In the eighth century BCE this went as far as creating a strong enough alliance to oust the king from his capital for a short period. After this hiatus, the Chou/Zhou regained its power which brought about the beginnings of the Eastern Chou/Zhou (as opposed to the earlier Western Chou/Zhou), since a new capital was set up in the more easterly lower Yellow River valley.

The history of the Chou/Zhou dynasty need not detain us here, but a few points might set the context for a more detailed look at the religious beliefs and practices. It was seen above that the whole Chou/Zhou dynasty was divided into Western and Eastern. The Eastern Chou/Zhou (771–256 BCE) is itself divided into two periods, the Spring and Autumn period as it is called,[34] from the eighth to the fifth centuries BCE (722–481 BCE), and then, some decades later, the Warring States period, from the fifth to the third centuries BCE (403–221 BCE). From a different point of view, the Chou/Zhou dynasty is divided into pre-classical times, from its beginning to about the mid-sixth century, and the classical period that followed. It is in the classical period that we meet the great philosophers. In the eighth century BCE, the Chou/Zhou capital was transformed to Lo-i/Luoyi, today's Loyang/Luoyang in Honan.

The Warring States period was probably enhanced by the use of iron, the Iron Age being dated roughly to the middle of the Chou/Zhou dynasty. By the time Confucius was born in the sixth century BCE four powerful states had emerged that were constantly at war in an endless struggle for further power. Increasingly, warfare became more ruthless and brutal, involving vast armies. It created a wretched existence for those caught in the middle, and a breakdown of normal social order and good government. The philosophy of Confucius was set against this backdrop. And yet, the period was not without its successes. Needham noted the advances in craft skills, the animal-drawn plough, the growth in markets, improved economy, military expertise, and irrigation, for example. He saw the period as one of political and economic consolidation.[35] Cultural changes were evident in the increased elaboration of decorated bronzes, in music, and by sophisticated artefacts that were buried with the dead. Clearly, civilized progress was accompanying the terrors of warfare.

In spite of the changes that were taking place at the political level, the religious traditions still maintained some of their earlier characteristics. The practice of hierarchizing deities and ancestors in Shang times was entrenched with the feudal system that itself had a clear, hierarchized bureaucracy. Sacrificial ceremony was as important as ever, for without it, the ruler of a state, or the king himself, might be defeated in war if he disrespected the gods. Religion and politics were, therefore, inseparable. As in Shang times, religious ceremony was a public and not personal occasion, undertaken by the nobility on behalf of the respective clans. As Maspero commented: "It was an expression of religious life in defined social grouping where each person's place was determined by his role in society – the lords to carry on the worship, the subjects to take part in it following their lord. It allowed no room whatever for personal feeling."[36] However, it is likely that the more personal problems of the peasants were presented to such as the local shaman-diviners, the sorcerers and magicians, who were believed to have power over disease, fearful phenomena, and so on, through their intercessionary powers with departed spirits and the spirits of nature.

For the early Chou/Zhou, Shang-ti/Shangdi remained the overarching, all-powerful supreme deity. Some myths about Shang-ti/Shangdi emerge from the Chou/Zhou period, and we know more about him through the poems of the *Shih Ching/Shijing*. He was a huge giant, evidenced by his occasional footprints left on earth. He had his palace in the constellation of the Great Bear, though he sometimes entertained guests on Earth. He had a family, and the ancestors of the powerful clans as his vassals. Life in his palace was thought to be the same as that in the earthly king's palace, and like the king ruled his subjects, so Shang-ti/Shangdi supervised the whole world, assisted by the *ti/di*, the deceased ancestors that were once great ministers and rulers themselves. Of these, five Lords stand out, the Blue Lord in the East, the White Lord in the West, the Red Lord in the South, the Dark Lord in the North, and the Yellow Lord, Huang-ti/Huangdi in the centre. A host of other nature gods was added.

As time went on Shang-ti/Shangdi was replaced by T'ien/Tian, "Heaven", though both deities seem to have existed as "conscious but relatively impersonal forces".[37] Later still, the name Shang-ti/Shangdi came to mean "high god" or "high gods", and a synonym of T'ien/Tian.[38] Above all, T'ien/Tian demanded moral righteousness in a ruler, and good government, for the ruler would have been chosen and, therefore, supported by him. The ruler was, thus, a vassal of God, to whom he owed constant allegiance. The idea that the earthly ruler held his place by the Mandate of Heaven was developed by the Chou/Zhou; after all, it was with such a theory that they had justified the overthrow of the Shang. Consequently, the king was sometimes called T'ien-tzu/Tianzi, "Son of Heaven". As T'ien/Tian regulated all life, so the king regulated the sacrifices and ceremonies that perpetuated that order as the

Mandate of T'ien/Tian. The king thus existed for the sake of good government of his people and linked Heaven and Earth. It was a concept that promoted further the idea of the unity of Heaven and Earth and the interconnectedness of all things. By late Chou/Zhou times Tsao Chun/Zaozhun, the god of the stove, the "Kitchen God", seems to have been well established, and was to remain an important deity throughout the centuries that followed. He was a "Master of Destinies" who kept an eye on the good and evil done by the inhabitants of the home. He kept a register of these actions and then reported them to T'ien/Tian. The length of an individual's life was then extended or reduced, depending on the report. In the words of the time: "*T'ien* inspects the people below, keeping account of their righteousness, and regulating accordingly their span of life. It is not *T'ien* who destroys men. They, by their evil doing, cut short their own lives."[39]

As in Shang times, there was an abundant number of other gods, nature spirits and ancestors, all the objects of attention in order to gain their benevolence and avert their hostility. Also to be found were the gods involved with human life – the god of marriage, of occupations, of the doors of the home, the hearth and the well, as we have seen probably existed in Shang times. It seems also that three grand deities were worshipped in Chou/Zhou times: T'ai-i/Taiyi "Grand Unity", T'ien-i/Tianyi "Heavenly Unity" and Ti-i/Diyi "Earthly Unity". These three presided over an increasingly larger hierarchized pantheon of gods. The overall God of the Earth, and the hierarchized other earth gods continued to flourish. There were also gods of the guilds of craftspeople. Belief in demons and evil forces continued, and rocks, mountains, trees, stones and swamps, and so on, were believed to be infested with demons ready to lead humans astray or devour them.[40] The actual *nature* of all these supernatural beings never really troubled the Chinese; they were all simply superhuman beings with inherent powers, but none too clearly demarcated. The fact that ancestors – once human beings themselves – became deified reveals how deities were rather like humans, not terribly reliable and prone to mood swings if all did not go well! It would have been impossible to pay respect to *all* these deities and spirits, hence the responsibility of the clan leader to conduct ceremonies for the main gods of his own clan, and the need for individuals to conduct their specific rites in their homes for their gods and ancestors. There must also have been considerable coming and disappearing of local territorial gods in a period that was infested with warfare.

Shaman-diviners remained at the official level as much as at the popular level of religion, but since there were official priests that oversaw ceremonies, the shamans were closer to the ordinary folk than the priests. They also came to be associated with ideas of immortality and the concoction of elixirs and drugs to procure it.[41] Priests assisted with ritual. Each head of state, each prince and the king himself, had his own official clergy. They were responsible for divining, for reciting prayers and carrying out sacrifices. They called the gods to the sacrifice and ceremony and had a certain amount of social esteem. Their offices were probably hereditary, the ritual prayers and ceremonial ritual being learned meticulously and passed on from generation to generation. There were different priests for different functions – prayer, sacrifice, the hunt, war, treaties and contracts, funerals, rites to the Earth God and many others. They are indicative of the importance placed on precise ritual and the proper means of conducting ceremonies involving gods, ancestors and the spirit world. Such official priests contrasted very much with the shaman-diviners, the sorcerers and sorceresses.

Because they were characterized by ecstatic dancing, trances, emotional outbursts and less precise ritual, shaman practices came to be looked on with fear and suspicion. The profession was normally a hereditary one, judging by the term for the diviners, *wu-chia/wujia*, "shaman-family" and included women as much as men. The shaman was important enough to be sacrificed if an urgent situation arose, the thought being that he could more speedily intercede for restoration of harmony! However much the nobility came to distrust and despise shamans, they were often quick to call on their services when sickness invaded a household. Specialized sorcerers were also essential for expelling evil forces such as at the great exorcism that took place at the end of winter and the beginning of spring to rid the old year of all malign evils. Then, too, princes would not venture out of their territories without a sorcerer to protect them. In later times, the state continued to have the same ambivalence in its attitude to shamans. At the popular level, however, they remained in demand. Shamans and sorcery diminished in popularity amongst the nobility by the end of the Chou/Zhou dynasty, but remained embedded in folk practices. It was particularly in the South that religious cultures clung to shamanism for a good deal longer than in the more sophisticated North. Astronomy and astrology were also a feature of religious practice. It was believed that the planets exerted their influence on human affairs.

The Chou/Zhou dynasty continued the practice of divination along late Shang lines, and diviners continued to be important in the functioning of the state. The diviners took to the use of yarrow stalks for divining, rather than the bones of animals and shells of tortoises as in

Shang times, though the richer persons might have resorted to the latter. It is likely that, as time went on, the practice of divination with yarrow sticks was adopted more widely by non-professional patricians, since it became a philosophical practice as much as a ritual one. This will be seen when the *I Ching/Yijing* is examined in detail in chapter 2. It was partly through the medium of divination that King Wu of the Chou/Zhou justified his overthrow of the Shang. As we have seen, Wu claimed that the Mandate of Heaven gave him the right to rule, instead of the unjust Shang ruler. But this meant that it was exigent to maintain harmony between state, Heaven and people. Richard Smith thus makes the point: "For this reason, the Zhou state, and all subsequent Chinese regimes made every effort to divine Heaven's will with the milfoil and turtle shell, to predict the movements of the sun, moon, stars and planets, and to interpret portents correctly. Chinese astrology, astronomy, divination and calendrical science coalesced into a single administratively-grounded science."[42] The trend in the Shang to focus divination at the court was reversed during Chou/Zhou times, and by the Spring and Autumn period, divination was widespread outside court circles.[43]

There was, thus, a good deal of continuity in religious tradition from Shang to Chou/Zhou times. The differences were of emphasis rather than radical alteration. But the religious cult became more elaborate under the Western Chou/Zhou. Ceremonies were characterized by sacrificial offerings of animals, prayer, incantation, dance and music. Ritual purity and perfection of detail were essential not to offend the gods and not to bring about disorder as a result. The specialism demanded for the ceremonies further entrenched the notion that the nobles were acting on behalf of a large number of people. But the ordinary people took no part in the proceedings. The aim was to ensure order in the world and support for the clan, not to assist individuals. It was the Earth God, in particular, who expected animal and sometimes human sacrifices – the latter usually supplied in the form of prisoners of war, though the custom of human sacrifice was certainly in decline by the later years of the Chou/Zhou. Girls were also sacrificed to the deity, the Count of the Yellow River.

No temples have been bequeathed to us by the Chou/Zhou. Where they existed, they were built of wood and clay and so have long disappeared. But in any case, apart from the palace temple and the mounds to the Earth God in the temple confines, other deities had altar mounds – usually square, since the earth was believed to be so – in open spaces. However, the temples for ancestors were always housed within a dwelling. After all, ancestors were part of the family and the clan. The royal temple, of course, was much grander than those of the nobility, though all were similar in structure. The royal temple would also have more shrines for ancestors, unlike leading nobility who would have had just three shrines for father, grandfather and great-grandfather.

Religious ritual was rhythmic; it complemented the seasons and agricultural cycles on the one hand, and the needs of ancestor worship on the other. It segmented the year[44] into patterns and balances that were predictable, and that were believed to bring about the necessary harmony for existence. By conforming to the rhythms of nature and the patterns for care and veneration of ancestors, life was ensured in a self-creative way. The religious festivals, especially, were intimately linked with agriculture. However, as feudalism gave way to imperial state control during Chou/Zhou times, and state organization reduced the number of feudal localities to ten principalities, religion shifted from the many small localities to major state centres, so removing ceremony, festival, and ritual, away from local practice.

The ritual surrounding death was extensive and meticulous. Whereas in Shang times the wives, servants, slaves, horses and a host of objects might be placed in the great tombs, fewer humans and animals were immolated with their masters in Chou/Zhou times. Often, only representations of these came to be used towards the end of the Chou/Zhou dynasty, except for the burial of kings and later emperors, when many real and costly items were placed in their tombs ready for an ancestral life with T'ien/Tian. But, being deprived of the right to sacrifice and carry out appropriate ritual to the higher gods and spirits, the fate of the souls of the peasants after death was a depressing one. In all, as Maspero commented, ideas of afterlife "were clumped together into such a confused mass in the Chinese mind that any description must falsify if it tries to define them precisely".[45] As Matthias Eder wrote: "We see that the Chinese dealt with the enigma of death in a confused way, baffled by this great dissonance in human existence."[46]

What, then, are the important features of ancient Chinese thought and practice that were a legacy for the centuries that followed? Perhaps the most important is an inherent affinity with nature and the natural world. Bodde rightly commented: "For the Chinese, this world of nature, with its mountains, its forests, its storms, its mists, has been no mere picturesque backdrop against which to stage human events. On the contrary, the world of man and the world of nature constitute one great indivisible unity."[47] Bodde considered that this perspective of nature stemmed from the agrarian nature of the Chinese existence in antiquity. So the ancient agrarian background of the Chinese instilled into their psyche a closeness to, and need for harmony with, all nature. It was a harmony that saw the same animation and spirit in nature as in human beings. Mountains, springs, rivers, trees – all had their animated forces that might or might not co-operate with humans. It was such beliefs that led to worship and propitiation of all kinds of gods and spirits through dance, chant, sorcery, sacrifice and shamanism. The corners of the home and the niches of the environment had their spirits good and evil – house deities, earth deities, territorial deities, demons, were abundant. But the dominant idea in these practices was a need to harmonize oneself, one's home, family and clan with natural and supernatural forces in order for life to run smoothly.

The ancient conception of an orderly universe in which all is harmonized in interconnected, though hierarchized, relationships is continuously reflected in Chinese thought. Nature is characterized by incessant, regular change that conforms to self-perpetuating rhythms, patterns and cycles: individual, familial and societal life needed to reflect the same kind of harmony. In social terms, the Chinese have accepted that such harmonious living does not necessarily mean equality of living. A hierarchized existence is as essential in the physical, earthly realm as in the divine or spirit world, and to experience harmony is to accept one's social position and function in society and family.

The human being is not estranged from nature or from a reality that is so ultimate that he or she is worthlessly lost. Reality is experienced in the patterns and harmonies of nature and life. Derk Bodde believed that it is ethics and not religion that inform the spiritual life of the Chinese,[48] and such a view is certainly evident in the meticulous expression of order, right behaviour, ritual practice, honour to ancestors, and so on, which have characterized Chinese life. Fulfilling the best in one's own nature and accepting the unique difference of oneself from another is what it means to be a relevant part of an interconnected and harmonized whole.

It was a belief in the capriciousness and overwhelming force that nature often displays that engendered the need to remain in harmony with nature, and to use the medium of shamans and sorcerers, as well as priests and ritual, to maintain the harmonious rhythms of familial, agricultural, political and societal life. The intimate connection between spirit and human worlds is reflected in the divinatory practices that have been popular from ancient to present times. Keightley's comment that "The oracular impulse lies deep in Chinese culture"[49] is indeed so. It is an impulse found in all kinds of expression from interpreting cracks on tortoise shells and animal bones in the ancient past, to the visits of people to the many fortune-tellers in temples in present times. Again, the underlying concept is one of creating and maintaining harmony between oneself and nature. This seems to have been the underpinning philosophy that informs Chinese beliefs. Indeed, the Chinese goal is harmony of the self with nature, and of Heaven with oneself. This would be true whether from a Taoist, Confucian or Buddhist perspective.

A profound belief in the spirits of ancestors – a belief that surfaced as much in political intrigue and status as in popular religious worship in later times – characterized ancient Chinese religion. Ancestor veneration, especially, united the living and the dead in the *present*, not in a mere remembrance of the departed by the living, but in a mutual reciprocity emerging from the belief that each could affect the other in the here and now. It is a theme that will be reiterated in the chapters to come. Ancestor veneration has been a dynamic and continuous aspect of the Chinese psyche, one that held together families, clans, territories and dynasties in the long years of Chinese history, and one that was coupled with Confucian respect for familial ties. What emerged was a reverence for the ancient past and retention of ancient beliefs in the present psyche.

The continued interaction between the living and the dead meant that the living were protected by their ancestors, who remained interested in the affairs of the family. Conversely, the dead continued to be cared for by the living, with sacrificial offerings bestowed with respectful and meticulous ritual. Ancestor veneration gave particular emphasis to the role, unity and stability of the family. It also engendered filial respect and reverence. Bishop's comments concerning this fundamental belief are particularly apt: "Religion was predicated on a view of reality as monistic and moral and a belief in the continuity of life and organic natural processes. There was no sharp division between a person and his ancestors. Life flowed on from one generation to another. Similarly, there was no absolute break between past, present and future."[50] It is important to note that ancestor reverence was essential to the ordinary person. Bodde called it "the most vital and sincere form of religious feeling" in early Chinese civilization.[51]

Veneration of ancestors was as orderly and hierarchized as the rest of the Chou/Zhou culture. The homage paid to a person in life was mirrored in equal veneration in death, reflecting that person's position and status. The importance of sons cannot be overemphasized in this patriarchal tradition where male ancestors were important for the further protection of the family. As Eder stated: "Ancestor worship is not only care for the dead; it is care for the living as well. The ancestor soul is the family's most favorably disposed guardian-god, the worship of whom at the same time enhances the social standing of the family."[52] Filial piety, or *hsiao/xiao*, was essential in this process, and respectful obedience to parents and ancestors was a particularly ethical expression of Chou/Zhou life. It was a sign of virtue, *te/de*. On the wider scale, ancestor worship linked the clan, and bound it as a religious unit as much as a social one. Thus, bringing a new bride into a home was only legitimized after a sacrifice had been made to the ancestors: a trial period had to be undergone before such an important event could take place, and before a woman could be brought into the clan. So important was ancestor reverence that it did not differ fundamentally in principle with the rich and the poor. It was just that the poor had not so many ancestors to whom they gave offerings, and the offerings were according to their means. And just as the earth gods were notified of agricultural activities, so the ancestors were notified of all events, agricultural and otherwise. Ancestor reverence was essential to all Chinese religion.

The age of the philosophers

The sixth century BCE onwards under the Chou/Zhou witnessed a superb intellectual flowering, producing some of the greatest thinkers and philosophers in the world. Throughout the Chou/Zhou dynasty there had been a growing literati, and by the sixth century BCE such intellectuals had become increasingly concerned with more abstract thought, a sense of universal order, and an ideal social order. The projection of religion to an abstract level was probably influenced by the instability of the time, the corrupt Chou/Zhou rulers, and the feeling that T'ien/Tian was impotent in the face of the suffering of so many people. The literati, then, were beginning to be concerned with naturalistic, humanistic and ethical philosophy in contrast to ritualistic religion. Coupled with this was the desire of some to withdraw from the political arena, commune with nature, and follow a more cosmic path.

Theories of *yin* and *yang*, the complementary forces that govern life and whose interaction produces all the phenomena of life, are very old, as is the theory of Five Agents that informs all life, though both were developed considerably in the late Chou/Zhou period. *Yin* and *yang* were related to the agricultural year in particular, to its festivals, and to humans themselves; indeed, the theory was expanded to explain everything in life. The Confucians and the Taoists accepted these theories of *yin* and *yang* and the Five Agents to explain the universe and the way in which they dynamically supported life. They are theories important enough to need separate and more detailed examination in chapter 2. The late Chou/Zhou period also witnessed the rise of more metaphysical thoughts about life. What was behind all the flux and change of life? Was there something behind the constant transformations of *yin* and *yang* in the cosmos? For some thinkers, wealth and power, the ritual and pomp of ceremony were rejected for a naturalistic perspective of the cosmos. Coupled with this was a belief that life was precious and should be preserved. Death was not the inevitable fate of all. Then, too, the interconnectedness of life gave it a unity, and all things in that unity had their natural "way". With Confucius, Lao-tzu/Laozi and Chuang-tzu/Zhuangzi and others in the three centuries after Confucius, comes the age of classical China, the age of the great philosophers and thinkers in Chou/Zhou times.

The end of the Chou/Zhou dynasty came in 256 BCE after years of weakening power by the central government. Its semi-feudalism was to give way to a political unity in the form of the first Chinese empire begun by the Ch'in/Qin dynasty. The following chapter will deal with the book of divination that has been handed down to us from Chou/Zhou times, the *I Ching/Yijing*, with the well-known theories of *yin* and *yang*, and the important Five Agents that inform all life.

宇宙韵律

2 Rhythms of the Universe

Since ancient times, three major theories of the cosmos, still relevant today, have informed the Chinese view of the macrocosm of the universe and the microcosm of Earth and of the human body. They are the ancient text, the *I Ching/Yijing*, the related theories of the interaction of *yin* and *yang*, and the theory of the Five Agents. Each represents a *dynamic* view of cosmological change and transformation, and can account for the universe and all the manifestations contained within it without the need to posit any primal force or divine being to set its mechanisms in motion. This chapter will examine each of these influences and assess their contribution to the various strands of Chinese religion and identity. Before doing so, however, it is important to note that the *I Ching/Yijing*, *yin* and *yang*, and the Five Agents are not ancient ideas that were frozen in time, to be studied as relics of Chinese history and philosophy. Anyone who has had experience of acupuncture or of the practice of T'ai Chi Ch'üan/Taijiquan will find that on closer scrutiny these three influences are fundamentally present.

The Book of Changes: the *I Ching/ Yijing*

The *I Ching/Yijing* is one of the oldest known books and one of China's most prestigious texts, the oldest of the *Five Classics* of ancient times. The word *I/Yi* means "transformations", "changes" and *ching/jing* means "warp", that is to say, fundamental material like the warp on a loom. The *I Ching/Yijing* began, as we shall see, as a divination text over which layers of philosophical interpretation have been placed, so that today it can be used as an oracle of processes of change in one's life and surroundings, or as a philosophical and moral guide, or both. What it isn't is a straightforward fortune-telling oracle that will define what is going to happen in the future, about which nothing can be done. Used as an oracle, it is more a response to "How can I handle the situation in which I find myself?" The *I Ching/Yijing* is able to respond to such a query because it was, and is, believed to encapsulate all the patterns and transformations of life itself. It became a pseudo-scientific text that explained the law of existence in the interrelation and interaction of all things in the universe. It was believed to relate the individual, familial, societal, or royal situation to what was happening in the cosmos, and to suggest how co-operation with the prevailing cosmic forces might best be achieved. The psychologist Carl Jung was sufficiently impressed with the *I Ching/Yijing* to write the *Foreword* to Richard Wilhelm's translation of it. Here, he suggested that at any moment in time we are caught up in the particular conditions that obtain in the universe; we are like a series of connected atoms in a cosmic whole. How we are in one moment is not isolated from the rest of the universe but reflects our degree of harmony or disharmony with cosmic norms.[1]

Historical development

The *I Ching/Yijing* that we know today is the result of thousands of years of evolution. There are two ways in which we can approach it. First is the academic one of peeling away all its varied layers to reach its origins. Then there is the traditional acceptance of the text and what it means to those who revere it in the present, and to those who have accepted it as such during the long centuries of Chinese history. Both seek to discover the origins of the hexagrams – six short broken or continuous lines placed one on top of the other – and trigrams – three short broken or continuous lines placed one on top of each other – which are the major feature of the *I Ching/Yijing*.

Let us look first at the academic understanding of the text. For this we need to go back to the ancient practices of divination that were prolific in Shang and early Chou/Zhou times discussed in chapter 1. It is with the court diviners that the *I Ching/Yijing* began. Bone and bronze inscriptions from Chou/Zhou times have the results of oracles recorded in sets of six numerals similar to the hexagrams in the *I Ching/Yijing*. But even earlier, according to Richard Smith, "there is growing evidence to support the view that the Shang Chinese developed a numerical system capable of producing linear hexagrams even prior to the inventions of trigrams", Smith also believes that these early practices of Shang times were carried out with the use of milfoil or yarrow stalks.² Exactly when this system developed into the *yin* —— —— and *yang* ——— lines that are the foundation of the *I Ching/Yijing* is uncertain, but the system was in place well before the time of Confucius and encapsulated in a text that had sixty-four hexagrams, a brief statement about the image created by each hexagram and statements concerning each of the six lines of each hexagram. This early *I Ching/Yijing* was known as the *Chou I/Zhouyi*, "*The Changes of the Chou/Zhou*". It dates perhaps to the late second or early first millennium BCE, though there is no certainty of its age. There may, indeed, have been an oral transmission of some of its contents in the prognostications and sayings of the divinators before these were committed to written form. Linguistically, the *Chou I/Zhouyi* matches the language of Western Chou/Zhou bronze inscriptions,³ so a finer date of about 825–800 BCE is possible.

The *Chou I/Zhouyi* did not have any of the accompanying commentaries that make up the *I Ching/Yijing* we know today. It was likely a document for official divination and nothing else. Thus, it seems the original text was a divination system that served the purely pragmatic need for prognostication at the Shang and Chou/Zhou royal courts. Then, the original system was developed to provide philosophical and moral content in what became the *I Ching/Yijing*. Such content is provided by what are called the *Ten Wings* (*Shih-i/Shiyi*), the ten sections that are the *Appendices* to the work.

In the traditional view of the origins and composition of the *I Ching/Yijing*, four famous figures – Fu Hsi/Fu Xi, King Wen, the Duke of Chou/Zhou, and Confucius – are credited with its composition. The first of these, Fu Hsi/Fu Xi, was probably completely legendary. We met him in chapter 1 as an ancestor of the Chinese who was credited with introducing crafts to humankind, as well as the eight trigrams that form the basis of the *I Ching/Yijing* images. One of the *Ten Wings*, *The Great Treatise* (*Ta-chuan/Dazhuan*) tells us that when Fu Hsi/Fu Xi ruled the world, "he looked upward and contemplated the images in the heavens; he looked downward and contemplated the patterns on earth. He contemplated the markings of birds and beasts and the adaptations to the regions. He proceeded directly from himself and indirectly from objects.⁴ Thus he invented the eight trigrams in order to enter into connection with the virtues of the light of the gods and to regulate the conditions of all beings."⁵ From these eight trigrams composed of broken *yin* —— —— and *yang* ——— lines the hexagrams were formed – a traditional view that entrenched the thought of the trigrams as prior to hexagrams very firmly in most minds.

Next came King Wen, who was responsible for the addition of explanations to the hexagrams – the so-called *Judgements*. Tan/Dan, the Duke of Chou/Zhou, and son of King Wen, is believed to have added comments on the individual lines of the hexagrams. The *Ten Wings*, which contain an abundance of philosophical and moral content, are traditionally attributed to Confucius and his followers. The *Ten Wings* consists of seven texts, three of which are divided into two, thus making up the ten. While their content is often contradictory and varied, and not at all suggestive of a single author, their value lies in the philosophical analyses they provide, analyses that are essential support for an otherwise terse and extremely ambiguous text. What is important about the *Ten Wings* is that they provided the Chinese with a cosmological blueprint, a means of understanding the universe and of coping with its transformations. Maspero commented that these *Ten Wings* gave the Chinese of later centuries a philosophical vocabulary, and were the only parts of the *Five Classics* to deal with metaphysics.[6] However, the *Ten Wings* provided very fertile material for all kinds of interpretations of the older text – the latter being barely understandable as time progressed. If the *I Ching/Yijing* began as a divinatory text, the *Ten Wings* transformed it into a philosophical one also. As Rutt aptly comments, "the spell was cast more by the Ten Wings than by the *Zhouyi*".[7] By Han times, the *Ten Wings* had become an accepted appendage to the *Chou I/Zhouyi*.

While the traditional view of the authorship of the *I Ching/Yijing* is academically discounted, it matters not to the Chinese and to those who value it, that there is any discrepancy over its origins, or multifarious interpretations of the text. It is in its uses as an oracle, as a text suitable for meditation and as an indicator of rhythmic cosmic change that its value is judged and, as such, it has stood the test of time. What is sought from it are the means to create harmony within the context of a dynamically changing universe, and also to locate the moment in time with the ageless process of generation and regeneration of all things. The *I Ching/Yijing* is a composite, heterogeneous collection of Chinese wisdom gathered from the dawn of time and embellished in the long years of widened wisdom and understanding of the nature of life and the cosmic patterns of time.

Reality

The view of reality epitomized by the *I Ching/Yijing* is one of incessant change. Nothing in the universe can ever be static, but is *dynamically* and *perpetually* changing. However, such change is not haphazard but rhythmic, and the rhythms of the universe are subject to certain fundamental laws that ensure its transformations conform to certain patterns. Moreover, each rhythm may be different, but all are part of an organic whole. The aim is for all these different rhythms to be in harmony. Each one of us is involved in multiple processes of transformations in the forces of living and dying. But at any one time we have degrees of harmony or disharmony with the world around us and the cosmos at large. What the *I Ching/Yijing* is believed to do is reflect the changing resonances of the cosmos. If individuals are able to discover what those resonances are at a particular point in time, then they will have the potential to bring harmony to their lives and actions. But since change characterizes everything in the universe, then the situation at one particular time in life is different from that which is coming to be; each situation is one in process, only to be changed in the succeeding moment, hour, day, or spell of life. Such changes are rhythmic, patterned, and predictable, though not predetermined. They are self-perpetuating, endless, impersonal, and independent of any agent or prime mover.

Reality is represented in the *I Ching/Yijing* by what is *firm* and what is *yielding*. The former later became *yang* and the latter *yin*, and they represent the complements of activity and receptivity, of movement and stillness: the tension between these informs all the processes of life. Throughout our daily lives, thoughts advance and subside, arise and disappear. We advance to do this or that and retreat after our efforts. We are active during the day and passive during the night. And we know that the basis of our ability to advance, to act, to think well, to achieve, is dependent on the strength we acquire in the rest and stillness we have in sleep. Receptivity and passivity, stillness and calm are therefore the dynamic processes of change that prepare us for the more active times of our daily lives. And the tension between the two will always operate to create new experiences or different nuances of old ones. Reality, then, is the changes brought about by the dynamic tensions between the firm and the yielding. It is because things are coming into being and never static that events in the process of shaping up are perceptible. The *I Ching/Yijing* ascertains what is coming to be and offers guidance as to how to balance the activity and receptivity of the self in order to harmonize with events in a positive way.

The *I Ching/Yijing* accepts the firm as Heaven and the yielding as Earth. Heaven is the active, creative and energizing principle, eventually *yang*, and Earth is the yielding, the receptive and passive, eventually *yin*.

Heaven is light, incorporeal, the macrocosm and determines what happens on Earth. Earth is its complement, dark, corporeal and the microcosm that is receptive to Heaven. The complementary interplay between these opposites is the basis of all the other possibilities of change. Each individual is a microcosmic image correspondent to the macrocosm, a miniature of the universe. The *I Ching/Yijing* acts as the medium that illuminates the interchange between them.

The Eight Trigrams (Pa-kua/Bagua)

While it is important to bear in mind that the use of sixty-four hexagrams may have been prior to, or was contemporaneous with, the trigrams, it is easier to deal first with the trigrams. Each is an image of a process of change, composed of three lines of *yin* and/or *yang*. Like the hexagrams, trigrams are always read from the bottom, the bottom line representing Earth, the top one Heaven, and the middle one humanity. There are only eight different possible combinations, but it is the arrangement of them that is important. The earlier, primal, former or prior to Heaven arrangement is attributed to Fu Hsi/Fu Xi, and is an important symbol in some religious ritual. A second arrangement is traditionally that of King Wen, who rearranged the trigrams to represent motions of change through the year. These will be important points to bear in mind, since we shall return to them in the context of alchemy in chapter 6.

The two most important trigrams are *Ch'ien/Qian The Creative*, which consists of three *yang* lines ☰ . It is the symbol of Heaven, strength, goodness and masculinity. Its complementary opposite is *K'un/Kun The Receptive*, which has three *yin* lines ☷ , representing pure femininity, receptivity, passivity, devotion, and is the trigram of Earth. All the other trigrams are the "sons" and "daughters" formed from these two as the "father" and "mother". So we have *Tui/Dui The Joyous* ☱ , whose image is a lake, and whose two firm lines underlying the broken one makes the trigram one of stability. Thus, it is associated with joy, happiness and wisdom. *Li The Clinging*, whose image is fire, has a dark, *yin* line enclosed between two firm lines ☲ . It is thus a light-giving trigram associated with the sun, heat, evolution of consciousness, devotion and purity. *Chen/Zhen The Arousing* has the image of thunder and has a firm lowest line with two *yin* lines above it ☳ . It represents energy and light rising up, reaching through darkness, so it is associated with movement, speed, energy, power and impulse. Conversely, *Sun The Gentle* has a yielding bottom line with two firm lines above ☰. The images of the trigram are wind and wood, and it is a gentle trigram related to what is spiritual, to intellect and to the mind. It is also penetrating like the wind. *K'an/Kan The Abysmal* has water as its image. In this trigram, since the firm line representing light is enclosed in darkness ☵, the whole trigram is one of winter, darkness, instability and danger. The last trigram is *Ken/Gen Keeping Still*, whose image is the mountain. It signifies standing fast, with two yielding lines supporting the uppermost firm one, thus suggesting passive immobility at its roots ☶.

Importantly, none of the lines making up each trigram is static. The firm line is actively pulling apart until it divides and changes into a yielding line. The yielding line is moving together until it joins to form a firm line. Thus, change is operating all the time within the trigrams; they represent a fluid not static picture, constantly changing into each other and so depicting the flow of cosmic change. Each has its positive and negative possibilities, which would be relevant only to a specific situation in time.

The hexagrams

Traditionally and scholastically it has always been believed that the hexagrams were derived from combining two trigrams into the sixty-four possible combinations. However, it is possible that hexagrams were used before trigrams, the latter becoming important later for the understanding of the hexagrams.[8] It is also possible that hexagrams and trigrams were coexistent from very early times.[9] Each hexagram is given a "tag", a name, often relating to life situations, like *Youthful Folly*, *Opposition*, *Possession*, or social situations such as *The Marrying Maiden*, *The Well*, *Fellowship with Men*. Others depict personal characteristics like *Modesty*, *Enthusiasm* and *Grace*. The degree to which people relate the names to the explication of the nature of the hexagrams varies. Some, like Rutt, argue that they have no relation at all.[10] Others, like Stephen Karcher, see the tags as critically important in understanding the lines of the hexagrams.[11] Each hexagram also has a statement attached to it, and this, too, is variously rejected as having little to do with the lines of a hexagram, or as being critical to its understanding.

The traditional order of the hexagrams[12] is believed to alternate in patterns representing the rhythms of *yin* and *yang* in the cosmos, in life and in nature. Such rhythms are believed to be sequential, mirroring the ebb and flow of existence. Their specific order has a tendency to reflect opposing forces, each juxtaposed with the one before and the one following, in contrasting ways. This is because the pendulum of life experiences is never static. At each high point it has to swing back in the other direction, though perhaps with momentary rest before the change in the opposite direction occurs. So success can only be followed by failure, strife by peace, beginning by completion, abundance by scarcity, creativity by passivity and so on: the pendulum always swings back the other way. Understanding such a principle of life encourages optimism in moments of despair and caution in excessive success. The hexagram that emerges following consultation of the *I Ching/Yijing* places the individual psyche in the appropriate context of such ebb and flow, such process of change and transformation indicating in which direction life is flowing, and how best to deal with it. The hexagrams express very finely the permutations of transformations extant in the world of phenomena: they are images of states of change.

The intricacies of reading an individual hexagram need not detain us here, but it is worth pointing out that all its aspects are used to interpret its advice – the lower and upper trigrams that it contains, the "nuclear" trigrams within it,[13] the nature and position of each line and their relation to other lines, the lines that are in rapid processes of change from *yin* to *yang* or *vice versa*, for example. The whole balance of *yin* and *yang* in the hexagram is also crucially important to its interpretation.

Consulting the I Ching/Yijing

The traditional method of consulting the *I Ching/Yijing* is by the use of yarrow or milfoil sticks. It is the most complicated of methods using fifty sticks (though one is put to one side), and through divisions, subdivisions and countings the hexagram is built up from the bottom. It is the system used for ritual in temples.[14] This traditional method has been adapted for modern use in a number of ways. Perhaps the simplest is the extraction of one stick from a container of them. Each stick is numbered and the one drawn will provide the appropriate hexagram. But more common is the use of just twelve sticks, or of three coins. With the sticks, six bear a *yin* line and six a *yang* one. Six sticks are then drawn one by one to build up the hexagram from the bottom. The coin-tossing method, according to tradition, goes back to the fourth century BCE. Today, in the West, three like coins are used, and the "head" side is regarded as *yang* and the reverse side as *yin*.[15] The *yang* side of the coin is given three points and the *yin* side two. The three coins are then thrown down six times, the addition of their values resulting in a hexagram.[16] It is when the coins are cast, or the stick drawn, that is to say as the process is being carried out, that the statement of need is directed to the book.

The *I Ching/Yijing* has at the basis of its metaphysics the idea that the microcosm of Earth is a reflection of the macrocosm and that what happens in one affects the other. Neither is static, but interactive and mutually dynamic. Thus, there can be no fixed laws, but equally so, there is nothing chaotic. Between these two extremes there are ever-changing patterns and rhythms that inform growth and decay, coming and going, resisting and yielding, expansion and contraction, and so on. Going with the flow of things, rather than in the face of them, is the sensible means by which to live life. To the Chinese, the sage was the embodiment of one who could live life in this way. Like water that could find its way around obstacles, the sage travelled through life in the direction of the momentary cosmic flow of things, in harmony with the ever-transforming universe.

Joseph Needham called the *I Ching/Yijing* a "cosmic filing-system"[17] and a "mischievous handicap"[18] that rather prevented scientific development. *Scientifically* this may well be true. But those who use the *I Ching/Yijing* are hardly looking for scientific answers. On the contrary, they are trying to discover the degree to which their present space–time situation harmonizes with the interconnected cosmos. To assess the *I Ching/Yijing* scientifically, or even too academically, is to miss the *spiritual* connectedness with the cosmos that its proponents wish to achieve. The fact that it has stood the test of three millennia of time is quite remarkable, and is indicative of its continuing value.

Yin and *Yang*

If there is one theory emerging from China that is widely known in the West it is surely that of *yin* and *yang*, the theory of complementary opposites. Perhaps this is because, as one writer says, it is a concept that is "one of the most fruitful and useful ever devised by the mind of man for making sense out of the infinite multitude of diverse facts about the universe".[19] Its appeal thus has a good deal to do with our common-sense observations about the world around us, our understanding of which is based on relationships between opposites. We know what darkness is, for example, because we know what its opposite is, and *vice versa*. The Chinese view of the cosmos, of the heavens, Earth, human beings, the rhythms of day and night, the seasons, the phases of the day

– indeed all life, came under the dynamic power of *yin* and *yang* in all phenomena.

The Chinese were from antiquity a people who felt deeply about the rhythm of the seasons and the expression of nature in rhythmic patterns. Their whole existence depended on their ability to harmonize their society, agriculture and religion with the deeper rhythmic patterns of the cosmos. Even Chinese history seemed to follow the natural swing of the pendulum from one polarity to its opposite. Sarah Allan notes this in the early history of China. The Hsia/Xia, she writes, "were originally the mythical inverse of the Shang, associated with water, dragons, the moons, darkness and death, as opposed to the fire, birds, suns, light and life, with which the Shang were associated".[20] The waning and waxing of dynastic rule, of war and peace, of upheaval and stability are the *yin* and *yang* of Chinese historical patterns.

The origins of yin *and* yang

According to tradition, *yin* and *yang* were discovered by Fu Hsi/Fu Xi, the mythical founder of the Hsia/Xia dynasty, since they figured in the eight trigrams. However, the terms *yin* and *yang* were not used for some time: the earliest strata of the *I Ching/Yijing*, for example, does not refer to them. Nevertheless, the *idea* of bipolarity of two forces is clear from very early times. Indeed, according to Allan: "Within the Shang myth system, there was also a dualism, the antecedent of later *yin-yang* theory, in which the suns, sky, birds, east, life, the Lord on High were opposed to the moons, watery underworld, dragons, west, death, the Lord below".[21] Allan thus believes that the origins of the *yin* and *yang* theory lie in Shang times.[22] It is clear, too, that the whole concept of balance and rhythm that informs the *I Ching/Yijing*, and its hexagrams and trigrams, blends well with the *yin* and *yang* theory, even if we do not know when the two were first associated, though early Han times are the most likely. What we do know is that there is little evidence of the terms *yin* and *yang* before the school of Tsou Yen/Zou Yan who developed it.

In the late Warring States period of the fifth to third centuries BCE many different schools of philosophy sprang up. One school was the *Yin–Yang* school, and another the Five Agents school. By Han dynasty times, both these were thoroughly coalesced. The *Yin–Yang* school probably originated in the realms of those who practised magical arts, divination, magic and the like. These were the *fang-shih/fangshi* who were highly important in the development of religious praxis in many forms. The founder of the *Yin–Yang* school, Tsou Yen/Zou Yan, is mentioned by Ssu-ma Ch'ien/Sima Qian in his historical *Shih Chi/Shiji* about the end of the second and beginning of the first centuries BCE. Indeed, this is the only source to mention Tsou Yen/Zou Yan by name; references to him are otherwise indirect, and none of his own writings is extant. He is likely to have been a Confucian, and this is perhaps one reason why his theory of *yin* and *yang* was wholeheartedly accepted by Confucians.[23] The *Shih Chi/Shiji* says of him:

> Thereupon he examined deeply into the phenomena of increase and decrease of the yin and the yang, and wrote essays totalling more than one hundred thousand words about strange permutations, and about the cycles of the great Sages from beginning to end. His words were grandiose and fanciful. He had first to examine small objects, and extended this to large ones until he reached what was without limit. . . . Moreover, he followed the great events in the rise and fall of ages, and by means of their omens and (an examination into their) institutions, extended his survey backward to the time when Heaven and Earth had not yet been born, to what was profound and abstruse and not to be examined.[24]

What Tsou Yen/Zou Yan did was to set out a cosmology that defined the whole universe as the intermingling of the two forces of *yin* and *yang* and, as we shall see below, of the Five Agents.

Yin

Yin, often referred to as "White Tiger", is the yielding, receptive aspect in life. Thus it is the feminine essence, is gentle and beautiful, but also negative, cold and dark. It is autumn and winter time, from which its opposite emerges in the spring. Thus, cosmologically, it is the chaos of darkness from whence the light of creation was born: in some schools, it therefore precedes *yang* as the eternally creative element from which *yang* emerges. *Yin* is the mother aspect, passive, soft, wet, the flesh of the body, the shady, cool side of a valley, mountain, river bank or garden. Yet, such general passivity and receptivity are not weaknesses, for they can be more enduring than their opposite of *yang*.

Yin is the valley and the womb; it is depth and descent, receiving and accepting; yet from it all emerges. Jean Cooper puts this rather well when she says: "It is because it is the lowest, humblest place that the valley receives the full force of the waters which fall into it from high *yang* places. Majestic waterfalls and turbulent mountain torrents, for all their power, come down to the lowly and are absorbed by it and converted into the deep-flowing, broad, quiet and irresistible forces of the rivers, lakes and oceans, the *yin* principle."[25] *Yin* is also square, its strict sides symbolizing immobility and passivity. The moon is *yin*, as is silver, the colour connected with the moon. Pearls, since they are obtained from water, are also *yin*. The physical spirits that survive after death are called *kuei/gui*, and since they return into the earth, they too are *yin*. In the human being, instinct, emotion and intuition are *yin*, as well as flexibility, openness and calmness. *Yin* is everything that is esoteric. Negatively, however, it can be weakness and stasis, pettiness and small-mindedness. The eighteenth-century Taoist Liu I-ming/Liu Yiming had the following to say about the flexibility of character that is the nature of *yin* in a person:

> Flexibility is docility, yielding, self-mastery, self-restraint, self-efface-ment, humility, selflessness, consideration of others, absence of arbitrariness, pure simplicity, genuineness. Those who use flexibility well appear to lack what they are in fact endowed with, appear to be empty when they are in fact fulfilled. They do not take revenge when offended. They seek spiritual riches and are aloof of mundane riches; they do not contend with people of the world.[26]

Yang

Yang emerges from *yin* as the light that arises from darkness. It is the spirit, the intellect, the father, and thus male, and is the active principle in life. It is aggressive, hard, heat, dryness, the bone of the body, the hard, dry stone of the home, the south, sunny side of a valley or river bank, and the spring and summer time of the year. It is symbolized by the sun and is sometimes known as "Blue Dragon". It is round, indica-tive of its active ability to move. Roundness is also the symbol of Heaven, which is also *yang*. Gold, associated with the sun, is *yang* as is jade. The *shen* spirits that rise from the body at death into new life are *yang*, unlike their *kuei/gui* and *yin* counterparts that are held in death. *Yang* is the right side of the body, the side that wields the sword, hence its aggression. *Yang* is experienced in the transcendence that sometimes floods the mind at odd times in life. The Taoist Huang-ch'i/Huangqi, from Yüan/Yuan dynasty times, explained this well:

> It may also happen that while you are reading books or reciting poetry, personal desires suddenly vanish and a unified awareness is alone present – this too is one aspect of the arising of yang.
>   Also, sometimes when friends gather and talk, they reach a communion

of the inner mind, and suddenly yang energy soars up and the true potential bursts forth – this is also one way in which yang arises.

Furthermore, even when playing music, playing games, drawing, fishing, cutting wood, plowing fields, reading books, if you can harmonize spontaneously based on the natural essence, without seeking or desiring anything, there will be a serenity and contentment, clearing the mind so that you forget about feelings – this is in each case a form of arising of yang.[27]

However, despite the positivity of such transcendent experience, over-excitement, overdoing the experience, transforms into negativity. Similarly, firmness that becomes overbearing can become self-destructive. Cultivating the firmness of *yang* is the goal, but it has to be in the right ways. Liu I-ming/Liu Yiming explained what this means:

What is firmness, first get rid of covetousness. Once covetousness is gone, firmness is established, and the pillars of the spiritual house are firmly stationed. Once the basis is firm and stable, there is hope for the great Tao.

What is firmness? Cutting through sentiment and clearing the senses is firmness. Not fearing obstacles and difficulties is firmness. Putting the spirit in order and going boldly forward is firmness. Being harmonious but not imitative, gregarious yet nonpartisan, is firmness. Not doing anything bad, doing whatever is good, is firmness. Being inwardly and outwardly unified, working without ceasing, is firmness.[28]

Here, then, the characteristic of *yang* as the rising principle in life is applied to the spiritual evolution of the human being, and the goal of harmony of the inner and outer self. Liu I-ming/Liu Yiming's words show clearly how *yang* implies progress and growth in the best possible dimensions of living.

The interplay of yin and yang

Yin and *yang* are complementary essences or forces. Just as we cannot understand darkness without light or *vice versa*, and just as we need the variances of dark, light and shadow to see well, so *yin* and *yang* cannot exist without each other. So in being mutually dependent, *yin* and *yang*, like all opposites in Chinese thought, are complementary rather than oppositional. Further, *yin* and *yang* are alternating, even "pulsating"[29] creative forces representing the interplay between physical and spiritual, emotion and intellect, passivity and activity, the yielding and the firm, resistance and generation. Rather than opposition between the two, there is polarity in unity, like two sides of one coin – a harmonized unity of opposites. There is tension between them and a mutual play and inter-action that makes them too close to be outright opposites. And in that interaction there is never a state of perfect *yang* or *yin*. The goal may be balance between the two, but whatever exists is simply dominated by one or the other; it is the varying degree of *yin* or *yang* present in an entity, or in a period of time, that makes it what it is. Lao-tzu/Laozi spoke of such mutual dependency thus:

> Everyone sees beauty as beauty only because there is ugliness.
> Everyone knows good as good only because there is evil.
>
> Therefore having and not having arise together.
> The difficult and the easy complement one another.
> Long and short contrast with each other;
> High and low depend on each other;
> Sound and silence harmonize with each other;
> Before and after follow one another.[30]

Not only, then, is our understanding of the world based on the inter-play of polarities but, in the Chinese view of things, nothing can ever be wholly one polarity as opposed to its complementary opposite. All males have a certain amount of the female within their physical and psychic make-up, as do women have a degree of masculinity. Quite contrary to most western thought it is not the triumph of good over evil, of light over darkness, of the divine over the demonic that is the Chinese goal, but the perfect balance between *yin* and *yang* polarities that enables the self to transcend them in activity. Evil is but temporary disharmony, just as night is the temporary suspension of day.

The continuous transformation and rhythmic patterns of *yin* and *yang*, their waxing and waning, coming and going, rising and falling, are related to all phenomena in the universe. To use Chung-Ying Cheng's words: "*Yin* is always the phase of difference, and *yang* always the phase of identity in the process of change (*yin*). Therefore *yin* represents the potentiality changing into the actual and *yang* the actuality changing into potentiality."[31] The degrees of balance and tension created by *yin* and *yang* account for all things. Thus, *yin* and *yang* are the qualitative essences found in all entities in the universe, constantly reacting with each other. Their energetic activity is that of *ch'i/qi*; it is the energy that is necessary for life, and for things to come into being. Their interaction controls the cycle of seasons, *yin* being the passive, cold seasons of autumn and winter, spring and summer being *yang*. So when winter is at its deepest – the time of maximum *yin* – *yang* begins to ascend once again, as far as the height of summer. *Yin* and *yang* affect all aspects of life, even the temperament of an individual, the nature of a society, war, and religion. They make life possible, their interaction creating the relativity necessary for existence. Rest and motion, contraction and expansion, advance and retreat are the dynamics of the universe.

The interrelation of the macrocosm of Heaven and the microcosm of human affairs was a critical one in Chinese thought. The ruler, especially, could influence natural events positively or negatively by proper or improper behaviour. Thus, it was exigent that he conducted his political and religious responsibilities at the correct times. The agricultural year was meticulously planned to coincide with the seasonal *yin* and *yang* changes. It was by such means that the *yang* of Heaven and the *yin* of Earth were balanced and harmonized. It was the *Yin–Yang* school, especially, that stressed the need for unity between the ruling power and the *yang* and *yin* of Heaven and Earth. There were even high government ministers who were responsible for advising the king on the ways in which *yin* and *yang* should be harmonized. A text known as the *Monthly Commands* set down exactly what the ruler should do in each month of the year. In the first month of spring, for example, the ruler was instructed thus:

> He [the sovereign] charges his assistants to disseminate [lessons of] virtue and harmonize governmental orders, so as to give effect to the expressions of his satisfaction and to bestow his favors to the millions of people. . . . Prohibitions are issued against cutting down trees. Nests should not be thrown down. . . . In this month no warlike operations should be undertaken; the undertaking of such is sure to be followed by calamities from Heaven. This avoidance of warlike operations means that they are not to be commenced on our side.[32]

The importance of harmonizing such affairs of state with the macrocosm of Heaven is underpinned by an acceptance of the interrelation and interdependence of all things. It is a belief that is fundamental to Chinese religious and philosophical thought, and points to the unity of all existence.

The idea of the relativity of opposites, reflected so much in nature and life, made sense to the Chinese psyche. The world that we experience is one of multiplicity and plurality in which we differentiate between all things through a system of categorization by language and experience. In order to exist in the world we have to know what things are and what their properties are. We need to know that if something is hot that it can burn, or that if music is beautiful, we may enjoy it. These perspectives that we have in life are *relative*: that is to say, we can only know what one thing is or means in relation to something else, usually its opposite. These are the dualities of life that help us to make sense of it. In much eastern religion, and certainly in classical Taoism and Buddhism, the ultimate goal in life is one that is involved with transcending these dualities. This is not to say that such dualities do not exist, that they are not there, but that we need to overcome the desires for, and aversions to, one thing rather than its opposite. The perfect balance between *yin* and *yang* brings this about. The enlightened being is at the point of equilibrium between all opposites, and is able to flow in any direction in life without losing that equilibrium.

Since the relativity of opposites forms a considerable part of our space–time understanding of the world, if we focus on one thing too much we automatically highlight its opposite: anything taken to its extreme will produce its opposite. If, for example, we concentrate on the good in life, we become even more aware of evil. If we imagine any pair of opposites pictorially as connected by a straight line, they become, as Capra described them, "extreme parts of a single whole".[33] The interdependence of polar opposites is what is behind the *yin* and *yang* principle. Their relativity means that nothing can exist in its own right. Laotzu/Laozi put this simply:

> That which contracts
> Must first expand.
> That which is weak
> Must first be strong.
> That which is cast down
> Must first be raised up.
> Before something is taken away
> It must first be given.
>
> This is called discernment of things.
> The soft and weak overcome the hard and strong.[34]

Human beings are constantly at some point other than the central equilibrium between all kinds of polarities. Only when dualities are transcended can the true perspective of reality be known. Cooper pertinently points out: "No observation in the realm of duality can see the whole and therefore cannot be absolutely right. It is little wonder that so many of our judgements, both individual and social, produce such unfortunate results when they are based on the erroneous assumption that we can see the whole."[35] In fact, the alternation between *yin* and *yang* suggests that if you want to achieve something you should start from its opposite! Again, Lao-tzu/Laozi said:

Yield then overcome;
Bend and become straight;
Empty and become full;
Wear out and become new;
Have little and gain much;
Have much and be confused.[36]

Taking the gains and losses in our stride is the moral of a story told by Lieh-tzu/Liezi. An old man and his son lived together at the top of a hill. They were very poor. One day their horse strayed away. The neighbours came to express how sorry they were. But the old man said: "Why would you see this as misfortune?" Not long afterwards the horse returned bringing with it many other wild horses. This seemed good fortune indeed, so the neighbours all came to congratulate the old man. But the old man asked: "Why would you see this as good luck?" Having so many horses, the old man's son took to riding, but he fell off a horse and broke his leg. The accident left him lame. Once again, the neighbours gathered round to commiserate with the old man, but again he said: "Why would you see this as misfortune?" Some time later, war broke out and, of course, his young son was not able to go because he was lame.

The dominance of yang

Despite all that has been written above, it would have to be admitted that *yang* generally appears to be superior to *yin*. Graham, for example cites an early list of *yin* and *yang* characteristics from the ancient document *Ch'eng/Cheng*. Here, politically insignificant states are *yin* as opposed to important ones that are *yang*. And in terms of character, to be base as opposed to noble, being stuck where one is as opposed to getting on in the world, being controlled by others instead of controlling, are all *yin* in nature.[37] Metaphysically, too, *yin* is chaos from which *yang* as light and intellect emerges. In the Taoist rite of exorcism it is the *yang* energies that defeat and drive out the *yin kuei/gui*, and *yang* ritual items are used throughout.[38]

So while *yin* and *yang* can never replace each other, there is what Bodde called "a cosmic hierarchy of balanced inequality" that informs the *yin* and *yang* relationship.[39] Given that the polarities of *yin* and *yang* probably arose from the observations of the seasons, Bodde comments, "it would be surprising indeed if the early Chinese, living in North China, with its rigorous winter climate, would have preferred the cold-bringing *yin* to the life-giving *yang*. Yet, confronted by the inexorable diurnal and annual alternation of the two, they were wise enough to see in them a pattern of movement necessary to the cosmic harmony rather than two irreconcilable warring forces".[40] The inconsistencies of hierarchizing *yin* and *yang* do not seem to have bothered Chinese philosophers too much.

The Five Agents

So far, we have seen that the *I Ching/Yijing* and the theory of *yin* and *yang* posit cyclical motions of change that underpin all life. The third theory supporting this concept is that of the Five Agents – Wood, Fire, Earth, Metal and Water. The Five Agents are known collectively as the *wu-hsing/wuxing*. *Wu* means "five", but the word *hsing/xing* is more problematic. Traditionally it has been translated as "Elements" much in line with the Greek and Indian conception of the elements of earth, air, fire and water as the constituents of manifest existence. But Chinese *hsing/xing* has a much more dynamic meaning. This can be seen instantly in its root meanings – to prosper; to begin; to increase; to rise; to raise; to walk; to do; to act; to travel.[41] Thus, *movement* is characteristic of each of the Agents. They are *activators*, each with its particular kind of movement. It is for this reason that the translation "Agents" more readily describes their cosmological function. Tsou Yen/Zou Yan called them *wu-te/wude* "Five Powers", because he related them to the rise and demise of dynasties. They were also called Five Processes, indicative of their properties – Fire rising and burning, Water saturating and sinking, for example.[42] In pre-Han times they were called Five Materials (*wu-ts'ai/wucai*),[43] and from Han times onwards they were referred to as Five Phases, an appropriate term given the cyclical dominance of each of them in turn in all dimensions of life, as we shall see below.

Such descriptors illustrate two points. The first is that the origins and growth of the concept of the Five Agents were not neatly linear and, second, that the Agents could be applied in a variety of ways. Indeed, it is this last point that will be taken up in more detail below, for the theory of the Five Agents is very much alive in a number of fields in the present day and age. In all, the term *Agents* is perhaps the most all-encompassing, and does the least to confine the overall use of all Five. The reader should note, however, that the terms Elements and Phases are widely used, the latter term by more modern, academic sources, though it is somewhat time orientated; the former being increasingly discarded because it is not suggestive of the dynamism of movement.[44] In martial arts, especially in T'ai chi Chüan/Taijiquan, however, the term "Elements" is the norm.

The Five Agents, then, are *active* motivators. They are mutually functional, bringing into being and ending the phases and changes evident in the world. Air is excluded for it is the all-pervasive oneness of *ch'i/qi*, the vital breath or energy from which *yin* and *yang* and the Five Agents themselves emerge. Instead, Wood is included because of its more obvious functional and indispensable role in existence, for it represents growth and the ability to flourish. So the Five Agents are both abstract principles and dynamic forces. The former prevents their being reduced to basic, static substances, and the latter ensures their active roles in informing the interconnection of all phenomena. All phenomena in life will correspond to one of these Agents.

Like the theories underpinning the *I Ching/Yijing* and *yin* and *yang* the Five Agents allow for the cyclical motion of change and transformation in all life. But in each repetition of a cycle the space for change is infinite; there is renewal without identical copying, alternation with difference. Just as no springtime can be exactly the same as any other period of springtime in the past, so change characterizes the changeless cycles of the seasons, night and day, darkness and light, and the many dualities that make up existence. Again, such a view of the universe makes it self-creative and self-sustaining. However, these three theories ensure that while plurality is self-evident in the universe, the totality of that plurality is interconnected and interrelated by the forces that inform it.

Historical development

It is not difficult to see how the theory of the Five Agents arose from observing nature. Earth was seen as the central Agent, the one that united the other four. These four were linked easily with the seasons and the four cardinal points. It is perhaps amongst the *fang-shih/fangshi* that such correlations began and from whom the theory originated. But Richard Smith notes that: "A number of Shang rituals, spiritual agencies, and terrestrial organizations were categorized according to groupings of five, indicating a possible affinity with later pentadic correlations in China."[45] This would make the origins of the theory very ancient indeed.

Our earliest sources of information regarding the Five Agents are two texts, the *Lü-shih Ch'un Ch'iu/Lüshi Chunqiu*, which contains what is called the *Monthly Commands* (extant also in the *Book of Rites*), and the *Hung Fan/Hongfan* or *Grand Norm*, found in the *Book of Documents*, the *Shu Ching/Shujing*. The *Lü-shih Ch'un Ch'iu/Lushi Chunqiu* is the eclectic *Annals of Spring and Autumn*, composed in the late third century BCE by numerous scholars, and reflects the views of late Chou/Zhou philosophers. It is in this document that the phases of the Five Agents are correlated with dynasties and colours. Thus, the legendary Yellow Emperor ruled by the Power of Earth with yellow as his colour. Earthworms and mole-crickets appeared before he rose to power to indicate the ruling Agent. Grass and trees appeared when Yü/Yu came to power. So Wood became his ruling Agent, and green his associative colour. Similarly, T'ang/Tang the founder of the Shang dynasty, was associated with Metal and the colour white, since knife-blades appeared in water. The appearance of a fiery flame and a red bird holding a red book in its mouth made King Wen rule by the Power of Fire, with red as his colour. The *Lü-shih Ch'un Ch'iu/Lüshi Chunqiu* believed that Water would be the Power associated with the next ruler, along with the colour black, before the cycle revolved again to Earth. The idea that ruling powers followed the natural fixed sequences of the Five Powers was sufficient for the first Chinese Emperor Ch'in Shih Huang-ti/Qinshi Huangdi in 221 BCE to claim his right to rule in alliance with the ascendancy of the Power Water. Accordingly, he accepted black as his imperial colour. The succeeding Han dynasty then reverted to Earth and the colour yellow.

The *Monthly Commands* connected the Five Agents more finely with the months of the year, with appropriate colours to be worn, and with the musical notes to be played. Climatic disasters would ensue if conformity to the patterns of the dominant Agent were disregarded. According to the *Hung Fan/Hongfan*, the *Grand Norm* or *Great Plan*, such cyclical changes in dynastic rule were the result of the waxing and waning of the cycle of Five Agents, and not, as was so prevalently thought, entirely due to the morality and moral degeneration of rulers. Of the Five Agents, the *Hung Fan/Hongfan* states:

> The first is named water, the second fire, the third wood, the fourth metal, the fifth earth. The nature of water is to moisten and descend; of fire to burn and ascend; of wood, to be crooked and straight; of metal, to yield and to be modified; of earth, to provide for sowing and reaping. That which moistens and descends produces salt; that which burns and ascends becomes bitter; that which is crooked and straight becomes sour; that which yields and is modified becomes acrid; sowing and reaping produce sweetness.[46]

The cosmological cycles of the Five Agents were extended to directions, planets, deities, animals, emperors, mountains, musical tones and all kinds of phenomena.

The individual responsible for these ideas was, again, Tsou Yen/Zou Yan, so Ssu-ma Ch'ien/Sima Qian's *Historical Records* tells us. While the *Yin–Yang* and Five Agents theories seem to have existed separately at first, it was Tsou Yen/Zou Yan who brought about a coalescing of the two, though there are differences in nature between the two theories.[47] What Tsou Yen/Zou Yan did was to introduce the movement integral to the *yin–yang* concept into the Five Agents theory. By Han times the *Yin–Yang* school and the Five Agents school were interchangeable names. It was an important correlation of two strands of thought that had an enormous impact. The interrelation of Heaven, Earth and human affairs became such that the seasons and the general welfare of humankind could be affected by the proper or improper actions of the ruler – he who embodied Chinese humanity. The coalescing of the two powerful theories of *yin* and *yang* and the Five Agents served to illustrate a direct correlation between the macrocosm of Heaven and the microcosm of the human.

The function of the ruler came to be shifted towards aligning himself with the natural sequences of the Five Powers during the cycle of the year, and it was the proponents of Tsou Yen/Zou Yan's school that provided the expertise in interpreting the ways in which the ruler could align himself with natural forces. Given such knowledge it would be possible for a ruler to act in such a way that no misfortunes could occur in the natural, corporate life, or in his own personal life. It was in this context that the *Monthly Commands* provided explicit guidance. Here, the Five Powers are correlated with the seasons, Wood with spring; Fire with summer; Metal with autumn; Water with winter. And the actions of an emperor – from governing down to the colour of his clothes and what he may or may not eat – depended on the prevailing Power. The balances of *yin* and *yang* throughout the year, combined with the Powers, regulated the life at court, the times when the ruler should reward or punish, the area of the palace in which to live, the colours to wear, the ritual to observe. While such practices declined subsequent to the Han dynasty, it is notable that even the last Emperor of China ousted by the Republic of China in 1911 was called "Emperor of [the Mandate of] Heaven and in accordance with the Movements [Five Agents]".

The cosmology of the Five Agents

The Five Agents theory depicts the rotation of the Agents in both a generating and a conquering cycle. In the generating or mutually producing cycle, Wood generates Fire; Fire generates Earth; Earth generates Metal; Metal generates Water; Water generates Wood. Here, the logical sequence is taken from ordinary observation of nature. Wood fuels a fire. Fire creates ashes and so forms earth. Earth provides the environment for metal that forms in its veins. Metal encourages underground waters or provides a surface for dew as a result of condensation. Water encourages the growth of plants and trees – the wood that feeds fire. And so the cycle begins again. Here, the generating cycle is linked with the seasons, too. The wood of spring generates the fire of summer. Fire generates the earth itself. The earth generates the metal of autumn, and from autumn we pass to the water of winter. The two different cycles are presented diagramatically as follows:

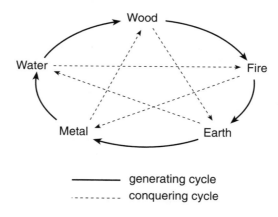

———— generating cycle
········· conquering cycle

In the conquering or mutually overcoming cycle, where the Agents overcome each other, Wood overcomes Earth; Earth overcomes Water; Water overcomes Fire; Fire overcomes Metal; Metal overcomes Wood. Again, the sequence is taken from natural observation. Wood overcomes earth as the roots of trees and vegetation take over, or as the plough overcomes it. Earth overcomes water by obstructing its path, as in dams, or by filling rivers with mud and silt. Water overcomes fire by destroying it completely, and fire is the element that can melt metal. Metal then overcomes wood by chopping it. The logic of the order here in the context of ancient Chinese culture is noted by Graham: "Among

Chinese proto-scientific concepts the conquest cycle stands out as independent of all correlations, and probably derives directly from observation of the five basic resources at the workman's disposal. Struggling with water, fire, metal, wood or soil, there is little room for disagreement as to which of the others is most required to dam, quench, melt, cut or dig the resisting material."[48]

The *Huai-nan-tzu/Huainanzi* combines the generating and overcoming cycles to show that each of the Agents passes through a rising and declining cycle – the *yin* and *yang* of each Agent. When at its zenith, each Agent can generate the next one, but at the same time can overcome the Agent that is at its weakest. Throughout the cycles each Agent follows the one that it cannot overcome:

Birth	Wood	Fire	Earth	Metal	Water
Zenith	Water	Wood	Fire	Earth	Metal
Ageing	Metal	Water	Wood	Fire	Earth
Immobilization	Earth	Metal	Water	Wood	Fire
Death	Fire	Earth	Metal	Water	Wood

So at its most potent, each generates the one that begins its rise, and conquers the one that is in demise: each has an active and passive phase. Importantly, what this table shows is that there is continued interaction between the Agents. Since the Five Agents were the constituents of all phenomena, they were believed to be present in the three realms of Heaven, Earth and humanity. Their mutual interaction and balances and imbalances at any one time had a profound effect on human existence. Given the rise and decline of each individual Agent, it followed that the early cosmologists saw human and natural events as being dictated very much by the particular phases of the Five Agents. Such was the case not only on the larger canvas of historical dynasties, but also on the cyclical events of the days, months, seasons and years, even the human body. While one Agent might be predominant at a particular time of the day, month, season or year, the relative strengths and weaknesses of the others also had their effects.

The Agents were also connected with the trigrams of the *I Ching/Yijing*. Thus we have: *Ch'ien/Qian* with Metal, *Sun* with Wood, *Tui/Dui* with Metal, *K'an/Kan* with Water, *Li* with Fire, *Ken/Gen* with Earth, *Chen/Zhen* with Wood and *K'un/Kun* with Earth. The operation of *yin* and *yang* determines the seasons and the dominating Agent for that season. While the trigrams and hexagrams of the *I Ching/Yijing* stood independently for some time as cosmological schemes,[49] by early

Han times the process of applying the theories of *yin* and *yang* together with the Five Agents in wider contexts was well in place. In the amalgamation of *yin* and *yang* with the Five Agents, the latter became the active Agents by which *yin* and *yang* could operate, and each Agent had its *yin* and *yang* cycle. Each of the Agents was assigned a *yin* or *yang* predominant force. Thus, Wood was lesser *yang*; Fire was great *yang*; Metal was lesser *yin*; Water was great *yin*. Earth, the central Agent, was the harmonizing point of them all. The fairly easy amalgamation of the different cosmological views was possible because of the Chinese view of an interdependent, interacting and interrelated universe that was ultimately a unity of its many parts.

The characteristics of the Agents

Wood (*Mu*) is the Agent associated with springtime when green leaves shoot out and vegetation revives from winter. It encompasses the ideas of expansion, of pushing upward, outward, budding forth and opening up. It is the Agent of beginnings, of youth, the sunrise, freshness and flowing energy. It balances with its opposite of Metal (*Chin/Jin*) the Agent of the autumn, when trees begin to lose their leaves, their branches becoming brittle, rigid and metallic. Metal suggests processes of binding, contraction, crystallization, restraint, withdrawal and inward movement. It is the beginning of *yin*. Fire (*Huo*) is clearly the Agent of summer. It is associated with vibrant growth and expansiveness to the point of maturity and accomplishment. Its warmth and heat are contrasted by the coldness and darkness of its opposite Agent of Water (*Shui*), the Agent of winter. Water is fluidity, dissolution, levelling, spreading, enveloping. It is *yin* at its fullest and oldest. Water was an important symbol in Taoist philosophy because of its naturalness, its ability to achieve its goal by gently wearing away its rocky banks, or adapting itself to fit any vessel. Water and Fire were always especially important, and became crucial to the processes of inner alchemy when linked with the *I Ching/Yijing*.

The Agent Earth (*Ti/Di*) is special in that it is central and pivotal to the other Agents. It is a preserving Agent. Since it is at the centre, it is the point of interaction for all the other Agents. Everything revolves around it and so it is balance and harmony, the point of change between the seasons, between *yin* and *yang*. Wood grows from earth, fire rises up from it, metals are found in it, and water is absorbed by it. In its central position, Earth is spatially at the centre of the cardinal compass points and in terms of time is dominant at a point between summer and autumn. Earth lends to the theory a cosmologically *spatial* dimension.

During the Han dynasty, the applications of the Five Agents begun by Tsou Yen/Zou Yan were extended not only to dynasties and historical cycles but to all manner of phenomena – the seasons, cardinal points of the compass, planets, bodily organs, calendrical signs, musical notes, colours, tastes, smells, numbers, and many other aspects. However, such correspondences necessitated the reduction of major phenomena also to five basic aspects. Allan suggests that the ancient Chinese division of the world into five geographical parts was the inspiration for the later significance of the number five.[50] Indeed, she points out that this geographical division amounted to four quarters and a central part, and that the number five was important in oracle bone inscriptions in Shang times. There were five major mountains and the deity Shang-ti/Shangdi had five ministers, perhaps thought to preside over the five geographical regions.[51] By Tsou Yen/Zou Yan's time, the number five had become a sacred number and five Confucian virtues were the underpinning morality of the state. Categorizing all things in groups of fives was an attempt to unify and systematize the known universe.

The theories of the Five Agents and *yin* and *yang* portrayed the phenomenal world as pulsating interchanges of different energies promoting and repelling each other in a multiplicity of combinations that result in what we view as life, material and immaterial, and also spiritual. Like the philosophical concepts underpinning the *I Ching/Yijing*, the Five Agents and *yin* and *yang* created an explanation for life in terms of perpetual rhythm and pattern.[52] Along with *yin* and *yang* the Five Agents theory underpinned later theories in alchemy, medicine, science, astronomy, geomancy, and art, for example. In medicine the *Huang-ti Nei-ching/Huangdi Neijing*, the *Yellow Emperor's Classic of Internal Medicine*, describes how the essential energy of the body, *ch'i/qi*, needed to be nourished by appropriate actions and living according to each of the four Phases and seasons of the year, to achieve a holistically balanced life: outward activities thus affect the internal functioning of the body. The body is viewed as a whole, its parts interactive and delicately balanced between *yin* and *yang* energies. Each of the Five Agents has its *yin* and *yang* organs.

The Five Agents are still used in modern Chinese medicine. In a standard textbook for modern-day practice of acupuncture and moxibustion, we find the words: "When the theory of the five elements is applied in traditional Chinese medicine, the classification of phenomena according to the five elements and their interpromoting, interacting, overacting and counteracting relationships are used to explain both physiological and pathological phenomena, and to guide clinical diagnosis and treatment."[53] In such medical practice the Five Agents theory and *yin* and *yang* are complementary to the extent that the use of one must include the other.

Importantly, these integrated theories placed the human being on a cosmic map. Angus Graham thus made the point that the cosmic view is an anthropocentric one where the individual "still stands at the centre of things in interaction with the rest, and has only to contrast A and B to respond to them immediately as superior and inferior, better or worse".[54] Needless to say, individual consciousnesses vary, and perception of interrelation with the rest of the cosmos is not for all. Again, Graham stated: "Man is in spontaneous interaction with things, but responds differently according to the degree of his understanding of their similarities and contrasts, connexion or isolation." [55]

With the trigrams and hexagrams of the *I Ching/Yijing*, *yin* and *yang*, and the Five Agents, we have a cosmological picture of the universe based on the interrelation of all things in the universe. Schirokauer points out that it was a very satisfying view of the world: "Not only did it explain everything, it enabled men to feel at home in the world, part of a temporal as well as spatial continuum. It provided both an impetus to the development of science and the basis for a sophisticated theoretical framework for explaining the world."[56] The three theories were generically Chinese. However, they provided such a systematic view of the universe that both Confucianism and Taoism accepted them as their fundamental cosmology. They are theories that came to be embedded deeply in the subconscious of Chinese culture.

儒家

3 Confucianism

East Asia is home to an ancient tradition that is known in those parts as *ju-chia/rujia, ju-chiao/rujiao, ju-hsüeh/ruxue* or simply *ju/ru*. In the West, this tradition rejoices in the name "Confucianism", a misnomer that is the result of misguided attempts by Jesuit missionaries of the seventeenth century to categorize an ancient Chinese tradition in terms of a system and label it an "*-ism*". Such transmutation misleads the western reader into accepting the mistaken premise that, as surely as other world faiths may have had their founders, so the arrival of one Confucius on the stage of China's history heralded the dawn of a new age and a new, hitherto unknown, religion for which he, and he alone, owned copyright. But founders of religion are seldom academics intent on developing a rigid philosophical system capable of withstanding robust cross-examination under intense critical scrutiny. Usually, their compelling motivation is generated by a vision that overwhelms them to such an extent that they must proclaim it to the world of their day. Sometimes, aspects of this vision simply do not add up; at others, the founder may have remained silent on matters that are later considered to be crucial to an understanding of reality, but that were not the founder's main concern at the time. The onerous task of defending the indefensible or explaining the inexplicable is invariably left to followers who are often some distance removed from the mind of the founder, no matter how honorable their intentions.[1] Even a great Confucian scholar of Theodore de Bary's stature admits to having problems answering the question, "What does Confucianism have to offer today?" His response invariably is: "Whose Confucianism are we talking about?" If it is the original teachings of Confucius in the *Analects*, then almost nothing said about Confucianism today speaks to that. Indeed, even the anti-Confucian diatribes of the last century spoke rarely to Confucius' own views but only to later adaptations or distortions of them.[2]

If Confucius can be said to be the founder of a tradition known as Confucianism, then he functioned in a way unlike any other religious founder either before or since. Although it cannot be denied that a distinctive school first arose under the aegis of Confucius, his position was hardly that of Lord or Saviour; rather, his contemporaries viewed him more as a "sage-teacher". Nor is it thought that at one point he created and introduced a totally new belief-system. Indeed, his role, and that of his contemporaries, was to nurture an extant tradition already deeply rooted in Chinese culture. Jacques Gernet has gone so far as to state: "If the term 'Confucianism', coined by Westerners, has any meaning at all, it is clear that it goes far beyond the actual personality or teachings of the great sage."[3]

The *ju/ru* tradition

Since Confucius is credited with being an outstanding *ju/ru* of his day, it is fitting that we now turn our attention to that designation. Robert Eno has characterized Confucius and his followers as "masters of dance", though he stops short of calling Confucius "Lord of the dance".[4] With the fall from grace of dispossessed aristocrats in antiquity, and the resulting change in status from warrior to that of religious participant, with religious ritual, rites and ceremonies replacing the sword, it is inevitable that the word *ju/ru* should have acquired a pejorative bent. When we meld to this the fact that etymologically the word has associations with a meaning "weaklings"/"cowards", it is difficult to see the term ever being used in a complimentary sense. However, we will do well to remember that Chinese words may have various meanings, and *ju/ru* also has the nuance "soft", "gentle", "enduring".[5] Language is also dynamic, with words changing their meanings over time and, in a truly excellent synopsis, Xinzhong Yao traces the various meanings of the word *ju/ru* throughout the course of history.[6]

Regardless of the original purpose and function of the *ju/ru* tradition, by the Autumn and Spring period (722–481 BCE) there was a decline in cultic practices. This period saw many *ju/ru* entering social life, taking with them their skills in state rituals and education. In time, the term *ju/ru* began to be applied to those who made a profession from their knowledge. They demonstrated expertise in wide-ranging fields, which included poetry, ceremonial ritual, history, music, and even, as Yao notes, archery.[7] Certainly, Confucius was an outstanding *ju/ru* of his day. Equally certainly, his day witnessed a fundamental change in the social and cultural functions of *ju/ru*, giving the term a meaning far removed from earlier masters of dance and magic.[8] Let us now turn to the man himself and examine his teachings.

Confucius

If we were to characterize in one word the Chinese way of life for the last two thousand years, the word would be "Confucian". No other individual in Chinese history has so deeply influenced the life and thought of his people, as a transmitter, teacher and creative interpreter of the ancient culture and literature and as a moulder of the Chinese mind and character.[9]

These arresting words describe the most significant figure ever to set foot on the stage of Chinese history. Confucius was born in 551 BCE to a once aristocratic family in the small East China state of Lu, and he died in 479 BCE. He was probably one of the rising class of scribes noted above, who were learned men, though not necessarily of the nobility class. Ironically, though Confucius is a name familiar to every western reader, his real name was not Confucius at all; this is simply the Latinized form of K'ung Fu-tzu/Kong Fuzi, a reverend title for K'ung-ch'iu/Kong Qiu or K'ung Chung-ni/Kong Zhongni.[10] Although he failed in his lifetime to bring any degree of order to society, and was unable to convince even one ruler of his teachings, his ideas were accepted by many, and were later to affect Chinese society immensely and fundamentally. He held only a minor government post, which he abandoned in order to travel from state to state in order to find a ruler that might accept his ideas. Unsuccessful, he retired to his home state of Lu and spent his time teaching. Indeed, his life ended in disappointment and ineffectiveness. It was only posthumously that fame was accorded him. Julia Ching summarizes the position well: "Were we to judge him on the basis of his achievements in public office, we would not even give him a footnote in history."[11]

Confucius must have died feeling something of a failure in life. He left a legacy to his disciples and a whole way of thinking and living for all the Chinese generations after him, but he was never to know that. Indeed, it is true to say that there is no consensus of opinion in the East or West over an evaluation of the worth and works of Confucius.[12] He was certainly a deeply humanistic man, and as Herrlee Creel commented: "He took as his basis, therefore, neither theological dogma nor religious hope but the nature of man and society as he observed them."[13] Although he is the most well-known Chinese teacher in western thought, there is also disagreement amongst western philosophers over whether, strictly speaking, Confucius really deserves the title "philosopher". Those who deny him this role see a thinker who simply offered humanity a practical wisdom, bereft of the analytical and conceptual language framework that one normally associates with philosophy.

Nor is there consensus of opinion in either eastern or western scholarship over whether Confucianism can truly hold claim to be called a religion. Notwithstanding the perennial problems besetting attempts to define what precisely constitutes a "religion", it has long been pointed out that the tradition that answers to the name Confucianism "has no priesthood, no church, no bible, no creed, no conversion, and no fixed system of gods. It has no interest in either theology or mythology".[14] However, it is well to bear the problem of definition in mind in any discussion of whether or not Confucianism can be said to be a religion, for the very question places western value judgments on an eastern belief system. We should be wary also of the mistaken premise that all religious traditions are of one type and that this type is informed by a theocentric framework. In western language, the term "religion" implies at least some elements of a commendatory nature, attributing high-minded principles to both the belief system in question and the believer. The Chinese language, however, has no such resonance, with the word for religion implying reliance on superstition, rituals and the like.[15] Accordingly, Chinese scholars who hold Confucianism in high esteem tend to describe it as a philosophy, whilst those who do not, identify it as a religion. The Italian Jesuit missionary Matteo Ricci (1552–1610), who adopted a conciliatory attitude to Chinese customs and usages, had to admit that matters of religion were of no great concern to the Chinese.[16]

Putting aside the politically motivated Anti-Confucius Campaign of 1973–74, it can be concluded that Communist China holds conflicting views over how to regard both Confucius and Confucianism. It is well known that Confucianism no longer holds the dominant position it once occupied in East Asia.[17] This said, Xinzhong Yao draws attention to the current situation in mainland China, "where the Confucian tradition is in general defined as a feudal ethical system". Yao advises that, "the perception of Confucianism has also started to change, as indicated

by a group of recently published articles in which a number of prominent intellectuals confirm the close link between Confucianism and
religion in one way or another."[18]

Those who would deny the existence of any such links are swift to
point out that nowhere in Confucian literature is there to be found a
single reference to one word that can be translated as "religion". Such
critics are either unaware of or unmoved by the fact that the absence of
a term for "religion" within the sacred literature of the world's faiths is
by no means unique to the Confucian tradition; were this a valid crite-
rion for classification, then most of the world's great religions need to
be reclassified as *secular*! Nor is absence of evidence evidence of absence.
Were this the case, then the fact that the term "Buddha-nature" is unattested in the *Lotus Sutra* means that the most important of the Mahayana
sutras has nothing whatever to do with Buddha-nature, one of its fundamental concerns! Neither do these critics pause to consider why at least
one chapter on Confucianism appears in every worthwhile publication
on Chinese religions. Ninian Smart[19] once identified seven dimensions
of *religion* that help to characterize the term in relation to Confucianism.
Although considerable overlap is immediately conspicuous, the dimensions are categorized as:

1 The Practical and Ritual Dimension

Every tradition has practices long associated with it, and
Confucianism is no exception. These are performed regularly and
precisely and may include worship, preaching, prayer, sacrifice,
meditation or the like. In some cases, these are known as ritual practices, to be effectuated with unwavering precision, as is the case with
Confucianism. The precise way these rituals are enacted is not open
to discussion, and the attention to detail given to their performance
in the form of study sometimes becomes almost a ritual in itself. Not
all practices are necessarily ritualistic in nature, and the practice of
stilling the mind has long been a feature of Hinduism, Taoism,
Buddhism, and Sikhism among others. Cave drawings in China,
furthermore, attest to yogic meditation practices in East Asia long
before the advent of even Taoism, let alone Buddhism, on the Chinese
mainland.

Ritual is hugely important in Confucianism. It will be seen
presently that *li* is a key term in the tradition, and at least one scholar
translates it as "the spirit of ritual".[20] The *Analects* (1: 9; 12: 2; 13: 4;
14; 44) has as its central focus "the noble man", the *chün-tzu/junzi*,
a "son of the ruler", "superior man" or "gentleman", whose qualities

include his cultivation of riteness. Here, he is expected to exhibit a deep respect for disciplined observance of the social and religious forms that should govern the common life. Furthermore, one of the Confucian *Classics*, the *Classic of Rites* (*Li Chi/Liji*), contains three early texts that were not compiled until the turn of the millennium. One of these is the *Book of Rites* or *Rituals* (*Li Chi/Liji*), which includes instruction on ritual and the rites. It directs its attention to the family rituals that, in turn, are informed by an ancient ancestral cult. At all times, deceased members of the family are to be remembered and honoured in ritual observance. Between the times of the Han and T'ang/Tang dynasties, this text informed Chinese society. Convinced that Confucianism needed a religious element, in 630 the ruler of the T'ang/Tang dynasty (617–907), T'ai-tsung/Taizong, ordered the establishment of Confucian temples throughout China. Ritual observance in what by now had become restored as the state religion included ritual dances, music and prayer. Guided by ancient rites, these temple rituals also included animal sacrifice.

2 The Experiential and Emotional Dimension

Recent research by Daniel Goleman has identified the human condition as having, in a sense, *two* minds, the rational mind and the emotional mind – one that thinks and one that feels.[21] Accordingly, we develop two different kinds of intelligence, rational and emotional. Ironically, it is not the rational mind, with its capacity for reason, deliberation and reflection that is the more powerful facet of the thinking process, but the impulsive, often illogical, emotional mind, which can, and often does, overcome rational thought. We can recognize Goleman's thesis[22] in our daily behaviour. The potency of music to arouse the emotions and generate an inner dynamism is ever conspicuous in this dimension, where feelings are never cold, and believers never pay mere lip service to acts of worship. There are those who would argue that the emotional dimension is surely manifest in the daily rituals conducted in Confucian temples. This cannot be denied, but orchestral concerts frequently evoke equally high emotional states amongst audiences, with no necessary religious connection.

World religions are rife with moving accounts of conversions, visions, theophanies, enlightenment experiences and journeys to the netherworld, all of which have immense appeal to the emotional mind, and all of which are absent from Confucianism; Confucius was no Muhammad. But Confucius was no Moses either and, though he may well have appealed to Heaven for authority, nowhere does he claim his words to be the direct revelation of a personal God.

3 The Narrative or Mythic Dimension

It is here that we encounter some of the greatest stories ever told, handed down (orally initially) from generation to generation. Some of these stories are historical accounts of the lives of the respective founders and leaders, others were never intended to be taken literally. Since the heart is moved far more by myth than by logical argument, and since, as just suggested, the emotional mind is more powerful than its logical counterpart, the creation and other myths of the world's great faiths feature prominently. There is certainly nothing fictitious about the life of the Prophet Muhammad, the crucifixion of Jesus or the Enlightenment of the Buddha, though each and every aspect need not necessarily be historically correct.

One of the Confucian *Classics* is the *Odes* (*Shih Ching/Shijing*). Also known as the *Book of Poetry* or the *Book of Songs*, the *Odes* comprises some three hundred and five songs, each with the moral message, "Have no depraved thought". The narrative dimension is conspicuous here, with 160 poems in one section describing daily life in thirteen different states. The poems also contain love songs, but the content material mainly centres on the court and court life. There are also accounts of historic or legendary figures, as well as details of liturgies, though miraculous nativity stories are conspicuous by their absence. While the mythic dimension is not always evident, the narrative dimension of Confucianism is transparent.

4 The Doctrinal and Philosophical Dimension

This is the intellectual side of religion that underpins the narrative dimension. The once oral traditions of the world's faiths that had long been confined to memory, were later committed to writing. These written testimonies become the seedbed for analysis, and the roots for justification of doctrines that arise from these analyses. They provide the fuel for, sometimes bitter, disputes. There is a saying in Judaism that where you have nine rabbis present, you will also have ten different opinions, but Judaism is not alone in disagreement over contentious issues. Differences of opinion are rife amongst Confucian masters. A religion's leaders are thinkers who want answers, but the questions they raise seldom evoke one answer that is acceptable to everyone, hence hotly disputed issues arise and schisms appear within.

Philosophical speculation abounds in Confucianism. Confucius himself never tired of appealing to "the Mandate of Heaven", for it was Heaven that was responsible for maintaining balance and harmony in the world: harmony and balance were not simply left to chance. Heaven was considered to be the force responsible for ordering both, but Heaven was informed by humankind's actions, both good and bad. Indeed, humankind was the prime mover in the disturbance and restoration of harmony. This being so, an internalizing rationale for one's behaviour and beliefs was essential: this was following the path or way, the *tao*, the harmonizing of one's inner self with the way nature meant people to be, and the way society ought to be. *Tao* was the right way, the moral way, the way that led to health and well-being for all.

Although Confucius himself did not seem to be interested in the metaphysical problems of a search for ultimate Reality, or the ultimate fate of the self as these came to be seen in the Taoist interpretation of *Tao*, Neo-Confucians later became deeply concerned with metaphysical knowledge in their quest to find the relationship between self-cultivation and the "heavenly" or cosmic order. We have a choice of seeing the *way* of Confucius as a purely humanistic path through life, or of seeing it as the *Way* of Heaven, of T'ien/Tian.

Xiong Shili's (1885–1968) early move from Buddhist studies to Confucianism found him striving to restore the true *Tao* of Confucius as the very heartbeat of Chinese religions. In Xiong's vision for Modern Confucianism, there was room for western learning, as well as for philosophy and science. So much more could be written about the place of Confucianism in the doctrinal and philosophical dimension. Suffice it here to give mention to the highly philosophical last section of the *I Ching/Yijing* (the *Book of Changes*). In fact, it was to this work that Xiong looked for a metaphysical basis to Confucian ethics.

5 The Ethical and Legal Dimension

The ethical dimension to religion is woven into the fabric of the tradition in question and is ubiquitous throughout Confucianism. The *Analects* has as its central focus "the noble man", the *chün-tzu/junzi*, whose cultivation of riteness has already been acknowledged. His ethical dimensions include his manifestation of virtue in forms that benefit the people (15: 34; 20: 2), his ability to command respect because of his own respectful or reverential manner (6: 30), and his kindly, generous, and forbearing manner in dealing with the people (18: 2; 11: 24).

Confucius changed the understanding of the concept of *li* from an outward conformity to ritual practice to an inner attitude of mind. Additionally, he gave the word a moral dimension by externalizing it as conformity to high moral and social norms. In order to govern effectively, rulers and officials needed to be men of character and educated, gentlemen/virtuous men (*chün-tzu/junzi*), all of which attest to the importance given by Confucius to the ethical dimension.

6 The Social and Institutional Dimension

This discipline could well be described as the sociology of religion, for religion is usually expressed in the group situation. Here we have the workings of a religion – how it actually functions among its believers, a fundamental aspect of the teachings of Confucianism. All of the previously attested dimensions find expression in the group situation, embodied in the workings of groups of like-minded people. But it is not always the religious leaders who are the mainstay of their faiths; charismatic visionaries are soon recognized for their true worth, taking their beliefs and practices forward, sometimes in diverging ways, on new courses. Whether Confucius or his followers can truly be described as "charismatic" is still disputed.[23]

The social dimension of religion is manifest in Confucianism's association with social stability and moral uprightness. Confucius believed in developing the intrinsic *humanity* in each person, and raising awareness of the need for a sense of propriety. The development of an altruistic concern in everyone found expression in the so-called Five Relationships of Confucianism. This doctrine of social and moral order is known as the "rectification of names" (*cheng-ming/zhengming*). Again we can look to the *Analects* and "the noble man", the *chün-tzu/junzi*, for examples of exemplary social behaviour. These include his sense of confidence and trust in relations with the people (12: 7; 13: 4; 15: 25), his reasonableness in making demands on the people, according to the seasons and circumstances (19: 10), as well as his zeal for learning, and readiness to take responsibility for the education of the people (6: 20; 13: 4; 13: 29).

7 The Material Dimension

Invariably, the previous dimension finds expression in material form, often in iconography or as a religious building, as is evident in the Confucian tradition. Sometimes such buildings are marked by their simplicity, as is the case in Islam. In 630, the ruler of the T'ang/Tang dynasty (617–907) in China, T'ai-tsung/Taizong, decided that Confucianism needed a material religious dimension, and he ordered the establishment of Confucian temples throughout the realm. Confucius was given divine status, and Confucianism restored as the state religion. Besides erecting statues of Confucius over the centuries, the names of Confucian dignitaries were recorded on tablets and set in the profusion of temples that by this time had been given state patronage.

Despite attempts by the Chinese government to suppress resurgence in popular religion (in the interests of modernization), evidence of this resurgence is found manifest in many folk temples throughout Hong Kong, where one finds statues of Kongzi (Confucius), Laozi (Lao tzu), and the Buddha alongside those of traditional Chinese immortals as objects of veneration.[24] There are also tens of thousands of initiates today worshipping a cult figure (Lin Zhao'en, 1517–98) in over a thousand temples throughout south-east China and south-east Asia. Restoration of these still functional temples began as recently as 1979, and the cult is still thriving today in post-Mao China.[25]

These dimensions of religion are not compartmentalized, stand-alone categories. The intellectual side to religion underpins the narrative dimension. Often, the narrative and ritual dimensions to religion overlap, as found in the *Analects* (1: 9; 12: 2; 13: 4; 14; 44), where "the noble man", the *chün-tzu/junzi*, is expected to demonstrate deep respect for disciplined observance of the social and religious forms that should govern the common life. The social and institutional dimension in Confucianism becomes manifest in building and art forms worldwide, while the practical dimension is also evident here, as it is in the ethical and legal dimension. There is also overlap with the latter and the ritual dimension.

To our knowledge, neither Ninian Smart, nor anyone else for that matter, has ever suggested that all seven dimensions of religion need be present in a tradition in order to identify that tradition as *religious*, or that all faith communities have any necessary interest whatever in all seven. We have pointed out dimensions that are clearly present in Confucianism, with the Ritual, Ethical, Social, and Material dimensions being the most obvious, and those that, equally clearly, are not. In this light, rather than joining the "it is/it is not religion" argument, we may be better employed concentrating on the distinctiveness of the religious dimension of Confucianism, a deliberation recognized by Yao.[26] Yao argues that "the distinctiveness of Confucianism as a religion lies in its humanistic approaches to religious matters, such as beliefs, rituals and institutions, and in its religious concerns with secular affairs, individual growth, family relationships and social harmony".[27] What did emerge in Confucianism was the idea that each person should know his or her role in life and effectuate it without friction to others, in a way that would be of benefit to other individuals and to society at large. Family cohesiveness and mutual support became paramount as the fabric and essence of Chinese societal life.

Famous interpreters of Confucius were to consolidate and expand Confucian ideas. In the centuries that followed his death, Confucius became a role model, and by the end of the first century BCE he had become regarded as the teacher *par excellence*, a man venerated by the scholarly class. In 59 CE the Emperor formalized this by decreeing that sacrifices could, indeed should, be offered to K'ung/Kong.[28] Recognition that Confucius, by this time, had become a cult figure in a distinctive school is manifest in the evocation of the word *K'ung-chiao/Kongjiao* ("the cult of Confucius"), as well as in the somewhat critical appellation *li-chaio/lijiao* ("the ritual religion").[29]

The *Analects*

Details of the life of Confucius need detain us only briefly here. Hagiography has played an enormous part in embellishing and distorting the life of one of China's greatest figures, and it is necessary to rely on the collections of conversations compiled by later followers. These conversations are those recollected as having taken place between Confucius and his disciples or between Confucius and the rulers of various feudal states that he visited. The Chinese word for "conversations" is *lun-yü/lunyu*, a title normally translated into English as *Analects*. It is the *Analects*, a rambling collection of sayings and anecdotes, to which one must look to provide a picture of the man. His words are no less applicable today, despite the passage of time. So important was this text to the Chinese that many memorized its sayings: even peasants preserved some of them as proverbs. A few examples will suffice:

> Those who are possessed of understanding from birth are the highest type of people. Those who understand things only after studying them are of the next lower type, and those who learn things from painful experience

are the next. Those who have painful experiences but do not learn from them are the lowest type of people.[30]

Honourable people are modest in what they say but surpassing in what they do.[31]

Honourable persons seek things within themselves. Small-minded people, on the other hand, seek things from others.[32]

Bereft of a philosophy or ideology, this unstructured and unsystematized collection of sayings and anecdotes known as the *Analects* has as its central focus "the noble man", the *chün-tzu/junzi*, a "son of the ruler", "superior man" or "gentleman". It is such a portrait of the noble man, so appealingly portrayed, that gives interest in the *Analects* endurance.[33] Theodore de Bary has summarized the qualities of the noble man as follows:

1 His manifesting of virtue in forms that benefit the people. (*Analects* 15: 34; 20: 2)
2 His ability to command respect because of his own respectful or reverential manner. (6: 30)
3 His cultivation of riteness – a disciplined observance of the social and religious forms that should govern the common life. Respect for rites and respect for the people are all of one common piece. (1: 9; 12: 2; 13: 4; 14: 44)
4 His kindly, generous, and forbearing manner in dealing with the people. (18: 2; 11: 24)
5 His sense of confidence and trust in relations with the people. (12: 7; 13: 4; 15: 25)
6 His reasonableness in making demands on the people, according to the seasons and circumstances. (19: 10)
7 His zeal for learning and readiness to take responsibility for the education of the people. (6: 20; 13: 4; 13: 29)[34]

The debate as to whether Confucian beliefs were based on a religious or totally humanist framework still engages scholars today. Primarily, it seems, Confucius was interested in ideal ethical social living and, therefore, his ideas contain no doctrines of afterlife, priests or scriptures, and he had little to say about the concept of God. However, mention in the *Analects* of Heaven, T'ien/Tian, illustrates that he seems to regard T'ien/Tian as the source of virtue, *te/de*. Howard Smith has suggested that there was possibly a "deep sense of man's dependence upon a supreme deity"[35] that underpinned his social, ethical and political perspectives, but if Smith is right here, it is difficult to know how far Confucius took this, given his emphasis on social concerns. The earliest biography of the great thinker was not undertaken until centuries after his death, and even his famous *Analects* were compiled long after his demise. Perhaps we need to take for granted his acceptance of the ritualistic respect given to the gods and ancestors, and certainly later Confucianism became very ritualistic. Also the chaos of the time needs to be borne in mind along with the scepticism that accompanied it concerning the nature of the divine beings and supreme God who seemed to be absent. Such factors may have influenced Confucius in his promulgation of a more humanistic and social ethic, rather than an overtly religious one.

Teachings

The master said, "At fifteen, my heart was set upon learning; at thirty, I had become established; at forty, I was no longer perplexed; at fifty, I knew what is ordained by Heaven; at sixty, I obeyed; at seventy, I could follow my heart's desires without transgressing the line."

Analects 2: 4[36]

As a whole, Confucius' teachings later influenced Chinese society on dramatic levels. He must have been an outstanding teacher, if unorthodox. He taught that any person could become a *chün-tzu/junzi*, a "son of the ruler", "superior man" or "gentleman" – noble, unselfish, kind, just – irrespective of birth; this term is discussed 107 times in the *Analects*. Such an idea was perhaps to be expected, given the instability of social order in the times in which he lived, but he trained his students to become gentlemen and chose them from all walks of life, rich and poor. However, this tended to impose class structure by education rather than birth, and Confucians never courted any notion of equality. He came to accept that correctness in aspects of life, and proper behaviour in every person, would bring about the kind of stability necessary for a wholesome and peaceful existence. Such concern was to be generated by an inner moral strength of character that set an example and aided others in becoming the same. External standards for living life, though necessary, were not felt to be sufficient.

An internalizing rationale for one's behaviour and beliefs was essential: this was following the path or way, the *tao*, the harmonizing of one's inner self with the way nature meant people to be, and the way society ought to be. *Tao* was the right way, the moral way, the way that led to health and well-being for all. Confucians of all ages saw the entire spectrum of nature and life as one organic whole, comprising a multitude of interconnected parts. As is the case in the human body, the malfunction of just one of these parts leads to disharmony of the organic whole. Harmony and balance were not simply left to chance, however; Heaven was considered to be the force responsible for ordering both. Never viewed as either some form of deity or even a catalytic agent that implements irrevocable destiny, Heaven was informed by humankind's actions, both good and bad, for humankind was the prime mover in the disturbance and restoration of harmony.

The norms of correct social behaviour were termed *li*, adherence to which was required from state and family; *li* is propriety or the ritual associated with it. In the establishing of a gentleman, it can also mean etiquette or courtesy. This is rather a simplistic rendition of a highly complex term, however, and commentators are not of one mind regarding a precise definition. Herrlee Creel noted that the original meaning of *li* was "to sacrifice",[37] suggesting its original use in connection with correct ritual practice in the service of the gods and ancestors. Theodore de Bary highlights the problem of definition, when he analyses just one instance of the term in the *Analects*:

> Courtesy not in keeping with what is rite becomes laborious bustle; caution not in keeping with what is rite becomes timidity; courage becomes brashness; and forthrightness becomes rudeness (8:2). Here some translators render li as "the rules of property" (Legge), or "the prescriptions of ritual" (Waley), while Lau, apparently to avoid overdetermination, translates it as "the spirit of ritual". As before, we have difficulty combining form and spirit in one expression.[38]

Accordingly, it is necessary to be fully aware of the context before becoming over-eager to translate the term in question. If it was the father's place to maintain *li* in his household, then it was the duty of king and government to inform the people of the conduct required by *li*, and the resulting expectations of public conduct. Discord in the cosmic order, and hence *li*, could be instigated by humankind's discordant thoughts and subsequent actions, whether motivated by evil or simply the result of ignorance. Any fool could cause disharmony, only the wise could restore it. Unsurprisingly, in Confucian thought the wise were to be found only among the Confucian sages, their wisdom having been drawn from studying the Confucian *Classics* and other Chinese sources. Wisdom was viewed as the cornerstone of harmony.[39]

In Confucian eyes, the next logical step on the road to the establishment of social harmony was obvious. One simply had to identify those worthies who, through self-realization, had found harmony in their own lives and place them in positions of government. As surely as night follows day, one form of harmony would lead to another, and the restoration of ancient social order would be assured. After all, to govern effectively, rulers and officials needed to be men of character and educated, gentlemen/virtuous men (*chün-tzu/junzi*), and these criteria should not preclude the poorest man from rising to high-ranking places in the government, to assist the hereditary rulers. If Confucius can be said to have portrayed the ideal man, then that worthy was depicted as an attainable ideal. What Confucius did was to internalize the concept of *li* and make it an inner attitude that was naturally expressed by the true gentleman, rather than an outward conformity to ritual practice. But he also gave the word a moral dimension by externalizing it as conformity to high moral and social norms. Those who could do this were the individuals that could make society effectively moral. And there were certainly moral outcomes of his teaching. It was the Confucians who managed to oust the last vestiges of human sacrifice, and who stressed the need for universal education.

Logical as this may have seemed to Confucians, they need only have looked to the Master's own life to see that this idealistic position, entirely peculiar to Confucianism, was untenable. It is not simply a question of those elected to positions of authority being "the right people", but the right people must be elected at the right time. Surely, if the people chosen to govern are not the right ones, then as a result of their poor, or even immoral, decision making, the times throughout their period in office will bring disharmony. But, more than this, as Benjamin Schwartz illumines, even when those appointed are unquestionably the best people, if the time is not right, their considerable efforts will amount to little.[40] As we have seen, Confucius' achievements in public office are hardly worthy of mention, his life ending in disappointment and ineffectiveness. It was only posthumously that fame was accorded him. With the passing of time, the limitations of his idealistic vision became all too apparent; again and again the suitability of superior men to govern effectively – even if they had undoubtedly found self-realization in their private lives – was called into question.

If Neo-Confucians later became deeply concerned with metaphysical speculation in their quest to find the relationship between self-cultivation and the "heavenly" or cosmic order, as noted above, Confucius himself did not seem to be interested in the metaphysical problems of a search for ultimate Reality, or the ultimate fate of the self as these came to be seen in the Taoist interpretation of *Tao*. As has already been noted, we have a choice of seeing the *way* of Confucius as a purely humanistic path through life, or of seeing it as the *Way* of Heaven, of T'ien/Tian. But however we see it, the same concepts of propriety, love, loyalty, sincerity, moral rectitude, wisdom and correct social interaction characterize *Tao* as the products produced by it in successful interactive living.

Essentially, Confucius believed in the right kind of actions and behaviour between king and minister, father and son, husband and wife, elder brother and younger brother and between friend and friend – the so-called Five Relationships of Confucianism. Thus, Confucianism is associated with social stability and moral uprightness. This doctrine of social and moral order is known as the "rectification of names" (*cheng-ming/zhengming*), a doctrine that led to study of the relationship between substance (*t'i-i/tiyi*) and function (*yung/yong*). His message was one advocating the intrinsic *humanity* in each person, and the need for a sense of propriety in all dealings in life. The need for an altruistic concern for others in each person was an important element of his teaching. Indeed, at the heart of Confucius' message is to be found what has been called, not unreasonably, *The Negative Golden Rule*:

> Zigong asked, "Is there one word that one can act upon throughout the course of one's life?" The Master said, "Reciprocity (*shu*) – what you would not want for yourself, do not do to others." *Analects* 15:23[41]

Confucius also propounded a doctrine of moderation that later became formalized in Chinese philosophy as *The Doctrine of the Mean (chung/zhong)*. Commentators on the *Analects* are of one mind that *chung/zhong*, one's own moral nature, and *shu*, treating others as one would oneself, are two sides of the proverbial coin, called *jen/ren*. Since they address the required moral behaviour for both the individual and society, this could well be the "thread" that Confucius claimed runs through his teaching.[42] *Jen/ren*, "love", is an inner quality, one that proceeds from the heart of an individual and that externalizes as serenity and grace in living. It was what Howard Smith termed the "inner dynamic" of *li*.[43] *Jen/ren* is goodness in the sense of its outgoingness to others; it is benevolence and humanity in its fullest expression in an individual. It was a central concept of Confucius' teachings, and might be said to be the fundamental characteristic from which all other qualities develop. Indeed, the doctrine of *jen/ren* was germane to Confucius' mission; he defined it as loving others, personal integrity and altruism.[44]

Confucius imparted his teaching directly to a body of students. Whether, as the *Shih chi/Shiji* (the *Book of Poetry* or *Songs*) attests, Confucius boasted 3000 students, or merely 70, is not the point at issue. What is noteworthy here is the fact that Confucius was the first to accept students regardless of social or financial status. His objective was not the receipt of fees from the sons of aristocrats but the transmission of values to worthy disciples. Accordingly, he instructed them not only in the precise knowledge of ritual observance – a prerequisite for all gentlemen – but also in the sophisticated art of the acquisition of *jen/ren*.

The Confucian *Classics*

As the doctrine of *literati*, Confucianism may well be called a tradition of books, in the sense that it takes the sacred writings of the ancients as the source of values and ideals. It has been agreed that the Confucian classics contain the core of Confucian doctrines, the root of the late Confucian schools and sub-schools, and the fountain-head of all the Confucian streams. Indeed, without a proper knowledge of Confucian classics, it would be impossible for us to draw a full picture of Confucianism.[45]

Confucianism was to become the orthodox doctrine of China for most of that country's long history. In retrospect, later ages were to look back at the figure of Confucius, who looms so large in the history of Chinese thought and practice, and accord him all sorts of greatness, wisdom and sagacity – indeed, veneration amounting to divine status. Later ages were also to accord Confucius words with which he had no necessary association. Modern scholarship acknowledges the fact that many of the so-called Confucian *Classics* are indeed contemporaneous with that worthy, though others precede his lifetime. Whatever their genesis, there is no doubt that later editing, over a considerable period of time, dramatically changed the original texts, whether or not the originals were penned (or, at least, edited) by Confucius. Nevertheless, we cannot overestimate the worth of the Confucian *Classics* to any responsible study of Confucianism.

The year 213 BCE found the Chin/Jin emperor issuing a decree that a unified system of writing should be introduced immediately, while earlier books should be put to the torch. It was an act that created problems for future scholars, for whatever texts survived, or emerged for the first time, could not be interpreted without considerable difficulty. The later Han dynasty did its level best to rectify this unhelpful situation, and in 125 BCE study of the *Classics* became obligatory for students in the imperial college. The Confucian school was thus restored to favour and the texts were quite literally carved in stone. Nevertheless, earlier forgeries were not always easy to identify, whilst various traditions differed in interpretation and commentary. Although modern scholarship no longer accepts this view, tradition ascribes the *Five Classics* to the pen or, at very least, the editorial scrutiny of Confucius. A sixth *Classic*, the *Book of Music* no longer exists.

The Book of Changes: the I Ching/Yijing

As detailed in chapter 2, the oldest of the Chinese *Classics*, the *I Ching/Yijing*, predates Confucius. Its prestige in China has been unrivalled since its incorporation into the Confucian *Classics* during the Han dynasty. Recognizing the fact that its responses are believed to be morally geared to the evolution of the self and of society, it is not difficult to see why this manual on how to meld one's life-condition and establish a right balance and harmony in life came to be associated with the teachings of Confucius.

The Odes (Shih Ching/Shijing)

Appropriately also called the *Book of Poetry* or the *Book of Songs*, the *Odes* comprises some three hundred and five songs, each bearing the tenet, "Have no depraved thought". Tradition has it that Confucius compiled the work from over three thousand songs in order to produce a text that could be used for educational purposes. Although modern scholarship has questioned this tradition, there is no doubt that Confucius did use them in his teaching. All three official versions of the *Odes* are now lost to the sands of time, and it is likely that the extant compilation, named the *Poetry of Mao* after its compiler, predates Confucius. The subject matter is arranged in four sections, with 160 poems in one section describing daily life in thirteen different states. The poems also describe courts, festivals, hunts, banquets, even dances, and contain love songs. Additionally, they give accounts of historic or legendary figures, and details of liturgies.

The Book of History/Documents (Shu Ching/Shujing)

It is in these ancient documents that one encounters examples of what most scholars today consider to be forgeries, at least in the oldest chapters. Ironically, it was also this *Classic* that was long considered as the most important. It was believed that Confucius had placed in it accounts of royal and governmental speeches in chronological order, and he was also credited with introducing each chapter. Confucians gained great solace from its teachings, not only because they saw it as reflecting the times in which they lived, but also because they considered its doctrine to be germane to all manner of Confucian thought.

The Classic of Rites (Li Chi/Liji)

This work, the date and provenance of which are hotly disputed, contains three texts compiled at the turn of the millennium, but based on earlier materials, *viz*:

1 The *Ceremonials* (*I-li/Yili*), an instruction book of etiquette for the nobility detailing how one should or should not behave on formal occasions.

2 The *Book of Rites* or *Rituals* (*Li Chi/Liji*), comprising 49 sections that range from instruction on ritual and the rites, government and education, to music and poetry. This text is preoccupied with the family rituals that, in turn, are germane to an (originally noble) ancestral cult that dates back to the dawn of Chinese history. Not only are deceased members of the family to be remembered and honoured in ritual observance, but they are, at all times, to be kept informed of those rites of passage effectuated on earth for the living members of the family. Between the times of the Han and T'ang/Tang dynasties, the text became the mainstay of Chinese society.

3 Finally, there is the *Institutes of Chou/Zhou* (*Chou-li/Zhouli*), which depicts an idealized form of government in Chou/Zhou times.

The Spring – Autumn Annals (Ch'un-ch'iu/Chunqiu)

Traditionally associated with three commentaries, the Tso/Zuo (*Tso-chuan/Zuozhuan*), Kung-yang, and the Ku-liang, the annals are so-called because they depict the period between 722 and 481 BCE, what has become known as the "Spring and Autumn Period". The work chronicles the decline of ancient political and moral order in Lu, Confucius' native state. It was long thought that the *Annals* were a personal record of Confucius' condemnation of the moral decadence of his age, though modern scholarship has refuted this. Nevertheless, Confucians still look on the *Annals* as a guide for moral world order. On a metaphysical front, the annals introduced into Confucian teachings the concept of *yin* and *yang*.

Confucian development

So what does Confucianism have to offer today? Theodore de Bary raises some interesting points in addressing this vital question:

> What purpose is served by freezing the definition at some moment far in the past, when what we want to know is something about the role of Confucianism yesterday or today? Again, since the question, as we have it, is one raised all over East and Southeast Asia, the answer could well take many forms: Korean, Japanese, and Vietnamese, as well as Chinese. Strictly speaking, we would need to consider in each case how Confucianism was understood and practiced – how it came to be transmitted, interpreted, accepted, and acted upon in this time and place.[46]

We will do well to heed de Bary's warning that though China is the homeland of Confucianism, the ancient tradition was never confined to those shores. Any comprehensive survey that either ignores or evades its spread to East and south-east Asia (not to mention North America, Europe, and the rest of the world), cannot be considered a responsible one. Scholars of Chinese philosophy in general and Confucianism in particular have proposed a variety of paradigms that they see as reflecting their views as how best to study the development of Confucianism. These range from the twofold paradigm of Fung Yu-lan to the fivefold division favoured by some modern scholars. Following Yao's rubrics in the main,[47] we propose a system that divides the stages of Confucian evolution into five perspectives.

Confucianism in formation

In this initial period of development, the extant tradition already deeply rooted in Chinese culture becomes nurtured by Confucius and his contemporaries, and developed by his successors. Here, in the Spring and Autumn period, Confucianism takes on a classical presentation (*ju-hsüeh/ruxue* or *ju-chia/rujia*) with its proponents, led by Confucius, viewing the extant tradition in a new light, a light that shone as a beacon on the road to peace and harmony.

The succeeding Warring States period (*ca.* 403–221 BCE) saw China in the throes of political upheaval. The larger states were consuming smaller and weaker ones, a disturbing and unsatisfactory state of affairs that eventually led to the unification of China. Not only individuals, but also the rulers themselves were seeking the advice of philosophers on how to govern well or just survive in times of turmoil. The responses given to this question saw the rise of three main strands of thought. One group, led by authors of some of the passages in the *Tao Te Ching/Daodejing*, advocated a return to primitive times, with a rejection of all social conventions and institutions including wisdom, humaneness (*jen/ren*) and righteousness (*i/yi*). This, they argued, would develop filial piety (*hsiao/xiao*) and fraternal love (*ti*).

Pessimists mentioned in the *Analects* such as the Gatekeeper at the Stone Gate (14:41) and the Tillers at the Ford (18:6) are included in the second group of advisers, who could well be described as "No-hopers". Their limited vision foresaw nothing but doom and gloom for the future of the world, so what was the point of offering any positive advice? The third group certainly saw a future for the world; equally certainly, they advised that the world would have to change in order to secure any meaningful future. Differences in outlook amongst the third group led to the evolution of three major schools in Chinese philosophical thought – Confucianism, Mohism and Taoism.

Confucianism evolved as a major school under the direction of Meng-tzu/Mengzi and Hsün-tzu/Xunzi. We have noted already the concerns of Benjamin Schwartz when he drew attention to what he termed, "the problem of founders and leaders".[48] His point was that it is extremely difficult to extricate the original teachings of the founders from the various interpretations of the followers. In most religions, after the death of the founder society is left with the discordant voices of followers, totally dedicated to their leader, yet differing in how they interpret his teachings. The two outstanding pupils of Confucius that follow are a case in point.

Meng-tzu/Mengzi and Hsün-tzu/Xunzi

Meng-tzu/Mengzi (Latin Mencius) (371–289 BCE?) and Hsün-tzu/Xunzi (313–238 BCE?) were passionate in their loyalty to the teachings of the master. Both saw humanity and righteousness as high moral values particularly in kingly government. They adored Confucius and offered their total support to his advice on education, the reification of names, and respect for social distinctions. They were unequivocal in their belief that every man could become the "superior man", irrespective of birth but, ironically, this is also where they parted company. Meng-tzu/Mengzi took as his starting point what he interpreted as the Confucian inference that, in order for such a premise to have warrant, human nature must be inherently good, an issue on which, frankly, Confucius was virtually silent. Meng-tzu/Mengzi was passionate about humanity, particularly the concept of righteousness arising in the family before spreading onto the world stage, though he offered no advice as to how this should be effectuated. Nor did he show any interest in religious beliefs or practices, though he did approve of shamans and he believed in the inner flowing vital force or *ch'i/qi*.

In support of his position (which he also believed to be that of Confucius), that human nature is inherently good, Meng-tzu/Mengzi argued that humanity cannot bear to see others suffer. He used the analogy of a child falling into a well. His point was that onlookers will act instantly to save the child, not because they find the child's cries annoying, nor in order to impress the child's parents or even neighbours, but because human nature, being inherently good, cannot stand to see suffering. He went as far as to say that anyone who lacks the basic human qualities of commiseration, shame and dislike, and the ability to discern right from wrong, is not a human being.

Meng-tzu/Mengzi firmly believed that inherent within humankind is the innate knowledge of what is good and the innate ability to do good. He developed his argument by advocating that humankind is born with what he called "the four beginnings":

> The mind of commiseration is the beginning of humanity; the mind of shame and dislike is the beginning of righteousness; the mind of civility and courtesy is the beginning of ritual; the mind that distinguishes between right and wrong is the beginning of wisdom. People have these four beginnings just as they have their four limbs . . . If those people with these four beginnings within themselves know how to develop and fulfill them, they will be as fires beginning to burn or streams beginning to flow.
>
> *Mencius* 2A. 6[49]

Hsün-tzu/Xunzi, meanwhile, took quite the opposite view, holding that the human being's nature is innately evil. Far from having to develop a basic nature in order to become a sage, the human being must curb natural tendencies to do evil by dedicating time especially to education, discipline and rites. For Hsün-tzu/Xunzi, Heaven is no more than another name for nature, bereft of ethical principles, impersonal and controlling natural law without fear or favour. Meng-tzu/Mengzi, on the other hand, saw Heaven as the spiritual power whose support is essential to government and individual alike. In fact Meng-tzu/Mengzi was the first to speak of "humane government". Meng-tzu/Mengzi and Hsün-tzu/Xunzi were contemporaries, and at the time the latter was probably the more influential, admired by many for his vision and clarity of thought that found expression in his erudite Confucian philosophical essays. Some of his pupils rose to the highest possible positions in government and elsewhere; ironically, it was also his pupils who were partly responsible for his downfall. With people mindful of their brutal use of power during the Ch'in/Qin dynasty, as well as Hsün-tzu/Xunzi's insistence on the evil nature of humankind, Hsün-tzu/Xunzi fell from favour and was eventually excluded from the line of Confucian transmission. It was Meng-tzu/Mengzi, not Hsün-tzu/Xunzi, who, by the time of the Sung/Song dynasty was being spoken of as "the second sage", his name forever linked with that of Confucius.

Confucianism in adaptation

The Ch'in/Qin dynasty was governed by the Legalists. Under their direction, the Ch'in/Qin finished building the Great Wall, produced a simplified and uniform written language, and extended military influence beyond existing Chinese boundaries. The Legalist position could not have been further removed from a Confucianism that considered rites and music to be important to society. Having no time or place for the Confucian concept of *li*, and hence no room for what they saw as fanciful talk of an "inner realm", the Legalist position was a purely pragmatic one based on a system of reward for those who delivered, and severe punishment for those who did not. Its ideal was the formation of a powerful state, generating a fearsome war machine capable of withstanding any threat from without, and having no place for Confucian values such as contentment and harmony from within.[50]

The Ch'in/Qin also established the first unified Chinese empire, introducing a system of provinces still evident today in twenty-first century China; gone forever were the old feudal domains. In order to obviate any form of criticism, the Legalist government ousted all Confucians from office and in 213 BCE books of the ritual schools were put to the torch. However, the government's refusal to brook any form of criticism led to its being hoist by its own petard. Within fourteen years, the Ch'in/Qin dynasty had been overthrown, and in 206 BCE the leading revolutionary Liu P'ang/Liu Pang founded the Han dynasty. The Ch'in/Qin dynasty had banned Confucian teachings, doing its utmost to destroy all its books. Ironically, it was an action indirectly responsible for returning Confucianism to favour under the Han. Those books held in official archives had been spared the torch, while other Confucian books had been hidden from sight or imprinted on minds. Confucian *Classics* were once again coming into circulation but they were in dire need of commentary and explanation. With Confucian scholars eminently capable of providing both, it was they who increased in importance, gaining influence at court and hence the ear of Liu P'ang/Liu Pang (now Emperor Kao-tsung/Gaozong).

The second stage of evolution saw Confucian thinkers of the Han Dynasty recovering from the persecutions of the Ch'in/Qin and, in 136 BCE, Confucianism was made the official state philosophy. The country's leaders began taking Hsün-tzu/Xunzi's point that Confucianism offered the most balanced form of social theory available. They made the case that Legalism may well have a place in government in times of war, but it should not be considered a serious permanent option. Confucians began to show their competence in conducting court ceremonials, alongside their knowledge of state administration. One Confucian scholar demonstrated his awareness of statesmanship by reminding the new emperor that, whilst it is possible to conquer an empire on horseback, it is impossible to rule from the saddle. This was in response to Kao-tsung/Gaozong's rebuke of a Confucian scholar, who repeatedly held up the *Book of History* and the *Book of Odes* as examples *par excellence* of correct behaviour. Kao-tsung/Gaozong was impressed, and the year 195 BCE found him in the role of the first government official ever to offer sacrifice to Confucius. With their new found influence, Confucians began replacing Legalists in government office. Nevertheless, it was the new Taoist religion that curried favour with early Han emperors and empresses, and the first hundred or so years of Han rule saw a Taoist majority in government.

Although Confucianism had become a major school with numerous manifestations in the Warring States period, it was merely one school among many. Confucian scholars now set about restoring and editing as many lost and fragmented texts as possible, often adding their own lengthy commentaries, particularly on the classical texts. At the same time, Han Confucians adapted their doctrines in recognition of the threat from other schools. They were aware that times were changing and that Confucianism could not survive in isolation. Accordingly, Confucian scholars began to address the needs of the empire and the doctrines of the other schools. There followed a reforming and a renewal of Confucian doctrine in the light of the influence of the schools of Legalism, Mohism, and Taoism, as well as the school of Yin–Yang and the Five Agents. One of Hsün-tzu/Xunzi's outstanding pupils, Han Fei (d. 233 BCE), had earlier become the most prominent scholar in the Legalist school.

A certain scholar, Tung Chung-shu/Dong Zhongshu (176–104 BCE), won the ear of the young Emperor Wu (r. 140–86 BCE). His advice was to follow only the teachings of Confucius, as exemplified in the *Six Classics* (the sixth *Classic* being the no longer extant *Classic of Music*) and to dismiss all non-Confucian officials from government. So impressed was Emperor Wu with the thrust of thought of this scholar that he immediately appointed Tung/Dong as chief minister of a princely state. In 136 BCE, Wu made Confucianism the state orthodoxy, making it the basis for state education. Unlike Ch'in/Qin times, punitive measures were never taken against those who wished to study the teachings of any of the "hundred schools", but the recruitment of those who wished to be considered for government office depended on an examination system that tested the candidates' knowledge of Confucianism and the *Six Classics*.

Given this edict, the glorification of Confucius was inevitable, and the temptations offered by forgery great. By the middle of the first century BCE, Han scholars intent on immortalizing Confucius produced a new type of literature, commonly referred to as apocryphal. This *we-shu* (or "woof" of a fabric) they argued was penned by Confucius during his lifetime as a supplement to the *Six Classics* or six "warps" (*ching/jing*). For the Han forgers, the six woofs complemented the six warps and encapsulated Confucian teaching in its entirety. In apocryphal works such as the *Ch'un Ch'iu/Chunqiu*, otherwise known as the *Annals of Spring and Autumn*, Confucius is elevated to the heights of adoration, someone for whom no praise is too high. In another, the *Expository Charts on Confucius*, Confucius is accorded divine status. Held to be the son of a god who rejoiced in the name of "the Black Emperor", Confucius is depicted here as a foreteller of the future and the worker of many miracles. "If these views had prevailed, Confucius would have held in China a position similar to that of Jesus Christ, and Confucianism would have become a religion in the proper sense of the term."[51]

These views did not prevail, however, for Confucianism was too pragmatic to harbour mystery and superstition, and the movement fell into disrepute after a hundred years or so, at the end of the second century BCE. Rational scholars who brought about its demise, denying Confucius any powers beyond those of a sage, formed a group called the Old Text school. This school evolved in opposition to the New Text school, supported by Tung Chung-shu/Dong Zhongshu, whose versions of the *Classics* were written in a script familiar in the Han dynasty. The Old Text school owes its name to its insistence on being in possession of the oldest versions of the *Classics*. These versions predate the burning of books in 213 BCE and were written in a script long outdated by Han times.

By the end of the later Han dynasty, scholars of the New Text and the Old Text schools were directing their attention and exhausting their energies on exegesis of the Confucian *Classics* (*ching-hsüeh/jingxue*) as well as debating the teachings of Confucius. The huge void created by the burning of books left Confucian scholars little time for doctrinal examination of the *Classics*, and the doctrine of human nature was the only philosophical consideration that evolved in the Han. Against the teachings of both Meng-tzu/Mengzi and Hsün-tzu/Xunzi, Yang Hsiung/Yang Xiong (53 BCE–18 CE) argued that human innate nature is both good *and* evil, not simply one or the other, and the way life is led will determine which aspect is cultivated. Simple as this statement may be, it nevertheless forever focused the attentions of Confucian scholars on the insurmountable problem of human nature.

It was during this period of adaptation that the doctrine of the inter-action between Heaven and humankind was developed – a metaphysical exposition that formed the spine of the new Confucianism. Since Heaven, as the transcendental reality, is the source of human life, humankind must reflect Heaven's principles in order to secure its Mandate. Heaven has dominion over Earth, just as surely as an earthly ruler governs his people, a husband his wife, etc. But such earthly authority must be effectuated in a moral, humane way in order for *yin* and *yang* to be in harmony, life to be sweet and the harvest plentiful. To act in an immoral or indifferent manner towards one's subjects or family will bring about a disharmony between *yin* and *yang* that will ensure that the crops fail at the same time as human relations break down. Evil will then become the dominant force in the world and Heaven will remove its Mandate. Although Tung/Dong did not agree with Meng-tzu/Mengzi that human nature is innately good, their differences were nominal, and Tung/Dong explicitly compared his theory of human nature with the thought of Meng-tzu/Mengzi. He argued that, as surely as *yin* and *yang* operate in Heaven, since humankind is a replica of Heaven, then *yin* and *yang* must operate similarly in the mind of the human being. Accordingly, Tung/Dong identified two elements of the human mind which he designated *hsing* (humankind's nature) and *ching/jing* (human emotions).[52]

Tung/Dong saw the principles of Heaven and Earth as manifest in the Confucian *Classics* and he urged the young Emperor Wu to apply them to his rule. An admirer of all the *Classics*, Tung/Dong held the *Spring and Autumn Annals* above the others, convinced that Confucian scholars had philosophized over Heaven and humankind in order to produce this work. For Tung, virtuous rule, moral education and the Mandate of Heaven were indivisible, a point he made time and again in his work *Luxuriant Gems of the Spring and Autumn Annals*, echoing an earlier sentiment attested in the *Book of Poetry* and the *Book of History*.

In early Taoist history (third and fourth centuries CE), a philosophical movement arose that focused on the study of three ancient "mysterious" texts, known to, but not peculiar to, Taoism – the *I Ching/Yijing*, the *Tao Te Ching/Daodejing* and the *Chuang-tzu/Zhuangzi*. By the time of the Wei-chin/Wei-jin dynasties (220–420), an eclectic culture had become transparent in the melding of Taoist philosophy with Confucianism as well as Confucian influence on Taoist principles: "In each way Daoism and Confucianism came together in what is known as Dark Learning or Mysterious Learning (*hsuan-hsueh/xuan xue*). This was to have a lasting influence upon the later development of Chinese thought."[53]

经典道家

4 Classical Taoism

What is Taoism?

Taoism is the most complicated of the Chinese religions, mainly because it is multi-faceted, varied and diffuse, but also because its many strands are themselves complex with origins that are obscure. But what can be said is that at the heart of Taoism is the word *Tao*; it is the *-ism* that is problematic. The term Taoism was first used to refer to a religious school of thought in the second century BCE when the historian Ssu-ma T'an/Sima Tan mentioned the school of *Tao-te/Daode*. The Chinese used the word *tao* in a variety of ways for it simply meant "way". Tao-*ism*, however, refers to religious beliefs and practices that centre around the concept of *Tao*, which will be examined in greater depth below. Tao-*ism* is concerned with two interrelated strands; one is *Tao-chia/Daojia*, which is classical, philosophical and mystical Taoism, and the other is its more overtly religious, ritualistic and institutional expressions, *Tao-chiao/Daojiao*.[1] In this chapter we shall concentrate on the former and leave religious Taoism for chapter 6. However, it is important to remember that both are overlapping approaches to *Tao* and that a neat division between the two is neither appropriate nor academic.

The Chinese character representing the word *Tao* is made up of two parts, one is the ideogram for a human, and the other for forward movement; combined they suggest a "way". In Taoism, that "way" becomes ultimate – the *Way* of the universe, Reality at its ultimate, and existence as what emanates from that Reality and returns to it. Essentially, Taoism has always been a highly fluid phenomenon, evolving, diversifying, returning to past ideas, developing new ones and absorbing from its changing environments. The historian Ssu-ma T'an/Sima Tan, noted above, demonstrated well the eclectic nature of what he termed Taoism in his own day: "As to its techniques, it conforms with the great yin and yang; it selects the good points of the Literati and Mohists; it chooses the essentials from the School of Terms and the School of Totalitarians." Taoists, he says, "change with the times and respond to the transformations of things-and-beings".[2] Thus, Taoism is a religion that has no formulated, characterized sets of beliefs, for it is too all-encompassing for such definitive dogma. There are many pathways in Taoism, sometimes to the same goal and sometimes to different goals. And throughout its long history, it has been heavily influenced by Confucianism, Buddhism and popular religion. Indeed, for many Chinese the boundaries between each have always been thoroughly blurred. Allinson makes the valid point – and one that will be reiterated in different ways throughout this book – "we are reminded of the generalized folk saying that every Chinese person is a Confucian, a Taoist, and a Buddhist. He is a Confucian when everything is going well; he is a Taoist when things are falling apart; and he is a Buddhist as he approaches death".[3] Nevertheless, Taoism has always been close to the psyche of the Chinese people.

While the roots of religious Taoism are complex, those of classical Taoism are less so, despite its antiquity. Nevertheless, no single source or sources can be traced. Rather, we have to reckon with a variety of like-minded ideas: some were gathered together here and there in written form, others were preserved in oral traditions and even in sayings from everyday life. When, centuries later, there was sufficient evidence of such an, albeit somewhat diverse, body of thought in Chinese society, some term was necessary to describe this "school" of thought, and that term was *Tao-chia/Daojia* or Taoism. But, while traditionally, the roots of Taoism are traced back to three major thinkers – Lao-tzu/Laozi, Chuang-tzu/Zhuangzi and Lieh-tzu/Liezi, it is done so anachronistically. In fact, none of these three would have referred to himself as Taoist.

Lao-tzu/Laozi and the *Tao Te Ching/Daodejing*

Apart from the Bible, no other book has been translated as often as the *Tao Te Ching/Daodejing*. This is so despite the brevity of the text – a mere eighty-one very short chapters, many amounting to just a few lines. It is an exquisite text, profound and yet delightful in its simplicity and serenity. Traditionally, its author was Lao-tzu/Laozi, "Old Master" "Old Boy", "Old Fellow", and his real name was perhaps Li Erh/Li Er. Unfortunately, the *Historical Records* of Ssu-ma Ch'ien/Sima Qian at the end of the second and beginning of the first century BCE, and our only source of the life of Lao-tzu/Laozi, provides only a sketchy and rather unclear picture that is a mixture of what he took to be fact, with added legend. From this account we learn of Lao-tzu/Laozi's mother's conception after she had seen a shooting star and the birth of Lao-tzu/Laozi with white hair sixty-two years later. According to Ssu-ma Ch'ien/Sima Qian, Confucius was supposed to have visited Lao-tzu/Laozi, an occasion that came to be accepted in both Taoist and Confucian circles. Tired of the decadent life he witnessed in society and of the deteriorating Chou/Zhou dynasty, Lao-tzu/Laozi left for the western borders of China, travelling on an ox or on an oxcart. It was at the Western Gate, at the request of the gatekeeper of the border pass, that Lao-tzu/Laozi wrote down the content of the *Tao Te Ching/Daodejing* in five thousand Chinese characters, before disappearing to the West. By the middle of the third century BCE, Lao-tzu/Laozi was accepted as the person responsible for the text, and it was therefore known originally as the *Lao-tzu/Laozi* .

Today, we are faced with a variety of views concerning the nature, authorship and dating of the text of the *Tao Te Ching/Daodejing*. Traditionally, the text is accepted as a mystical writing informed by belief in *Tao*, and *Tao* is believed to be anything from an "ultimate vision of an Absolute" and an anthropomorphic deity,[4] to a cosmogonic force that sustains the world. Others focus not on *Tao* itself, but on the *experience* of the individual, the "oneness or some kind of mystic union with the ultimate ground of reality" that provides meaning for life.[5] Others reject the mysticism of the text, and even the concept of *Tao* as a metaphysical abstract. Such scholars also stress that the *Tao Te Ching/Daodejing* is about *experiences* but not of a mystical, ultimate Reality.[6] According to this view, the *Tao Te Ching/Daodejing* is all about "self-cultivation", "inner cultivation" and *Tao* refers to the inner experience that results from meditative praxis. Harold Roth, for example, believes that such inner cultivation "is at the very heart of the *Laozi*".[7]

Similar are the ideas of Mark Csikszentmihalyi, who argues that *Tao* is a term that linked together different groups as the term expressing the principles and goals of their practices. To him, *Tao* was a "common denominator", "a way of speaking about a unitary phenomenon that appeared in different guises once it was constructed in different traditions".[8] Regardless of the original historical setting of the *Tao Te Ching/Daodejing*, however, and important as such scholarly perspectives are, we should not eschew what the text has become, and what it has meant, and means now, to the Taoist religion. It would be a mistake not to value the mystical dimension of the text, given its long historical interpretation as such, concomitant with *Tao* as a unifying ultimate Reality.

The *Tao Te Ching/Daodejing* is divided into two, the first part dealing – or rather beginning – with the word *Tao* and the second part with the word *Te/De*, "Virtue" or "Power". *Ching* means "prestigious book" or "classic". Clearly, it is a text that aims to dislodge normal thought patterns, despite containing pragmatic advice for rulers. Angus Graham described it as a "masterpiece of a kind of intelligence at the opposite pole from the logical".[9] However, its terseness makes it a difficult text, its meanings only hinted at, like peaks of mountains whose valley depths are hidden in mists. It is, thus, an ambiguous text open to different literal, figurative or manipulative translations. This is especially so since the ancient characters in which the text was written contain no indications of grammar at all. So it is a difficult text to translate and can be translated in a variety of ways.[10] Transmission of the text, too, has been anything but pure, with a legion of past commentators and competing political and philosophical views informing its transmission. It is not surprising, then, that some can see the *Tao Te Ching/Daodejing* as a completely humanistic and atheistic text, while others centre on *Tao* as a cosmogonic, eternal force that sustains the world[11] and one that is present as the energy and force extant in each individual entity, making each what it is.[12]

So did Lao-tzu/Laozi write the text? Traditionally, the answer is yes; academically, we would have to say that it is very unlikely. Its sources were probably multiple – sayings, bits of poems, fragments of this and that – all woven together by its compilers to suit and enhance their particular philosophies. The bottom line is that there is unlikely to be any connection at all between a man called Lao-tzu/Laozi and the *Tao Te Ching/Daodejing* that he is said to have written. LaFargue considers that a number of small informal schools, each grouped round a teacher, contributed to the text, in which case the aphorisms of the *Tao Te Ching/Daodejing* are relevant to the life-situations of their own time.[13] If this is the case, then is it right to lift those aphorisms into modern contexts and to interpret *Tao* that occurs within them as a unifying force and source of the universe? Whatever the origins of the text, it is clear that it has stood the tests of time and context in providing meaning for life. If the aphorisms gave spiritual sustenance in the distant past, there is much to be said for their ability to do so in the present, albeit in different contexts and with different meanings. This, indeed, is how the *Tao Te Ching/Daodejing* has taken its place in the passage of time: if there were originally separate statements like so many different beads, they have become strung together in what is now regarded as a more unified text. When, then, did the *Tao Te Ching/Daodejing* come into being? The traditional date of about 500 BCE and the time of Confucius can be dismissed. The Guodian version of the text,[14] though not the traditional version, shows that some form of it must have been present before 300 BCE, so this suggests a date of the fourth century BCE, in the Warring States period, but bits and pieces may belong to oral traditions stretching back to the sixth century.[15]

In the content of the *Tao Te Ching/Daodejing* there are many juxtaposed themes. Central is the concept of *Tao* that can only be vaguely depicted in negative terms as opposed to the power and potentiality of *Te/De*. Egoistic activity based on desires is balanced with the goal of egoless, spontaneous action. Outward strength is balanced with the goal of a soft and yielding nature; external force with inner power; the masculine with the feminine; verbosity with silence; fullness with emptiness; the contrived with the natural; Being with Non-Being; plurality with oneness; knowledge with ignorance. The *Tao Te Ching/Daodejing* searches out the spaces not the forms, like the space that makes a door possible, and the emptiness within a pot that makes it what it is. The concepts of the sage, and rulership according to sage qualities, are central issues, yet these sections are balanced with those that praise the meditative life. The two, in fact, are seen as complementary. The externalized values of conventional living by Confucian virtue and ethics are portrayed as degeneration from the experience of *Tao* and *Te/De* within all life, for *Tao* is beyond language and conventional thought. Returning to a *Tao*-orientated life ensures right action from inner naturalness, not from outward conformity. And the more Confucians stressed the need for moral action, the more evidence that would be of its decline!

Chuang-tzu/Zhuangzi

The work of Chuang-tzu/Zhuangzi, given the same title as his name, is a delight to read. Instead of the terse depth of the *Tao Te Ching/Daodejing*, we find a plethora of stories, amusing incidents and anecdotes on which to feed the mind. Wilhelm called Chuang-tzu/Zhuangzi "a splendid figure in Chinese intellectual and spiritual life".[16] In contrast to the vague identity of Lao-tzu/Laozi, in Chuang-tzu/Zhuangzi a refreshingly vivid person comes across, with an evolved sense of humour and wit, and the ability to convey profound thoughts through simple imagery. Burton Watson pointed out that humour is rare in Chinese philosophical literature, but in the *Chuang-tzu/Zhuangzi* "it is the single most potent device employed by the writer to jar the reader out of his mundane complacencies and waken him to the possibility of another realm of experience".[17] Yet the work has a somewhat elusive nature that challenges conventional thought, and he loved discourse and discussion – especially if there could be no right answer!

As in the case of Lao-tzu/Laozi, the second to first century BCE historian Ssu-ma Ch'ien/Sima Qian gives a biography of Chuang-tzu/Zhuangzi in his *Historical Records*. He tells that he was born in the town of Meng, located today in the province of Honan/Henan. His real name was Chuang Chou/Zhuang Zhou; -*tzu*/*zi*, the honorary title of "Master", was added later. He worked at the Lacquer Garden, though it is not clear what this was. Ssu-ma Ch'ien/Sima Qian states that he was offered an important post at the court. However, Chuang-tzu/Zhuangzi declined. He likened acceptance to the sacrificial ox that was well fed, well nourished and well decked. But at the moment of sacrifice the animal would certainly wish to be an ordinary creature of the field. Just so, Chuang-tzu/Zhuangzi saw no value in a privileged life at court. His reply was blunt: "Go away! Don't mess with me! I would rather enjoy myself in the mud than be a slave to the ruler of some kingdom. I shall never accept such an office, and so I shall remain free to do as I will."[18]

From the *Chuang-tzu/Zhuangzi* it is known that Chuang-tzu/Zhuangzi was married and had children, and his wife's death is the subject of one discussion. He does not appear to have been wealthy, and was more concerned with inner riches of the self than outward materiality. While he shunned political life, he seemed to have had a good enough knowledge to be aptly critical of it. Living in the difficult age of the Warring States period of Chinese history, it is small wonder that the turbulence of the age drew forth his distaste of ruling parties of his day.

Turning to the authorship of the *Chuang-tzu/Zhuangzi*, there are similar problems to those that beset the *Tao Te Ching/Daodejing*. The *Chuang-tzu/Zhuangzi* is a composite work, and it is only the first seven chapters, called the *Inner Chapters*, which are fairly consistently ascribed to Chuang-tzu/Zhuangzi himself. Of the remaining twenty-four chapters, some have been ascribed to an author heavily influenced by the thought of Lao-tzu/Laozi, others to eclectic and syncretic Taoists of the early Han dynasty, disciples of Chuang-tzu/Zhuangzi and others.[19] Chapters 8–22 are generally recognized as the *Outer Chapters*, and the remaining Chapters 23–33 are sometimes set aside as *Mixed Chapters*.[20] The whole work, then, is well described as "a catch-bag, an anthology of stories and incidents, thought and reflections which have gathered round the name of Chuang Tzu".[21] The dates of Chuang-tzu/Zhuangzi are fairly well established as somewhere in the mid-fourth and early part of the third centuries BCE, traditionally 369–286 BCE. However, the other contributors of material to the *Chuang-tzu/Zhuangzi* lived much later, and it was centuries later that the text reached a completed form.

The *Inner Chapters* deal with many topics – the need to transcend conventional knowledge and worldly concerns; the folly of definitive rights and wrongs; spontaneity in living one's life; problems of living an enlightened life in the working world, the advantages of being useless and unemployed; living by the innate power within the self rather than by outward conventions; death; statecraft and the ideal ruler. The content contains a rich mixture of tales about rich and poor, kings, sages, robbers, potters, butchers, carpenters and many others. And beggars and cripples are treated in exactly the same way as kings and sages. Underlying all is the focus on *Tao* as that which makes possible the flight of the self to unlimited freedom in the natural spontaneity of life lived within the reality that is *Tao*. Such spontaneity is reflected particularly and superbly in the spontaneous character of the content in the *Inner Chapters*. Additionally, Chuang-tzu/Zhuangzi uses what has been described by some writers as a "dizzying array of literary techniques" in the *Inner Chapters*.[22] The term "dizzying" is a pertinent one, since it conjures up the desired effect of throwing the mind out of its logical and normal thought patterns.

Those who reject the metaphysical concept of *Tao* as a cosmic force in the *Chuang-tzu/Zhuangzi*, as in the *Tao Te Ching/Daodejing*, take a much more individualized view of any mysticism that might be present in the texts. Self-cultivation is usually the tack that such writers take in viewing the texts in this way. Thus, for example, Allinson considers self-transformation to be the underlying theme of the *Inner Chapters* of the *Chuang-tzu/Zhuangzi*. As he sees it, Chuang-tzu/Zhuangzi's purpose is one of "silencing the analytical thinking reflexes of the reader and simultaneously empowering the reader's dormant intuitive or holistic mental functions".[23] The transformation here is from the controlled mind, "to the absolute freedom of the mind to move in any direction that it fancies" – the aim of the text, as Allinson understands it.[24] Clearly it is a relevant aim whether one wishes to retain a unifying and mystical *Tao* in the *Chuang-tzu/Zhuangzi* or reject it.

Lieh-tzu/Liezi

Very little is known about the life of Lieh-tzu/Liezi. He seemed to have lived in poverty and as a recluse in the principality of Cheng/Zheng, where he remained for forty years before being forced to leave because of famine. It was then that his disciples are said to have written the book that bears his name, including a few scant details about the sage. Chuang-tzu/Zhuangzi refers to him so there must have been some prior tradition about him, perhaps a collection of his sayings. But, despite the portrayal of Lieh-tzu/Liezi in the *Chuang-tzu/Zhuangzi* as a real person, there is no evidence to suggest that he existed outside legend. The book that bears his name, the *Lieh-tzu/Liezi*, was probably compiled several centuries after his supposed lifetime. Many now date the text to around 300 CE or later, though the first commentator was Chang Chan/Zhang Zhan in the second half of the fourth century CE.[25] About a quarter of the text is found in other sources of the third and second centuries BCE. So a good deal of the content of the *Lieh-tzu/Liezi* is gleaned from older sources like the *Chuang-tzu/Zhuangzi*. Also, like the *Chuang-tzu/Zhuangzi*, the *Lieh-tzu/Liezi* contains tales and legends, parables and miracles, humorous anecdotes and jokes, but also a good deal of reflective philosophy, presented through the medium of prose and rhythmic verse. Magic and mystery are interwoven. There are deep messages to be gleaned from episodes relating to life; dream and reality; knowledge and ignorance; the extraordinary; destiny and freedom; and morality. All these topics are dealt with in order to explain the nature of *Tao* in life. The *Lieh-tzu/Liezi* is less critical of Confucius the man than the *Chuang-tzu/Zhuangzi* is at times, but artfully uses words put into the mouth of Confucius himself to criticize Confucian values.

Such, then, is the philosophical foundation of Taoism, retrospectively cast back to three ancient sages and the works ascribed to them. We now need to turn to the heart of their philosophy and examine the concept of *Tao* as they understood it and as it has since been understood.

Tao

In chapter 25 of the *Tao Te Ching/Daodejing* there are the following words about *Tao*:

> Something formless, yet lacking nothing,
> There before Heaven and Earth.
> Silent and void,
> Standing alone and unchanging,
> Revolving, yet inexhaustible.
> Perhaps it is the mother of the universe.
> I do not know its name
> So I call it Tao.
> If pressed, I call it "Great".

It was noted earlier that the Chinese ideogram for *tao* contained the sign for moving on, as well as a head. It indicated moving step by step, of walking feet, possibly in rhythmic movement.[26] The use of the character for the head combined with a foot suggests a "way", "path", "road", or even "method", with the head suggesting, perhaps, that it should be a thoughtful way forward. Thus it can be used in the sense of a political way, a social way, a religious way, or the way of Heaven. It can include the manner in which one goes along the way in the sense of "to lead" or "to guide". It can also mean "to speak", "to tell" or "to instruct".[27] It is a very old word that can obviously be used in a quite mundane sense. But from ancient times, it could be used in the sense of the way of humanity, with connotations of morality, virtue and righteousness. In one of its more abstract meanings, and in a metaphysical sense, it can mean "Way" or "Truth" in the sense of a doctrine, or a principle.[28] Here, the meaning of the word is deepened, and it is in this sense that we shall need to look at the concept in Taoism, where the term was projected to its metaphysical ultimate. In Taoism, *Tao* represents ultimate Reality.

The Confucians used the term *Tao* in the sense of social order, and as a foundational ethical principle. Here, it is a right way in the political, social and moral activities of life. In this sense it could be furthered through knowledge, study, discipline and excellence in living. It could be nurtured in culture and propriety, and success in pursuing the Way would bring its rewards in life through right societal behaviour. Such a conception of *Tao* has nothing of the metaphysical connotation that Taoists gave it. In Taoism it is the Way of all nature, the deep natural-ness that pervades all and makes everything such as it is. It is the ultimate

Reality that informs all things. Yet, the ultimate Principle that is *Tao* in the pre-religious Taoist sense is essentially *impersonal*: it cannot reward or punish, favour the good or condemn the bad. *Tao* is a unifying ultimate Principle, not a being. The Way of the Confucians is a describable Way; the Way of the Taoists is essentially metaphysical – the still, underlying, unity that is the source of all motion, change and plurality in the universe, the point at which opposites meet and the harmony between them all.[29]

Tao is the undifferentiated Void and potentiality that underpins all creation, immutable, unchanging, without form. It is indescribable Reality, eternally nameless, but experience of it, and of its profound emptiness, is the goal of the Taoist. The opening of the *Tao Te Ching/Daodejing* has the words: "The *tao* that can be spoken of is not eternal *Tao*. The name that can be named is not the eternal Name." There are a variety of ways in which the Chinese characters can be translated here, but really, they all amount to the same thing, and that is to say that if you can speak about, tell of, or express *Tao*, then you do not really know what *Tao* is.[30] The same is reiterated in the *Chuang-tzu/Zhuangzi*: "The great Way is not named" and "The Tao that is clear is not the Tao."[31]

Tao is that which begins all things. It is their potentiality, the unchanging "that", which underlies all things as their source, giving impulse, form, life and rhythm to the changing plurality of the cosmos – the last, depicted in the *Tao Te Ching/Daodejing* as the "ten thousand things". So we are told in chapter 34 of the *Tao Te Ching/Daodejing*: "Great *Tao* flows everywhere, filling all to the left and to the right. The ten thousand things depend upon it for existence; it rejects none of them. It accomplishes its purpose silently and claims no fame." Contrasted here is the unchanging, unnameable absolute Reality that is *Tao* with the impermanent, changing world of names and forms, differentiation, opposites and dualities. But the two are not incompatible: the former is the unchanging Source, the latter the ever-changing world that proceeds from it. Chuang-tzu/Zhuangzi, particularly, associates *Tao* with the ebb and flow of change in the universe. It is the inexplicable, rhythmic, pulsating, dynamism of *Tao* pervading life with which the true Taoist needs to become in tune with in life. For Chuang-tzu/Zhuangzi, *Tao* is the means by which the soul is nourished and is able to return to its source. But while the *Chuang-tzu/Zhuangzi* emphasizes that *Tao* transcends all language and thought, it sees the immanence of *Tao* in all things down to a blade of grass.

In essence, *Tao* is that which makes things as they are – the flying of birds, the flowing of rivers to the sea, the blowing of the wind. Yet *Tao* is not itself a thing; it is *no-thing*, even though experience of things as they are, is also experience of *Tao*. It contains all, performs all things, sustains all and permeates all, and nothing can be separate from it. It is the "is-ness" of all things, all forces and all subtleties, the rhythms of existence, the patterns of nature, the order of the cosmos. Chuang-tzu/Zhuangzi tells us that: "The great Tao has both reality and expression, but it does nothing and has no form".[32] *Tao* simply operates, but it does so neutrally. It cannot control events; it simply is the transformations and changes that take place in existence as well as the source of them. The course that *Tao* takes is such as it is; nothing can alter it. *Tao* is Non-Being (*wu*) in the sense that it is beyond form and beyond all that exists. In contrast, it is the changing world of things or "Being" (*yu*) that has names for this and that, and differentiation of matter. Entangled in such a world of matter, of "Being", the ego is stimulated by desires for some things more than others, and loses *Tao*.

Such is *Tao* as a mystical principle, but it has to be remembered that there are other views of it. It is worth reiterating the opposite opinion of *Tao* posited by Michael LaFargue. He believes it is a mistake to see such a unifying and underpinning metaphysics in the *Tao Te Ching/Daodejing*. He strips *Tao*, and associated words like *Te/De*, stillness, emptiness and oneness, of their cosmic and metaphysical character and reduces them to the "concrete practice of self-cultivation".[33] Such terms, he believes, refer to a "hypostatized state of mind" of the experiencers, not to some principle or doctrine of *Tao* to which they conformed.[34] Perhaps he is right, but then it would still have to be claimed that *Tao* subsequently became something more than a quality of mind, and came to be accepted as a metaphysical principle underlying all creation. This was certainly the understanding of the term by Wang Pi/Wang Bi, the major early commentator on the *Tao Te Ching/Daodejing*, who understood *Tao* as Non-Being (*wu*) in the sense that it is beyond form and all that exists.[35] Yet, Chad Hansen goes as far as to say that in the *Chuang-tzu/Zhuangzi* there are many *taos*. "The *Zhuangzi* contains references to great *dao*, extreme *dao*, mysterious *dao*, heavenly *dao*, the ancient king's *dao*, its, his or their *dao*, emperor's *dao*, human *dao*, sage's *dao*, the *dao* of governing, moral *dao*, the *dao* of long life, the master's *dao*, the *dao* you cannot (or do not) *dao*, the gentleman's *dao*, this *dao*, authentic *dao*, artificial *dao*, my *dao*..."[36] and so on. Hansen's point is that there is not just *one Tao* but many, and that it has been a mistake to understand one ultimate principle as the true meaning of *Tao*. It is an interesting point, but the wide use of the word *tao* in any text need not preclude one metaphysical principle being posited in addition, and it is the *evolved* conception of *Tao* with which Taoism became concerned.

Creation and reversal

Tao, then, is the potential for all things and that to which all things will return – the utter silence of the primordial Void. It is cosmic totality, Void, or chaos (*hun-tun/hundun*) that projects itself outward to form the whole of the universe and then reverts back to chaotic completeness.[37] It is always present throughout all creation, "deep and always enduring", chapter 4 of the *Tao Te Ching/Daodejing* tells us. The inactive stillness of potentiality in the Void exists alongside the spontaneous activity of *Tao* in life. Thus, chapter 37 says that: "*Tao* exists in nonaction, yet nothing is left undone." The inseparability of these two aspects is critical to the understanding of the nature of *Tao*. In chapter 42 we have the words: "*Tao* produced the One. The One produced the Two. Two produced Three. And Three produced the ten thousand things. The ten thousand things support *yin* and embrace *yang*. They achieve harmony by the interplay of these forces." So from *Tao* comes One, the cosmic energy of *ch'i/qi*, a concentration of powerful creative potential. Graham described it as a "pool of energetic fluid".[38] Nothing will be able to exist without it, for it will permeate the universe in both *yin* forms and *yang* forms.[39]

From *ch'i/qi* come the two, *yin* and *yang*. The spontaneous interaction between these two forces produces all in the universe. At this point, the two are merely potentially present, not yet dynamically active.[40] The interplay between *yin* and *yang* produces the three, *yin* and *yang*, plus the results of their combination as the third.[41] Girardot points out that since *hun-tun/hundun* or chaos still obtains when the "three" are present, it is a state of cosmological unity in which the "two" are "mysteriously balanced by a third term that unites them perfectly". He suggests this is a paradisical form "associated with the undifferentiated or embryonic condition of wholeness at the beginning", a sort of "ordered chaos", as opposed to absolute chaos,[42] and a "paradise condition of the harmonious unity of the one and the two".[43] Girardot also thinks it possible that the "three" might refer to *ch'i/qi*, though the latter is usually seen to be the One.[44]

The combination and interplay of *yin* and *yang* produce the "ten thousand things" that emerge from the three. The expression, "ten-thousand things", is synonymous with all the phenomena that emerge in the universe. The sophisticated and complex combinations of varying degrees of *yin* and *yang* bring about the whole of the material world and all the ever-changing subtleties contained within it. As far as the *Chuang-tzu/Zhuangzi* is concerned, the "ten thousand things" in creation are all equal. *Tao* runs through all things and unifies them all so that no one thing is more important than another.

Such views represent the concept of creation as reflected in the *Tao Te Ching/Daodejing* and the *Chuang-tzu/Zhuangzi*. While *Tao* is nameless, and has no consciousness and volition, it represents all organic order – the on-going patterns and rhythms of all cosmic existence. It is dynamic in that it informs the myriad patterns and created entities of existence, animate and inanimate, gross and subtle. Taoists hope to experience such immanence of *Tao*, not by the intellect, logic or empirical knowledge, but by intuitive awareness of the essence of things – the beginning of *return* to *Tao* and the ultimate goal of the Taoist sage. Return is a process of transcending or "forgetting" the ten thousand things – the dualities of life, the self; and even the fact that one's self exists – until the unity of existence is experienced. Then, the self becomes one with *Tao*, eternal, immortal, "sitting in forgetfulness" as the *Chuang-tzu/Zhuangzi* puts it, in the emptiness of the mind that is the emptiness of *Tao*, transcendent to all differentiation and dualities of existence.

The idea of return is part of a cyclical process that is reflected in the macrocosm and the microcosm. The process of creation is not an evolutionary forward movement, but a cyclical movement of emanation and dissolution, of Being and Non-Being, of arising and decaying, of life and death. There is no beginning and no end, merely arising and dissolving in rhythmic patterns. The Taoist goal is return to the root, to the beginning, to the empty spirit, to nature, as far as the old commentators understood it.[45] Creation in Taoism is understood as a cosmic force that emanates beyond itself into the myriad manifestations of existence through a process that changes from Void to spirit, spirit to vitality, vitality to essence and essence to form.[46] All manifested existence is, then, like the energy radiated out from a centre that is ultimately formless, non-dual Reality, and it is only in relation to that centre that anything can obtain its level of reality. To return to the centre is to return to a state of non-differentiation and non-duality. The active vitality that emanates from the centre to the myriad phenomena is *Tao* manifest as *Te/De*, a concept that will be examined in detail below. In order to return to the source, to *Tao*, it is necessary to experience *Te/De* in every moment of life. This is "going with" the flow of existence and it is this

Classical Taoism

that enables the Taoist sage to return to the source, the Void of *Tao*, by a reverse process of form > essence > vitality > spirit > Void. The goal of the sage, then, "is to reach through order to the inner organism of the world, to its hub, its empty and vague center, which is Tao in its essence".[47]

From all that has been said above, it is clear that unity underpins the cosmos through the essence of *Tao*. Every entity has its own innate nature, but *Tao* unites all those natures into one. The multiplicity of the world is held in potentiality in the unformed *Tao*, and it makes no difference to the unity of all things whether they are in potential or realized form or part one and part other. In the end, all is *Tao*; unity exists in multiplicity, a unity that underpins all change.[48] It is the unifying *ch'i/qi* that is the source of the plurality of existence, though it permits individuation and differences in innate potential. There is a mutual arising and dependency of existence according to Taoism that demands a unifying principle that informs its interconnectedness. So while *Tao* underpins everything, it still permits the differences that make reality multifaceted and spontaneously expressed. There is a difference in the self-expression of all things, a "naturalness" (*tzu-jan/ziran*) in the way that things spontaneously are and act. Thus, the reality of external differences is not denied; it is just that their separateness is not as deep as we think. It is when we are involved with the dualities of life and forget the unity that informs them, that we have an incorrect perspective of reality. According to Chuang-tzu/Zhuangzi: "Tao is obscured when men understand only one of a pair of opposites, or concentrate only on a partial aspect of being. Then clear expression also becomes muddled by mere word-play, affirming this one aspect, and denying all the rest."[49]

It is the Taoist sage standing at the centre between all opposites who has the correct view of things as neither this nor that, but as *Tao*. Experiencing *Tao* in this way is experiencing the essence and harmony of all the myriad things within existence – something that can be done only at that central point of *Tao* around which all revolves and from which all emanates. In such a state, or lack of it, rational forms of knowledge are left behind, emotions are stilled, definitions are abandoned, classifications are forgotten.

Te/De

The Chinese character for *Te/De* consists of three symbols; first, ten eyes and a curve, suggesting perfection (since ten eyes failed to see a curve), secondly the heart, and thirdly, a foot going forward. Combined, as Star comments, "Te is not so much 'perfect-heartedness' but its *expression* and the action that gives rise to it".[50] This leaves a meaning of something like "perfect-hearted action", or "straightness of heart in action". Waley noted, too, the earlier connection of *te/de* with the idea of planting and potentiality, as in the planting of seeds. In this sense, it is the "latent power" or "virtue" in an entity.[51] Confucius used the term to signify virtue in the sense of correct living according to *Tao*, the right way. Later Confucians came to emphasize *te/de* as moral rectitude in living one's life, but especially in relation to the community, both polit- ically and socially. But the Confucian sense of moral living is not the way in which one should see the word virtue. It is more like "virtuality", if ungrammatical, because in the Taoist sense of the word it is that power and potential in things that makes them what they are. It is the *Taoness* within, the true nature of something, which is activated exteriorly. *Te/De* is the force of life that flows from *Tao*. This is certainly the way in which Lao-tzu/Laozi understood the word – "something sponta- neous, original or primal, that which is timeless and infinite in every individual living being".[52]

So *Te/De* is the functioning of *Tao*. And it functions in the wind that blows; the soil that nurtures; the growth of the seed; the growth, and even the decomposition, of the human. Essentially, it is a *natural* and *spontaneous* potential, not a forced innate drive. Nor can such a poten- tial be acquired from without; it exists naturally, instinctively, and is primal in all things. It is by means of *Te/De* that *Tao* can be experienced. The ability to be at one with the innate virtuality of what one is, is the ability to "go with" the flow and essence of things. It is the ability to experience *Tao* emanating out into the universe, and it will also be the means of experience of returning to *Tao*. To be able to experience the virtuality of something is to connect with the Source in different dimen- sions; it is to experience *Tao* in human, animal, plant and inanimate objects. It is an inward, mystical experience of the natural essences of things, a simple and natural experience that can be accomplished by "forgetting" conventional standards and conditioned ways of thinking and acting. Listening to the innate virtuality of the self, rather than directing energies to the outward ten thousand things, makes such "forgetting" possible. It will lead to an understanding of the nature of things such as they are, to a greater understanding of what life is and a concomitant freedom and happiness.

The particularization of *Tao* as *Te/De* in any thing does not suggest that it has to be perfect or even good. It is simply such as it is. It is often emptiness rather than materiality that reveals the *Te/De* of something, the empty space in a jar that provides its function, the empty spaces of doors and windows that make a home. Oshima believes operating from the heart rather than the mind brings about the pure awareness that allows one to "flow with" the wind, with *Tao*, and to feel at home with the direction in which *Tao* is taking one.[53] But *Te/De* is not static, for it represents the processes of change and transformation in all things. Such cyclical process has been described by Roger Ames as "an endless spiral that evidences, on the one hand, persistent and continuing patterns and, on the other, novelty, with each moment having its own particular orbit and character".[54] This is an important point, because the change and transformation do not revert to old patterns but to new, unique formulations. Therefore, Chuang-tzu/Zhuangzi, for one, despised the fixed conventions that suggested there could always be one answer, one right way, in all situations of *x* or *y*. Going with the flow of life means understanding this shifting and dynamic nature of reality and moving with it, not against it.

Reversal is an important concept in the *Tao Te Ching/Daodejing*. For something to shrink it must first expand, to fail it must first be strong, to be cast down it must first be raised, and for someone to receive, someone has to give. It is believed to be an invariable law of nature that reversal is the way things must be – just as hurricanes don't last forever or rain for eternity. So if we want to be strong we have to begin by recognizing that we are weak; whatever we want, we begin with its opposite – a point echoed again and again throughout the *Tao Te Ching/Daodejing*. And in the *Chuang-tzu/Zhuangzi* it is an ability to flow with such continuous change that is seen as essential. Hence, Chuang-tzu/Zhuangzi wished to turn the tables on conventions that crystallized and rigidified approaches to life that could never be natural.

Wu-wei: non-action

Broadly speaking, *wu-wei* means "not acting", though its specific meanings are wide and a little ambiguous. The word *wei* means "to be; to do; to make; to practise; to act out; to cause".[55] It can also have the nuance of meaning of acting out, as if on a stage, or to pose, make a show of. The addition of the negative *wu* means not to do these things. Paul Carus, therefore, suggested that *wu-wei* means "to do without ado", "to act without acting", "acting with non-assertion".[56] Such suggestions indicate admirably the sense in which the *Tao Te Ching/Daodejing* uses the term to mean acting without inner egoistic involvement with the action. It is action carried out externally from the still inactivity of the ego within. It is thus unforced and natural action of the kind that has no ulterior drives and motives behind it. It is the art of accomplishing much with the minimum of activity. That is why chapter 37 of the *Tao Te Ching/Daodejing* states that *Tao* is of the nature of *wu-wei*, of non-action, yet leaves nothing undone. *Wu-wei*, then, is the ability to act with minimum forced effort by going with the natural flow of things, in short, being in tune with *Tao* and its expression as *Te/De*. When heavy snow covers the branches of trees, the branch that can bend, like the willow, does not break. Just so, the art of taking the natural and softest path through life, with the minimum of show, force, assertion or parading of oneself, is acting according to *wu-wei*, and incurs less wear and tear.

Clearly, the *Tao Te Ching/Daodejing* does not suggest that *wu-wei* as inaction should be no action at all, total *laissez-faire*, since it states that nothing is left undone by *wu-wei*. And it is worthwhile recalling that the *Tao Te Ching/Daodejing* is full of advice to rulers on the way to conduct statecraft and military affairs. It is *interference* that is wrong, the egoistic imposition of the will of a human being or human groups in a matter that can be better solved by more natural, moderate means. Water, for example, is weaker than stone, but in time will wear it away. *Wu-wei*, to quote Liu Xiaogan, is "the balance between minimal effort and best result".[57]

When actions are carried out in the *wu-wei* sense, they are harmoniously aligned to natural laws. They are not aggressive or forceful, violent or ego-motivated. Thus, they are usually right actions, and should reap harmonious results, even though they are not done with moral intent. Moreover, liberated from the constraints and conditionings of usual patterns of thought, there is a sense of freedom in natural, effortless action that is devoid of concern for selfish end products. Such freedom involves the letting go of normal response patterns, the ability to give way, yield, and be receptive. And all it is, is an ability not to go against the grain of things in the multiple situations life presents. It is an ability to use the natural potential of one's own self, one's own *Te/De*, to fulfilment. Such living is far from passivity. The *Tao Te Ching/Daodejing* expected rulers to operate according to *wu-wei*, with sage-like qualities, but not to abrogate all activity: *wu-wei* is not a recipe for idleness. Much of the *Tao Te Ching/Daodejing* is a manual of how to govern well, how to maintain order amongst subjects, how to organize farming, trade, and the army. But, in order to govern well the laws of nature cannot be disregarded, and the natural path – the more subtle way to look at things – is the way of *wu-wei*.[58]

Again, the ultimate level of humanity is that of the Taoist sage. Much is said of the sage in the *Tao Te Ching/Daodejing*, especially in connection with *wu-wei*. The sage keeps in the background, but is always ahead, detached, but at one with everything, acts selflessly, but is fulfilled (chapter 7). The sage refrains from acting and people are reformed. He enjoys peace and finds that people around him become honest. He does nothing and people become rich, and when he has no desires people revert to a more natural life (chapter 57).

Tzu-jan/ziran: naturalness and spontaneity

Chapter 76 of the *Tao Te Ching/Daodejing* points out that at birth we are weak and gentle, soft and supple. At death we are brittle and stiff. The same can be said of young tender plants that become withered and dry at death. So, to be stiff and unbending is to encourage death, but to be soft, yielding and flexible is to encourage life. To be flexible, adaptable, and to find ways around force and confrontation is to embody naturalness. This is living life according to *tzu-jan/ziran*. *Tzu-jan/ziran* (*tzu/zi* "self" and *jan/ran* "such") means "natural", "spontaneous", "so of itself", "so on its own", "just-so-ness" and, nominally, "naturalness", "spontaneity". It is *Tao* that exhibits this and, indeed, *is* this, *par excellence*, and so all humanity needs to adopt the same principle in order to achieve harmony and oneness with *Tao*. Liu Xiaogan argues that naturalness is the "cardinal and central value of Taoism, while *wu-wei* is the essential method to realize it in social life".[59] So *wu-wei* is the means by which naturalness is actualized, because it is intimately involved with human behaviour.[60] It is not wrong occasionally to drift like the waves on the sea, or like the breeze and the wind (*Tao Te Ching/Daodejing* chapter 20). And it is essential to respect the naturalness that is part of the created universe. In chapter 29 we are told that we cannot control and improve the universe, and if we try to, we will ruin it. To gain naturalness in life, we need to nourish *Te/De* in the body, the family, village, nation and the universe (chapter 54). Naturalness and *Te/De* go hand in hand. The *Chuang-tzu/Zhuangzi*, too, endorses naturalness as the way to experience life.

Go side by side with the sun and moon,
Do the rounds of Space and Time. . . .
Be aligned along a myriad years, in oneness, wholeness, simplicity.
All the myriad things are as they are,
And as what they are make up totality.[61]

For Chuang-tzu/Zhuangzi, excess in living inhibited the experience of naturalness. A simple life engendered awareness and openness to the natural way of things. The *Lieh-tzu/Liezi*, too, extols naturalness: "If nothing within you stays rigid, outward things will disclose themselves. Moving, be like a mirror. Respond like an echo."[62]

Naturalness, then, is that hidden undercurrent in life that we find when we set aside for a short time the normal constraints of living, the stresses and strains, the things for which we strive in long-term and short-term goals, and just stop. It is only when we are still, caught perhaps in a moment of warm sunshine, a smile, the song of a blackbird, a midnight sky full of stars, that the pendulum passes through the still point and permits a glimpse of another way of life:

Be the stream of the universe!
Being the stream of the universe
Ever true and unswerving,
Become as a child once more.[63]

Naturalness and spontaneity is acceptance of the moment as it is, and response and adaptation to that moment that is completely natural. Such, in fact, is the way the universe is, the way night follows day, and the seasons follow each other. Being assertive and purposeful about everything are inimical to balance and harmony in life. Such, indeed, was the message of the *Chuang-tzu/Zhuangzi*. The spontaneous character of nature is indicative that there cannot be fixed principles in approaching life. Each moment is different, and it is the ability to correlate the self in harmony with the situational moment that is the key to spontaneous living. In achieving inner harmony through taking the softer paths through experience with minimum effort, then maximum health, strength and benefit to others are achieved.

The *Tao Te Ching/Daodejing* sometimes referred to naturalness as the *uncarved block*, that is to say, the natural state of something before it has been worked by an agent, that which is left in its natural state, be that a part of nature, a way of life, or whatever. All nature and all life have the stillness of *Tao* at their source. The uncarved block is the individual immersed in *Tao*, the one who has returned to the primordial state, what Girardot calls "the chaotic matrix of fertility present in the earth".[64] In the *Chuang-tzu/Zhuangzi* withdrawal to solitude and the quiet life of the hermit is the ideal, where the mind is allowed to turn meditatively inwards on itself to *Tao* and away from the anxieties and stresses that normal sense-stimuli bring.

The goal of the Taoist is to experience the flow of *Tao* increasingly until it pervades all life: when this happens, the individual is able to live life in the fullness of the moment. Happy, contended, serene, moderate and in harmony with all, those who achieve such a life-style attain to *Tao*. Chapter 18 of the *Tao Te Ching/Daodejing* describes how the decline in a life focused in *Tao* brought about the kind of sophistication in society that necessitated rules for order, piety and relationships. Chapter 80 deals with a social utopia that can be experienced when a sophisticated life-style is exchanged for a simpler one. The *Tao Te Ching/Daodejing* does not suggest that there should be no involvement in the political scene. But rulers should be sages, able to rule unobtrusively, and have the capacity to withdraw when a task is completed. Reaching stillness within, so characteristic of *Te/De*, automatically influences others. Hence the importance for the sage-ruler to possess *Te/De* himself, for when he does, strife in his lands will be minimal, and then he will be able to refrain from action. Thus, Ivanhoe sees an, "intimate relationship" between *Te/De* and *wu-wei* in the ruler.[65] Apart from being a book about *Tao*, then, the *Tao Te Ching/Daodejing* is also a manual for ruling, for *Tao* can act through the sage-ruler to make rulership as spontaneous and natural as *Tao* itself. In the *Chuang-tzu/Zhuangzi* and the *Lieh-tzu/Liezi*, as noted above, there is far more antipathy to involvement with politics. But, generally, the *Chuang-tzu/Zhuangzi* considers state institutions to be an imposition on individual freedom, particularly because they impose uniformity on society, allowing no room for individual differences. Such was the *Chuang-tzu/Zhuangzi's* view of Confucian regularity that inhibited natural spontaneity and replaced what was natural with artificiality. A good ruler is a charismatic one that fulfils the needs of his people but wants nothing in return.

The ideal person is a *sheng-jen/shengren*, a holy or perfected person. This is the person that can operate from a point of naturalness, not interfering with the just-so-ness of other things in creation. The sage is successful because he never strives; is modest, and thereby achieves greatness; accords respect to all, and so is honoured; asks for nothing, yet has the universe. For knowledge of *Tao* one does not have to seek it out, go anywhere, or study; it is simply there. With the deeper understanding that *real* knowledge of *Tao* brings, the ego is transcended, the emotions are controlled, and the self is not swayed by the "this and that" of existence. External modalities cease to have an effect, and equilibrium is maintained. For the sage, a complete lack of desire permits experience of the stillness within that is *Tao*. It is utter contentment and complete identification with *Tao* and the dynamism of its immanence in the universe. The release of the self from the world of desire brings about the highest gain of all.

佛家

5 Buddhism

The Advent of Buddhism in China

A casual visitor to the study of contemporary Chinese religions might well conclude that in China today there is little place for Buddhism. Perhaps the visitor could be forgiven for drawing this conclusion since the profusion of Buddhist sects and schools that once proliferated mainland China no longer obtains. He or she might add that, whereas T'ien-t'ai/Tiantai still exists as the Tendai school in Japan, and Hua-yen/Huayan is known in that country as Kegon, these no longer feature as separate schools in China. The more serious student, however, will be all too aware that Buddhist *influence* on Chinese beliefs and practices over the years has been considerable. Time and again, Taoist priests pressed Chinese rulers to purge Chinese modes of thought and expression of Buddhist influence; time and again this very influence penetrated Taoism itself. If China offered hospitality to schools of both Theravada and Mahayana strands, then in some cases this hospitality was short lived. Early Buddhism never really gained a foothold in China as a distinct school, while the attraction of Indian Mahayana imports in schools such as San-lun/Sanlun (Three Treatises) and Fa-hsiang/Faxiang (Yogacara) proved ephemeral. Wei-shih/Weishi and Tantric Buddhism also flourished but briefly in China, the demise of which need not detain us.

If we expect to find evidence of a seamless transmission of Indian Buddhism to mainland China, we must yet again be mindful of the fact that it is culture that shapes a religion and not the converse. In India, at the approach of a monk, every head would bow, but a Chinese emperor bows to no one, hence the monks had to concede this point and bow themselves. The Chinese had a strong work ethic, whilst the *Vinaya Pitaka* (Early Buddhism's "basket of discipline", which set out a detailed code of conduct for the monastics' daily lives) expressly forbade monks to work (out of deference to creatures of the soil) – an edict that caused Confucians to label them "economic parasites". Clearly, such publicity would have won Buddhist monks few converts, and they were anxious to redress this accusation. Their changing attitudes are reflected in the fact that sixth-century T'ien-t'ai/Tiantai monks are attested bringing in the harvest, while the eighth-century Zen monk Pai-chang/Baichang (Jap. Hyakujo) went so far as to state: "A day without work is a day without food".

The advent of Buddhism in China occurred during the first century of the common era, at the time of a flourishing Han dynasty (206 BCE–220 CE). Its appearance initially heralded the release from spiritual imprisonment of a Chinese people long (four centuries) suffocated by the confines of Confucianism. Although Buddhism provided a spiritually impoverished people with an enormous potential for creative energy, paradoxically it also provided highly refined answers to questions that the Chinese had not raised: the problems for which Buddhism offered resolutions were not Chinese problems. The Indian mind was preoccupied with suffering, its cause and its cure – a concern that had never arisen in Chinese thought, since all deceased ancestors were venerated, regardless of *karma*. Chinese thought centred on harmony with nature, while Indians sought to flee the world. As Henri Maspero showed, the two doctrines were, in fact, fundamentally at variance at almost every point:

> The Taoists sought the survival of the human personality; Buddhism denied the very existence of the personality: for the Buddhist there was no Me. Taoists claimed to make the body last indefinitely and to render it immortal; for the Buddhists the body, like all created things, is essentially impermanent, More than that, it has only a nominal existence – is a mere "designation", as they say – and the only things which have a real existence are the simple elements which make it up.[1]

Clearly, there was a huge gulf between the two mindsets. Furthermore, the grammatical framework within which questions and answers were set was diametrically opposed to the linguistic structure of Chinese. The discursive, repetitive nature of Indian Buddhist literature, replete with abstraction, was at variance with Chinese literature, where familiar metaphors, directness and concrete imagery abounded. Equivalent concepts and distinctions were absent from Chinese thought, an absence that rendered their vocabulary bereft of the terminology necessary for meaningful translation of Buddhist texts and discourse, as Maspero illumined:

> But Buddhism is rather a complicated religion for oral preaching; and the work of translation which alone could really make it known proved to be extremely difficult. In Han times the Chinese language, though it had been made pliant by an already considerable literature, could still express philosophical ideas only with difficulty. What was most troublesome was that, since the words were invariable, it was impossible to render precisely those abstract words in which the Buddhist vocabulary abounds, so translators had to put up with approximations. Even physically, moreover, the task of translation was carried out under irksome conditions. The missionary, even if he learned spoken Chinese, could not learn how to write it; he had to accept the aid of a team of natives who were meant to put his oral explanations into the correct written characters.[2]

Given these problems, there was room in translation for a multitude of errors and misunderstanding. Some Indian monks were illiterate in Chinese, and correspondence with the Chinese scribe was only possible through an interpreter: "In these conditions control largely escaped the foreign translator, and it was possible for his Chinese assistants to introduce into their writings terms, ideas, interpretations, which perverted the meaning of the original text."[3] Indeed, meaningful translations of Buddhist documents and intelligible interpretations of Buddhism did not appear until long after the demise of the Han dynasty, when translators who knew both languages began working on the Sanskrit texts.

It was not until the early fifth century that an Indian Buddhist, Kumarajiva (344–413), organized a translation bureau that produced works (both new translations as well as rewritings of previous poor translations), which were immense in terms not only of quantity but quality also. Buddhism now began to rival Taoism in earnest, and subsequent translation centres produced enormous volumes of literature until the early eighth century. Fletcher and Scott make the point that: "Kumarajiva supported and further clarified the Mahayanist doctrine of shunyata. He brought Mahayanist ideas into the mainstream of Chinese thought, and paved the way for the development of the Ch'an School, the precursor of the Japanese Zen tradition."[4] The spiritual climate of China provided the Mahayana with an opportunity to develop that was not offered on its Indian mother soil. Tolerance in the interpretation of its doctrines was the hallmark of the Mahayana, and educated Chinese of the early centuries began to regard Confucianism, Taoism and Buddhism as representing the religious mind of China. Indeed, as surely as the rise of the Mahayana in India saw Buddhism being reinterpreted by some as a school of Hinduism, so did its appearance in China, to which it brought a new doctrine of salvation, result in its identification with a barbarian variant of Taoism; the first Buddhist recruits were Taoists.

Despite Buddhism having stricter discipline and more profound doctrines bereft of alchemy, in the eyes of the Han Chinese, then, the points of contact were so numerous that Buddhism was but another sect of Taoism. The absence of sacrifice in public ritual and the importance given to meditation in private practice, as well as respiratory exercises and fasting, were recognized as common ground. In its oldest translations, Buddhist technical vocabulary is widely acknowledged to be borrowed from Taoism. For example, at his Enlightenment the Buddha is said to have obtained the *Tao*; the six *bodhisattva paramitas* (cardinal virtues) are described as *tao-te/daode* or virtues of the *Tao*; the Chinese felt that Buddhism showed a new path to immortality, equating Buddhist *nirvana* with Taoist enlightenment, referring to them by the common title, *wu-wei*, or "Non-Action", the precise state of the highest of the Taoist Immortals. They also likened the *arhat* or sage (Skt. *arahant*) to the Taoist *chen-jen/zhenren* or pure man, a title found in the hierarchy of the immortals. To the deep consternation of Buddhists, they found themselves being regarded as followers of an inferior variant of Taoism, devotees who had simply misunderstood their master. Nevertheless, it is true to say that early Buddhists in China benefited from this misunderstanding; perhaps it is not stretching things too far to say that Buddhism entered China under the cover of Taoism,[5] and the two religions developed alongside one another in imperial China.

The central notions that the missionaries brought to China from India and Central Asia had a twofold pedigree, being the principal tenets of Early (Hinayana) Buddhism, as well as Mahayana. Early Buddhism implanted into the Chinese mind the importance of meditative practice (with which it was already thoroughly familiar), and themes of practical morality, but the Mahayana had a far more difficult task, as Henri Maspero noted:

> (Mahayana Buddhism) supplied metaphysical theses which first astonished and then enchanted the Chinese, not much indulged on this score by their own philosophers. The fundamental thesis of the Greater Vehicle, as it was spread in China, was that every man is right now in the condition of the perfectly accomplished Buddha, a condition which he has no need to attain since he had never left it; but he does not know this and through his ignorance he creates for himself the evil conditions of the sensible world, pure illusion which the knowledge of the Buddha dispels.[6]

The Buddha-condition may be realized through meditation, as the Dhyana school advocates, or by having complete faith in the Buddha's affirmation that all things have Buddhahood, as attested in the *Lotus of the Wonderful Law*, or by other means. Recognition and application of these teachings leads to the devotee's becoming Buddha, who has saved all living creatures whilst in the Domains of Meditation as a *bodhisattva*. This was the message that the Chinese mind had to comprehend and accept.

The Lotus Sutra

The *Lotus Sutra*, or to be precise, *The Sutra of the Lotus Blossom of the Wonderful Law*, is a translation of the Sanskrit title, *Saddharma-pundarika-sutra*. The Chinese title is *Miao-fa-lien-hua-ching*, which in Japanese reads *Myoho-renge-kyo*. Of unknown origin and authorship, the *Lotus Sutra* is unquestionably one of the most influential of all Mahayana scriptures, being revered over the centuries by Mahayana Buddhists throughout eastern Asia, particularly in China, Korea and Japan. It is likely that it originated in some form in India or central Asia, probably compiled in a local dialect, before translation into Sanskrit enhanced its credibility and authority. The first Chinese translation, from the Sanskrit, occurred in 255 CE; other Chinese translations followed in 286, 290, 335, 406 and 601, but it is the 406 CE translation of Kumarajiva that has won universal acclaim and is generally accepted as the most authoritative text. Other early translations were made in Tibetan, Mongol, Manchu, Korean and Japanese, while recent translations into English and other European languages have rendered the *Lotus Sutra* accessible to the western reader. The scripture today is regarded as one of the most influential religious books in the world.

In typical *Prajnaparamita (Perfection of Wisdom)* imagery, the cosmic drama of the *Lotus Sutra* unfolds against a backdrop that transcends time and space, depicts philosophical concepts in concrete terms, but above all affirms the true ideal of the Mahayana – the way of the *bodhisattva* – to be the one and only vehicle to enlightenment. At first, the reader could be forgiven for mistaking the *Sutra* for a historical record, but this was never the authors' intention. In the first chapter, the Buddha Sakyamuni's close disciple, Ananda, is depicted recalling events that occurred at Eagle Peak on the outskirts of Rajagriha in northern India. Mount Gridhrakuta finds the Buddha in a plausibly historical setting preaching the *Lotus Sutra* before his audience. As Ananda begins to describe the form and number of the assembled company, however, the reader finds himself lifted from the stage of world history and elevated to the stage of cosmic drama. The assembly comprises earthly and heavenly beings. Only the mind-shattering numbers that are cited at every juncture surpass descriptions of their multifarious forms. In the words of Burton Watson:

> Again and again we are told of events that took place countless, inde- scribable numbers of kalpas or eons in the past, or of beings or worlds that are as numerous as the sands of millions and billions of Ganges rivers. Such "numbers" are in fact no more than pseudo-numbers or non- numbers, intended to impress on us the impossibility of measuring the immeasurable. They are not meant to convey any statistical data but simply to boggle the mind and jar it loose from its conventional concepts of time and space.[7]

Once free from these restrictions, the mind is able to appreciate the realm of the cosmic myth. The second chapter of the *Lotus Sutra* continues by affirming that, whereas Sakyamuni's earlier teachings had accepted unequivocally that there are no less than three vehicles to salva- tion – that of the *sravaka* or voice-hearer, who attains enlightenment through hearing the words of the Buddha directly and by eventually becoming an *arahant*; the *pratyekabuddha*, who reaches that goal of life unaided; and the way of the *bodhisattva* – Sakyamuni now contends that only the last of these three vehicles is the true path to enlightenment. His explanation for such an apparent change of heart is that his earlier teach- ings, prior to their culmination in the *Lotus Sutra* were provisional, an example of his "skill-in-means" (*upaya kausalya*), and only given because they were appropriate to the levels of consciousness of his audi- ences at the time. The Eternal Buddha – for this is how Sakyamuni is later presented in the *Lotus* – now recognizes that the assembled company is eminently capable of receiving the true message, and delivers it accordingly: no longer is there the need to resort to any "skilful means" as a matter of expediency. To demonstrate the necessity for employing his earlier strategy, there follows, in the third chapter, the famous parable of the burning house, wherein a father entices his chil- dren from danger with promised gifts entirely appropriate to their respective levels of consciousness, only to replace them ultimately with more important and precious ones.

It is in the sixteenth chapter, in fact, that Sakyamuni reveals himself as the Eternal Buddha who transcends time. He is not, as was previously thought, a historical personality, but one who is both omniscient and omnipresent in the world, helping others in their quest for enlightenment. His apparent disappearance and reappearance at various points in time is merely another example of his skilful means by which he prevents the taking of his presence for granted, and the consequent diminishing of effort on the part of those seeking enlightenment. He then illustrates his point in the parable of the good physician, whose sons refuse any antidote for the poison they have consumed until their father's temporary departure.

The *Lotus Sutra* has a venerated place in Mahayana scripture and, for many Buddhists, the *Lotus* both encapsulates and surpasses the teachings of Sakyamuni Buddha. But familiarity with the text is of no avail unless its power is translated into practical living. Again and again these schools make this self-same point; again and again it is the practice that translates the dynamism of the *Lotus Sutra* into the dynamism of life: "No matter how many words and phrases of the text one has committed to memory, no matter how eloquently and aptly one may be able to interpret them, if one cannot apply the teachings of the text in one's daily life and translate them into practical and concrete terms of action, then one's understanding of the sutra is valueless."[8] Kumarajiva's translation into Chinese of this outstanding Buddhist text provided a vehicle for the propagation of Buddhism in China.

The T'ien-t'ai/Tiantai (Jap. Tendai) school

The establishment of the supremacy of the *Lotus Sutra* amongst all Sakyamuni Buddha's teachings is directly attributable to the work of the sixth-century Chinese Buddhist school, T'ien-t'ai/Tiantai. Appropriately known as the "Lotus school", the Chinese name literally means "School of the Celestial Platform". Together with the Hua-yen/Huayan school, the T'ien-t'ai/Tiantai tradition forms one of the two major doctrinal systems of Chinese Mahayana Buddhism. The fundamental problem facing Chinese Buddhist thinkers of the fifth and sixth centuries was how to reconcile a plethora of doctrinal differences presented in a vast collection of texts favoured by a variety of schools. The T'ien-t'ai/Tiantai school, the first of the great multi-system schools, addressed this problem, emphasizing exegesis together with meditational techniques employed in the *chih-kuan/zhiguan* method, using both *mandalas* and *mudras*. Its focus addressed the synthesis of a unified system of belief for many of the different teachings of Buddhism, melding all the divergent views of the other schools. Hui-ssu/Huisi (515–76) is said to be the founder of the school, which takes its name from its place of origin on a mountain in Chekiang in south-east China. However, it is Hui-ssu/Huisi's student, Chih-i/Zhiyi, also known as T'ien-t'ai/Tiantai, from whom the school takes its name (as well as Chih-k'ai, 538–97), who is credited with being the school's first great systematic architect.

In order to give itself credence by way of Indian pedigree, as was common in East Asian traditions, the school took Nagarjuna as its first patriarch. The founder of the *Madhyamika* system was arguably the greatest of all Buddhist thinkers and is often referred to as "the second Buddha". T'ien-t'ai/Tiantai derived its doctrine of the three truths from Nagarjuna's thesis that all *dharmas* are empty of inherent existence, and hence *sunyata*. With the benefit of Chih-i/Zhiyi's thrust of thought, the T'ien-t'ai/Tiantai school proposed that the teachings of Sakyamuni Buddha be classified into five periods and eight teachings. Although modern scholarship no longer accepts Chih-i/Zhiyi as the author of the final synthesis, it has never denied that it was Chih-i/Zhiyi who gave the system definition. For the T'ien-t'ai school, this synthesis demonstrates that the words of the Buddha were carefully chosen to suit the level of consciousness of his audience, and that his teaching was evolutionary in nature, being directly proportional to the increased consciousness of his listeners.

In this light, Chih-i/Zhiyi's system opens with the assertion that, in chronological sequence, the Buddha's teachings that occupied the three weeks following his Enlightenment were incomprehensible to his listeners. Accordingly, in the second period that lasted twelve years, the Buddha reappraised his teaching and taught only what his students could understand: this included the Four Noble Truths, the Noble Eightfold Path and the theory of Conditioned Arising. The third period lasted eight years and introduced the fundamental teachings of the Mahayana: these included the twin pillars of wisdom and compassion, as well as the concept of absolute and relative. A twenty-two year long fourth period embraced the teachings of the *Prajnaparamita sutras*, including the concept of *sunyata* (emptiness) and the false notion of all opposites.

On Chih-i/Zhiyi's view, it would have been entirely inappropriate for Sakyamuni to present his teachings in the same way to different audiences with different levels of consciousness. As surely as no responsible mother would dream of giving the same answer to a question from her four year old as she would to her eighteen year old child, neither did the Buddha give the same response to audiences with differing levels of consciousness, even when their questions were identical. Appropriately, on one occasion, we find him assuring a Hindu audience at their first meeting of the existence of a permanent soul or *atman*, which was total anathema in relation to his other teachings. Had he expounded his views on *anatman* (no soul) at their very first encounter, his audience would have simply evaporated into the mist of day. Accordingly, it was not until the last eight years of the Buddha's life (Chih-i/Zhiyi's fifth period) that the Buddha expounded the complete and perfect truth in the *Lotus Sutra*.

Nevertheless, it is not suggested that the Buddha's teaching was purely one of chronological progression. Indeed, Sakyamuni is depicted as having taught his truths contemporaneously throughout his life. The T'ien-t'ai/Tiantai school has identified four teaching methods – the sudden method for the most receptive students; the gradual method for those less gifted; the secret method whereby many hearers would be present though only one would comprehend the teaching; the intermediate method wherein the teaching would have different meanings for different students, though all would hear the same words. Additionally, four different categories of teaching have been isolated, again delivered by the Buddha throughout the course of his ministry. These include the teachings of Early Buddhism, teachings of both Early and Mahayana Buddhism, teachings aimed particularly at *bodhisattvas*, and what are described as "round" or "complete" teachings found only in the *Lotus Sutra*.

On this view, not only does the *Lotus Sutra* represent the culmination of the Buddha's thoughts, but, as noted above, all of Sakyamuni's earlier teachings are regarded as provisional, merely a "skilful means" (Skt. *upaya kausalya*), entirely appropriate to the unevolved levels of consciousness of his audience at any given time, but never intended to be regarded as ultimate truth. According to the T'ien-t'ai/Tiantai school, it is the *Lotus Sutra* alone that contains the ultimate truth of Sakyamuni's teaching, a truth that at one and the same time transcends all his earlier teachings, and yet unites them. This ultimate truth, revealed in the *Lotus* alone, affirms the existence of the inherent Buddhahood in every sentient being, and the consequent assurance that all sentient beings can become Buddha. Moreover, this scripture presents the nature of Sakyamuni as ongoing.

Objections against the *Lotus Sutra* that "Mahayanists have not a shred of real evidence to show that the Buddha ever delivered any of the addresses attributed by them to him ... the unprejudiced cannot doubt that they are the invention of a later period", and "We may say, then, that the Lotus never had any direct connexion with Sakyamuni"[9] have done nothing to quell the fervour for study of the *Lotus*. Indeed, not only has this Buddhist scripture attracted more commentary than any other, but its legacy has also left its mark on the classical literature of both China and Japan. Its appeal undoubtedly lies in its unequivocal affirmation that Buddhahood is universally accessible to everyone; it is not reserved for the chosen few – "elitism" is not in its vocabulary. Nevertheless, scholars have not been slow to point out that: "The sutra never mentions the Buddha-nature, and the concept of it derives from sutras of the *tathagata-garbha* tradition that appeared later than the Lotus Sutra."[10] Accordingly, critics have attributed T'ien-t'ai/Tiantai's position to its deriving the concept of Buddha-nature from *sutras* that were compiled later than the *Lotus* (i.e. the *tathagata-garba sutras*) and retrojecting the idea back into the much earlier *Lotus*.[11]

The decline of Buddhism in China and the consequent demise of the *Lotus Sutra* saw the sixth T'ien-t'ai/Tiantai high priest, Miao-lo/Miaoluo, reaffirm the efficacy of the *Lotus*, and it was returned to pre-eminence. Its similar standing in Japan, where the school was known as Tendai, was the direct result of the efforts of Saicho (Dengyo Daishi, 767–822), a student of one of the disciples of Miao-lo/Miaoluo. Saicho founded the Tendai school of Buddhism in Japan in the eighth century. There are no fundamental doctrinal differences between the Chinese and Japanese forms of the school, though Saicho refuted the teachings of all the other Buddhist schools.

I-nien san-ch'ien/yinian sanqian (Jap. ichinen sanzen)

T'ien-t'ai/Tiantai propounded an immense philosophical system that incorporates what are known as the Ten Worlds or life-conditions. Known as *ichinen sanzen*, and based on the *Lotus Sutra*, this doctrine is basically an explanation of the unity and interconnectedness of the universe: "*Ichinen sanzen* literally means 'a single life-moment possesses three thousand realms', and explains the relationship between the Ultimate Truth . . . and the everyday world. With this principle, T'ien t'ai demonstrated that everything in life – mind and body; self and the environment; the living and the non-living; cause and effect – are all integrated in the life-moment of the ordinary person."[12]

The T'ien-t'ai/Tiantai school formulated the theory by adding ten factors related to physical and spiritual activities of life in each of the Ten Worlds and the three realms of existence. Accordingly, it arrived at the conclusion that in each and every life-moment, three thousand categories are formed, only to change in the next moment. In other words, every thought, word and deed in every moment of every individual's life is inextricably bound to the whole of the cosmos: "One thought is the 3,000 worlds", and: "The whole world is contained in a mustard seed" is how T'ien-t'ai/Tiantai masters have expressed the concept.[13]

These ideas are very much an elaboration of the general Buddhist doctrines of impermanence, and the concept of the constant flux and state of becoming of everything in existence. All is interdependent and relative to something else: what the T'ien-t'ai/Tiantai school did was to quantify this process. But the theory of *ichinen sanzen* goes further than this in seeing each life-moment as being inseparably bound to all the phenomena in the universe, making the whole universe condensed into just one life-moment of any individual. Conversely, each life-moment of a person will have an effect on the whole of the universe to which it is so inextricably bound and, thus, can affect the universe positively, negatively or neutrally. It is a theory of the unity of the universe, suggesting that the macrocosm of the cosmos is held within one moment of life but, at the same time, the essence of each individual pervades the whole universe. T'ien-t'ai/Tiantai accepted that this was the knowledge to which the Buddha awakened at his Enlightenment – knowledge of the fusion and mutual relation of all things, knowledge of the mystic realm of life.

The interface between each life-moment and the rest of the cosmos may be likened to the surface of a frothy stream, the surface of which forms conglomerations of bubbles. No sooner do these bubbles form than they break off to make new patterns that immediately disintegrate to reform new ones – a process that continues *ad infinitum*. So there is no end to the *samsaric* cycle, no final *nirvana*, no escape from the continuous round of birth and death, rebirth and redeath.

The Ten Worlds

Each and every individual is believed to have ten life-conditions which he or she encounters from moment to moment in everyday existence. These life-conditions are known as the Ten Worlds, and most people are believed to spend the best part of their lives in what are known as the six lower worlds, which are hell, hunger, animality, anger, tranquillity and rapture. Hell is what is experienced by the sufferer trapped in a frustrating job or relationship where the only escape often seems to be self-destruction or the annihilation of others. This festers self-doubt, loss of self-esteem and the wishing of ill to others. Hunger is the insatiable craving for food, success, power, sex, wealth and much more, none of which gratifies: it is the *tanha* (craving) that Sakyamuni identified. Animality completes what are known as the *three evil paths* and is the amoral instinctive world of self-preservation and survival with no consideration for others. The *four evil paths* include anger, temporary madness, when our ego has been affronted, our reputation has been tarnished, our position challenged, our importance sullied. Tranquillity and rapture are certainly more harmonious: equally certainly, they are just as transient and just as dependent on environmental circumstances.

The four higher worlds, learning, realization, *bodhisattva* and Buddhahood, are known as *the noble paths*, but these are paths that can be journeyed only with considerable effort. Learning and realization or absorption are similarly concerned with the meaning of life, and similarly threatened by delusions of grandeur that these states may induce. *Bodhisattva* has its own pitfalls, which though they may manifest themselves in the altruistic dedication to helping others through life's trials and tribulations, can lead to the detrimental effect of exhausting one's energies on others, resulting in the eventual collapse of one's own health. The highest state of all is Buddhahood, said to be characterized by boundless wisdom, courage, compassion and life-force. Although this highest state is impervious to environmental circumstances and is in a sense indestructible, it is nevertheless transient, just like the other nine worlds. In the state of Buddhahood, moreover, the negative aspects of the lower worlds become transformed into positive ones so that we become angry against injustice, hunger for world peace and so on. These are the life-conditions through which we regularly move. They apply to everyone: there can be no exceptions.

Acceptance of the theory of *ichinen sanzen* places a much wider interpretation on the law of *karma*, an interpretation that holds that the actions of each and every individual have repercussions not only for the individual concerned but also for the whole cosmos. Since each action must, of necessity, arise in a cosmic moment, it must have its effect on the universe in that moment. Every action, therefore, will accrue its reaction instantly, though often in a latent form that will not manifest itself until some time later. As surely as the theory of *ichinen sanzen* holds that every life-moment is inextricably linked to the whole of the cosmos, so is each of the Ten Worlds inextricably bound to the others, for without any one of the Ten Worlds there can be no others. It is not, then, a theory of progression, whereby one ascends from the lowest hell-state over a period of time, gradually evolving over the years (or even lifetimes) through each of the Ten Worlds. It does not suggest that we leave the previous life-condition behind forever until we reach Buddhahood, where we remain until death. On the contrary, it is a teaching of *realization*, the realization that in each and every world, even in the life-condition of hell, the potential for Buddhahood is always present. Just as surely, the potential of the other nine worlds is always present, even in the tenth world.

Hua-yen/Huayan

Known as the *Flower Garland* school, Hua-yen/Huayan is the second of the great multi-system schools that appealed to the intellect. It takes its name from the *Avatamsaka Sutra*. The school spanned three centuries of China's history, but it was the third patriarch, Fatsang/Fazang (643–712) who proved to be the school's first great architect. At the start of this chapter, we said that Buddhist influence on Chinese thought over the years has been considerable; nowhere is such a statement more conspicuous than in Hua-yen/Huayan's influence on later Neo-Confucianism. For this school, reality has two facets, the noumenal (*li*) and the phenomenal (*shih/shi*), aspects that are directly comparable to the *li* and *ch'i/qi* that we shall encounter later in Neo-Confucian metaphysics.

To the fourth Hua-yen/Huayan patriarch, Ch'eng-kuan/Chengkuan (738–839), reality could be viewed in four different ways – a theory known as the *dharmadhatu* or *Dharma*-realm. On the first view (held by Early Buddhism's Abhidharmists), reality is seen as differentiated phenomena or *shih*. The Madhyamika and Yogacara positions that inform the second view concentrate on the nature or *hsing* underpinning all phenomena, while scriptural support in the form of the *Lotus Sutra* (among others) is found for the third view, which holds that principle and phenomena are interconnected. The fourth view, as exemplified in the *Avatamsaka Sutra*, attests to the interconnection, indeed, the interfusion, of all phenomena in the cosmos. Such a position is best depicted in the vision of Indra's net, a point illumined by Robinson and Johnson who describe the vision as, "a net of fine filaments stretching in all directions with a jewel at each interstice of the net. Each jewel reflects all the other jewels in the net, which means that each reflects the reflections in all the other jewels, and so on to infinity. This viewpoint is said to be that of a Buddha. Thus, much of Hua-yen metaphysics is concerned with the phenomenology of awakening: what the cosmos looks like to an Awakened one."[14] As surely as the mind reflects the multiplicity of all phenomena with which it is confronted, given that all phenomena are empty of inherent existence, and because the cosmos and the Buddha are one, then each and every phenomenon in the cosmos will not only reflect every other, but will interpenetrate all existence. Building on Nagarjuna's fusion of the emptiness of all *dharmas* with the law of Dependent Origination, Fa-tsang/Fazang equated all phenomena in the cosmos with the mind and body of a Buddha. The Buddha in question is Mahavairocana, which means, appropriately, Great Illuminator.

In 704, Fa-tsang/Fazang was summoned to the court of Empress Wu Tse-t'ien/Wuzetian in order to explain the basic teachings of the school. He used an analogy by way of illustration, committing his explanation to writing in an essay entitled *Essay on the Golden Lion*. His position is similar to that found in the early Hindu texts, the *Upanisads*. Fa-tsang/Fazang argued that whilst the lion itself is clearly phenomenon or *shih*, equally clearly, the gold is principle or *li*. In this case, the *li* just happens to take the form of a lion, but this form is purely arbitrary and *li* can take any form that is appropriate to the situation in which *li* finds itself. Furthermore, the gold is in no way confined to one or more parts of the lion, but permeates every single molecule of the image. In this light, the gold is seen to manifest itself in every organ. Since there can be no golden lion without the gold, and since every organ (indeed, every molecule) is empty of inherent existence, the golden lion must exist in each and every organ. Fa-tsang/Fazang's point is that since each and every phenomenon (*shih*) in existence is simply a manifestation of *li* (principle), then every phenomenon must be interfused with every other phenomenon.

Fa-tsang/Fazang next gave a practical demonstration of the school's position regarding the mutual identification of all phenomena. At the court, he set in the middle of a room an image of Mahavairocana Buddha, illuminated by a fiercely burning torch. This he surrounded by eight mirrors positioned at the eight principal points of the compass. Finally, one mirror was placed above the illuminated Mahavairocana image and one below. Escorting the Empress Wu around the room, Fa-tsang/Fazang demonstrated that in each mirror there was a reflection of the illuminated Buddha image, as one would expect. In every mirror there was also a refection of the images shown in all the other mirrors. Furthermore, as in Indra's net, the multiplicity of images reflected in each and every mirror was reflected in all the others.

Of all the Buddhist mindsets, Hua-yen/Huayan thought alone concentrates on the relationship between one phenomenon and another. Not only are *li* (ultimate principle) and *shih* (phenomenon) completely interconnected with each other, but so is each and every phenomenon in the universe. All are reflections of the mind of the Buddha, which is why Hua-yen/Huayan is known as the perfect teaching of the Buddha.[15]

Devotional Buddhism

From the late fourth century onward, our sources attest to the presence of Devotional Buddhism in China along with its attendant characteristic features. Finding expression in the cult of Amitabha, and centred on invocation of the Buddha's name, it is generally found in combination with other Buddhist beliefs and practices. Indeed, late imperial times witnessed some form of Ch'an – Pure Land syncretism practised in most Chinese monasteries. It was not until the sixth century that Pure Land Buddhism became established in China as a distinct religious movement.[16] Although it endured as a formal school in China only until the ninth century, it has long been recognized as the most popular movement in Chinese Buddhism. A first encounter with Devotional Buddhism is likely to leave the reader confused over whether he or she is reading about one of the main schools of the Mahayana, or an aspect of all schools in that tradition. There is good reason for this. It is perhaps a curious fact that the Buddhist schools in India that argued for the integrity of Devotional Buddhism – where faith in, and devotion to, the Buddha took precedence – were the very schools that had historical associations with the *Madhyamikavada*, for whom Wisdom had always held pride of place. This close association with the upholders of the Wisdom tradition meant that, though there was always a place in Buddhism for simple faith in, and total devotion to the Buddha, this was, for centuries, very much a *second* place. Ever in the intellectual shadow, Devotional Buddhism in India and central Asia never gained recognition as an independent school. In East Asia, however, a characteristic form of popular Buddhism evolved, centred on the cult of Amitabha, the Buddha of Infinite Light, which found expression in a variety of sects and movements known collectively as "Pure Land".

This said, the integrity of Devotional Buddhism was upheld, albeit in the Indian tradition outlined above, by no less a person than the founding father of the *Madhyamikas*, Nagarjuna. The debt owed to Nagarjuna is immense, for it was his spiritual insight that identified two possible paths that the would-be Buddhist could tread – the difficult path of self-reliance and the easy path of dependence. For Nagarjuna, the former comprised the practice of the Ten Perfections and the Four

Abodes of Mindfulness, while the latter depended solely on the compassion of the two Buddhas, Amitabha, the Infinite Light, and Maitreya, the Loving One. Although both are held to be Buddhas, strictly speaking Maitreya is not a Buddha but a *bodhisattva*. Semantically, the word *bodhisattva* means one whose essence or being (*sattva*) is perfect Wisdom (*bodhi*), but the term took on the meaning of one who has delayed his *parinirvana* (final extinction, the objective of the enlightened), for the salvation of humankind. In both Theravada and Mahayana traditions, Maitreya's domain is the Tusita Heaven, where he is on the brink of achieving Supreme Enlightenment. This will take place on Earth beneath a tree, during his final rebirth, towards the end of the present world-period. Maitreya is sometimes worshipped as a Buddha, and sometimes as a *bodhisattva*. In China, where he is widely popular, he is known as Mi-lo-Fo/Miluofo, the "Laughing Buddha", a recognized Zen "holy fool", identical with Pu-tai/Budai, a tenth-century Chinese monk.[17] The *bodhisattva par excellence,* however, is Avalokitesvara, the *Bodhisattva of Compassion,* for whom the *Karandavyuha* is our primary source material. In the Far East, only Amitabha is more popular, and the *Lotus Sutra* attests that Avalokitesvara can incarnate in any form. Since the tenth-century, China has depicted Avalokitesvara in female form as the goddess Kuan-Yin/Guanyin, known in Japan as Kwannon, "Regarder of the Cries of the World". We shall meet her again when we look at popular religion in chapter 9.

In many ways, it was inevitable that Devotion should find its way into the Mahayana tradition. The whole doctrine had expanded to such epic proportion that its profound philosophy could no longer look to science for verification. Since empirical knowledge could no more verify this immense doctrine, the scientific stage of this world became too small to portray the eternal and universal truth. Therefore, the doctrine of the Mahayana looked to a backdrop of infinite proportions, where space and time have no bounds, where the heart can be unlimited in its compassion – the realm of the cosmic myth. Ironically, it was this need to expand into the realm of cosmic dimension, where boundless compassion was enacted through myth upon the universal stage, which was one of the factors that brought about the demise of Buddhism in India. It became customary in Devotional Buddhism to worship the Buddhas. This took the form of praising him, paying homage to him, meditating on him and asking him if the worshipper could be born as a Buddha in the future. All such worship results in the accumulation of merit.

In meditation, the name of the Buddha or *bodhisattva* is either repeated silently, or chanted; power has always been believed to be in the name of a person or deity. Sometimes longer formulae are recited, e.g, "I pay homage to (or take refuge in) Amida/Amitabha Buddha":

Namu Amida Butsu (Jap.) or

Om Namo Amitabhaya Buddhaya (Skt.)

Commonly referred to by the Japanese word *nembutsu*, the Chinese term is *nien-fo*, and recitation became an important feature in fifth-century East-Asian Buddhism. In certain Buddhist traditions it is believed that just one such act or thought of devotion will bring salvation. To the eastern (non-Buddhist) mind, this was simply a form of Hindu *bhakti* (Buddhism has even appropriated the term *bhakti* to describe Devotional Buddhism), and it ceased to be regarded as anything different.

Amitabha/Amida

Also referred to by this name in China, Amida is the Japanese form of the Sanskrit names for the supramundane ruler of Sukhavati, believed to be a paradisical Land of Bliss in the western part of the universe. Known in Mahayana Buddhism as Amitabha (Infinite Light) or Amitayus (Infinite Lifespan), the texts portray this saviour creating the Land of Bliss from the force generated by his "Original Vow" to save all humankind. To those who recognize him as saviour is given the assurance of rebirth therein, where they will remain until they realize *nirvana*. Without mention in the Pali Canon, Amitabha is a creation solely of Mahayana Buddhism, though nowhere does Indian Mahayana accord him special veneration. Indeed, the religious lore into which Amitabha and Sukhavati are woven is a familiar Mahayana backdrop. Portrayed are "extraterrestial" Buddhas, of which Amitabha is only one, rejoicing in the legion of cosmic realms, of which Sukhavati is only one. These have been created by the generation of their past *karma*. The theme that believers may be reborn in these celestial regions is also a common Mahayana notion.

Devotees regard Amitabha as Buddhahood itself, the embodiment of Wisdom and Compassion *par excellence*. In India, Nepal, Tibet and Mongolia, the Buddha of Infinite Light was worshipped at the *Sambhogakaya* level as a purely transcendental figure. In China and

Japan, Amitabha achieved recognition as the Ultimate in Wisdom, Compassion and Infinite Love, not even "marginalized" as one of the Buddha's five principal *Sambhogakayas*, as Amitabha was in the countries mentioned above. In the Far East, Amitabha is, at one and the same time, immanent and transcendent, the supreme personification of the *Dharmakaya*, the Truth Body of the Buddha.

Unmentioned in texts that list the Buddhas who walked the earth, Amitabha is considered by eastern scholars to be a myth. Whether Amitabha was ever a historical figure should not detain us here; it is not the point at issue. Many sacred texts contain mythological elements that are unlikely to be historically accurate, but that is not their function. The purpose of such literature is not to record a historical truth, but to point the way to the truth. As Sangarakshita warns us: "We must not forget that Amitabha is the main object not of any system of philosophy but of the Buddhism of Faith and Devotion. What we are therefore concerned with here is an attempt not to convince the head but to move the heart. Since the heart is moved much more powerfully by a myth than by an argument the Buddhism of Faith and Devotion is necessarily in form mythical rather than historical, akin more to poetry than to logic."[18]

However, with the shift from the Indian Mahayana to the East-Asian cults of China, Korea and Japan, where veneration of Amitabha gave rise to a distinct sect in Mahayana Buddhism, the backcloth changes; so much so that scholars have looked to Iran rather than India for the origin of a number of features endemic to Pure Land Buddhism, yet inimical to Indian Mahayana.[19] The rise of the common era, moreover, witnessed widespread belief that, because of humankind's decadence, the end of the world was imminent: salvation was quite beyond one's own efforts and could only be brought about by devotion to and intervention by some powerful saviour.

Scriptures

The principal scriptures of Devotional Buddhism are rather short and fall into two broad types – those that extol the spiritual qualities of Amitabha and the virtues of rebirth in his Land of Bliss, and those that describe techniques that enable the practitioner to visualize Amitabha in his transcendental domain. The principal scriptures are the Larger and the Smaller *Sukhavati Sutras*, or the "Array of the Happy Land" (both believed to have been compiled in north-west India around 100 CE), and the *Amitayurdhyana Sutra*, or *Sutra of Meditation on the Buddha of*

Infinite Life. The first Chinese translation of an Amitabha myth dates from the early third-century CE.

The Larger *Sukhavati Sutra* opens in a geographical setting well known to the Indian reader. In the course of the Buddha Sakyamuni's conversation with his companion, Ananda, and as the Amitabha myth unfolds, the scene transcends the familiar Vulture's Peak in Rajagraha and moves to a stage of cosmic proportions. The kernel of the text and, indeed, the core of the teaching of the Pure Land school, are the forty-eight vows made by Dharmakara, once a powerful king who renounced his kingdom to become a monk, and who resolves to attain perfect knowledge as a condition of his entering Sukhavati, a Happy Land eighty-one times more immeasurable than the ideal Buddha-country he has had described to him by his teacher, the Buddha Lokesvararaja. Ananda is told that Dharmakara not only fulfils all his vows and has achieved his goal of attaining Supreme Enlightenment, but is now the Buddha of Infinite Light, Amitabha. As such, he is preaching the *dharma* in Sukhavati, leading countless beings there, simply by their having entrusted their own salvation and enlightenment to his care, as Dharmakara's eighteenth, Primal, Vow attests: "If, when I attain Buddhahood, sentient beings in the lands of the ten directions who sincerely and joyfully entrust themselves to me, desire to be born in my land, and call my Name even ten times, should not be born there, may I not attain perfect Enlightenment. Excluded, however, are those who commit the five gravest offences and abuse the right Dharma."[20]

An account of the career of Amitabha is followed in the *Sutra* by a description of the Happy Land itself, which ranks among the finest examples of descriptive writing anywhere to be found in world litera-ture.[21] Sukhavati is portrayed as an immense plain, "level as the palm of one's hand", inhabited solely by gods and men, with jewelled ponds and trees, exquisite flowers raining down from the sky, celestial music, surrounded by golden nets with lotus flowers made of jewels. The imagery is also a fine example of the Buddha's "skill-in-means" (*upaya kausalya*), for this is not merely a literal description of some celestial realm to which devotees aspire, but a literary device for presenting the enlightenment of *nirvana* to ordinary people, who think in imagery of our every-day world, and to whom metaphysical expositions of reality are unintelligible.

The *Sutra* goes on to extol the virtues of Amitabha, whereupon the names of his associates, the *bodhisattvas* Avalokitesvara and Mahasthamaprapta, appear for the first time. The cosmic myth next describes, in literary imagery of mind-blowing proportions how, through the grace of Amitabha, Sakyamuni's companion Ananda, as well as every living being is allowed to view the Happy Land of Sukhavati. Rebirth in Sukhavati, the *Sutra* explains, is dependent on the accumulation of good *karma*, though all but the gravest sinners may enter this Land of Bliss, where even the birds' songs echo the *dharma*.

The Smaller *Sukhavati Sutra*, on the other hand, emphatically denies that good *karma* is a necessary condition of rebirth in Sukhavati. This text describes Sukhavati in similar, if far less splendoured terms than the larger *Sutra* (which is eight times its length). Herein is found residing Amitabha, now rejoicing in his other name, Amitayus, the Infinite Life. Of the Happy Land, Sakyamuni tells his companion:

> Beings are not born in that Buddha-country of the Tathagata Amitayus as a reward and result of good works performed in this present life. No, whatever son or daughter of a family shall hear the name of the Blessed Amitayus, the Tathagata, and having heard it shall keep it in mind for one, two, three, four, five, six or seven nights . . . they will depart this life with tranquil minds. After their death they will be born in the world Sukhavati in the Buddha-country of the same Amitayus, the Tathagata.[22]

According to the Smaller *Sukhavati Sutra*, rebirth is assured those who have complete faith in Amitayus at the moment of death. This state of mind is rewarded by the appearance of the Buddha, and transportation of the soul (essentially a non-Buddhist concept!) to Sukhavati, where it is reborn from a lotus flower thanks to Amitabha's grace.[23]

The Larger and Smaller *Sukhavati Sutras*, together with the *Amitayurdhyana Sutra, the Sutra of the Contemplation of Amitabha Buddha*, are the texts that form the heart of Far Eastern Devotional Buddhism. The last named *Contemplation Sutra* describes meditations employed in order to visualize Amitabha in the transcendent beauty of Sukhavati. All three texts feature the Buddha, Sakyamuni, but he is never portrayed as the main object of devotion: rather, his role is that of one who introduces Amitabha to an audience and illuminates his greatness. The highly developed Mahayana Doctrine, with its sophisticated belief in the *Trikaya* (the three bodies of the Buddha – physical, shining transcendental, and truth), rendered the direct worship of Sakyamuni out of the question. Other influential texts fall into two broad divisions – those that regard a Buddha as the central object of worship, and those that place a *bodhisattva* in that position. Outside the *sutras*, the *Tannisho*[24] and the *Shoshingi*[25] are the two most quoted documents in Pure Land Buddhism, while the writings of Ippen Shonin (1239–89), founder of the Jishu (Time Sect) are also very popular.[26]

In order for the devotee to be saved by Amida and welcomed to the Pure Land through pronouncing the Name, NAMU-AMIDA-BUTSU, in all sincerity, the devotee cannot know what is good or bad for him. All is left to Amida. That is what I, Shinran, have learned.[27]

By definition, a "Pure Land" in Mahayana Buddhism is a land that has been purified by *bodhisattvas* in preparation for their future appearance there as Buddhas. Said to be as "numberless as the sands of the River Ganges", these Pure Lands bear witness to the leading of all sentient beings to Buddhahood as part of the purification process. In contrast, the realms from which unenlightened sentient beings come are called "Impure Lands" in recognition of the blind passions of the three defilements – greed, anger and delusion – to which we are all subject. The concept of a "Pure Land" is not peculiar to Mahayana Buddhism, for early Buddhists recognized what they termed a *buddhaksetra* (Skt.) or *buddhakkheta* (Pali), a realm wherein the teachings of Sakyamuni Buddha predominate. For the Mahayana, however, with its *bodhisattva* ideal, these worthies, who will become Buddhas, must be accommodated in a veritable galaxy of Pure Lands, since each has accumulated sufficient merit from past *karma* to generate a personal Pure Land, more especially since no two Buddhas can preside over the same Buddhafield. Although Sukhavati is only one of many Pure Lands (others include Abhirati and Vaiduryanirbhasa, as well as Maitreya's Tusita Heaven and the Potalaka Mountain of Avalokitesvara), it is also the best-known, and is described in detail in the Larger and Smaller *Sukhavati Sutras* as well as in the *Kuan wu-liang-shou ching* of central Asian origin.[28]

Pure Land Buddhism

There can be little doubt that indigenous Taoism played no small part in the development of Pure Land Buddhism in China. From the outset, Sukhavati was associated in the eastern mind with the K'un-lun/Kunlun mountain prominent in Taoist thought, and current Taoist religious practices were known to include visualization techniques and invocation recitals with supramundane beings in mind. The rise of Pure Land Buddhism in China, as founded by T'an-luan/Tanluan (476–542) and developed by Tao-ch'o/Daochuo (562–645) and Shan-tao/Shandao

(613–81) owes much to the widely-held view in currency throughout the East at the beginning of the common era that, due to humanity's decadence, the downfall of the world was not only inevitable but imminent. This pessimistic eschatology came to be called "the final phase of the Doctrine" (Chin. *mo-fa,* Jap. *mappo*). Widespread persecution of Buddhism in sixth-century China leant its full weight to this feeling and created a situation where serious study of the Buddhist scriptures as a means to enlightenment became all but impossible. As a consequence of both these conditions, a simpler solution was sought, which answered the problem in a stroke.

As the days, as well as the charisma, of Sakyamuni Buddha began to distance themselves in time from the memory of Buddhist minds, the path to enlightenment became increasingly difficult, and certain texts espoused a declining view of history where *mo-fa/mappo* (the age in which we currently live!), marked the third and most degenerate stage of the Buddha's *Dharma*, wherein no individual could attain enlightenment in a Single Lifetime. In fact, with a degenerate people, led by a government and a clergy who were no better, any hope of realizing enlightenment as a result of one's own efforts became unthinkable. Appropriately named "The Latter Days of the Law", all that remained of the Buddha's memory were his teachings: practices were a thing of the past and "enlightenment" a mere word. With people becoming ever aware that the attainment of enlightenment was now something beyond their power, a simple way to salvation was needed. The time was ripe for the emergence of a Buddhist teaching that claimed to be tailor-made for such disconsolate times, and in the sixth century the Pure Land tradition developed in East Asia.

The *raison d'être* of the Pure Land tradition, of which there are a number, is that if salvation is quite beyond one's "own power" (Chin. *tsu-li/zuli,* Jap. *jiriki*), then clearly there is a need to look outside oneself to a powerful saviour, thus "relying on the strength of the Other One" (Chin. *t'o-li/tuoli,* Jap. *tariki*).[29] Hase Shoto notes that:

> By participating in and allowing oneself to be permeated by this power, one transcends the world of causal necessity (*karman*). Implicit in the Pure Land teachings concerning the power of the Original Vow is the belief that, even if the escape from this world of *samsara* (the round of birth and death of unenlightened existence) is possible through inspired insight alone, the ground of the possibility of that insight depends in turn on something higher or deeper than mere human insight: the divine power (Skt., *adhisthana*) of the Buddha.[30]

This, of course, is a major departure from the teachings of other schools of Buddhism. The essence of Pure Land Buddhism is that it parts company with earlier forms of Buddhism that follow the difficult path of wisdom (*prajna*), meditation (*dhyana*), and austerity (*sila*) as the means to salvation, and advocates what is termed "the easy path" – total dependence on the salvific power of Amida Buddha, with the hope of attaining rebirth in his Pure Land. In other words, all Pure Land Buddhists place *t'o-li/tuoli* ("Other Power") above *tsu-li/zuli* ("own power"), which they consider to be not only difficult but, given the limitations of human capabilities, for most people, ineffectual.[31] Indeed, Shinran had such little confidence in human goodness and such faith in the salvific power of Amida that he reversed an earlier saying of Honen: "Even a bad man will be received in Buddha's Land, how much more a good man", to read "Even a good man will be received in Buddha's Land, how much more a bad man."[32]

The simplicity of such an appeal was immediate and widespread, and by the middle of the eighth-century it was not only the common people of East and south-east Asia who had made Amidism a powerful movement, but the upper classes too. The attractiveness of the belief that *nirvana* was inevitable for those reborn in the Pure Land was great indeed, particularly when the said rebirth simply required devotion to Amitabha. As time passed, however, the mercy of the *bodhisattva* Kuan-yin/Guanyin became just as important as the Buddha's saving grace. Contemplation of Amitabha to this end became widely popular amongst ordinary people. Accordingly, the invocation of his Sacred Name (Chin. *nien-fo*, Jap. *nembutsu*) as part of the formula

Homage to (or refuge in) the Buddha Amitabha

constantly chanted in the vernacular, sometimes up to a hundred thousand times a day, became the norm. Not all were convinced of this, however, and some made the point that Amitabha's "Original Vow", made eons ago while still the *bodhisattva*, Dharmakara, affirmed that the Buddha's grace was a gift for every genuine believer; *nien-fo/nembutsu*, therefore, was not the means but the end – a way of expressing one's gratitude for Amida's salvation, not a device for invoking it. On this view, what is all-important is faith in the Other Power, *not* in the *nien-fo/nembutsu*. Accordingly, the practice of chanting the formula is *not* a prerequisite for birth in the Pure Land, but that which naturally arises spontaneously out of gratitude for the wonder of the vow, thus promoting the arising of what is referred to throughout East Asia as "the entrusting mind" essential to Pure Land devotees.[33]

The formula *nien-fo/nembutsu* is a rendering of the original Sanskrit *nama amitabhuddhaya*, which means "Adoration of the Buddha of Infinite Light", the recitation of which is not only an expression of adoration by Amida's followers, but an affirmation of their total conviction that Amida has the power to grant them rebirth in his Land of Bliss. More than this, the chant is a metaphysical formula, representing a state of consciousness wherein all dualities cease, and subject (the devotee) and object (of adoration, Amida) become one.[34]

Reciting the name cannot be termed a religious practice. This is not to say that any or all such practices cannot be undertaken as a spontaneous act(s) of gratitude to Amida, which is, of course, the purpose and function of *nien-fo/nembutsu*, but any suggestion of their being used solely, or even partly, for self-aggrandizement can only be self-defeating. Used in this manner, such practices are seen to resort once more to "own-power" and, yet again, the ego raises its ugly head. It remains for the devotee simply to trust in the wisdom and compassion of Amida Buddha and to reflect on Amida as the supreme reality embracing all things, though this cannot be achieved without a measure of contemplative mindfulness. In so doing, the Pure Land Buddhist's total acceptance of Amida and his *dharma* brings recognition of the distress of our human condition as well as our true place in this world of suffering. With this comes also the assurance of the salvific "Other Power" of Amida with the promise of enlightenment to come which, given human limitations, is beyond the power of humanity.

The entrusting mind echoes the familiar Buddhist resolve to "let go", to "abandon" or "cease attachment to" the egocentricity that impedes enlightenment, whose only Triple Treasure is "I, Me, and Myself"! Filled with false-pride, the ego deceives us into an inflated sense of self-importance. Instead of recognizing our true place in this world, and acknowledging the worth of others, we vindicate our own misdemeanours, at the same time as we revile the shortcomings of others, setting ourselves up as the centre and standard of the Universe, around which the whole world revolves. Philip Kapleau makes the point graphically when he says:

> Sitting astride the senses is a shadowy, phantom-like figure with insatiable desires and a lust for dominance. His name? Ego, Ego the Magician, and the deadly tricks he carries up his sleeve are delusive thinking, greed and anger. Where he came from no one knows, but he has surely been around as long as the human mind. This wily and slippery conjurer deludes us

into believing that we can only enjoy the delights of the senses by delivering ourselves into his hands.[35]

It is the ego that feeds the darkest depths of our hearts and minds, promoting our evil desires, overt and covert passions, our greed and delusion. It is the ego also that tolerates, even encourages the dark side of our nature, by justifying the need for power, wealth and fame, forever interpreting our selfishness as "good intentions" – not that we can see this, indeed we would be quite horrified to learn that we have any evil whatever within us, as we continue to feed the ego with deception, remaining blind to our failings as we embark upon yet another "ego-trip". The Infinite Light of Amida Buddha, however, because it is infinite, can see through the masquerade into our darkest depths, leaving us shorn of the tinsel that deceives us into thinking that we are, in some way or other, superior to our fellow human beings.

The theme of an agitated mind is recurrent throughout Chinese Buddhism. Much of the problem is certainly one of ego, whereby we are convinced that only we know what is really important, and so we place unbelievable strain on ourselves, rushing through those chores we believe to be less important, like eating properly and spending time with those we love, so that we can get on with that which we alone know to be all-important – meeting that next target. Once the restless mind is weaned away from this treadmill of ignorance, belief in an ego that constantly has to be satiated becomes vacuous. This lack of subjectivity is also advocated in the texts, but it is no easy task. Observing the state of mind we are in at any given time, as the mind meanders its way through its galaxy of mood swings, embracing in turn both positive and negative thoughts, should be done objectively and dispassionately. As a scientist views a subject-study without passion, so should the Buddhist observe the mind, without pride or criticism, and without any thought of having ownership of the anger, worry or love, which becomes voiced in the words, "*my* worry" or "*I* am worried". With such a detached view, the practitioner becomes able to analyse the reasons why the emotion in question is dominating one's thoughts, and act accordingly.

For the Pure Land Buddhist, the root of the problem lies not in trying to fathom how to eliminate the ego (which will always be there anyway, no matter how hard we try to negate it), but in releasing the stranglehold that the ego has on our lives as it develops and encourages our blind passions, anxieties and egocentric tendencies. Once we loosen the ego's grip and see it for what it really is, it can no longer constitute a *karmic* impediment to enlightenment. But we cannot do this alone! Our ego convinces us that we have the "own-power" to overcome anything (which it would do, since it is hardly likely to promote its own demise!), but this is a contradiction in terms, since it would mean relying on the ego to overcome the self-same egoism. Dependence, therefore should not be on the vicissitudes of a fickle ego using "own-power", but on the all-embracing Infinite Light of Amida by means of "Other-Power". John Crook puts the point beautifully: "The ego cannot lose itself, it sometimes just gets lost. The practitioner is overcome by emptiness in much the same way, one may suppose, as a blackbird is overcome by its song. Such rare moments are known as 'enlightenment experiences'."[36]

If our *karma* is favourable, our lives assume a pattern whereby we can accept that the arising of the entrusting mind is, at one and the same time, the sole condition for rebirth in the Pure Land. It is a guarantee of enlightenment in the life to come; it is not *nirvana* itself. Seen in this light, through the mind of the wisdom and compassion of Amida, it is clear that the arising of the entrusting mind in an individual embraces not only recognition of the efficacy of Amida's vow to save all sentient beings, but realization that our ego can make no contribution whatever to our own enlightenment, let alone that of others.[37] After all, this is simply a natural progression from the Theravada and Mahayana Buddhist concept of *anatman*, which contends that there is no such thing as a permanent, unchanging self, and if there were (as Hindu *Advaitists* hold) then this most certainly would not be the ego.

So what religious practices have to be followed to this end? In a word, none! Recitation of the *nien-fo/nembutsu*, though considered by the Pure Land tradition to be a contemplative participation in the Buddha's Infinite Light, imbued with all the virtues and power of Amida himself, is no more a prerequisite than traditional Buddhist meditative practices (which are considered by many Pure Land Buddhists to be too demanding anyway), and ethical prescriptions. Originally, the purpose of meditation forms in the *sutras*, such as the *Amitabha-samadhi*, was to effectuate the visualization of Amida Buddha and his Pure Land, and they are said to have been successful, but nowadays their function is seen as an expression of joyful gratitude to Amida Buddha and his *dharma*. This said, there are still Pure Land Buddhists today who employ meditative techniques involving statues, paintings or *mandalas*, as well as following at least some of the galaxy of visualization exercises found throughout the traditional Pure Land *sutras*. Erik Zurcher adds a note of caution:

However, in spite of its doctrinal simplicity, Amidism in China developed an elaborate and characteristic liturgy, with hymn singing, the chanting of spells, collective prayer, and penitential ceremonies that in many variations have continued until the present ... As may be expected, Pure Land devotionalism appealed to the lay public, and the collective activities of lay believers, both male and female, often in the form of pious societies or congregations organized for common prayer and the performance of good works, always have played an important role.[38]

Inevitably, as time passed, more philosophical Buddhist doctrines began to make incursions into the simplicity of Pure Land Buddhism. The "One Vehicle" doctrine of the *Lotus Sutra* began to appear, as did certain esoteric aspects of Tantric Buddhism. The influence of Ch'an Buddhism, meanwhile, with its ideal of an inner Buddha-nature within each individual, led to the belief that the Pure Land to which Amitabha devotees aspired was not to be sought in some western paradise in a distant part of the universe, but within oneself. At the same time, Sukhavati came to be viewed as the embodiment of Mahayana Buddhism in general, and the Enlightenment of Sakyamuni Buddha in particular – in a stroke removing Sukhavati from the realm of the cosmic myth and transforming it into the most popular object of veneration in East Asia.[39] Ch'an Buddhism also appropriated the Pure Land formula, "Homage to (or refuge in) the Buddha Amitabha" in meditation and, as we have said already, by late imperial times, most Chinese monasteries bore witness to Ch'an – Pure Land syncretism in some form or other.

道教

6 Religious Taoism

Historical development

Following the ancient "Three Dynasties" of the semi-mythical Hsia/Xia, the Shang and the Chou/Zhou, China passed into its imperial phase in 221 BCE with its first Chinese Emperor, Ch'in Shih Huang-ti/Qinshi Huangdi.[1] More important for our purposes was the following long Han dynasty, which stretched from 206 BCE right down to 220 CE,[2] and whose advent ended the period of classical China. With imperialism came state-controlled religion and it was Confucianism that was accepted as the state doctrine. However, beyond the state religion, the seeds of religious Taoism were sprouting in the form of magical praxis at the popular level. The Han was a time of great eclecticism, with engagement in spiritualism, the supernatural, magic, divination, alchemy and the quest for immortality. The theories of *yin* and *yang*, the Five Agents, and the unifying energy of *ch'i/qi* were accepted from Chou/Zhou times, and served to explain the natural rhythms of the cosmos and all life. Such ideas permeated the whole of society.[3]

The roots of religious Taoism lay very much in the diverse practices of people known as *fang-shih/fangshi*. They practised divination, medicine and magic in their early history and, later, astronomy, geomancy, exorcism, astrology, biology, metallurgy and music. Some were specialists in practices promoting longevity and immortality. They flourished in many circles of society for several centuries, for their individual specialisms were very broad. Outstanding was the fact that they were the expert diviners of their times.[4] They gave vibrancy to the theory of an interconnected universe in which the macrocosm of Heaven was reflected in the microcosm of Earth by supplying magical ritual for the ordinary individuals' needs – rain, stable crops, a healthy family. They evolved eventually into the *tao-shih/daoshi*, the specialist priests of religious Taoism.

A number of other movements of the Han period also require mention as part of the building blocks in the development of Taoism.[5] The Huang-Lao school of the second century BCE was the main school of Taoist thought of its day, though it was probably not a comprehensive belief system.[6] It was heavily influenced by the *Tao Te Ching/Daodejing* but combined its thought with a search for longevity and hopes for a future messianic figure. The Huang-Lao school influenced the important second-century BCE highly eclectic text called the *Huai-nan-tzu/Huainanzi*. This consists of twenty-one essays covering metaphysical and philosophical inquiries into the nature of the universe and its origins.

The beginnings of an organized religious Taoism occurred in the socially turbulent early or mid second century CE, in north-west China. Lao-tzu/Laozi is believed to have appeared to Chang Lin/Zhang Lin at his mountain retreat. Later, Chang/Zhang became known as Chang Tao-ling/Zhang Daoling and he began what was known as Five Bushels of Rice Taoism, because adherents paid an annual tax of five bushels of rice. It was a healing cult over which Chang Tao-ling/Zhang Daoling became the hereditary "Celestial" or "Heavenly Master". It was to be the beginning of the Celestial Masters or Perfection of Orthodox Unity school of Taoism, which is the major Taoist school to the present day. Communal confession of sins characterized the movement, as well as communal ceremonies and festivals to mark seasonal occasions. Talismans were used to heal the sick or, rather, the sins that were believed to cause sickness.

Another, very similar, Taoist movement of interest was Way of Great Peace Taoism, also of the second century CE, but in eastern China. It was a messianic movement that also grew out of the misery of the turbulent political and military instability of the time. It was founded by three Chang/Zhang brothers[7] and was intensely missionary, focusing on confession, repentance of sins, meditation and chanting. In particular, confession of sins helped to restore the harmony between the *ch'i/qi* of the body and that of the universe in the same way as Chang Tao-ling/Zhang Daoling's movement.[8] Adherents wore yellow turbans in defiance of the blue/green colours of the Han. They wanted an overthrow of the Han and a new "yellow" dynasty of Earth. The massive number of converts to this movement aroused the suspicion of the Han rulers, and when in 184 they rose in rebellion against the Han, they were eventually crushed, but not before they had seriously weakened the dynasty.

An influential scripture of the second century was the *Scripture of Great Peace*, the *T'ai-p'ing Ching/Taipingjing*.[9] It was a messianic text that told of a Celestial Master who would bring peace, and it probably influenced both of the movements mentioned above. Its ideas reached back to the classical ideas as much as forward to the development of later ideas in Taoism.[10] The end of the Han dynasty saw China divided into Three Kingdoms. It was a time that witnessed the growth of the Celestial Masters school, and the earliest texts of religious Taoism that emerged from this sect. One reason for the success of the school was its meticulous organization, not only in its earthly bureaucracy, but also in its official hierarchy of deities and spirits. After the fall of the Han, the school gained state recognition. A particular feature of the Celestial Masters movement was its "registers" of deities, immortals and spirits that were granted to those who rose through its echelons. These registers became talismans, contracts with deities who would guarantee protection.[11] The school also insisted on "purity chambers" for its adherents, places for ritual meditation. Important was the idea of the creation of a "Spirit Embryo" within the body, an embryo that could be nurtured and that could develop into a post-death immortal.

After the Three Kingdoms and the brief Chin/Jin dynasty, China was divided into two, with a succession of dynasties in both the North and the South. In the fourth century, the great naturalist and alchemist Ko Hung/Ge Hong gave his literary name Pao-p'u-tzu/Baopuzi, "the Master who embraces simplicity", to a major work with the same title, completing it in 317. He has been described as "the greatest alchemist in Chinese history"[12] and while he may have been a Confucian outwardly, he seems to have been a Taoist at heart and his influence on Taoist thought and alchemy is considerable.

We should not think that the rise of religious Taoism saw the demise of classical ideas such as those of the *Tao Te Ching/Daodejing*. Some Taoists centred more on philosophical and metaphysical themes, turned their backs on conventional and political thought, but did not seek disengagement with society. They just sought free inquiry and independent thinking. These were Neo-Taoists, whose ideas were coloured not only by past classical thought of the *Tao Te Ching/Daodejing* and the *Chuang-tzu/Zhuangzi*, but also by Buddhist and Confucian concepts. Schools like The School of Pure or Light Conversation and schools of Mystery Learning typify this kind of thought.

From 316 to 581 China was divided between non-Chinese rulers in the North, and six successive Chinese dynasties in the South. Two very important schools of Taoism emerged during this period. The first was the Shang-ch'ing/Shangqing school. Its foundation lay with celestial revelations of scriptures, originally to Yang Hsi/Yang Xi, and then to two others between 364 and about 370. What eventually emerged was a whole corpus of texts that became the basis of a school that, a century later, was established on Mount Shan. Isabelle Robinet described these important scriptures as, "ultimately sacred and pre-cosmic. Issued from the void, they took shape and were written by divinities eons before they were revealed to humanity".[13] Their revelation matches the stages of divine form on Earth and they provide the essential link between Heaven and humanity. The school is thus sometimes called Mao Shan Taoism, and the spiritual centre there was a prototype of the monasteries that were to follow. Like earlier movements, the school was messianic in nature, and was influenced by both Celestial Masters Taoism and by the ideas of Ko Hung/Ge Hong. Life in the Heaven called Shang-ch'ing/Shangqing was the goal of its adherents, and meditative visualization of the many gods both within and without the body was the major means to it. In particular, self-cultivation could lead to salvation for everyone. Thus, the school is important for its emphasis on an inner, interiorizing process of discovering *Tao*. Yet it also courted external alchemy techniques,[14] though its interiorization of religion and visualization of the inner body may also have influenced the development of inner alchemy – both to be explored below. The school was a blend of the rational/intellectual character of the Celestial Masters, who originated in the North, and the southern more cosmic/spiritual ethos.[15] The school was at its height by early T'ang/Tang times, but declined thereafter, disappearing in the nineteenth century.

The second important school of this period was the Ling-pao/Lingbao school. Its beginnings are traced to revelations of new scriptures to Ko Ch'ao-fu/Ge Chaofu at the end of the fourth or beginning of the fifth century in south-east China. The content of the scriptures reveals a good deal of Buddhist influence – universal salvation, *karma* and the idea that present good actions can aid the fate of deceased ancestors, compassion, and the doctrine of Heaven and Hell. But also influential were Confucian values, particularly in the concept of the perfected and enlightened sage. The school is important because of its emphasis on merit-giving externalized ritual, its liturgies informing Taoist practices to the present day.

From the Shang-ch'ing/Shangqing school came the first attempt at a

Taoist canon of scriptures, the *Tao-tsang/Daozang*, the collecting and collating of many texts. This canon underwent many recensions throughout the following centuries, the final result being highly lengthy and very heterogeneous. Like the three "baskets" of the Theravada Buddhist scriptures, the Taoist ones are divided into three "caverns" or "grottoes". In all, the wide range of texts caters for every aspect of religion, "from that of a sick peasant requiring an exorcism to that of a refined aristocrat seeking sublime spiritual union".[16]

By the sixth century, then, organized Taoist movements with specific rituals, fasts, festivals and ceremonies were in existence. It was during the T'ang/Tang dynasty, from the seventh to tenth centuries, that religious Taoism flowered, aided by the eclecticism of the time, which allowed Buddhism and Taoism to flourish alongside Confucianism.[17] Confucianism engendered the emphasis on ethics and morality, Buddhism concepts of rebirth and compassion, and Taoism attitudes to nature and the cyclical phases of life. But the heyday of Taoism was during the reign of Emperor Hsüan-tsung/Xuanzong (712–56), for he promoted Taoism and the cult surrounding Lao-tzu/Laozi. Always rivalled by Buddhism, at least in T'ang/Tang times, Taoism was the more popular and infiltrated all facets and areas of society. Thereafter, the fate of Taoism waxed and waned, depending on political, state support. By the time of the Sung/Song dynasty (960–1279), Taoism had evolved more or less to its fully established character, and its influence had spread into many localities and to wider groups of people, resulting in a multiplicity of practices.[18] In the final decades of the Sung/Song, however, three new schools of Taoism emerged – Complete (or Perfect) Reality (or Realization, Perfection) Taoism, which has survived to the present day; Grand Unity Taoism; and Great Way Taoism. In the thirteenth century, Complete Reality Taoism became by far the most popular religion of northern China. Adherents practised inner alchemy, celibacy and self-cultivation to empty the mind – all with the goal of immortality.[19] Very important in the centuries that followed was the consolidation of the mutual influence between Confucianism, Taoism and Buddhism.

Alchemy

The dream of long life, of the continued existence beyond the grave and of immortality, fired the imaginations of the Chinese as much as it had in many other cultures. The goal was to replace the physical, mortal, perishable body with an equally physical, but imperishable body that developed gradually within the body framework. It was alchemy that provided the means for such transformation. While alchemy was a facet of the broader character of Chinese religion, in Taoism it was a search for a quantifiable, qualifiable and immutable *Tao* that could be replicated within the human body.

In its infancy, alchemy was the process by which base metals were transmuted into gold and, by extension, the transmutation of the mortal body into an immortal one. Thus, even external alchemy has a religious foundation.[20] Some alchemy was laboratory based and is termed "outer", "external" or *wai*, which is contrasted with "inner", "internal" alchemy or *nei* that takes place within the body. The word for "alchemy" is *tan/dan*, meaning "cinnabar", "elixir" or "pill". So we have both *waitan/waidan* and *neitan/neidan*. Outer alchemy was laboratory based and believed it necessary to ingest substances to transmute the mortal body into an immortal one. Inner alchemy believed transmutation could take place in the body itself without the aid of substances. Some alchemists, however, engaged in both, and the overlap in terminology and ideas is considerable. Both had the aim of purification of a basic material to the point of perfection. Central to both was the interrelating reciprocity of the macrocosm of Heaven and the microcosm of Earth, so both types tried to replicate the pulsating and rhythmic forces of the macrocosm within the laboratory or the human body with precision timing according to the phases of the day, night, moon, and so on. The range of praxis covering the two kinds of alchemy is enormous, and the legion of alchemical traditions couched their recipes in deliberately obscure and symbolic language to preserve their secrets.

In part, alchemy owes its beginnings to the old shamanic practices as described in chapter 1. The shamans could enhance life through spells to ward off illness, disease and malevolent spirits. Then, too, there are traditions of sages that defied age and death and enjoyed immortality. But it was particularly to the widely skilled *fang-shih/fangshi* that alchemical practices owe considerable debt. Their skills in magical healing and attempts to prolong life through herbs and minerals were to have a significant effect on the development of alchemy, and those interested in longevity and alchemy were the forerunners of the great alchemists. They created potions for immortality from plant, mineral and animal sources. They advocated breathing techniques, gymnastic exercises, dietetics, and sexual practices for the promotion of longevity, and kept alive the notion of the spirit world that invaded the human realm.

The foundation of much alchemical practice was the belief in the possibility of creating a drug, a pill or an elixir that would prolong life indefinitely, reverse the aging process and permit an immortal existence. The search for *The Golden Elixir* from all kinds of materials, but especially gold, jade and cinnabar, resulted in countless deaths, not least of emperors themselves. The meticulous preparations of the laboratories, the exact dimensions and orientation of the cauldrons, the heating and cooling phases and the rhythms of *yin* and *yang* and the Five Agents made the processes highly complex. A read of Ko Hung/Ge Hong's *Pao-p'u-tzu Nei-p'ien/Baopuzi Neipian* shows just how intricate the recipes were, and there were even extensive purificatory rituals to be engaged in before attempting to make an elixir.

By T'ang/Tang times, outer alchemy had reached its zenith and inner alchemy gained credence. Inner alchemy was more concerned with the nature of the human body and its own abilities to house the cauldron, furnace and ingredients that could create immortality within the self. The Taoist view of the inside of the body is one of a microcosm that reflects in its entirety the macrocosm of the universe. Imagine a journey through your own body that is like a journey through the earth, the stars, the planets and the whole universe. Inside the body are the mountains, lakes, oceans and plains of the earth, the spirits and deities that inhabit the heavens, and the primordial essences that are the stuff of the universe before it ever came into being. The outcome of such a belief is that the body is an expression of *Tao* and the physical being itself has the means to experience *Tao* and return to it. Two kinds of souls existed within the body: *yang, hun* souls could rise up to the heavens after death and become *shen*, spirit, while *yin, p'o/po* souls descended into the grave of the earth, where they eventually disintegrated with the corpse. Clearly, the former were purer and encompassed the spiritual energies of an individual, so only they could become *hsien/xian* "immortals". Tu Wei-ming emphasizes superbly the importance of souls when he says: "To the Chinese, souls are neither figments of the mind nor wishful thoughts of the heart. They have a right to exist, like stones, plants and animals, in the creative transformation of the cosmos."[21] Such a complex structure of multiple souls informs the interrelation of the macrocosm and microcosm, the existence of a three-tiered universe of Heaven(s), Earth and Hell(s) and ancestor veneration.

To Taoists, life occurred when the breath of the universe, *ch'i*/qi, combined with the innate essence, *ching/jing*, of an individual. Conversely, their separation meant death. Working for the death of the body are three cadavers and nine worms that create illness and sap vitality, because they will be free from the body when it dies. *Yin* and *yang* energy channels in the body are blocked by them, but inner alchemy aims at creating a pure flow of energy, in line with cosmic energy, in the body. All the cosmic forces and tensions of good and evil, positive and negative, are mirrored in the body. So what Robinet termed "a sequence of nested enclosures in time and space" in the universe is also to be found on a microcosmic scale in the human body.[22] Such concepts of the body have been retained to the present day.

Critical to the understanding of inner alchemy are the three *cinnabar fields*[23] or *tan-t'ien/dantian*. The lowest is in the abdomen, below the navel, and is the place where the Spirit Embryo is "conceived". The middle one is below the heart and spleen, and the uppermost is in the head, between the eyebrows. Each is a *tan/dan*, a cauldron, and there are three "gates" that provide entry to each, as well as other gates that permit the passage of energy. Every organ or function of the body is presided over by one or more deities and by ministers – just like a state – and have to be harmonized and unified in the same way. The three cinnabar fields, in particular, correspond to the three great deities of Taoism, the *Three Ones*, whom we shall meet below. Thus, the body is host to the universe and, therefore, is host to *Tao*.

Also critical to the understanding of inner alchemy, to the experience of *Tao* and to the attaining of immortality through the development of a new spiritual self, a spiritual Embryo that develops into an immortal body, are the *Three Treasures – ching/jing, ch'i/qi* and *shen*. They are sometimes called Three Flowers, Herbs or Jewels. It is these Treasures that make life possible. Cosmically, they are the functioning of the energies of *Tao* in the universe, just as they are the life-giving essences of the body. Inner alchemy aims to restore each of them to the original and primordial purity that is *Tao*. Maintaining, purifying and unifying them brings immortality; allowing their energies to be absorbed by worldly desires, aversions, anxiety, stress, emotion, sorrow, excessive drinking and eating, for example, weakens them.

Ching/jing is the vital essence that generates all life, and is the vitality in, and the root of, any thing. At its coarsest level, it is male and female sexual fluids and other fluids of the body like saliva. But it is also the essence in the seed, and the essence that makes things what they are, just as it is the essence in the Void that makes the universe what it is. Normally, it is concentrated in the lowest cinnabar field. *Ch'i/qi* is vital breath and energy. Cosmically, it is the emanation of *Tao* in the universe, as much as in the body itself. Since it has many forms, both material and subtle, there are many *ch'i/qi*s. They are cause and effect in the changing rhythms of all that exists. Livia Kohn puts this admirably: "It is a continuously changing, forever flowing force, an energy that can appear and disappear, can be strong and weak, can be controlled and overwhelming. *Qi* is what moves on in the changing rhythm of the seasons; *qi* shines in the rays of the sun; *qi* is what constitutes health or sickness; *qi* is how we live, move, eat, sleep."[24] So while it can mean the air that we breath, and the breath itself, it can also be indicative of energy and vitality. Michael Page likens it to a cut diamond that reflects different lights, yet is the same diamond.[25] The cosmic importance of *ch'i/qi* cannot be overestimated. It is the *One* in the Taoist process of creation, the first subtle entity that emerges from *Tao*. As such it is also *Te*, the expression of *Tao* in the whole cosmos. Divided it is *yin* and *yang*, and therefore informs the rhythms of rise and fall, ascent and descent, advance and retreat and the swing of all things between polarities. It is what makes possible all the changes and transformations in the universe and what, at the same time, interrelates and unites all the changing phenomena. It is also the causative nature of the Five Agents. It makes you what you are and I what I am. Ultimately it is the subtle link between all things and *Tao*. In the body, it is generally associated with the middle cinnabar field.

Shen is spirit, the soul, the psyche, the spiritual aspect in the self. Cosmically, it is the Void, the undifferentiated *Tao* of primordial chaos. In the body, *shen* is associated with the heart as the seat of emotions, with the mind, the deepest consciousness, and with the nervous system. However, though connected with the heart, it functions through other organs also. *Shen* is the part of us that is intimately *Tao* and the means by which we can experience *Tao*. It is the means of return to the primordial state of *Tao* from whence we sprang. Located in the uppermost field of the body, in the head, it is the flower that needs to develop from the roots of *ching/jing* and the stem of *ch'i/qi*.

At the beginning of his classic *Understanding Reality*, the eleventh century Taoist Chang Po-tuan/Zhang Boduan began his teaching with the following words:

> If you do not seek the great way to leave the path of delusion, even if you are intelligent and talented you are not great. A hundred years is like a spark, a lifetime is like a bubble. If you only crave material gain and prominence, without considering the deterioration of your body, I ask you, even if you accumulate a mountain of gold can you buy off impermanence?[26]

The creation of a *new* and *physically spiritual* body was the ultimate aim of the inner alchemists. It was as early as Han times that the belief arose in the possibility of developing an immortal foetus, an embryo, within the body. It was thought to be subtle, light, and yet physical. It was given many names – the Spirit Embryo, Golden Embryo; the Holy Embryo; the Immortal Embryo; Golden Elixir; the True Person Cinnabar of the North; the Golden Pill; the Pearl. It is formed after a long period of inward concentration. It is the True Self and is formed when *shen* is purified and unified with *ch'i/qi* and *ching/jing*, the three being indistinguishable and united. The proper circulation of energies in the body feed and nourish it until, when fully developed, it is able to leave the body like the butterfly that leaves the chrysalis. For its formation, there must be an emptying of the self in the sense of a cessation of egoistic involvement with the world, so that the central equilibrium of the self, "an undefined opening anywhere in the eternity of time and the infinity of space",[27] is experienced. As such it is the central "point" of the universe – the same axis as the *Tao* that is centripetal to all life. The whole process of creating then nourishing the Spirit Embryo through its "conception", its growth, and its release into the Void, is what inner alchemy entails.

There were countless inner alchemical traditions for encouraging the growth of a Spirit Embryo. Some practised sexual alchemy, in which intercourse without male ejaculation, and the extraction and gathering of energy from a female partner, were believed to maintain, build up and conserve coarse *ching/jing*.[28] Some combined both sexual and inner alchemy traditions: indeed, the goal informing both is the same. But it is inner alchemy that has remained important to much Taoist belief and practice. Inner alchemy is the process of successive refinement of *ch'ing/jing*, *ch'i/qi* and *shen* in the furnace of the body.

The harmony of the inner body, a calm inner state, a still mind, and freedom from extraneous influences, are general characteristics of inner alchemy that are reminiscent of the *Tao Te Ching/Daodejing* and the *Chuang-tzu/Zhuangzi*. Chapter 10 of the *Tao Te Ching/Daodejing* talks of keeping the spirits within, and keeping the One, the unity of all the deities within. It talks about making breathing as soft and gentle as an infant's, a purified vision of the inner self, of realizing the feminine through control of the "gates", and of the mysterious white light that penetrates all within. These are concepts highly akin to the practices of inner alchemy.

The harmony advocated by texts such as the *Tao Te Ching/Daodejing* is brought about in the body by the union of opposites, creating utter equilibrium. The goal is to preserve, restore and transmute the energies within into their natural state that existed at conception, to their natural primordial state of *Tao* that existed before awareness of the world dissipated them. It is a spiritual refinement that aims to produce from such purified energies, the immortal, spiritual body within the physical outer frame. The goal is *return* to *Tao* by *reversal* of the process of creation. It is a reversal that starts with the state of the human self as it is, and refines it back to its state in the Void, as *Tao*. This is a return to the Source that one really is. It is a return from some point on a circle to the centre of it. As opposed to evolution from the Void and from subtle to gross manifestation in the ten thousand things, and the generative cycle of the Five Agents, *involution* occurs. This is back from the gross to the subtle and the Void, and the reverse, destructive order of the Five Agents. So, just as the gestation of *Tao* produces the One, the Two and the Three, and then the ten thousand things, there is a gestation within the self in the sense of a rebirth that reverses the process and returns to *Tao*.

Meditation in the forms of visualizing the circulation of breath or energy in the body, stilling and emptying the mind, "sitting and forgetting" as Chuang-tzu/Zhuangzi put it, are the means of returning to *Tao*. It is essential that the inner self is brought into harmony in order to align it with the harmony of the universe. It is essential to rid the mind of its subject – object consciousness, so that the interrelation of all things in the universe is experienced along with all as a movement of *Tao* in life. Visualization of the deities in the body, especially the Three Ones, the Three Primordial energies, is particularly important, but especially their unity, their *Oneness*. This is called "Guarding the One", that is to say, keeping everything within the body – the whole cosmos in other words – unified. Guarding the One is concomitant with return to *Tao*, being at home with *Tao*, and not allowing worldly concerns to lose that sense of oneness.

Two processes in particular are essential to alchemy. One is the firing process and the other is the transmuting of the Three Treasures. In the firing process, which is the means of transmutation in the body, the middle *yin* and *yang* lines in the trigrams of *Li* ☲ and *K'an/Kan* ☵ respectively are interacted with each other to effectuate the restoration of the new, pure *yin* and *yang* trigrams of *Ch'ien/Qian* Heaven ☰ and *K'un/Kun* Earth ☷. The process is sometimes referred to as the "immersion of Fire in Water". It is through such interaction that transmutation of the Three Treasures takes place. All the *yin* and *yang* balances in the body must first be harmonized.

Casting back to chapter 2, we noted that there were two *Pa-*

kua/Bagua or eight-trigram arrangements, the first was with the trigrams in the original, primal "Yellow River Map" (*ho-t'u/hotu*) of Fu Hsi/Fuxi. The second was King Wen's arrangement that represented the motion of change throughout the cycle of the year. In inner alchemy, the earlier one is regarded as the state of purity that needs to be brought about by the alchemical process. The later one represents the pattern of life as it is – the process of ageing. Changing from the latter to the former is what the process of reversal is all about. The aim of inner alchemy is to transform the later arrangement to the primal one by the extraction of the *middle yin* and *yang* lines of *K'an/Kan* and *Li* respectively and to use them to recreate pure *Ch'ien/Qian* and *K'un/Kun* (but on a reversed North – South axis). It is the *middle* lines that are being transformed. The process is, thus, one of separation and restoration. A new, *yang Ch'ien/Qian* has to be generated as the means to allow the immortal to rise to Heaven.[29] Put in another way, the *yang* in the middle of Water is taken to fill the *yin* in the middle of Fire, so reproducing Heaven. The *yang* in Water is the ultimate vitality within the body; the *yin* in Fire is the energy of mind. In the transmutation process, the *yang* vitality is what is changed into subtle form. Of course, the other trigrams also have to be transformed until the primal arrangement of the *Pa-kua/Bagua* is achieved.[30] The *yang* being within the *yin* represents the enlightened real consciousness being entrapped in worldly consciousness. Extracting it and replacing the middle *yin* line of *Li* restores the ultimate Reality of Heaven.[31]

In the transmutation process of inner alchemy, the Three Treasures of *ching/jing*, *ch'i/qi* and *shen* are transmuted from their coarse states to their refined and subtle states in the furnace of the body and in the cauldrons, the cinnabar fields. Throughout the process, the stilling of the mind is essential. Initially, coarse *ching/jing* is gathered in order to build up energy. The "gate" to the lowest cauldron is opened and, there, the coarse *ching/jing* is then refined or transmuted into a subtle state. Once refined, it is able to pass through the second "gate" into the middle cinnabar field. Here, *ch'i/qi* is nourished and refined in the same way by means of the subtle *ching/jing*. These subtle forms then pass through the third "gate" to the uppermost cinnabar field for the same transmutation process of coarse *shen* – the animating spirit of the mind – to subtle *shen*. Now, all the "gates" are open and subtle *ch'i/qi* is able to move to all three fields uninterrupted. It does this in two orbits or circuits, a microcosmic, lesser one, and a macrocosmic, greater one. The Three Treasures are now united in subtle form. They become one, and it is through their union that a Spirit Embryo is able to be born, nourished and eventually liberated. The whole process of refinement or transmutation reverses the evolution of creation, Void > spirit > vitality > essence > form, to one of involution, form > essence > vitality > spirit > Void.

Transmutation is a process of harmony within the self, and with the outer cosmos. The adept "dissolves the imperfect coagulations of the soul, reduces the latter to its *materia*, and crystallizes it anew in a nobler form. But he can accomplish this work only in unison with Nature, by means of a natural vibration of the soul which awakens during the course of the work and links the human and cosmic domains".[32] The "tiny pearl" of the Spirit Embryo is itself the formless and undifferentiated reality that is *Tao*. It is the original energy of pre-creation. Nourished by equanimity, harmony, balance, and stillness of mind it develops; until, developed, it is able to leave the body. Whereas the body remains in the world of the human, the spirit is liberated to roam in the cosmos – eventually completely so, when the body sheds its life. Experience of *Tao* is experience of the Void, of utter emptiness and yet utter fullness, because *Tao* is the unity of all opposites. There is at once both unconsciousness – of the world as a separate entity from the self – and yet real consciousness of *Tao* as, and in, all things. It is a return home, a return to the Source, a return to the centre of the circle, the central point between all dualities. The pure energy created in the self returns to the primordial energy of the cosmos.

Life beyond Earth

Chinese religion has always been replete with traditions about ancestors, deities, immortals and sages. That life existed beyond the visually present beings on Earth was accepted from the earliest times. The most fundamental belief was in the ongoing existence of each mortal being in an afterlife in which the same kinds of needs were present as in earthly existence. But whether ancestors, deities, immortals, sages – and the distinction between these often overlapped – all needed attention in their various hidden worlds.

Ancestors

The veneration of ancestors was essential to Chinese culture. It provided the link between the living and the dead that made sense of life, and it accentuated the role of the family unit by encouraging respect of the younger for the elder and for the deceased, entrenched by customary rites. With justification, considering its influence, Thompson describes the presence of the veneration of ancestors in China as "the very warp of a high culture throughout millennia of time".[33] Ancestor veneration provided a continuum between life and death on the one hand, and kept the dead in the context of life in the world on the other.[34] Stephen Teiser puts the position succinctly:

> If the system works well, then the younger generations support the senior ones, and the ancestors bestow fortune, longevity, and the birth of sons upon the living. As each son fulfills his duty, he progresses up the family scale, eventually assuming his status as revered ancestor. The attitude toward the dead . . . is simply a continuation of one's attitude towards one's parents while they were living. In all cases, the theory goes, one treats them with respect and veneration by fulfilling their personal wishes and acting according to the dictates of ritual tradition.[35]

While the lineage of the ordinary folk was maintained through the veneration of its immediate ancestors, the lineage of kings was essential to the credibility of their ruling power. Here, founding ancestors *were* important, essential enough to be deified, and remembered in an official way through religious ritual. Here, too, it was not just the immediate ancestors who were remembered, but the whole patrilinear line, represented by wooden tablets in the official temple. It is around such ancestors, who were believed to found monarchical lines, that myths grew. These were the ancestors that became deified, who dwelt in the lands of the gods, and who could intercede with the gods on behalf of their descendants. In ancient times it was sacrifices to such deified ancestors that procured their blessings. For an emperor, the legitimization of his rule and the whole fabric of political, economic and social life that came from it, were authenticated by the reciprocal interaction of ancestors with the living.

Great mythical ancestors were created to explain the beginnings of the world. P'an-ku/Pangu, for example, hammered and chiselled the basis of the world for thousands of years until he became exhausted and died, at which point his body was divided up to add the refined characteristics of the world. Three ancient figures are depicted as the ancestors of the human race, though they are semi-divine at the same time. They are called the Three August Ones, and are Fu Hsi/Fu Xi, Nü-kua/Nügua and Shen-nung/Shennong. The three were facilitators of human civilization. Shen-nung/Shennong was human in form, but the other two were part animal. Together, they were the creators of agriculture, farming, weaving, music and writing. To these can be added

Yü/Yu the Great, who gave knowledge of mining, the *yin* and *yang* of metals and the nature of the cauldrons used for their smelting.

Deities

Deities are specialists in power, and providing the credibility of the deity is maintained by a belief in its power, then that deity is recognized through ritual practice. Conversely, where such power appears to have waned, the deity becomes obsolete. Unlike the ancient semi-divine ancestors noted above, there are often no legends at all to accompany many of the deities. Others, however, have notably a variety of colourful tales attached to them. There is a certain pragmatism attached to the polytheistic worship of deities that has characterized Chinese religion in general from its ancient past. Early belief in the deities and spirits associated with natural forces, along with localized gods of the earth, locality, city, district and home, indicate well how much deities were associated with the ongoing lives of the people. Given the emphasis on the family and importance of territorial safety, each area had its own traditions about gods so that consistency in legends is impossible to find. Yet, at a deeper level, it has to be said that however much pragmatism informs the worship of many deities, philosophically they are all united by *Tao*, emanate from *Tao*, and are infused by *Tao*: the kaleidoscope of myriad divinities must, ultimately, be united as one. However, in some ways, philosophical and mystical Taoism was an intrusion into a world of polytheistic animism, which has never really left the ordinary folk. The old shamanic view of the necessity of placating and not offending the spirit world made the assistance of deities crucial. Belief in a plurality of deities rather than more philosophical contemplation of a mystical unity that underpins them was, therefore, pragmatic. In Palmer and Xiaomin's words: "Believing in the Taoist deities is a little like playing the lottery. You just never know when you might be blessed!"[36]

In addition to the Three August Ones were the Five August Emperors – the Yellow Emperor, Huang-ti/Huangdi; Chuan Hsü/ Zhuanxu; Yü/Yu or K'ao-hsin/Kaoxin; Yao; and Shun. Space does not permit a detailed analysis of each, though the Yellow Emperor is important enough to be the exception. Yao and Shun were humans; the remainder were divine beings. Since deities could arise from all sorts of sources, many were once humans. But if they were not, then they are usually found to have been anthropomorphized to the extent that humanized legends can be ascribed to them. Those who were previously humans and posthumously rose to the status of gods had sometimes met their deaths unjustly or prematurely. Then, too, there were celebrated men like General K'uan/Kuan, who became a famous deity. Not all gods were immortal: this was a status characterizing only the greatest deities. Many of the lesser ones were subject to *karmic* rebirth in the same way as mortals.[37] It is easier for the human mind to relate to all such beings than to the mysterious *Tao* and, thus, it was such deities that fired the human imagination more than a metaphysical principle. There was much interchange between Taoist and Buddhist concepts of deity. Nowhere is this more apparent than in the lavish concept of Buddhist hells that became part of Taoist belief, each hell with its own special administrator. The mixture of Taoist and Buddhist concepts of deity is exemplified well in the iconography of their respective temples.

The Yellow Emperor, Huang-ti/Huangdi, deserves special attention. He was hailed as the first ruler of China from about the end of the second century BCE[38] and as founder of the Hsia/Xia rule. In the Taoist tradition he is the greatest Ancestor of all, and was believed to have been adept at longevity and the arts of immortality. He was, therefore, considered the founder of alchemy. *The Yellow Emperor's Classic of Internal Medicine*, written in about the fourth-century BCE, incorporates some of his alleged ideas on immortality and long life, but it was compiled by a number of writers. Other texts, too, have been attributed to this legendary Emperor. In the "Biographies of the Immortals", the *Lieh-hsien Chuan/Liexian Zhuan*, it is said that he could speak when only a small child, that he could foretell the future, and that he had the qualities of a sage. He knew the innate nature of all things, and was highly respected by the gods. Following his death and burial, a landslide on the mountain opened his coffin. Inside, there were only his sword and his slippers. But the same text also recounts how a dragon descended to take Huang-ti/Huangdi to Heaven. He strode onto the back of the dragon and was lifted up into the sky. His courtiers hung on to the whiskers of the dragon, hoping to accompany him, but were dropped when the whiskers became loose.[39]

The Yellow Emperor is also credited with the founding of the Chinese calendar, rites of sacrifice and funerals, the compass and musical scales, among other things. His interest in, and protection of, humanity earned him the reputation of a benevolent, moral ruler, and tales about him show his wisdom and sagacity, as well as his fight for justice as much against the gods as unjust humans. Today, the Yellow Emperor has been the inspiration of a new religion founded in the twentieth century in Taiwan. Under a new name Hsüan-yüan chiao/Xuanyuan jiao, "Yellow Emperor Religion", its adherents have combined aspects of Taoism with

Confucianism and Mohism, and seek to return to former Chinese values. Politically, they hope for the reunification of the Chinese empire.[40]

It would be impossible here to give full coverage of the deities that cluster the Taoist pantheon. However, since they are modelled on the official bureaucratic structure of the empire, they are hierarchically arranged, though without any one definitive hierarchy! Nevertheless, the more power a deity has, the higher in the pantheon it is placed. While there are subtle and highly celestial deities, there are also innumerable deities that fit into the administrative scheme of things, responsible for tasks from the most menial to the more prestigious. But we should remember that alongside this complex bureaucracy runs the theory that rhythmic transformation and change takes place irrespective of any divine interference. Deities have prescribed functions, but *Tao* operates impersonally and independently of all. Nevertheless, for the individual who needs an anthropomorphic conception of what divinity is, for those needy times of assistance, for help with illness and sickness, for safety in the home and success in business, there are the deities. For everything in nature – the wind, the lakes, the clouds, the stars, the flowers – and in the locality – the home, the place of work, the city – there are protective deities. Indeed, we have the same principle of spirits mirroring all earthly phenomena that we saw at the outset, in ancient China.

Out of this great complexity of deities only a few would be relevant to each individual. There would be no need to contemplate the entire host of them. The home is crucial to the integrated life of its inhabitants, so house gods and gods of the wider locality would be important. Students would favour the god of literature, and professions, too, have their associative deities. The status of a spirit, immortal, or deity, is not static. Just as in earthly bureaucratic systems one can rise from lowly status to the higher echelons, in the divine world too it would be possible over a great length of time for a spirit to rise to divine status. Such would occur by the meticulous fulfilling of one's allotted functional role.

The highest deity is Tai-i/Tai-yi, "The Great One", "Supreme Unity" or "Supreme Oneness", introduced in Han times. It came to be the unity, the One, of the *Tao Te Ching/Daodejing*, the One that produces the two. It is the formless beginning of all things, the cosmic unity that is generated by *Tao*, the energy by which all is created and sustained. By late Han times it had become personalized, a personification of *Tao*, and was thought to reside in the Pole Star. But it retained its formless state in inner alchemy, where it remained the ultimate Void into which the adept was eventually liberated. It was, however, diversified into a triad of three deities, the highest deities in the Taoist pantheon.

Three Celestial Venerables form the official triad of deities in religious Taoism. They are all *t'ien-tsun/tianzun*. *T'ien/tian* means "Heaven" and *tsun/zun* "venerable", "honoured" or "worthy". The whole expression, then, means "Celestial" (or "Heavenly") "Venerables" (or "Worthies"). Their creation was a contribution of the Ling-pao/Lingbao school of Taoism, perhaps influenced by the Buddhist *trikaya* doctrine of the three *kaya*, or bodies, of the Buddha.[41] The three Celestial Venerables are also known as the Three Pure Ones, the *san-ch'ing/sanqing*, whom we have met above in connection with alchemy, for they are located in the three cinnabar fields of the body. Here, they represent the primordial energies of *ching/jing*, *ch'i/qi* and *shen* and the unifying of the three that result in return to *Tao*.[42] There are also the Three Rulers, Officers or Agents, *san-kuan/sanguan*,[43] who are much more closely appropriate to the daily lives of ordinary Taoists than the Three Pure Ones. They have been venerated since early times, and featured in a Celestial Masters' rite by which people confessed their sins to the three. Even more revered popularly are the three stellar gods of longevity, health and blessing – happiness in general. These are Fu, Lu and Shou. They are found in Chinese homes, on the roofs of temples, in the workplace, in Chinese restaurants, and are to be found, too, in some shops and garden centres in the West.

During the Han and Six Dynasties periods, Lao-tzu/Laozi became deified as Lord Lao, and was important enough in many cases to be worshipped alongside the Yellow Emperor, particularly in the cult in the early Han, known as Huang-lao Taoism – a name that combines the two personages. In his deified status Lao-tzu/Laozi is independently known as T'ai-shang Lao-chün/Taishang Laojun, Supreme Master Lao. As Kohn points out, for the *fang-shih/fangshi* he was a master thinker and practitioner of the art of longevity and immortality. But it was in official circles that he was to become the great cosmic deity, and the personification of *Tao*. For messianic sects of Taoism, too, he became the ultimate saviour.[44] In his cosmic divine dimensions, Lao-tzu/Laozi was believed to exist before the cosmos, preceding creation, but appearing to sage-kings in various ages.[45] An inscription dated to the end of the Han dynasty depicts Lao-tzu/Laozi as a cosmic deity, dwelling in the centre of Heaven in the Big Dipper, and being coexistent with the primordial *Tao*. In his deified form, Lao-tzu/Laozi incarnates or communicates with humankind, bestowing scriptures and guidance, and acting as the teacher of dynasties. Each school or tradition created its own image of the deity[46] and by T'ang/Tang times Lao-tzu/Laozi had lost much of his cosmic character in favour of being a deity that was felt to be much closer and accessible to ordinary people.[47] But to both Complete Reality and Celestial Masters Taoism the divine Lao-tzu/Laozi was, and still is, the central deity.

Some prominent female deities also emerged in Taoism. Hsi Wang-mu/Xiwangmu "The Queen Mother of the West" is the most significant goddess of these, reaching her most popular status in T'ang/Tang times. She is an interesting goddess because her origins reach back into antiquity, and her portrayal in T'ang/Tang times, where she is mainly associated with the Shang-ch'ing/Shangqing school of Taoism, retains much of her ancient character.[48] She was instrumental in assisting the transcendence of desires and egoism that impeded immortality, and was the major mediator between Earth and Heaven. The Queen Mother of the West features widely in the literature of the T'ang/Tang dynasty.[49] Earliest references to her are perhaps on Shang oracle bones[50] and, much later, in the *Chuang-tzu/Zhuangzi*. Later still, in the time of the Warring States, there seem to have been a number of different traditions that suggest a plurality of goddesses by the same name. But by T'ang/Tang times, all these had been subsumed under one title for one goddess,[51] and she headed the list of female goddesses in Shang-ch'ing/Shangqing Taoism. She champions women, nuns, the recluses, female Taoist adepts, and is the Queen of female immortals especially. She is worshipped at many shrines and immortalized archaeologically on stone inscriptions, having become a respectable, aristocratic goddess, though she never seems to have lost some of her more primal character.

Another prominent female deity is the Empress or Queen of Heaven, Ma-tsu/Mazu or T'ien-shang Sheng-mu/Tianshang Shengmu, "Holy Mother in Heaven". She is a beautiful goddess, a true mother figure, who takes care of sailors, travellers, women and children. As a young girl she was devoted to meditation and holy texts. She came from a fishing family and, one day, her father and brothers were out at sea in a terrible storm. She meditated, and her *hun* souls left her body. As they were about to lose their lives, her father and brothers saw her white figure gliding to their boat. She began to tug them back to safety. However, her mother came into the room and, finding her still, shook her. Her souls returned, but before she could drag her family to safety. Only two brothers survived to tell the tale. Ma-tsu/Mazu died young and celibate, a woman with great spiritual power. Her mummified body was entombed in her native village in a temple built for her that lasted right up until the time of the Cultural Revolution in the last century. Her cult began in a small way, but in the centuries after her death (which probably occurred in the tenth century), and when many miracles were attributed to her, she rose in the official list of deities. She became a national deity, and was eventually given status in one of the stars of the Big Dipper. She became Queen of Heaven in the seventeenth century and is widely worshipped, but she has remained the patron saint of sailors and commerce to this day. Sailors in the area where she lived, and those wider afield, sometimes carry her picture on their boats.

Religious praxis

Religious Taoism embraces many beliefs that have filtered down from antiquity through centuries of trends, turbulence, superstitions, philosophies and traditional and locational practices. Touched deeply in its many twists and turns by Buddhism and Confucianism, it has also remained close to popular experiences, needs and customs, even though, at the same time, it was important to the higher echelons of society. Taoist religious praxis is characterized by the kind of pragmatic pluralism that enables the worshipper to approach Buddhist deities as much as Taoist ones when the occasion arises. The choice of deity is determined by the needs of the moment, not by any conformity to specific religious institutional practice. Despite such diversity, however, there is an underlying rationale that seems to be present in any aspect of Taoism or Chinese religion in general, and that is to create, or restore, and maintain the balances and harmonies that exist between Heaven, Hell and the human realm. Many Taoist practitioners are the mediums by which such balance and harmony is effectuated. Just as in ancient times, the theories of *yin* and *yang* and the Five Agents underpin the ritual of religious Taoism in the search for that harmony. But the seriousness of the goal of harmony does not inhibit the means by which it is brought about. For Taoist religion is replete with ritualistic expression that surfaces in colour, music, rhythm, dance, symbols and imagery while, at the same time, it maintains a certain amount of structure through centuries of lineage and meticulous transmission of traditions. All this serves the purpose of bringing the world of humanity in balance with the supernatural forces of the cosmos.[52]

In its appeal to the masses, in its earliest forms, religious Taoism gave the Chinese populace a religious focus that answered immediate needs. However, in the centuries that followed, religious Taoism became enmeshed in popular practice that was both Taoist and more broadly

Chinese. This admixture of beliefs and practices has remained characteristic, and it is really impossible to extract religious Taoism in the modern and post-modern world from popular Chinese practices. Strictly Taoist praxis is only for priests: for the rest of the populace the blurring of the distinctions between Buddhist, Confucian and Taoist practices has been endemic. According to Asano Haruji, offerings currently used in Taoist ritual are also used in Buddhist, Confucian and popular ritual, though the methods and meanings may be different for each. Such Taoist ritual in Taiwan, Asano Haruji has found, will even include the more popular practice of blood sacrifice.[53]

Influenced by Buddhism, religious Taoism has a doctrine of salvation for all. Hitherto, the goal had been immortality for the few, but in religious Taoism existence after death could be influenced by the way in which life was lived in the present. Since the afterlife was modelled on the earthly one – albeit that it was believed to be the other way around – there were many places to be filled in the hierarchies of the heavens and hells in the post-death experience while awaiting rebirth. This is just one good example of the fusion of Buddhist and Taoist ideas. Since popular Taoism is so all-embracing and syncretic, there is no set doctrine prescribed by a particular religious institution to follow: there is a compass point through life, but no ordnance map to dictate the pathways. There are, then, considerable local variations in ritualistic praxis. It may well be that a Taoist or Buddhist specialist may conduct ritual, in which case the longstanding formalities of strict tradition will be followed. Nevertheless, such specialists are not always necessary, and a master of ceremonies who is neither may well preside over ritual. Even where such specialism is employed, the Taoist or Buddhist priest or monk always remains closer to the needs of the ordinary people than to the ritualistic traditions – a point, according to Maspero, that has virtually always been the case.[54] While Taoism, more than Buddhism or Confucianism, was closest to the people, ordinary folk would find it difficult to designate themselves as Taoist or Buddhist, and would certainly not be at pains to differentiate between the two. It is a matter of pragmatism that at one time a particular Buddha or Buddhist *bodhisattva* may be more appropriate to approach than a Taoist deity. Since those in the divine world have different functions, it always makes sense to take one's problems to the divine being that specializes in that area.

Two major schools of Taoism are extant today, Complete Reality[55] or Ch'üan-chen/Quanzhen, and the Celestial Masters, or Cheng-i/Zhengyi, Perfection of Orthodox Unity school, to give it the name by which it was known after the fourteenth century. From these two schools a large number of sub-schools have emerged. Differences between them are characterized by differences in the texts that they transmit. Complete Reality Taoism is a monastic tradition, its best-known monastery being the White Cloud Monastery in Beijing. It is a tradition that exemplifies well the eclectic nature of religious Taoism, considering its Zen-like meditative practices, its emphasis on emptiness of mind like Buddhism, both mixed with Taoist inner alchemy. Nevertheless, its goal is not enlightenment as in Buddhism, but immortality, despite the influence of Buddhism in so many other Taoist doctrines. The most influential sect to emerge from Complete Reality Taoism is the Lung-men/Longmen sect, an inner alchemy school that probably emerged in Ming times.[56] The other major school, the Celestial Masters, is expert in colourful and complex rituals for funerals, festivals, exorcisms, healing, and the use of charms and talismans. Its priesthood is a hereditary one, in which the specialist texts, along with their powers, are meticulously transmitted. But the priests are only used on special occasions: at other times they disappear into the backdrop of ordinary society.

Priests of the Celestial Masters tradition, therefore, are the specialists in ritual. Some are *Black-head* priests, so-called because of the formal black caps they wear. They are the more orthodox practitioners, the priestly elite, who bring specialist knowledge, power and ritual practice to occasions. They can heal and perform exorcisms, too, but one special function is the ritual for the dead. Then there are *Red-head* priests, so-called because they wrap red cloths round their heads or waists during ritual. They rarely perform death rites and are more involved with medium divination than *Black-heads*. Priests often share their work with Buddhist monks – a point that demonstrates well the lack of any firm demarcation of religious affiliation amongst the populace.

A particular feature of Taoist religious praxis is the use of spirit mediums where the medium's body is taken over by a god or spirit, and he becomes a tool, a puppet, or a "divining youth" of the god, and the means by which that deity conveys a message. The medium is, thus, possessed, and often resorts to severe mortification of the flesh in order to demonstrate, spectacularly, that this is so. It is often *Red-head* priests who will interpret the messages delivered by the deities to the mediums. Exorcism is also a feature of religious Taoism, the more intensive ritual being undertaken by *Black-head* priests, the lesser by *Red-heads* or others. The exorcist is often like a magician, or sorcerer, who has acquired skill in the procuring of power from the gods and the ability to use it. While there is often little to distinguish between Taoist and Buddhist temples, at special ceremonies the usual deities are moved to one side in order to accommodate the Three Pure Ones, who are the most important divine guests at any significant ceremony, though space for other high-ranking deities is also made.

On occasions of special ritual, when the temple is filled with ritual specialists and surrounded outside by devotees, the atmosphere is particularly charged: "The blaze of votive lamps and candles, the swirling clouds of perfumed smoke and the richly coloured garb of the officiants sometimes produce a powerful effect, especially if the voices are good and the sweet music of flutes replaces the rather harsh music of clarinet, drum, cymbals and 'wooden-fish drum', although this, too, may be impressive."[57] At large festivals the senses are dazzled in a charged and emotional atmosphere. The rationale informing all ritual is the creation of harmony between the three realms of Heaven, Earth and the underworld. It is considered sufficiently important to necessitate the utmost care and meticulous detail in order to be efficacious. The most prestigious of rituals is the *chiao/jiao* or "offering", which may last several days, and is held for a variety of reasons. It is especially at the sixty-year *chiao/jiao*, at the end of one cycle and the beginning of a new cycle of time, that the ritual is at its most magnificent, for at this time there is a need for renewal of the whole community into a new cycle of time. The pageant of ritual that makes up a *chiao/jiao* is too lengthy to describe in full here.[58] Suffice it to say that it is full of dramatic representation and symbolism, frenzied beatings on drums and the bangs of firecrackers, creating a spectacular scene. There is fire-walking, possessed mediums, great processions, drama, puppet shows, and a throng of people who come from far and wide, and even from overseas for the occasion.

Immortals[59]

The idea of immortality in China is an ancient one, with legends of those who have transcended death to live in heavenly realms, or of those who live in lonely parts of mountains and forests. Some were believed to have had apparent rather than real deaths. Such concepts were widespread in Chinese thought in the third century BCE. But, according to Robinet, the belief in physical immortality is witnessed on Shang bronze inscriptions dated to as early as the eighth century BCE, and talk of the isles where plants for immortality grew was present in court circles in the fourth century BCE.[60] In time, the status of immortals rose to exceed that of the earth gods. It came to be believed that, through excessively good merit, some mortals could bypass the hells after death, and take their place in the ranks of heavenly beings, from where they would be able to rise in status, eventually becoming full immortals.

The Chinese character for immortal is *hsien/xian*, which is usually translated as "immortal", even as "genie". It can also mean "perfected" or "transcendent". It refers to a person who has lived such a holy and spiritual life that he or she has transcended normal patterns of existence and has taken on the nature of a saint. The Chinese character *hsien/xian* is itself composed of two characters, one for "human being" and the other for "mountain". Put together, the image is of a mortal being who dwells in the mountains, or of one who transcends. Thus, as Schipper points out: "Phonologically, the word *hsien/xian* derives from the root meaning 'to change, evolve, go up,' or even 'to dance.' This recalls the themes of transformation, of ascension to heaven, and of dance which, in the ritual, allows one to take possession of a sacred space."[61] Schipper's words here are reminiscent of the shamanic dances and flights of the shaman to the realms of the spirits and gods. But one characteristic seems to pervade the concept of an immortal, and that is the easy-going, free and spontaneous nature of those who realize such a level of spirituality.

Not all immortals are portrayed as secretive, mystical beings. They might ride the winds and sip dew, but many are depicted as colourful characters. It is especially in the popular mind that these more accessible immortals are held dear. These are the immortals that engage in earthly events, appearing to uphold justice and defend the weak. It is these who are artistically portrayed in art and iconography, and who take on profoundly anthropomorphic personalities. They sip dew, which might also, on occasions, be wine, or may be seen playing the lute. They are merry people, at ease with each other and with themselves, existing in perfect contentment.

Of all the immortals, eight are particularly special. They are found in a prominent position in most Taoist temples, where they have the special function of warding off evil. They are found in the home, at celebrations like weddings and anniversaries, or represented in dance at the beginning of theatrical performances. They are depicted on paintings, vases, plates, teapots, and can be found in craft shops and garden centres in the West. Such is their importance that they are not just a Taoist phenomenon, but are popular in the wider context of Chinese religious life as a whole. Since these Eight Immortals defend the weak and uphold justice they illustrate that the life-condition of the truly good person can be turned from one of poverty to riches or from oppression to joy. In short, they provide hope, and the Immortals are always ready to intervene in the human situation to turn hope into reality. Given the hardship of the peasants and lowest strata of Chinese society, the tales of the Eight Immortals were welcomed as illustrations of how persecutors could themselves be punished and how the rich could be brought low. The tales of the Immortals are ones in which happiness follows sadness for those who are virtuous.

The Eight Immortals are examples of those who have reached the ultimate goal but who have remained in the world, or returned to it, to help others, rather like the Buddhist concept of *bodhisattvas*. They participate in the lives of ordinary folk, disguising themselves to perpetrate justice. They have very different characters, but generally they are funny, happy, free, and often drunk. Their purpose in the many tales and anecdotes about them is manifold. Apart from championing justice, sometimes, for example, they provide an explanation for a geographical feature like the grottoes of Ching Ling/Jingling, explained by their digging and burrowing through the mountain in search of a precious pearl.[62] But they are champions of Taoism, helping people to understand the functioning of *Tao* in the world. Then, too, the characters in the stories reflect the daily life of ordinary people – the oil seller, woodcutter, beggar, local commissioner, for example. Of the Eight, however, some have always been more popular than others: Lü Tung-pin/Lü Dongbin, Ti Kuai-li/Diguaili and Chang Kuo-lao/Zhang Guolao, the first three, are far more important than the rest. Some of the Eight only occur in the context of the others in their group, but the important ones are portrayed in tales individually. Their characters span social boundaries of rich and poor, official and peasant, male and female, old and young, the healthy and the sick. The origins of the tales of the Eight Immortals date back to T'ang/Tang times, though the tales about them were developed more significantly in Sung/Song times. But it was not until Ming times that the official legends about the Immortals were finalized.

Sages

The Taoist sage is the culmination of years of effort by the adept, and is the concluding phase of life on Earth that culminates in immortal life beyond it. There are many terms used for the sage, *sheng-jen/shengren*, "sage" or "saint", the term used in the *Tao Te Ching/Daodejing*; *chen-*

jen/zhenren, "true", "real" or "perfect being";[63] *shen-jen/shenren*, "spirit being"; *chih-jen/zhiren*, "perfect being",[64] the terms found in the *Chuang-tzu/Zhuangzi*.[65] While inhabiting Earth, the sage has the means to traverse beyond it in the same way as immortals. He is at one with *Tao*, but his involvement in human affairs can range from the rule of the sage–king of early texts like the *Tao Te Ching/Daodejing* to instruction of disciples on lonely mountainsides. This two-fold nature of the sage epitomizes the distinction between those involved in life, and those who withdrew from it to solitude. The term "sage" is, therefore, an all-embracing one, though it encompasses for all sages the status of imminent immortality, and the ability to be both this-worldly and other-worldly, the perfect pivot between Heaven and Earth.

It is the ability to be astride this and the other world beyond ordinary life that links sages with the shamans of the ancient past. With the sage we find none of the ecstatic and wilder activities of the shaman, but the thread of continuity between the two is not that difficult to see. Indeed, when they become immortals they will have all the skills of shamans, many of which they acquire in pre-immortal state. They acquire power over nature and time, and act in unconventional ways. So, in a way, we have come full circle from the shamans of ancient times to the sage as the ultimate goal of the Taoist adept, and to immortals, especially, who bear so many of the characteristics of shamanic practices.[66]

The sage is the culmination of earthly life and the medium for transcendence to the heavenly one. He is at the same time in the world and beyond it at the pinnacle of reality, *Tao* itself, and he has the freedom to wander at will from one to the other. His egoistic self has vanished, and he is ageless like the sun and moon. Like the shamans of old, the Taoist sages leave the confines of the world for the splendours of the heavens. Such wandering in the universe "leads out of the entanglements of given laws into a freedom in which the rules of tradition no longer prevail".[67] The sage journeys beyond the ordinary self and even beyond the transcendent self. It is a journey that ultimately loses the self in utter tranquillity and serenity, stillness and emptiness.

Because the sage has become empty of individual personality and selfhood, he is like a pure tube through which the light of *Tao* pours into his being. The rhythm of the universe floods through him, linking him to the ten thousand things with which he is in total harmony. Perfect simplicity and innocence to all things pervades the mind and being of the sage. Thus, he conforms to the transformations of *Tao* as they occur in the universe, knowing that they will take their own courses in an orderly rhythm: and he is totally harmonized with such rhythm. All conventional knowledge is dispelled for a state of ignorance that, paradoxically, opens the mind to the entire universe. It is a process of "forgetting the forgetting", that is to say, forgetting all conventional knowledge even to the extent that you have forgotten that you have forgotten it. Thus, the mind becomes truly empty and freed from its own volition. It is in this state of no-self, of utter emptiness and Void, that *Tao* is found. "The Tao takes over the identity that once was the individual's alone."[68] Gazing out into the vastness of the universe with its myriad stars and galaxies, the sage is an atom of that whole being, flowing with it, feeling its cosmic energy in his whole being. It is a return to one's cosmic beginnings and tuning of the self to the ongoing pulses of creation.

The sage has the perfect balance between *yang* outer activity and *yin* inner passivity. The English poet William Wordsworth captured this when he wrote: "With an eye made quiet by the power of harmony and the deep power of joy, we see into the heart of things". And with inner serenity, the sage is able to act in the world without ever losing the calm serenity and stillness within. For the sage is at the centre of the circle, he is at that point where dualities cease to exist. He is the equipoise, the balance between the this and that of all opposites and all things, and between *yin* and *yang*. The sage has not *found Tao* for he had never really lost it. He simply experiences it as himself and all things. It is in the living, breathing and eating of the day, in the clouds, the moon, the winds, the morning mists, the song of the bird. *Living* is *Tao* and is experience of the interconnectedness and unity of all.

新儒家

7 Neo-Confucianism

Scholars of Chinese philosophy in general, and Confucianism in particular, have proposed a variety of paradigms that they see as reflecting their views as how best to study the development of Confucianism. This chapter takes up the internal developments in Confucianism and follows naturally on from the initial discussions in chapter 3. While the stages of Confucian evolution can be discussed in a number of different ways, the division adopted here is fivefold, the first perspective being the so-called transformative period.

The transforming face of Confucianism

The middle of the first century of the common era heralded the advent of Buddhism on the stage of China's history, bringing with it a belief system previously unknown in China, and offering a way to end suffering by means of compassion. In introducing the Chinese mind to the concept of *karma*, Buddhism offered a rational explanation for the state of human existence, an explanation that impressed even Confucian scholars. Additionally, Buddhism addressed hitherto unknown metaphysical concepts, including the ultimate nature of cosmic Reality. It also offered a means to effectuate transcendence of the self, and operated a celibate monastic order that released the bonds of a stifling Confucian family hierarchy. The fall of the Han dynasty was followed by three and a half centuries of disunity. With no central government, and hence no government posts, the need for candidates for office to study the Confucian *Classics* was no longer apparent. Clearly, the threat to Confucianism was great, and Buddhism lost no time spreading its wings. Recently emerging Ch'an/Chan Buddhism, with the promise of enlightenment for everyone through meditation, proved particularly appealing; now everyone could believe that they had Buddha-nature within them.

Nor was meditation peculiar to Buddhism, for Taoism had also developed meditative practices. The reunification of China at the end of the sixth century found intellectual and spiritual China under the influence of both Buddhism and Taoism. There is a profusion of Taoist texts that attest to the fusion of Taoist and Buddhist ideas; just one illustration will suffice, supposedly penned by no less a dignitary than Chang San-feng/Zhang Sanfeng, the alleged founder of the Chinese art of T'ai Chi Ch'üan/Taijiquan:

> The rootless tree,
> Its flowers so red.
> Pick all the red flowers till the tree is empty.
> *Shunyata is samsara;*
> *Samsara is shunyata.*
> Know that the true *shunyata* is found in the midst of *samsara*;
> And when one fully understands the nature of *shunyata*,
> *samsara* disappears.
> The *dharma* lives forever, never falling into emptiness.
> This is called perfect enlightenment,
> And one deserves the title of great hero.
> The ninth patriarch achieves salvation
> And ascends to heaven.[1]

Evidently, the Buddhist concepts of *shunyata* (emptiness) and *samsara* (rebirth) were quite acceptable in a Taoist text.

Where conflict did arise, Taoists sought comfort in the formulation of the incredible doctrine of *hua-hu*, wherein the Buddha was but an incarnation of Lao-tzu/Laozi, who had gone to India to convert the barbarians before he became the Buddha. Accordingly, with both Buddhism and Taoism having a common source, there could be nothing improper in a foreign deity (Buddha) and the native deity (Huang-Lao Chün/Huanglaojun) being worshipped by the common man at the same altar. Clearly, the insistence of Early Indian Buddhists that the Buddha Sakyamuni was a mere mortal was becoming ever less cogent. For the Chinese masses, therefore, a rather muddled theology arose that informed popular religion, a religion that borrowed freely from the teachings not only of Taoism and Buddhism, but Confucianism also, the last named having become the official religion by the time of the T'ang/Tang and Sung/Song dynasties.

Recent research by Kenneth Dean of McGill University has discovered tens of thousands of cult initiates worshipping in over a thousand temples throughout south-east China and south-east Asia; the cult figure in question being Lin Chao-en/Zhao'en (1517–98). Despite attempts by the Chinese government to suppress such resurgence in popular religion (in the interests of modernization), restoration of these temples began as recently as 1979, and the cult is still thriving today in post-Mao China. Lin Chao-en/Lin Zhao'en had formulated what he called "The Three in One Teachings", the success of which eventually found him with devotees elevating him to the status of "Lord of the Three in One", a title in which he (albeit, posthumously) rejoices today. Lin Chao-en/Lin Zhao'en's attempts to popularize Confucianism included the melding of Confucian teachings with the philosophical speculations of Ch'an/Chan Buddhism, as well as the alchemical practices peculiar to Taoism. The popularity accorded Lin Chao-en/Lin Zhao'en's efforts today is irrefutably attested in Dean's research.[2] It has been noted earlier that there is a generalized folk saying that every Chinese person is a Confucian, a Taoist, and a Buddhist. He is a Confucian when everything is going well; he is a Taoist when things are falling apart; and he is a Buddhist as he approaches death. It was a point made by Robert Allinson who added: "While this may have been intended to be taken cynically, it has been taken by some to indicate a kind of practical wisdom. This kind of practical wisdom is further illustrated in many folk temples in Hong Kong where one can see statues of Kongzi (Confucius), Laozi (Lao Tzu), and the Buddha set up alongside those of traditional Chinese immortals as objects of veneration."[3] Such fusion of the three religions is a phenomenon that will be reiterated throughout this book.

Although T'ai-tsung/Taizong, the model ruler of the T'ang/Tang dynasty (617–907), believed himself to be a descendant of Lao-tzu/Laozi, hence favouring Taoism, he reinstituted Confucianism as the state religion, at the same time offering state patronage to all Buddhist temples and monasteries. He also was convinced that Confucianism needed a religious element, and to this end in 630 he ordered the establishment of Confucian temples throughout the realm. Ritual observance by government officials effectuated within them included ritual dances, music and prayer. Guided by ancient rites, these rituals also included animal sacrifice. The aim was to elevate Confucius to divine status, and over the centuries, besides erecting statues of Confucius, the names of

Confucian dignitaries were recorded on tablets and set in the temples that proliferated the land. This said, it must be conceded that, from the fall of the Han dynasty (c. 220) until the middle of the great T'ang/Tang empire (c. 740s), Confucianism benefited mainly from a continued writing of the commentaries on the *Classics* that was begun in the Han, with little else to commend it. One of the reasons for this lack of progress was that, with Buddhism enchanting the Chinese mind and permeating Chinese life, intellectual minds were entranced with what the Buddha taught, rather than what Confucius thought. The arrival of Buddhism on the stage of Chinese history had presented a huge challenge to the Chinese mind, for it was the first high culture it had encountered; all previous insurgents had been barbarians, for whom philosophical and metaphysical debate had not been a priority.[4] With the most brilliant minds now occupied with the deeply penetrating thrust of Buddhist thought, the influence on Confucianism was considerable. Taoism was also making its presence felt, and among the many schools of thought that obtained at that time, accusations of being "pro-Buddhist" or "pro-Taoist" were frequently levied against Confucian scholars.

We now enter the period of development that is usually called Neo-Confucianism in western literature, in order to mark its departure from traditional Confucian Learning. Confucian Learning is a simplified rendition of *Tao-hsüeh/Daoxue* or *Li-hsüeh/Lixue* – terms that translate as "The Learning of the Way" or "The Learning of the Principle" respectively. This new form of Confucianism evolved in direct response to the growing challenge of the other Asian religious belief systems, Buddhism and Taoism. Although it is important to see philosophical developmental trends in their "setting in life", there are dangers inherent in rigidly following a chronological approach to intellectual development. It would be a mistake to assume that the Neo-Confucians were intent on creating Neo-Confucianism; on the contrary, they were totally loyal to the original Confucian vision.[5] Wing-tsit Chan illumines the broad canvas embraced by this evolution, when he says that: "The Confucian movement that began in the Sung dynasty (960–1279) was marked by its wide sphere of interests, including political and educational reforms, the compilation of comprehensive histories, the pursuit of classical scholarship and textual exegesis, the reaffirmation of Confucian morality and ethics, and the study of metaphysics and epistemology."[6] Clearly, the Neo-Confucians were loyal to their origins, albeit that these were wide-ranging in character.

The period of the Sung/Song–Ming dynasties witnessed a revival in

Confucian authority over every aspect of Chinese life. Thinkers directed their attention to purging Confucianism of each and every superstitious element that had infiltrated their belief system from Buddhism and Taoism. At the same time, the great contribution that Buddhist philosophy and Taoist spirituality could make to Confucianism was recognized and appropriated, resulting in a reevaluation of the Confucian position on the universe, society and the self.

The place of women in Confucian culture

Because of a dearth of recorded material, two problems immediately arise in any attempt to analyse the position of women and the transmission of Confucian culture during the Northern and Southern Sung/Song dynasties. We do know that there are records that attest to the fact that a woman's station in life was determined, and maintained, from an early age. There are records of young girls being trained as attendants, laundry maids, servants, kitchen maids and the like, while the capital cities of Sung/Song China did not deny enterprising common women the opportunity for self-employment. There is also evidence of success stories from those who established themselves as owners of restaurants, wine shops and teahouses. Nevertheless, it is now recognized that:

• Earlier studies, that have claimed to examine critically the role of women in Chinese society, have been hampered by restricted vision. Their view is unrepresentative of the true picture in China, for they almost totally ignore the vast majority of working women who struggled to survive in the villages and small towns. A dearth of historical records in this respect has restricted the attention of sociologists to female members of the nobility and gentry. This is, of course, perfectly valid in itself, but empresses and princesses can hardly be said to be truly representative of China's womanhood. Even here, records are incomplete for, while the plight of the working woman was evident for all to see, mansions with many rooms were not open to public viewing.

• Again, outside of elite families, family life was a matter of survival. For the former, the label "Confucianism" may well have had meaning, but for the common man, full of pragmatic concerns about everyday life, exactly what was or what was not "Confucianism" may have mattered little. Accordingly, despite official prohibitions, it was not unknown for (sometimes fatal) fights to break out in large working-class families following the death of the family head. Invariably, this was followed by internal family feuds that resulted in permanent schisms developing in the once united family; such behaviour was, of course, far removed from the Confucian ideal. Sung/Song writers invariably laid the blame for such bickering firmly at the door of the womenfolk in the family.

The parameters of female behaviour during the Sung/Song period have been delineated as "the priority of filiality, duties involved in managing the inner realm, separation of males and females, rights of property inheritance, and conjugal relations".[7] Males and females were not permitted to share the same toilet or bath, lest this should raise suspicion. The requirement to separate males and females even extended to the same household, and there are accounts of members of the same family being seated at mealtimes in different rows according to gender. Lineage rules were strictly observed, and there is testimony to the extent to which they were upheld: "A newly married son brought his wife some delicacies from the market. Refusing his favor, she took it to the elders and asked them to give him a flogging."[8] Clearly, the unfortunate husband had breached the requirements of the laws of lineage, which expressly forbade the giving or receiving of gifts directly from members of the opposite sex, even where the recipient is your wife!

Jian Zang is of the opinion that many such values and practices may have been extant in China prior to Confucianism and that these and other norms were appropriated by the early Confucians.[9] The wife of the financially solvent husband with a large family had a somewhat more restricted role to play in family life than the working wife in a small family. The latter could well attend to the financial affairs and business arrangements of an inept husband who, incompetent or not, could well find his role as head of the family usurped on his death by his wife, rather than his eldest son. Sung/Song legal codes were mindful of the need to sustain unmarried daughters, and catered for their needs by providing for their inclusion in inheritance laws. Doubtless, this influenced the practice of providing daughters with an equal share of the wedding expenses as their betrothed brothers, even though the daughter remained unmarried. Another practice that arose during the Sung/Song, out of economic necessity, was a widow's remarrying; the new man in her life was called "the continuing husband".

This dearth of recorded written material on the lives of rural women restricts our view to mere glimpses of their lot. Our limited vision is not helped by the fact that they were not accustomed to socializing outside extended family circles, unlike their urban counterparts. Nevertheless, the rural woman was involved in productive labour, working alongside men in the fields as well as selling her wares in the village. There was nothing wrong, *at that time*, with a woman being seen outside the home. Jian Zang, attests that coastal women were unfazed by the high seas, exemplified in the beautiful stories of Ma-tsu Lin/Mazu Lin (whom we have already met in chapter 6). She was a common rural woman who grew up in a fishing village. Gifted in spiritual healing, she soon won the hearts as well as the respect of the locals, but she had far more to offer than this. Ma-tsu Lin/Mazu Lin was well versed in astronomy, with an ability to predict the weather at sea, as well as having highly developed navigational skills. All of this enabled her to assist those in peril at sea and save countless lives. Her efforts did not go unnoticed or unrewarded. After her death, she became immortalized in popular religion as a cult figure, worshipped for generations as "the Protector at Sea", eventually becoming officially recognized in 1133 by Emperor Kao-tsung/Gaozong. We shall meet her again in chapter 9.

However, the passage of time saw not a diminution of the strictures imposed on women but an increase in their severity. It came to be considered unseemly for a woman to venture outside the home, for a housewife's place was in the kitchen, where she needed to be seen to be both competent and knowledgeable: "Do not step away from the stove" was the common edict. The ultimate sin was to be unfaithful to one's husband, at your (and your interfering parents') peril: "If a female has erred and committed adultery, give her a knife and a rope and lock her up in the cowshed; let her kill herself. If her mother interferes, divorce her. If her father interferes, take him to the officials and have him exiled. Erase his name from the genealogy and cast him off from the ancestral shrine in life and death."[10]

The perpetuation of the family line was held in high esteem; there is no suggestion that daughters were unloved, though it was not unknown for poverty in working families to invoke infanticide in the case of baby girls. The wife who bore her husband many sons was seen to have fulfilled the filial obligation admirably, as well as providing both family and state with an abundance of productive labour. A barren or sonless wife, on the other hand, was culpable of family extinction, one of seven reasons why a wife may legitimately be divorced according to Confucian theory. This said, divorce was not taken lightly in Sung/Song society and those who did divorce their wives were often castigated by society. Accordingly, it was not unknown for barren wives amongst the upper classes to procure concubines for their husbands.

The Five Masters

Early Neo-Confucian masters include Chou Tun-i/Zhou Dunyi (1017–73), Shao Yung/Shao Yong (1011–77), Chang Tsai/Zhang Zai (1020–77), Ch'eng Hao/Cheng Hao (1032–85) and Ch'eng I/Cheng Yi (1033–1107), collectively known as the Five Masters of the early Sung/Song period. This dynasty provided a safe and stable environment for Confucian thinkers that they had not known in former times of disunity. Accordingly, the mood was favourable for a re-examination of Confucian Learning and provided scope for new philosophical directions.

Chou Tun-i/Zhou Dunyi

Chou Tun-i/Zhou Dunyi was a man of great principle, who would speak out against injustice in front of any audience. The author of moral theses, his focus shifted Confucian thought from the exegetical studies that had permeated Han Learning to examination of the principles of philosophy (*li*), human nature (*hsing/xing*), and the heart/mind (*hsin/xin*). Under Chou Tun-i/Zhou Dunyi's influence, the fusion of Buddhist and Taoist thought in Confucian tradition is conspicuous in the Neo-Confucian adaptation of the Buddhist view of a constantly changing universe. This position is combined with the Taoist concept of *yin* and *yang* as well as the *I Ching/Yijing's* (the *Book of Changes*) teaching on the Supreme Ultimate. Not to be confused with the western "Godhead", the Supreme Ultimate is not found in Buddhist thought, but is a Taoist concept of a force used to produce *yin* and *yang*. Employed by Neo-Confucians to explain creation, it later became the cornerstone of Chinese cosmology.[11] The Neo-Confucian world-view (or, rather, "universal view"), held a position of non-duality; in other words, everything in the universe is one. Creation is considered to have come about by the manifestation of the Supreme Ultimate from Non-Being, which generates *yin* and *yang* that, in turn, generate the Five Agents. This profusion of cosmic forces, both on the macrocosmic level (the Way of Heaven) and the microcosmic level (the Way of Earth) bring into being masculine and feminine power from which creation evolves.

Considered to be the first of the Neo-Confucian philosophers, Chou Tun-i/Zhou Dunyi's thinking fuses Confucian, Taoist and Buddhist thought in other ways also. The Confucian assertion that, as the highest form of life, only human beings have the perspicacity to comprehend the universal principles is found in his teaching, as is the Buddhist assertion that the way to understanding reality lies in overcoming desire. Interestingly, these two assertions find expression in the *Book of Changes*, where the sage is held up to be the exemplary figure for humanity. The sage's acquisition of human virtues such as humaneness, sincerity and righteousness is depicted in the *Book of Changes* not in human terms, but in cosmic and worldly aspects of creation such as the sun, the moon and the four seasons. Accordingly, as portrayed in the *Doctrine of the Mean*, with tranquillity (the absence of desire), not activity, as their basis, these human virtues are seen to be in no way confined to humanity itself, but as the mainstay of universal order and harmony.[12]

Shao Yung/Shaoyong

Shao Yung/Shaoyong was also impressed with Taoism and Buddhism, but humaneness and righteousness did not feature in his teachings – factors that did not endear him to Confucian scholars. He agreed with Chou Tun-i/Zhou Dunyi's holistic world-view but he went one stage further in identifying the Supreme Ultimate with the heart/mind. Since all creatures emanate from the same source, he argued, the same principles must be common to all existence. Furthermore, by studying the *Book of Changes*, it is possible for the sage, from whom nothing is concealed, to determine and predict the nature of things. Shao Yung/Shaoyong held that, from the numerical patterns depicted in the *Book of Changes*, it is possible to discern the future order of the cosmos. It can only be done objectively, however, for our senses have the propensity to deceive rather than inform. An objective view of reality is only achievable by drawing on objective knowledge, knowledge informed by deliberating on everything learned from every source; this is the viewpoint of the sage.

Chang Tsai/Zhang Zai

Acknowledged to be the founding father of Neo-Confucianism, like those before him, Chang Tsai/Zhang Zai also was impressed by the *Book of Changes*. Its contents encouraged him to propound a new world-view theory that was accepted and developed by later Neo-Confucian scholars. He identified the Supreme Ultimate with *ch'i/qi*, the vital life-force. The life-force is said to have originated in a formless state known as the Great Void, soon to split into the two forces of *yin*

(Earth) and *yang* (Heaven). From the interaction between these masculine and feminine forces of *yang* and *yin* evolve all things in existence. He put forward the thesis that, because the vital life-force has two aspects (the void and the solid), so human beings have two aspects, the propensity to be mainly good or mainly bad, depending on the composition of one's individual *ch'i/qi*. His advice was for beings to serve both Heaven and Earth during their lifetimes: each should seek neither to end life prematurely nor strive to continue it beyond an allotted time span.

Ch'eng Hao/Cheng Hao and Ch'eng-I/Cheng Yi

Former students of Chou Tun-i/Zhou Dunyi, the two brothers complete the list of the Five Masters of early Neo-Confucianism. The abiding legacy of the brothers is the isolation of Confucianism from both Taoism and Buddhism, their combined teachings giving rise to a completely new system, a single school, known as *Lo-hsüeh/Luoxue*. For the brothers, the root of all social and moral problems stems from the discord between heavenly principle and human desires. The cultivation of one's heart/mind is the means to obviate such tension, melding the decree of Heaven with a fully developed nature. However, there were differences in emphasis between them; Ch'eng Hao/Cheng Hao developed concentration on Learning of the heart/mind, while Ch'eng I/Cheng Yi championed the Learning of Principle. For the former, learning involves far more than simply the acquisition of knowledge. He argued that if the universal principle exists in the heart/mind, then by extending one's heart/mind to all humanity, one's humaneness transcends all dualities, and what ostensibly appears to be a multiplicity of non-duality is seen in its true light as the one body of the universe – this is true learning, coming to know Heaven, not simply acquiring a multitude of facts.

Ch'eng I/Cheng Yi, on the other hand, saw the acquisition of knowledge as being of fundamental importance to one's spiritual development. The order and pattern transparent in the universe is directly attributable to the fact that, though every entity in the universe has its own particular principle or *li*, these individual principles are simply reflections of the one universal principle that is responsible for order rather than chaos in the universe. Accordingly, one must strive to acquire knowledge of individual principle, hence gaining an understanding of the universal principle and the reason behind all things. Ch'eng Hao/Cheng Hao's emphasis on humaneness and Ch'eng I/Ch'eng Yi's insistence on the investigation of all things later led to the emergence of two strands of thought in the evolution of Neo-Confucianism. The former's position was championed by Lu Chiu-yüan/Lu Jiuyuan and Wang Yang-ming (Wang Shouren), while the latter's stance was developed by Chu Hsi/Zhu Xi.

Chu Hsi /Zhu Xi

The name Chu Hsi /Zhu Xi (1130–1200) commands attention. His influence was second only to that of Confucius himself. It is in the thrust of this former student of both Taoism and Buddhism's thought that we find expressed the culmination of Neo-Confucianism in the Rationalist school. Unfortunately, as Angus Graham notes, he was under the mistaken premise that the whole of Neo-Confucian philosophy had been handed down by someone who was actually a Confucian – Taoist syncretist, a misunderstanding that was perpetuated throughout his lifetime.[13] He admired all of the Sung/Song masters, but his respect for Ch'eng I/Cheng Yi is conspicuous in the basis of his philosophy that centred on *li* or "principle". Wing-tsit Chan neatly points out the importance of a re-defined concept of *li* for the Neo-Confucians:

> In the classics *li* meant primarily order or pattern. In the *Meng-tzu* it referred chiefly to moral principles. But in the hands of the Neo-Confucians *li* came to denote a universal principle or law of being. The reinterpretation of this term forms the basis for many related theories, including "the investigation of things" (*ko-wu*), taken from the *Ta-hsüeh* (Great Learning), and the notion of "reverent seriousness" (*ching*) or the disciplined, pure, and alert mind that is a precondition of knowledge.[14]

For Chu/Zhu, everything in existence has its own unchanging essence or *li*, though its form or substance, *ch'i/qi*, will vary, its permanence being in no way guaranteed – echoes of the views of his predecessors. This philosophy enabled him to develop his doctrine of moral cultivation. The syncretic influence of Taoism on Chu Hsi/Zhu Xi is conspicuous in his comparison of the Great *Li*, the essence behind all things, with the *Tao*, the universal Principle. Xinzhong Yao notes an example of the unity created by such an essence: "Although everything has its own principle, this is only a reflection of the universal Principle … Zhu takes the moon as his example and says that there is only *one* moon in the sky but moonlight is scattered upon rivers and lakes and can be seen everywhere. It seems that each river or mountain has its own moon and has its special moonlight, but in the final analysis all moonlight comes from the same and single moon."[15] Chu/Zhu's comparison is a clear indication of the exploration of an interconnected and unified cosmos that many Neo-Confucians found attractive.

Buddhist influence is also apparent in Chu/Zhu's likening of *ch'i/qi* to bad *karma*. For Buddhists, the accumulation of negative *karma* in a person is due to the enactment of bad deeds and thoughts. Bad *karma* can be negated by accruing good *karma*, through doing good deeds and practising meditation. Chu/Zhu saw *ch'i/qi* as bad news, bad *karma* in fact. The way to overcome *ch'i/qi* was, according to Chu Hsi/Zhu Xi, to enhance one's knowledge, what he termed "the investigation of things".[16] Extending one's knowledge leads to the realization that it is *ch'i/qi* that fuels the ego with its attendant unworthy impulses. The fulfilment of this goal of knowledge has the effect of making one a sage, bereft of ego – not at all unlike buddhahood with its demise of the three defilements of greed, anger and delusion.

The Confucian tradition was never averse to protests from within: indeed, this was even encouraged at times, and the issue of the supposed merits of the examination system was no exception. There were those who favoured a return to the ancient moral order, wherein merit was identified, recognized and rewarded by society without the so-called benefit of any examination system. Other critics were also dissatisfied with the examination system, but for different reasons. Their objections find echoes in criticisms of examinations still voiced in twenty-first century Britain and the United States, and centre upon concerns about those candidates that succeed in passing examinations through learning by rote with little understanding, or by cramming, with next to no interest in anything beyond passing the examination itself. The Confucians of imperial China opted for a compromise, looking to the superior man exalted by Confucius found employed in the service of the state.[17]

Chu/Zhu taught that the path to becoming a sage was through study. His recommended, indeed required, reading was the *Analects of Confucius*, the *Book of Meng-tzu/Mengzi* (Latin, *Mencius*) and two chapters from the *Book of Rites*, the *Great Learning* and the *Doctrine of the Mean*: these became known as The *Four Books*, the mastery of which ensured the understanding of every situation. Prior to the Sung/Song dynasty, the set texts for Confucian Learning and state examination were inevitably the *Five Classics* and occasionally the *Analects of Confucius*. Chu Hsi/Zhu Xi changed all that, and in 1313 the imperial court of the Yüan/Yuan dynasty (1260–1370) decreed that the annotations and commentaries made by Chu Hsi/Zhu Xi on The *Four Books* were to become the basis of the state examination system. These annotations and commentaries were published in a book entitled *Sishu*

Jizhu. Given the importance accorded this new canon – a much smaller corpus of texts than the previously statutory *Five Classics* – it is worthwhile pausing to consider the composition of the *Four Books*:

- The *Analects of Confucius*. Compiled long after the demise of Confucius, as detailed in the last chapter, these fragmentary dialogues between Confucius and his disciples, or between Confucius and various feudal rulers, are all we have to provide a portrait of the master and his teaching. The work comprises twenty chapters divided into almost fifty (sometimes extremely brief) sections.

- The *Book of Meng-tzu/Mengzi* (Latin, *Mencius*). Taking as his starting point his belief that the nature of man is inherently good, Meng-tzu/Mengzi developed his argument by advocating that humankind is born with what he called "the four beginnings".[18] Again, this work recalls conversations between pupil and master, but its seven chapters are written in a far more animated manner than the *Analects*, and they are replete with apposite and illustrative anecdotes.

- The *Great Learning* is a brief chapter culled from the *Book of Rites* or *Rituals*. Between the times of the Han and T'ang/Tang dynasties, the *Book of Rites* became the mainstay of Chinese society. However, the *Great Learning* places less emphasis on ritual and more on moral strength and moral virtues as the backbone of good rulership. Rather than resorting to arms, laws, and power, peace may be brought to the world through the cultivation of moral principles and character, beginning with the individual, then progressing through to the family, the state and finally the world.

- Exactly how this may be achieved is outlined in the *Doctrine of the Mean*, another work culled from the *Book of Rites*. The key word here is "sincerity" for if one's mind is sincere, then one's character may become cultivated and one may become a sage. Such sincerity is developed by focusing on an inner life of harmony and tranquillity, which reflects the harmony and order of the universe. According to *The Doctrine of the Mean*, that enigmatic entity that rejoices in the name "the self" is in reality suspended between two polarities – the ten thousand things at the one pole and the pure centre of readiness or *chung* at the other. Neo-Confucians equated *chung* with *li* or principle. The self is shaped by the structured connections of the "self" between these polarities, particularly those behavioural traits steered by one's orientations that respond to the ten thousand things as well as showing an aesthetic appreciation of and appropriate reactions to *li*.[19]

Although generally considered to be the most important of the Neo-Confucians, Chu Hsi/Zhu Xi was not without his critics. The general criticism made was that his doctrine had no direction and was of no benefit to the state. The Practical Learning school of Ch'en Liang/Chen Liang (1143–94) and I Shih/Yi Shi (1150–1223) saw Zhu's doctrine of human nature as being anything but practical, and given more to aimless talk than beneficial advice. The Idealistic school of Lu Chiu-yüan/Lu Jiuyuan (better known as Xiangshan), and later Wang Yang-ming (Wang Shouren, 1472–1528), was similarly unimpressed by what it saw as an unnecessarily difficult and exegetical approach to sagehood, rather than a natural and harmonious appreciation of the natural order. The Idealistic school saw Chu/Zhu's doctrine of moral cultivation as being beyond the understanding of the common man and thus of no use to the people.

Taking the *Book of Meng-tzu/Mengzi* (Latin, *Mencius*) and the *Doctrine of the Mean* as its foundation, the Idealistic school argued that there is no principle outside the heart/mind and that the heart/mind contains all that is necessary to make virtuous and moral decisions. The Rationalist school's failure to recognize this was a source for further criticism. Wang Yang-ming (Wang Shouren) and the School of Mind were also castigated and blamed for the fall of the Ming dynasty. This came about as the result of a misunderstanding when Wang wrote: "In the original substance of the mind there is no distinction of good and evil". It was a statement that caused outrage in some circles that saw such an affirmation as directly violating the Neo-Confucian doctrine of the original goodness of human nature. Misguided students saw Wang's dictum as giving them *carte blanche* to act in ways that were not entirely commensurate with Confucian teaching, hence the castigation. Wang's abiding legacy to Neo-Confucianism was his doctrine of the identification of mind and principle; in other words, his conviction that the mind and principle are not only inseparable, but also identical: "To look for principle in each individual thing is like looking for the principle of filiality in parents. If the principle of filiality is to be sought in parents, then is it actually in my own mind or is it in the person of my parents? If it is actually in the person of my parents, is it true that as soon as my parents pass away the mind will then lack the principle of filiality?"[20] As Confucianism spread its wings, these criticisms were not confined to mainland China.

The dissemination of Confucianism

Chapter 3 noted that though Confucianism certainly was conceived in China, equally certainly, it was not forever confined to its Chinese homeland. It is important to remember that, as religions spread their wings to pastures new, it is always the culture that shapes the religion, never the religion that shapes the culture. Accordingly, the transmigration from northern China, throughout the Chinese mainland, initially to the rest of East and south-east Asia, and later to the rest of the world, saw local influences affect Confucianism to a greater or lesser degree. The Former Han Dynasty saw Vietnam, Korea and Japan first appropriate, and then modify, Confucian beliefs and practices. Local culture and tradition began to exert an influence on Confucian Learning worldwide, and the dawn of the twentieth century witnessed the appearance on the world stage of a variety of forms of Confucianism, all stemming from a mother culture, all expressing themselves in a way peculiar to native scholars' own understanding and experience of local culture and tradition.

Vietnam

The Chinese empire absorbed Vietnam in the days of the Han dynasty, in 111 BCE to be precise. In turn, Vietnam absorbed Chinese culture over the next millennium. Although retaining their own spoken language and customs, under China's control, the Vietnamese adopted Chinese writing for administration and educational purposes. In newly opened schools dedicated to introducing Vietnamese children to Chinese civilization, the teaching of Confucian ethics was included in the curriculum.

The expulsion of the Chinese from Vietnam in 938 found China now being regarded as an elder brother. Accordingly, the Vietnamese emperor adopted the title Son of Heaven from his Chinese namesake. Chinese rites and ceremonies continued to be observed, as was the Chinese custom of holding examinations in the understanding of Chinese culture that included Confucian studies. This was the benchmark for candidates seeking posts in government: a Confucian-trained civil service came into being. It is small wonder that interest in Confucianism increased, with concerns over righteousness and public-order behaviour pre-eminent in the minds of court officials.

The Vietnamese government both admired and adopted forms from the Han and T'ang/Tang laws that seemed appropriate to the Vietnamese people. In 1070 Hanoi, the first Confucian temple was built; others followed later. In time, scholars insisted that Confucian values become the norm – an edict effectuated by state decree. The five human relationships were emphasized and the "fathers of the people", as scholar-officials became known, advocated the appropriation of Chinese dress and manners.

Korea

It is not Vietnam, but Korea that lays claim to the richest Confucian developments outside China. During the Korean Koguryo dynasty (37 BCE–668 CE), a national academy for the study of Confucianism was established in the Kingdom of Paekche. From the Kingdom of Silla (365–935), students were encouraged to make the journey to China for the same purpose. Although Confucianism had entered Korea during the first century BCE, some four centuries before Buddhism, it was the latter that was still regarded as the state religion as late as the Koryo dynasty (918–1392). By these times, the infusion of Taoism, Buddhism and Confucianism into the country's cultural heritage was being referred to as "the legs of the three-legged stool".[21] By the end of the Koryo era, in their determination to exalt Confucianism, scholars began to revile Buddhism, and the succeeding Yi dynasty (1392–1910) found Buddhism playing very much second fiddle to Neo-Confucianism in Korean culture and society. Korean scholars were fascinated by the expositions of Neo-Confucians, not only studying their theories but also engaging in metaphysical and philosophical debate that led to the development of their own Korean doctrine:

> The Neo-Confucian concepts of *li* (principle), *qi* (material force), *xin* (heart/mind) and *taiji* (Great Ultimate) with their practical applications in meditative discipline and self-cultivation gained the hearts of Korean scholars and became the centre of academic study and debates. One of the first great Confucian scholars of the sixteenth century, So Kyong-dok (1489–1546) elaborated a monistic theory based on the conception of *qi* (material force), which can be said to be a Korean version of Zhang Zai's theory of material force and primordial harmony (*taihe*) and of Zhou Dunyi's cosmological deliberations. So Kyong-dok argued that the universe was composed of nothing but material force and that material force alone was the source of all things.[22]

Clearly, the Korean mind found Neo-Confucian doctrines intriguing, an intrigue that informed future philosophical and metaphysical speculation. As far as Neo-Confucianism is concerned, the two most well-known Korean philosophers are T'oegye (Yi Hwang 1501–70) and Yulgok (Yi I 1536–84). However, they were not of one mind concerning the central position of the relationship between principle and material force. T'oegye saw the relationship as a dual one whereas Yulgok favoured a monistic interpretation. This difference of opinion was the seedbed of the formation of two opposing schools, the School of Principle (Yongnam School) and the School of Material Force (Kiho School). The debates that ensued did much for academic discourse and little for everyday life, so much so that in the seventeenth century in the Ch'ing/Qing dynasty (1664–1911) attention turned to social reform and public welfare. This systematic theory and practice was termed *Silhak* or Practical Learning. The trend did not win universal acclaim, however, and it was eventually replaced by another academic system known as *Tonghak* or Eastern Learning. Introduced by Choi Je-wu (1824–64), as the name suggests, Eastern Learning favoured Oriental thought and eschewed Christian and other Western doctrine. Although the movement had become a religion known as The Religion of Heaven's Way (*Chondo-kyo*), Confucianism in Korea was a spent force by the end of the Yi dynasty (1910).

Japan

Confucianism did not become a prominent force in Japan until after 1600, when it made its presence felt by way of Korea. Kang Hang (1567–1618), a (prisoner of war) student of T'oegye is generally credited with being the messenger. Sung/Song Neo-Confucianism had previously reached Japan shortly after its appearance in China, but it failed to gain a foothold until much later. Confucianism of the Han variety was known in Japan long before this, and with it came belief in the Five Agents and the forces of *yin* and *yang*. It is well attested in Japanese literature that a family planning to construct a house would bear in mind the forces of *yin* and *yang* and build accordingly. Nevertheless, as in Korea, Confucianism had to overcome Buddhist influence before it became fully accepted, and in Han times Confucianism was regarded as a sect of Buddhism: by the time of the thirteenth century, Confucianism had still to make an impact on Japanese culture.

In the year 1600, the Tokugawa shogunate was founded, Tokugawa Ieyasu (1542–1616), the founder of the *bakufu* (government) system, being the first *shogun* (war lord) to rule over a unified Japan. Although records attest that it was certainly the Japanese emperor who *reigned*, equally certainly, it was the shogunate that *ruled*. The metaphysical and philosophical debates that informed Confucianism in Korea are inconspicuous in Japanese thought, which centred on a more pragmatic approach.

The first of the Tokugawa Confucian masters was Fujiwara Seika (1561–1619), a former priest at the major Zen Buddhist centre of Shokokuji. Through his Zen studies, as was the custom, he was introduced to Confucian texts, and he came to believe that human relationships are more important than anything. His attempts to study under a Confucian master in China were thwarted, but his knowledge increased courtesy of the erudition of Korean prisoners of war captured during Toyotomi Hideyoshi's invasion of Korea. He set the Koreans the task of copying the *Four Books* and the *Five Classics*, which he annotated in Japanese, a landmark in the history of Japanese Confucianism. At one time considered to be the founder of Tokugawa Neo-Confucianism, Seika today is looked on more as a middle man who helped Confucianism crystallize out of a Zen-influenced Confucianism found in the Gozan Zen temples of the Muromachi period. As surely as Seika saw Buddhism as renouncing the world, he renounced Buddhism. He favoured the teachings of the Sung/Song but was criticized for his emphasis on "stilling the mind", in which his opponents saw echoes of the Zen teaching on enlightenment. Nevertheless, his was an eclectic approach to Confucian studies: Yao illustrates this eclectic characteristic perfectly:

> He identified the common principles shared by Neo-Confucian philosophers, and combined them into a common system. He believed that "the emphasis on quietness" of Zhou Dunyi, "holding fast to seriousness" emphasised by Cheng Yi, "investigating principle exhaustively" propagated by Zhu Xi, "the simple and easy way" of Lu Jiuyuan, "quiet sitting" proposed by Chen Xianzhang (1428–1500) and "the innately good knowledge" of Wang Shouren, "are all from the same source but appear to be different in words".[23]

With Seika as his teacher, Tokugawa looked to *Shushigaku* (Studies in the philosophy of Chu Hsi/Zhu Xi) to ensure stability in society. However, it was the Japanese Neo-Confucian scholar, Seika's pupil, Hayashi Razan (1583–1657) to whom Tokugawa turned for a class structure that divided merchants, artisans, and farmers, from nobles and samurai – a division that remained the *status quo* until the late nineteenth century. Also given the priest-like name Doshun, Razan's advice was understood to represent the official Confucian position in Japan during the Tokugawa shogunate. Like his master, Seika, Razan rejected Zen Buddhism, for similar reasons. Unlike him, he was single minded in his admiration of Neo-Confucians, and the study of *Shushigaku* was the only way forward as far as he was concerned. This said, it was his general knowledge that brought about his appointment to the shogunate, rather than his having any expertise in Confucianism. As was customary, he was required to shave his head and wear priestly vestments, but any focus on the dissemination of Confucianism was not within his remit.

Razan recognized an affinity between Confucianism and Shinto, but Yamazaki Ansai (1618–82) kept the two belief systems separate. A faithful follower of Chu Hsi/Zhu Xi's teaching, Ansai set himself the task of restoring what he saw as the distorted interpretations of Seika, Razan and others. For Ansai, Chu Hsi/Zhu Xi's thought could not simply be transposed from China to Japan, but should be interpreted in the context of everyday Japanese life. The differences between Razan and Ansai resulted in the development of two major schools.

Among Japanese Confucian philosophers who came to prominence at this time is to be found the name of Kaibara Ekken (1630–1750). Although a supporter of Chu Hsi/Zhu Xi, he proposed that Principle as the Supreme Ultimate was the formal name for the primordial Vital Force. It was Kaibara Ekken who brought Confucianism into the homes of the common people. In Ekken's thought, there was no place for dualism: for him, Confucianism is a monistic belief system that melds heavenly principle with everyday life. This "great doubt" about the supposed dualism of Principle and material force is found expressed in his work *Taigiroku*. Although a samurai scholar, his studies and subsequent advice centred not on the Confucian classics but on an appreciation of nature and the basic moral principles and everyday conduct desirable in a Japanese household. Yamaga Soko (1622–85) went one step further, saying that such desirable conduct was exemplified in the samurai, whom he identified with the "true gentleman" whose "righteousness" was so staunchly applauded by Confucius.

Nakae Toju (1608–48), on the other hand, was deeply impressed with the thrust of thought of Chu Hsi/Zhu Xi's critic, Wang Yang-ming (Wang Shouren). For the latter, action speaks louder than words and Zhu's "investigation of things", though rational, was an inferior approach to one that centred on deeds. The Study of Wang's Learning, with its emphasis on the heart/mind, is otherwise known as the *Yomeigaku*, an ideology promoted by both Nakai Toju and Kumazawa Banzan (1619–91). Since Toju, following Wang, saw goodness, which he called the Divine Light of Heaven, in the most humble person (not only scholars), it was these to whom Toju turned. He won the ear of the common people and under his influence Confucianism came to be regarded as a religion by a Japanese people who worshipped a personal deity called the Supreme Lord Above. Nevertheless, it was the *Shushigaku* that gained precedence over the *Yomeigaku*, winning official recognition and becoming the State Orthodox Ideology in 1790.

During the Tokugawa period, a third school made its appearance felt. This was the School of the Ancient Studies, *Kogaku*. The teachings of Chu Hsi/Zhu Xi and Wang Yang-ming (Wang Shouren) were seen to have developed under Taoist and Buddhist influence, and were discredited. The Duke of Zhou, Confucius and Meng-tzu/Mengzi (Latin, Mencius) were considered as the true teachers of the Way. Ito Jinzai (1627–1705) and Ogyu Sorai (1666–1728) went one step further in identifying the *Analects* as "the foremost book of all". Whilst this had the admirable consequence of permeating the Japanese psyche with high Confucian moral principles, it had the adverse effect of stifling the way forward for Neo-Confucian Learning. Confucianism became reduced to "the art of government", and went into decline. The transformation of Japan into an industrial and military state saw Confucianism blamed by some for holding back the advance, but this was never its intention. Accordingly, whereas in the Chinese and Korean modernization process there was no room for Confucianism, Japan found room. The Meiji Restoration of 1868 had made Shinto the state orthodoxy, but not to the exclusion of Confucianism and other belief systems. Despite briefly falling into disfavour at the end of the Second World War, it continues to be seen as the influence of eastern morality balancing western science. Yao puts the point clearly when he writes:

> The Japanese pragmatic attitude toward Confucian Learning greatly affects the way in which the Confucian tradition develops and explains the unique image and functions that Confucianism has had in modern Japan. For most of the twentieth century the majority of the Chinese and Koreans see Confucianism as politically conservative and culturally backward, while in Japan, Confucianism is largely considered to have played an important role in the Meiji reformation and aided the acceleration of Japanese industrialisation and modernisation.[24]

However, as noted earlier, it is culture that shapes a religion, never *vice versa*. Although Confucian influence was conspicuous, Japan neither could not, nor would not appropriate Chinese thought in its entirety. Being an aristocratic society, any examination system that led to positions of government was always the preserve of the aristocracy and never available to the general public; the scholar never enjoyed the claim to fame accorded him in China. Although there could never be room in Japanese thought for a belief system that gave credence to criticism of a Japanese emperor, the Mandate of Heaven was introduced in order to lend support to the establishment; all Japanese emperors were considered to be divine by birth, and hence beyond rebuke.

Modern New Confucianism

The so-called "modern new Confucianism" (*xiandai xin ruxue*) that evolved during this last period of Confucian development is the result of the influence of world philosophical systems that obtain outside of China. Particularly influential here are contemporary Christian spirituality as well as European philosophical tradition. No study of recent Chinese philosophy that either ignores or evades discussion of the contribution made by the study of Chinese philosophy in the West can be considered a responsible one. This influence was recognized and fostered by many outstanding Chinese Confucian scholars of the twentieth century. The history of such study begins in the seventeenth century with the arrival of Jesuit priests in China. Their purpose was to persuade Chinese intellectuals and scholars of the truth of Christianity, but in their discussions they inevitably learned much about Chinese philosophy in general and Confucianism in particular. These teachings from the Confucian *Classics* they dutifully communicated to the intelligentsia of Europe as well as to their own order. More and more European philosophers gradually became interested in Confucianism, especially in England, France and Germany – an interest that accelerated with the publication of *Confucius the Philosopher* in the middle of the seventeenth century. However, in the very next century, the exchange of ideas between East and West came to an abrupt halt, brought to a close by the Rites Controversy's edict forbidding the participation of Jesuit priests in Confucian rituals. With no guidance from texts or tongues, misunderstanding of Confucian studies was given *carte blanche* in western thought for over two centuries, and even intellectuals of the ilk of Kant, Rousseau, and Hegel were guilty of seriously misrepresenting Confucian studies because of the ignorance brought about by a dearth of communication.

The fact that late nineteenth-century China fostered strong anti-western feeling among the public is graphically illustrated in a print from about 1890. Here, Christ is portrayed as a pig bound to a cross and transfixed by arrows fired by Chinese bowmen.[25] By 1911, however, the ancient Chinese empire, along with its attendant Confucian trappings, was no more, overwhelmed by the tide of westernization that swept East Asia. Confucianism took the full brunt of criticism from those seeking reasons for East Asia's playing second fiddle to western cultural supremacy. Modern China was no longer deemed to be a suitable home either for Confucianism or, for that matter, Christianity. Accordingly, the lecture tours of Bertrand Russell and John Dewey in China between 1911 and 1921 attracted only those Chinese intellectuals eager to learn more about western philosophy, rather than those keen to put forward their own Chinese viewpoint. The Revolution of 1911 also saw the diminution of previously endowed widow's Confucian privileges; these included the favourable position enjoyed by widows in respect to property rights. A gradual decline in the value attributed to women's material and cultural efforts in the commercial workplace (though not in the cottage industries) was offset, to a degree, in the appreciation afforded the female contribution to performing arts, in every sense of the term.[26]

At that time, the study of Chinese philosophy in the West as a living tradition of philosophical thinking was unimaginable. Already, Confucianism was being presented to western scholars and students alike as some kind of ossified tradition, of no possible relevance to the twentieth century. Departments of Chinese Philosophy were conspicuous by their absence from the universities of Europe and America, nor were these studies subsumed in Departments of Philosophy. Where these studies did obtain, they were to be found in either Departments of History or Asian Studies. Even where worthwhile translations of Chinese texts did appear, these were tainted by biased commentary, as Chung-ying Cheng attests:

> From the end of the nineteenth century to the middle of the twentieth century, Chinese philosophy was studied in the West in the fossilized form of texts translated from Chinese by nonphilosophical sinologists specializing in ancient Chinese culture. The two most well-known sinologists were James Legge, who translated all the major works of the Classical Confucianism into English, and Richard Wilhelm, who translated the *Yijing* and *Daodejing* into German. They did a great service in introducing Chinese philosophy to the modern West, but their comments revealed their Christian background rather than the living traditions and current issues of Western philosophy.[27]

The lack of respect in which Chinese philosophy was/is held by some western philosophers is largely attributable to ignorance: even today, some consider that Chinese philosophy is bereft of morality and truth. Part of the problem is the desire to compare *like with like*, but Chinese philosophy is *unlike* western philosophy, and the Chinese language is *unlike* any western language. The grammatical framework within which western philosophy operates is at variance with its Chinese counterpart, where comparable concepts and distinctions are absent. Accordingly, the persuasive (to the Chinese mind) arguments propounded by Chinese scholars have been wasted on (at least some) philosophers who operate outside the Chinese philosophical framework.

Confucianism now found itself in the role of a political football, with players on one side calling for the restoration of Confucianism as the state religion, informed by study of the Confucian *Classics*. On the other side, the overthrow of the Manchu Ch'ing/Qing dynasty in 1911 heralded the appearance of a strong anti-Confucian movement. By 1919, the May Fourth Movement had concluded that there was no place for Confucianism in the way forward for China, indeed, it was Confucianism that was responsible for the nation's ills. Accordingly, Chinese philosophers looked to their western counterparts as leading lights, showing the way forward to an inferior system.

> Since the beginning of the twentieth century, Western philosophy was absorbed in China faster than Chinese philosophy was studied in the West. Good examples of the Chinese reception of Chinese philosophy are found in Kang Youwei, Liang Qichao, and Wang Guowei. These Chinese philosophers tried to catch up with the current trends in Western philosophy. Hence, Bergson and Dewey were translated into Chinese and their thought contributed both to the formation of new Chinese philosophy and to the reconstruction of traditional systems of philosophy. Xiong Shili and Liang Shuming, for example, used Bergson to promote their understanding of Chinese philosophy and Western philosophy. With Fang Dongmei, Mou Zongsan, and Tang Junyi, a critical attitude towards specific Western philosophers was developed.[28]

These language translation developments helped overcome the previously mentioned linguistic obstacles to understanding, and as early as 1935 East/West philosophical dialogue was inaugurated in the University of Hawaii at Manoa under the instigation of Charles Moore and Wing-tsit Chan.

Meanwhile, back in China a critical eye was being cast over both Confucianism and the *Classics*. At one and the same time, two millennia of classical learning came to an abrupt end, while the intensity of feeling to these criticisms against Confucianism was so strong that Confucian intellectuals responded by introducing what became known as Modern New Confucian Learning. These Modern New Confucians fall into two main schools, Modern New Idealists and Modern New Rationalists. Their aim was to combine traditional Confucian values with the needs of the modern world. As Yao reminds us: "Xiong Shili (1885–1968), Liang Shuming (1893–1988), Fung Yu-lan (1895–1990), Qian Mu (1895–1990), Zhang Junmai (Carsun Chang, 1886–1969), and He Lin (1902–), to name but a few, stood out as the leaders of this new trend; their activities constituted the first phase of Confucianism in the twentieth century."[29] Led by Zhang Junmai, intellectuals at the 1923 debate on Science versus Metaphysics seriously called to question the conclusions reached by the May Fourth Movement when it unreservedly applauded western models of modernity against the supposed stupefying effects of Confucianism. The time was now ripe for modern reflective interpretations of all the ancient Confucian and non-Confucian texts in general and the thoughts of those great Neo-Confucian masters, Chu Hsi/Zhu Xi and Wang Yang-ming (Wang Shouren) in particular. The former's realism against the latter's focus on mind provided the main focus of attention for Modern New Confucians.

Xiong Shili's early studies of Buddhist teachings, particularly those that taught "Mere Consciousness", left him wholly dissatisfied with Buddhism. A move to Confucianism found Xiong earnestly seeking to restore the true *Tao* of Confucius as the fundamental *raison d'être* of Chinese religions. Influenced by Wang Yang-ming (Wang Shouren), Xiong also incorporated western learning into his vision for Modern Confucianism. His aversion to Buddhism is apparent in his proposing an active Confucian concept of *self*. Xiong also thought deeply about the relationship between metaphysics and morality, looking to the *I Ching/Yijing* (the *Book of Changes*) for a metaphysical basis for Confucian ethics. In Xiong's vision, there was scope for both philosophy and science, though their roles were quite distinct.[30]

Although, like Xiong Shili, Liang Shuming was influenced to some extent by Henri Bergson, he had no doubts that the Chinese ideal of living a life in harmony with nature was vastly superior not only to a western mindset that sought to *harness* the waters and *conquer* the mountains, but also to an Indian mindset that sought to flee the world, having no (at least for Buddhists) belief in a permanent unchanging self. Liang based his thinking on the thrust of thought of the Neo-Confucian Wang Xinzhai (1483–1541). Like those before him, he argued that knowledge is derived not only from intellect, but from intuition also. Accordingly, Confucian concerns with intuition again bear the marks of a culture superior to that of the western world. Liang's thought concerned itself with a comparative study of both human culture (the West/India/China) and human nature (different personality types). For Liang, the time would come not only for Confucian culture, but for a Confucian self also.[31]

Again like Xiong Shili, Fung Yu-lan distinguished between philosophy and science. He further distinguished between actuality and truth-and-reality, and used modern logical analysis to criticize and develop Chu Hsi/Zhu Xi's realist theory of principle (li). Fung Yu-lan's thrust of thought developed a metaphysical/philosophical system that blended traditional Confucian values with China's commitment to modernization. This found expression in the commitment of a faithful subject to a legitimate ruler. Fung Yu-lan's intellectual drive was fuelled by a deep dissatisfaction with the unsystematized structure of Chinese philosophical texts, as well as for their fondness for using aphorisms. These teachings he sought to reconstruct in the light of modernity, at the same time developing a profound philosophical mysticism with consideration of the concept of reality as its fulcrum.[32]

The dream of Modern Confucianism took an immense step forward in the declaration of commitment to world harmony. This coincided with the setting up of institutions that voiced as their mission the blending of different cultures and different traditions with a view to bringing about a humankind with unified thought. Working within a framework of the Confucian values inculcated in institutions of the Sung/Song and Ming dynasties, these colleges employ teaching techniques current in European universities, facilitating a humanities programme that encourages dialogue between eastern and western cultures. The leading light in this initiative to revive Confucianism has been Quin Mu, who became the inaugural president of the Academy of New Asia, Hong Kong.

He Lin is the least known Chinese philosopher of his generation, probably because he saw no need for the formulation of further philosophical systems. For He Lin, all of China's modern cultural problems could be traced to the nation's loss of philosophical direction. The answer, he proposed, was a philosophical universalism that sought to fuse western philosophical teachings with the Confucian philosophy of principle. Accordingly, the universally true idealist system proposed by Hegel should steer the Confucian doctrines germane to the School of Mind. There are no distinguishing features between mind and principle, he reasoned, and he sought to reinterpret the doctrines of the School of Mind with a view to formulating an idealistic framework that combined culture, nature and spirit, with a philosophical perspective of *Tao*. However, as far as formulating a philosophical system of his own was concerned, He Lin failed to see the need, probably because he was perfectly happy with Hegel's. One has to resist the temptation to smile when reading Jiwei Ci's explanation of why He Lin is probably the least known Chinese philosopher of his generation:

> In part, this reflected his apparent lack of ambition or ability to develop a philosophical system of his own. In spite of this, He was a strong believer in philosophical systems and left numerous clues as to what his system would look like had he built one. He Lin was a system builder without a system or, put another way, he provided pieces of a system, which lacked either full development or explicit connection.[33]

The opening chapters of the twentieth century heralded a half century of despair for China, riven by civil war and foreign oppression and culminating in the invasion by Japan in the Second World War. The formation of the People's Republic of China in 1949 and the Cultural Revolution in the 1960s sounded the death knell to any moves to make Confucianism the state religion and ideology. The status of both Confucius and Confucianism continues to be debated, and between 1960 and 1962 thirteen conferences were held to this end.[34] The International Society for Chinese Philosophy, as well as the *Journal of Chinese Philosophy* (founded by Chung-ying Cheng in 1965 and 1972 respectively), both contributed enormously to the introduction to the western mind of Chinese philosophy as a living tradition. The Society held conferences in 1995, 1997 and 1999 with this in view. In 1985, the International Academy of Chinese Culture was founded by academics from Peking University with similar aims. Among those vital and dynamic modern Chinese thinkers, currently dedicated to taking Chinese philosophy forward in the modern world, are to be found the names of Ye Xiushan, Jin Wulun and Chen Lai.

In modern times, the development of the study of Chinese philosophy in the West has been enriched beyond measure by both Chinese and non-Chinese philosophers alike. The list is long and includes such worthies as Wing-tsit Chan, Chung-ying Cheng (Cheng Zhongying), Antonia Cua (Ke Xiongwen), Fu Weixun (Charles Fu), Liu Shuxian (Shu-hsien Liu), Tang Liquan (Lik-kuen Tong), Qin Jiayi (Julia Ching), and Du Weiming (T'u Wei-ming). In recent decades, the fine work of these scholars has been enhanced enormously by academics who are not of Chinese descent, but who value the contribution that Chinese philosophy can make. Among these are to be found the names of Benjamin Schwartz, Friedrich Mote, Derk Bodde, William Theodore de Bary, Donald Monroe, and Chad Hansen. This list is by no means exhaustive,[35] but it is representative of the interest shown in Chinese philosophy by distinguished scholars who credit fully the value of Chinese thought in modern philosophical advances. It was Theodore de Bary who reminded us that the beginning of the twentieth century found Confucianism in China dominating not only family rituals and the imperial civil service, but the entire educational establishment.[36]

Never deemed to be theocentric, what is Confucianism's position today? T'u Wei-ming, one of its leading proponents, describes it as "an inclusive humanism", with its followers exhibiting what is best described as the fundamental principle of humaneness. On this view, Confucianism remains an invaluable source for those seeking meaningful answers to life, answers that have been meaningful in the past, are meaningful for the world today, and will be meaningful in the future. Many critics of Confucianism, on the other hand, would argue that it has no value whatever outside the realms of history. Mao Tse-tung himself saw the only place for Confucianism being alongside the relics in museums. The latter position is exemplified in the thought of the great intellectual historian Joseph Levenson, writing in the mid-1960s. For Levenson, modern advances on all fronts have restricted any useful contribution Confucianism may make to the history books, a tradition no more capable of addressing the problems of the twenty-first century than the traditions of Egyptian and Mayan cultures.[37] The histories of these ancient civilizations make fascinating reading for the historian and archaeologist, but they do not hold the same interest, nor provide the answers to life's problems, for anyone else.

Events have proved both Mao Tse-tung and Levenson wrong. A rise in interest in Confucian studies throughout East Asia makes nonsense of Mao Tse-tung's assertion that Confucianism had died with the 1949 revolution. Admittedly, China is lagging behind a Confucian revival that has gained prominence since the Second World War in Taiwan, Hong Kong, Japan and Korea, but advances are taking place in China also, a point noted by Berthrong, writing in 2000:

> In Hong Kong, New Asia College, founded by famous new Confucian scholars after the communist revolution of 1949, has become an integral part of the Chinese University of Hong Kong. Scholarly bookstores that would not have had a single positive book about Confucianism twenty years ago are now stocked with reprints and new editions of the

Confucian classics. Beijing University, the premier university in China, has just published its own new, multivolume critical edition of the thirteen classics. Along with classical studies, new editions of great Neo-Confucians such as Zhu Xi and Wang Yangming have also appeared.[38]

New challenges lie ahead, not least in the ecological crisis of the late twentieth century.[39] Perhaps we should allow Xinzhong Yao the final word on the place of Neo-Confucianism in China today, for his is a well-balanced, indeed, eminently sensible appraisal of the situation. His position is that Neo-Confucianism is not an ossified tradition as seen by Levenson, no more than a wholesale revival of the tradition. For Yao, New Confucianism is "essentially a moderation of the disagreement between Confucian traditionalism and moralism on the one side, and western democracy, capitalism and individualism on the other".[40]

禅宗

8 Ch'an Buddhism

Some time ago, a conference was being held on Japanese religions. The list of speakers included one scholar who had been invited to speak on Zen Buddhism. After he had been introduced, but before he began to speak, a conference member stood up and said: "If you will pardon my saying, this topic has no place at a conference on Japanese religions: Zen Buddhism is Chinese!" The member had a point, because the legacy of China to Ch'an (Jap. Zen) Buddhism is immense. It was here that Ch'an took seed, blossomed and maintained a maturity that it enjoys today. It was here that Ch'an developed the ability to retain its essence while ever adapting to new cultures worldwide.

As surely as Confucianism was not forever confined to its Chinese homeland, so Ch'an Buddhism spread its wings to Japan, where it found a new home, and a new name; no longer was it to be called Ch'an, but Zen. So familiar did the new name become to outsiders' ears that even today most people associate Zen Buddhism with Japan. Most westerners feel they have at least some familiarity with the way of Zen, where popular images of Japanese Zen gardens, Zen masters, martial arts, monks, meditation, even Japanese Tea Ceremonies, spring readily to mind. Indeed, many westerners would be quite surprised to learn that Zen Buddhism has any associations whatever with China. Even eminent scholars, writing on Ch'an Buddhism in China today, frequently prefer to use the term "Zen Buddhism", a phrase that chimes to western ears. Moreover, in sixth-century China, the Japanese word "Zen" was appropriated into common use and given a new richness of meaning.[1] But let us now examine Ch'an's roots.

Bodhidharma

According to the testimony of Tao-yuan/Daoyuan, in the standard Ch'an version *The Record of the Transmission of the Lamp*, one fine day some time in the year 520 CE, a certain Bodhidharma left the aforementioned Indian mother soil, and travelled East.[2] Of Judaeo-Christian traditions, it has been well said that if there had been no historical figure called Moses, it would have been necessary to invent him: the same may be said of Bodhidharma, for with no Bodhidharma there can be no understanding of the history of Ch'an and Zen. However, if the historicity of Bodhidharma is called to question, so too is the lineage which is reputed to have directly transmitted the Buddha-mind.

The Indian monk, Bodhidharma, is credited with personally introducing to China the form of Buddhism known as Ch'an. Bodhidharma is acclaimed by the faithful as being the first patriarch of Ch'an in China, and the twenty-eighth Indian patriarch in direct succession to the Buddha Sakyamuni, Siddhartha Gautama. However, the list of twenty-eight patriarchs who purportedly followed Sakyamuni, as if in some form of "apostolic succession", has no historical warrant: indeed, the entire Bodhidharma tradition is historically questionable. It is recognized today that, in their anxiety to prove a direct transmission of experience from Sakyamuni himself outside the *sutras*, later generations from the Golden Age of Chinese Ch'an, during the T'ang/Tang and Sung/Song periods, fabricated certain sensational events and retrojected them into the life and times of Bodhidharma. The same generation may also have credited Bodhidharma with these famous words:

A special transmission outside the scriptures;
No dependence upon words and letters;
Direct pointing to the mind;
Seeing into one's nature and realizing Buddhahood.[3]

For faithful Ch'an Buddhists, however, these words epitomize the very essence of Ch'an, and the fact that tradition attributes them to Bodhidharma melds the quintessence of Ch'an with the personage of the Indian monk. Indeed, Heinrich Dumoulin believes that the "special transmission" of which Bodhidharma purportedly spoke encapsulates the heart of Zen Buddhist aspiration: "This is the treasured heritage of Buddhism, the goal of the Buddha's quest: the insight born of enlightenment that he wished to share with all peoples. It is the fundamental conviction of those following the way of Zen that within Buddhism this special transmission has been especially entrusted to the Zen school."[4]

Indeed, for Ch'an Buddhism, the Ch'an patriarchate itself began with the first spiritual transmission. Tradition places Sakyamuni before a typical assembly of earthly and celestial beings, each waiting in silence, and in expectation also, for the Buddha's words of wisdom. But the World-Honoured One respected and retained the silence, instead holding aloft a golden flower without comment. With the dawn of a smile on the face of Mahakasyapa, who alone understood the Buddha's action, came the dawn of the wordless transmission that continued from generation to generation until it was brought to sixth-century China by Bodhidharma:

> At that the Buddha proclaimed, "I have the Jewel of the Dharma-Eye and now hand it to Mahakasyapa". This transmission is said to have continued unbroken from "heart to heart", to this day. What did the Buddha show? What was transmitted? What is the Jewel? The Buddha raising the flower? Mahakasyapa's smile? Endless speculations will not reveal it – it is to be discovered each for him or herself, in the course of Zen training.[5]

Perhaps Mahakasyapa was still smiling when he handed down the *Dharma* to the Buddha's devoted disciple, Ananda, who consequently became the second in line of the twenty-eight Indian Ch'an patriarchs; these included such notables as Nagarjuna and Aryadeva, and ended with Bodhidharma.

All schools of Buddhism are proud of their associations with Sakyamuni, and Ch'an is no exception. Indeed, the evident anxiety of Ch'an to trace the transmission of the *Dharma* directly back to Siddhartha, and the fact that Ch'an is so Chinese in style, are among the reasons why the historicity of the lineage has been called to question. This has long tempted certain scholars to focus their Zen studies not on the teachings of Indian *sutras* but on Chinese masters. As Ruth Fuller Sasaki attests: "Today we know quite clearly that Chinese Ch'an did not originate with an individual Indian teacher and that many of its roots lay deep in native China's thought."[6] This is an extremely interesting and important point. Although no scholar, to our knowledge, has questioned the historicity of Bodhidharma, his life has no attestable historical certainties. We know neither the date or place of his demise nor, for that matter, where he first set foot in China. Our earlier sources affirm that Bodhidharma preached the *Dharma* on Chinese soil but they do not tell us what he preached, nor the details of his meditation techniques. They tell us that his views were not received well, but we have no idea why.[7]

There are three credible historical texts, written by Yang Hsüan-chih/Yang Xuanzhi, Tao-hsüan/Daoxuan and T'an-lin/Tanlin, which bear reliable testimony to the historicity of Bodhidharma, but none of which provides a biography of that worthy, of whom, frankly, we know little. All three texts affirm that Bodhidharma was, indeed, among those who travelled across China preaching the *Dharma*, advocating meditation, and visiting temples. In a typically abrupt and direct exchange with Emperor Wu (502–550), however, Bodhidharma is depicted condemning the worth of building temples and reciting *sutras*. The meeting (which is not attested in *all* sources), presumably did little to endear him to the founder of the Liang dynasty, a practising Buddhist who was earnestly enquiring of Bodhidharma what merit his actions had accrued. Nor did Bodhidharma's later rejections of invitations to visit the northern court of Emperor Hsiao-ming/Xiaoming win him acclaim. After crossing the Yangtze river, but before handing down the mind-seal to his successor, Hui-k'o/Huike, who became the second patriarch of Chinese Zen, Bodhidharma is alleged to have remained seated for nine years in meditation facing a wall, until his legs wasted away after ceasing to function.

Another legend tells of the wrath of this wild-eyed, ferocious-looking, bearded figure, which manifested itself in his cutting off his eyelids, because he had fallen asleep in meditation. They fluttered to the ground only to arise as the first tea plant. Legend also has it that on no less than six occasions, Bodhidharma thwarted attempts on his life by miraculous means, though our sources do not attest why anyone should wish to take his life. It is generally supposed that the patriarch met his demise in 532 at a ripe old age, though most of his life, his teaching, and his method of meditation remain, like the figure, shrouded in mystery. A later account tells of an official named Sung Yun, who, returning to China from abroad, met Bodhidharma in Central Asia on the very day of Bodhidharma's death. In his hand the patriarch held one of his sandals; the other was found when they opened his grave.[8]

Hui-k'o/Huike

Equally arresting, even with the horrors of so-called twenty-first century civilization forever in our minds, is the account of how Hui-k'o/Huike (formerly Shen-kuang) became Bodhidharma's successor. Repeated entreaties by Hui-k'o/Huike to Bodhidharma, waiting outside the monastery of Shao-lin-ssu/Shaolinsi in the freezing snow, were at first ignored and then acknowledged with the assertion that still more was expected of him. Suiting the action to the word, Hui-k'o/Huike produced a sharp knife, severed his left arm at the elbow, and presented it to Bodhidharma. Convinced at last of his sincerity, Bodhidharma now enquired of Hui-k'o/Huike what it was that he wanted: "'My mind has no peace as yet! I beg you, master, please pacify my mind!' 'Bring your mind here and I will pacify it for you,' replied Bodhidharma. 'I have searched for my mind, and I cannot take hold of it,' said the Second Patriarch. 'Now your mind is pacified,' said Bodhidharma."[9]

The instant realization that now dawned on Hui-k'o/Huike is known in Chinese as *wu* (Jap. *satori*); the Japanese form is more familiar to western readers. Beyond intellect and conceptual thought, this indescribable state, in which one awakens to the Buddha-nature within, is one where all dualities cease, and no subject – object differentiation exists, since the common notion that there is an "I" that has to be appeased and satiated no longer obtains. The method employed here to induce the second patriarch's *satori* is said to be the first recorded instance of what was to become the characteristic *mondo* of Rinzai Zen (Chin. Lin-chi/Linji). The *mondo*, or "question and answer" method of instruction, takes the form of a dialogue between master and pupil, engaged in with such rapidity that the sequence of logical thought patterns is transcended and intuitive knowledge is attained instantly.

Our information is scant on the period immediately following the demise of Bodhidharma in 532, but if, with the transmission of the *Dharma* to Hui-k'o/Huike (487–593), there is the temptation to speak already of a "Ch'an school", then this is a temptation that must be avoided: clearly defined Ch'an schools did not materialize in China until the eighth century (by which time they were known as "Zen schools"). The historian, Tao-hsüan/Daoxuan, our main source for the period, tells that it was a middle-aged and well-educated Hui-k'o/Huike, well-versed in Taoism, Chinese classics, and Buddhist philosophy, who received the Buddha-mind from Bodhidharma in about 527. According to Tao-hsüan/Daoxuan, Hui-k'o/Huike also received the transmission of the *Lankavatara Sutra* (*Descent to the Island of Lanka*), though the historical worth of such a statement is, at best, doubtful. Evidently, Hui-k'o/Huike was the first to recognize the essence of the *sutra*, which focused on intuitive insight and self-enlightenment, though his efforts to disseminate this message were thwarted by the stance of those who supported the Wisdom *sutras*.

Even if it is premature to speak of a Zen school at this early stage, the

Bodhidharma tradition was certainly a part of the growing meditational movement of the time, even though the acclaimed uniqueness of Bodhidharma's method and its subsequent development must remain concealed from us forever. Equally certainly, the *Lankavatara Sutra*, with its emphasis on intuitive insight and self-enlightenment, exerted a considerable influence on the meditational movement in general, and the Zen tradition in particular. Realization of inner enlightenment, made possible by the *Tathagata*-womb which we all have, obviates recognition of any duality, since mental discriminations are transcended. Kenneth Ch'en adds:

> The *Lankavatara* also teaches that words are not necessary for the communication of ideas. In some Buddha lands teachings are transmitted by gazing, moving of facial muscles, raising of eyebrows, frowning, smiling, and twinkling of eyes. Here one sees a definite affinity between the *Lankavatara* and later Ch'an practices. Moreover, the tradition of gradual enlightenment followed by Shen-hsiu and his adherents might also be traced to this sutra.[10]

According to one source, before his demise Hui-k'o/Huike handed on the transmission of the *Lankavatara Sutra* to Seng-ts'an/Sengcan (d. 606). Although the *Diamond Sutra* took pride of place over the *Lankavatara* in the Southern Ch'an tradition, the Northern tradition favoured the *Lankavatara*; such was its importance that we even read of the "Lankavatara School" in early histories of the Ch'an tradition in China. Both the Northern and Southern schools emerged on the stage of China's history on January 15, 732 or thereabouts,[11] at the "Great Dharma Assembly" held in Honan province.

The genealogy in currency in early eighth-century China concludes the patriarchate with Tao-hsin/Daoxin (580–651), Hung-jen/Hongren (602–675), and the sixth patriarch Hui-neng/Huineng (638–713). However, the historical reliability of the chronicles of the Northern and Southern schools of Ch'an Buddhism on which we have to depend for this information is at best questionable. All agree on the names of the first five patriarchs, though neither their order nor (master–pupil) relationship can be substantiated with any degree of certainty. In the arresting words of Fung Yu-lan: "Such is the popular account of the early history of the Ch'an school. In actual fact, however, its development in India may safely be regarded as entirely imaginary, and even Bodhidharma, its alleged transmitter to China, looms uncertainly through the mists of tradition as a half legendary person."[12] Like countless other religious figures of history, Bodhidharma has had his story

Ch'an Buddhism

embellished with rich and fanciful elaboration, his wondrous works exaggerated at times out of all proportion, and transformed to the level of the sensational. Nevertheless, the formation of these accounts, even as legends, served the dual purpose of emphasizing the validity of the wordless transmission of the Buddha-mind from generation to generation, as well as showing how a new method of meditation introduced by Bodhidharma could continue and perpetuate this transmission.

Hui-neng/Huineng

What is certain, however, is that the attested dissent between the Northern and Southern schools over the authenticity of the sixth patriarch is a historical fact.[13] In 734 a Southern monk, Shen-hui/Shenhui (670–762), suddenly challenged the position of Shen-hsiu/Shenxiu, claiming that the fifth patriarch, Hung-jen/Hongren, had handed on the patriarchal robe not to Shen-hsiu/Shenxiu, but Hui-neng/Huineng (638–713). Kenneth Ch'en records that: "He also attacked the doctrine of gradual enlightenment held by Shen-hsiu and put forward his own position in favor of complete instantaneous enlightenment, contending that pure wisdom is indivisible and undifferentiated, to be realized completely and instantly or not at all."[14] While it is true that Zen masters teach such sudden enlightenment, Shen-hui's conviction would find little support today among Zen monks in Korea. Robert E. Buswell's study of monks in that country advises that they "routinely admit that they expect it will take upwards of twenty years of full-time practice to make substantive progress in their practice".[15] Sectarian controversy between the Southern and Northern Ch'an schools continued, with the Southern school, represented by the vociferous Shen-hui, becoming gradually the more powerful. Things came to a head when the Northern school charged Shen-hui with disturbing the peace, a charge that led to the banishment from the region of this now eighty year-old man. Public opinion was outraged at this heartless act: alienation of public support from the Northern school soon followed, and the Northern school fell from favour.

Nevertheless, it has been suggested that the aggressive behaviour of Shen-hui may account partly (but not entirely) for the fact that it was Hui-neng who came to be regarded as the symbol of the ideal that the Ch'an movement so earnestly sought. Although the final expression of Ch'an is found manifest in the *Sutra of the Sixth Patriarch*, the so-called *Platform Sutra* preached by the Sixth Patriarch, Hui-neng, we will do well to remember that the new movement that gained visibility within Ch'an in eighth-century China was not the vision of a single creative personality, but the culmination of decades of complex evolution.

The standard Ch'an history of the eleventh century, *The Record of the Transmission of the Lamp*, has Hui-neng gaining the approval of the fifth patriarch over Shen-hsiu/Shenxiu by a clever rewording of a stanza submitted by Shen-hsiu to the patriarch in his quest for a spiritual successor. Hui-neng had already made an initial impression by asserting that everyone (not just Northerners) possessed the Buddha-nature, an affirmation that was rewarded by his being appointed to the position of rice pounder.[16] The fifth patriarch, Hung-jen/Hongren, was swift to recognize the genius of Hui-neng, but slow to announce his decision to monks, whom he feared might become hostile to his selection. Instead, according to the standard Ch'an history, the patriarchal robe, the symbol of the transmission, was handed down in the secrecy of Hung-jen/Hongren's room. Historians have been quick to point out that *The Record of the Transmission of the Lamp* was compiled some four centuries (and many legends) after these events purportedly took place – events that are unmentioned in the eighth-century work of Hsüan-tse/Xuanze.

An interesting anecdote marks the beginning of Hui-neng's mission as a Ch'an master. Evidently, he came across two monks in dispute over a pennant flapping in the breeze. The one argued that the only thing making the pennant flap was the wind, since the pennant was an inanimate object. The other contended that since it was only the wind that was moving, there could be no flapping pennant. Hui-neng intervened by asserting that there was indeed no flapping pennant, but neither was there a flapping wind; the only flapping was in their minds! Heinrich Dumoulin summarizes the point well when he writes:

> Until the third and fourth generation Hui-neng and his disciples represent the apogee of Chinese Zen. These enlightened masters burn Buddha images and sutras, laugh in the face of inquirers or suddenly shout at them, and indulge in a thousand absurdities. Though they may behave like fools and possess nothing, yet they feel themselves true kings in their free mastery of enlightenment. They know no fear, since they desire nothing and have nothing to lose.[17]

Dumoulin's comments here are reminiscent of the Taoist immortals whom we met in chapter 6, and are an indicator of the blurring of boundaries between the enlightened Buddhist master and the Taoist sage/immortal.

Ch'an Buddhism

The Zen movement after Hui-neng

In Zen Buddhism today, the awakening of a Zen master is recognized and acknowledged or "sealed" by a process called "receiving the *Dharma* seal". This involves the master being given a transmission booklet by his teacher that traces the patriarchal lines back to Sakyamuni through the twenty-six Indian and six Chinese Patriarchs, and the various Zen lines in China, Korea or Japan. The demise of Hui-neng saw various transmission lines branching out, many of which are still extant.

Hui-neng's enlightenment coincided with the beginnings of the T'ang/Tang dynasty, and a now reunited China witnessed the dawn of the so-called Golden Age of Zen. The turn of the eighth century saw Chinese Buddhism begin to assume greater definition. Buddhism had long been seen as a religion in its own right, and had left Taoism far behind in popularity, a point noted by Isabelle Robinet: "Even at the time of its greatest development and imperial protection, Taoism remained far behind Buddhism in its influence; in Chang'an, the Tang capital, there were sixteen Taoist establishments in 722 as opposed to 91 Buddhist ones."[18]

Disciples of Hui-neng and his attendant teachings on sudden enlightenment were ubiquitous throughout China. These followers of the Sixth Patriarch held the conviction that the transmission of the Buddha-mind could be traced back to Sakyamuni through Bodhidharma; the movement later became known as the "Zen of the Patriarchs" (Chin. *tsu-shih ch'an/zushichan*; Jap. *soshizen*). As Heinrich Dumoulin illumines:

> The dominant figures in the Zen movement after Hui-neng are Ma-tsu, Pai-chang, Huang-po Hsi-yün (d. 850), and Lin-chi I-hsüan (d. 866). Standing in a direct master–disciple relationship to each other, these four individuals help us focus the core of the "Zen of the Patriarchs": the transmission of the Buddha mind outside the scriptures and sudden enlightenment through seeing into one's own nature and becoming a Buddha.[19]

It is customary for scholars to consider the above four generations of Zen masters as one, for it was in this period of Ch'an history that the Buddhism that once took seed in China reached its apogee.

The collected sayings of these four masters were collated in a volume entitled *The Collection of Four Houses* (Chin. *Ssu-chia yu lu/Sijiayoulu*; Jap. *Shike goroku*), which not only testified to the unity of the generation line, but to the advent of a "new Buddhism" in China. By the middle of the eighth century, these stories, discourses and sayings attest to the transformation of the legacy of India into what was unmistakably Chinese religion. The Indian Wisdom *sutras* – riven with paradox and dialectic – remained, but the teachings now speak of a reality in practical and tangible terms, using popular idioms familiar and meaningful to the masses, rather than those that could be realized only through abstract thought processes. Fletcher and Scott note the eclectic spin-off from such a trend: "What made Zen masters distinct was their use of common Chinese expression to bring Buddhism alive, through popular idioms that people could understand. Chinese poetry and folklore was used to illustrate Buddhist views. Taoism, being popular at the time, was often blended into expression, and conversely Taoism borrowed freely from Buddhist expression."[20] With the provinces of Kiangsi and Hunan lying "westward from the river" and "southward from the lake" at the centre of classical Ch'an, the powerful Rinzai (Chin. Lin-chi/Linji) sect emerged. Tung-shan/Dongshan arose as co-founder of the Ts'oa-tung/Caodong (Jap. Soto) line, while Huai-jang/Huairang was at the beginnings of the Rinzai line, though somewhat overshadowed by his disciple and successor, Ma-tsu/Mazu, who boasted 120 enlightened successors. Ma-tsu/Mazu (709–788) was one of the most influential Zen masters of the T'ang/Tang period.

Sectarian divisions in Zen did not become consolidated until a thousand years later in Japan (Meiji period, 1868–1912), and Tung-shan/Dongshan's attention to detail in the five ranks (positions in practice) consequently formed an integral part of *koan* practice – which will be explored below – in both the Soto and Rinzai schools. It was common at that time for Chinese students to move between the teachings of masters of a variety of lines, or even become disciples of masters of two different lineages. An outstanding master of the time, Shih-t'ou/Shitou (700–790) – once a student of the Sixth Patriarch, Hui-neng – and his contemporary, Ma-tsu/Mazu, would often exchange students. Shih-tou/Shitou's famous verse, *The Identity of Relative and Absolute*, remains a standard chant in Zen monasteries worldwide to this day.

If the period from the death of Hui-neng (713) until the persecutions of Emperor Wu-tsung/Wuzong in 845 was the high-water mark of Chinese Ch'an, then Ma-tsu/Mazu was the dominant figure during the third generation after Hui-neng, as the sources attest: "His appearance was remarkable. He strode along like a bull and glared about him like a tiger. If he stretched out his tongue, it reached up over his nose; on the soles of his feet were imprinted two circular marks."[21] Unsurprisingly, given this description, violence was not outside Ma-tsu/Mazu's remit; in the pursuit of enlightenment, he once forcibly twisted the nose of a distraught disciple to attain this end. Shouting *ho* (Jap. *katsu*) was another innovation he employed – a means to enlightenment later appropriated and promoted by the Lin-chi/Linji (Jap. Rinzai) sect. Indeed, the methodology became known as "stick and shout". Ma-tsu/Mazu is the last Chinese Ch'an master to be given the title "Patriarch". At the heart of Ma-tsu/Mazu's message lay the unshakeable belief that, since the mind is essentially pure, sitting in meditation in order to purify that which is already pure is folly. This is a lesson that he, himself, had been taught by his master, a teaching recorded in our sources:

> Ma-tsu was then residing in the monastery continuously absorbed in meditation. His master, aware of his outstanding ability for the Dharma, asked him, "For what purpose are you sitting in meditation?" Ma-tsu answered, "I wish to become a Buddha." Thereupon the master picked up a tile and started rubbing it on a stone. Ma-tsu asked, "What are you doing, Master?" "I am polishing this tile to make it a mirror," Huai-jang replied. "How can you make a mirror by rubbing a tile?" exclaimed Ma-tsu. "How can one become a Buddha by sitting in meditation?" countered the master.[22]

The so-called lamp-anthologies – huge collections of the teachings of hundreds of Zen masters – are replete with such anecdotes, some intriguing, some appearing to be diametrically opposed to the Buddhist Precepts. The following account (not to be taken literally) of Nansen Osho (748–834), one of Tung-shan/Dongshan's masters and a disciple of Ma-tsu/Mazu, stands in direct contrast to the climax of the *Vimalakirti Sutra*, where Manjusri, the *bodhisattva* of compassion, asks Vimalakirti what it means to enter the *Dharma* of nonduality, and unreservedly applauds his "thunderous silence":

> Nansen Osho saw monks of the Eastern and Western halls quarreling over a cat. He held up the cat and said, "If you can give an answer, you will save the cat. If not, I will kill it." No one could answer, and Nansen cut the cat in two. That evening Joshu returned, and Nansen told him of the incident. Joshu took off his sandal, placed it on his head, and walked out. "If you had been there, you would have saved the cat," Nansen remarked.[23]

The dictum from the *Rinzairoku* is equally well known, and equally paradoxical: "When you meet the Buddha, you kill him; when you meet the patriarchs, you kill them." Here, it must be clearly understood that the flowering of classical Chinese Zen witnessed not a development in devotion to Sakyamuni as the founding father of Buddhism, but a metaphysical transcending of all dualities. While knowledge is born of tuition, wisdom is the child of a single parent, intuition; in other words, your understanding must be your own, not something bestowed by the influence of someone else. This is the teaching here: anything that stands in the path of such transcendence must be summarily dealt with, including any image of the Buddha.

A case from the *Mumonkan* makes the point. In hostile mood, a typical Zen master from the T'ang/Tang period, one Te-shan/Deshan (otherwise known as Tokusan, 780–865), set out to vilify the notion that Buddhahood could be realized simply by seeing into one's own nature, thus rendering any study of the *sutras* redundant. Requesting lunch from an old woman on the way in order that he might "refresh the mind", Te-shan/Deshan was asked what reading materials he had in his pack. On being told that Te-shan/Deshan carried commentaries on the *Diamond Sutra*, the old woman replied, "I hear it is said in that sutra, 'The past mind cannot be held, the present mind cannot be held, the future mind cannot be held.' Now I would like to ask you, what mind are you going to have refreshed?" A stunned and dumbfounded Te-shan/Deshan later set fire to his commentaries![24]

The blows delivered by Te-shan/Deshan's use of the staff were part of his utilization of *upaya kausalya*, yet another example of the same "skill in means" employed by Sakyamuni, as a vehicle to enlightenment. "If you can speak, thirty blows! If you cannot speak, thirty blows!" he would shout at his disciples of the Lin-chi/Linji (Jap. Rinzai) sect. Another Zen master, Chu-chih/Zhuzhi, severed the finger of a disciple, who had the gall to emulate his master's custom of simply raising one finger in leading his disciples to enlightenment. As Chu-chih/Zhuzhi once again raised his finger before an amputee in agony, the disciple at once became enlightened.

Another of Ma-tsu/Mazu's disciples, Pai-chang/Baizhang (749–814), is credited with promoting Ma-tsu's vigorous training, and formulating and applying monastic rules to his *sangha*. We have repeatedly said that it is culture that shapes a religion – which presumably is why one doesn't find too many naked ascetics in the polar regions.[25] Similarly, while "a robe, and a bowl on a stone under a tree" sufficed the Indian mendicant, the dawn of Chinese Buddhism had seen Tao-hsin/Daoxin establishing a code of conduct for his five hundred disciples that necessarily demanded a day's work for a day's food; thus we subsequently find Hui-neng splicing wood and treading the rice mill for some eight months in order to gain sustenance.

Others followed suit, and though begging was not supplanted, additional activities included rice-planting, farming, and bamboo-cutting. It was the monastic rules of Early Indian (Hinayana) Buddhism that informed Chinese Buddhism (including Ch'an), rather than those of the less formalized Mahayana, but Pai-chang/Baizhang borrowed from both, thereby establishing a new eclectic order. This new form of monasticism was thus independent of existing Buddhist orders and peculiar to Ch'an, its simplicity winning the approval even of Confucians. Pai-chang/Baizhang certainly practised what he preached (alternating meditation and worship with manual labour), and in his advanced years he refused to eat when well-meaning disciples, who considered him too old to work, confiscated his tools. He produced two outstanding Zen masters in Kei-shan Ling-yu/Geishan Lingyou (Jap. Isan Reiyu, 771–853) and Huang-po Hsi-yün/Huangbo Xiyun (Jap. Obaku Kiun, d. 850): both became founders of Zen lines, albeit unwittingly.

Many western writers have taken the paradoxical contradictions that permeate the legion of aphorisms delivered by revered Ch'an and Zen masters at face value. This is because they have mistaken the lamp anthologies for historical documents that accurately reflect the circumstances of Zen monasticism. Accordingly, an image was presented to the West of a religious tradition that reviles all Buddhist scriptures, policed by a clergy that operates an intimidation policy. Its devotees are subjected to mental anguish and physical abuse, supposedly in the cause of enlightenment, while anything that could possibly be considered to be of worth, *including Zen itself*, is steadfastly put to the torch. Robert Buswell puts the record straight:

> But such texts were never intended to serve as guides to religious practice or as records of daily practice; they were instead mythology and hagiography, which offered the student an idealized paradigm of the Zen spiritual experience. Many scholars of Zen have . . . presumed that they provide an accurate account of how Zen monks of the premodern era pursued their religious vocations. They do not.[26]

It should be remembered that Zen is the language of poetry, and it should be read in this light: "What Indian Mahayana sutras state in abstract terms Zen does in concrete terms. Therefore, concrete individual images abound in Zen."[27]

The Five Houses

Thomas Cleary[28] reminds us that there is no "Zen Canon", carved in stone, from a body of holy writ whose teachings are to be memorized and recited piously. To look for the standard source book of genuine classical Zen is to look for something that doesn't exist, nor could it. Most Zen masters had no interest in history; they were more concerned with the needs of others than the deeds of themselves, and taught accordingly. Zen masters were never idolized as in other religions. Consequently, Buddhist teachings came to be regarded as collections of useful ideas, devices with no necessary literal truth. In this light, strictly speaking, there can be no "History of Zen". Nevertheless, ninth and tenth century China saw the rise of several groups of outstanding Zen masters whose names became associated with the so-called *Five Houses of Zen*, and it is in this direction that we must turn for the best examples of classical Zen Buddhism.

The year 845 saw China witness a persecution of Buddhism of unprecedented ferocity; by the end of the T'ang/Tang period, Zen alone flourished. The other outstanding figure in the third generation after Hui-neng was Shih-t'ou/Shitou, and from these two great disciples developed what later became known in South Chinese Ch'an as "The Five Houses". Not to be mistaken for different sects or schools within the Zen tradition (though they later became identified as such), these so-called Houses were really lines of family traditions or styles originated by Ma-tsu/Mazu and Shih-t'ou/Shitou and followed and developed by devoted pupils. To the line of Ma-tsu/Mazu belong the Houses of Kuei-yang/Guiyang and Lin-chi/Linji (Jap. Rinzai), whilst the Houses of Ts'ao-tung/Caodong (Jap. Soto), Yun-men/Yunmen and Fa-yen/Fayan (Jap. Hogen) are of the line Shih-t'ou/Shitou.

Among these Houses are to be found what became the two major streams of Zen Buddhism today, Ts'ao-tung/Caodong and Lin-chi/Linji. The fact that the earliest of the Five Houses, Kuei-yang/Guiyang, was short-lived, whilst the last to develop, Fa-yen/Fayan, was probably the least significant, does not detract from the fact that their contrasting styles had much to offer. It has been well said that mysticism, like all other human experience, is influenced by human life conditions; it is not conceived in a vacuum. In this light, far from posing a threat to the cohesion and stability of the Ch'an movement after Hui-neng, the arising of the Five Houses, with their attendant differences in practice, provided the very foundation necessary for the development of Ch'an Buddhism in China. In order of historical emergence, the Five Houses are Kuei-yang/Guiyang, Lin-chi/Linji, Ts'ao-tung/Caodong, Yun-men/Yunmen and Fa-yen/Fayan. It is prudent to look now at some of the distinguishing features of the Five Houses.

Kuei-yang/Guiyang (Jap. Igyo) and the circular figures

Early murmurings in the second half of the T'ang/Tang period featured talk of family traditions, providing the seedbed for the Five Houses. Not without its critics, this earliest of the Five Houses made use of ninety-seven circular figures to symbolize enlightened consciousness and, hence, reality. Opponents were quick to point out that, far from symbolizing the true nature of reality, such an *upaya kausalya* or skill-in-means device actually confused the issue since "the absolute emptiness and formlessness of all things" can hardly be represented by a number of different forms. Perhaps this is why the sect was short-lived.

Nevertheless, outstanding personalities in the Kuei-yang/Guiyang tradition, such as Yang-shan/Yangshan, became enlightened precisely by such a method, which they in turn introduced to their disciples. This rough and hearty sect saw Yang-shan amputate two of his fingers in order to convince his parents that he was serious about entering the monastery of Ta-wei/Dawei.

Lin-chi/Linji (Jap. Rinzai) and shouting and beating

By the time of the Sung/Song dynasty in China, the House of Lin-chi/Linji had become the most important of the Five Houses. Among the writings of the Zen schools, *The Collected Sayings of Lin-chi*, which records the founder's life and work, is held in high regard. It is of Lin-chi/Linji about whom we have the most reliable historical evidence. Lin-chi/Linji, a highly gifted and intellectual master, achieved enlightenment only after being subjected by his master to a series of shoutings and beatings, and this, in turn, became his code of practice for leading his pupils to ultimate Reality.

Koan practice

The *koan* (Chin. *kung-an*) is a Chinese invention that literally means "public notice or notification", a meaning that has long been all but ignored. Unique to Zen Buddhism, *koans* are not nonsense. These short, apparently paradoxical riddles, or slightly longer stories posed by the master, sometimes offer the pupil a choice between two possible answers, neither of which is acceptable at face value. As surely as the meaning and purpose of life cannot be resolved by use of the intellect, neither is it possible to solve the meaning of the *koan* by the same means. Since enlightenment cannot be realized by conceptualized thought processes, the *koan* is employed not to develop powers of conceptualization, but to disrupt the sequence of logical thought and so bring about enlightenment by inducing an altered state of consciousness. In such a state, the meanings of all *koans* will effortlessly be revealed. Scholars have long sought parallels amongst other religions, and the combination of a unique master–pupil relationship, essential for *koan* practice, and accompanying legendary anecdotes is also to be found in, among others, Hassidic Judaism. It has been argued that the Taoist text the *Chuang-tzu/Zhuangzi* is a textual *koan* in the literature of Zen. However, as Robert Allinson has shown, "such an argument is of necessity historically backwards, since Zen (or Ch'an) arises much later in history ... it would not be surprising to find that certain characteristics of the child were to be found in the generic make-up of the parent".[29] Ruth Fuller Sasaki, an acknowledged authority on the *koan*, has claimed:

> The koan is not a conundrum to be solved by a nimble wit. It is not a verbal psychiatric device for shocking the disintegrated ego of a student into some kind of stability. Nor, in my opinion, is it ever a paradoxical statement except to those who view it from outside. When the koan is resolved it is realized to be a simple and clear statement made from the state of consciousness which it has helped to awaken.[30]

In this light, *koans*, of which there are about 1700, with some 700 in frequent use, are not meant to have any meaning for the unenlightened mind that clings to the names and terms in conditioned human language and perception. Thinking about a *koan* pushes the mind beyond all logic and intellectualism, producing a tension that brings one to the limits of thought.

It is claimed that, long ago, awakening was far simpler to realize than today. Ch'an masters compared the immediacy of the pupils' responses in early days to those of a horse that reacts instantly to the mere sight of a whip. The advance of so-called civilization, however, saw a decline in immediate awakening, and a need for the introduction of the *koan*. Such devices included gestures, blows and shouts, as well as words and roars of laughter. The Buddha's awakening of Mahakasyapa by raising a flower, and Bodhidharma's quieting the first Chinese patriarch's mind, are examples of a variety of *koan* devices. Another well-known *koan* asks, "What is the sound of one hand clapping?" Also: "If you meet someone along the road who has realized the truth, you may not walk past the person in silence, nor speaking. So how should you meet this person?" *Koans* in the form of short stories include the tale of the goose that grew increasingly large inside a bottle until it was too large to leave. The *koan* asks how the owner removed the goose from the bottle without harming either.

All *koans* arose from the teachings of Chinese Ch'an and Japanese Zen masters to their pupils, and the records of interchanges between them were gathered and formulated. Frequently, they were based on actual events within the masters' experiences. There is no one "answer" to the *koans*: individual spontaneity is expected and non-verbal responses are encouraged. Normally associated with the House of Rinzai (Lin-chi/Linji), the *koan* is not peculiar to this school; Dogen was introduced to the *koan* during his stay in China, and though less popular in Soto Zen (Chin. Ts'ao-tung/Caodong), the use of *koans* is not unknown here. Conversely, some eminent Rinzai (Chin. Lin-chi/Linji) masters have ignored the use of *koans* in their teachings, though the efforts of Hakuin Ekaku (1685–1768), who introduced a systematized structure to the classification of *koans*, offered this method a rejuvenation that has been maintained to the present.

Dokusan and *sanzen*

Traditionally found in all Zen schools, *dokusan* today functions mostly in the Rinzai Zen (Lin-chi/Linji) school. This is the formal, private meeting between master and pupil. Here, the pupil is given the chance to express any concerns s/he may have over meditation techniques. The master then has the opportunity to assess the progress of the pupil in regard to meditation in general, and *koan* practice in particular. It is in such personal encounter that the master will determine whether the pupil is ready to progress to the next *koan*. In former times, the term for the formal interview with the master specifically on *koan* practice was *sanzen*, whilst *dokusan* was reserved for discussion about other forms of practice. Today, however, both technical terms are virtually synony-mous.[31]

Kyosaku

Again peculiar to (but not to all forms of) Rinzai Zen (Lin-chi/Linji), the *kyosaku* or "encouragement stick" is not a punitive device for inflicting pain and humiliation before one's colleagues. Sometimes found up to a metre long, its purpose is to return the mind wandering in *zazen* ("sitting meditation", a term discussed below) to its focus. What is more well known in the West as a "butterfly mind", is referred to in Zen as a "monkey mind" – an apt description for the mind that jumps around from one place to another, much like the antics of our forest cousins. Accordingly, a monitor will patrol the *zendo* (meditation hall), periodically giving a sharp thwack to any meditator who appears to be day-dreaming – or, worse, snoozing. Not all masters make free use of the *kyosaku*, and some have openly criticized it.

Rinzai Zen (Lin-chi/Linji) not only eschews all the established cere-monies and rituals of religion but also conventional intellectualism. However, Rinzai and the school known in western civilization as "Western Ch'an" do not reject understanding the purpose and function of meditation in general and *koan* practice in particular. Zen masters try to break down all the traditional, conventional ways of thinking. It may be done in ways that seem odd to a westerner. A visitor to a Zen monastery, for example, may be kept waiting outside all day and all night, as in the case of Hui-k'o/Huike, whom we met earlier. Such actions are designed to apply a blow to the mind, just as Rinzai Zen (Lin-chi/Linji) teachers may also apply one to the body of a pupil from time to time. This kind of teaching was thought to be thoroughly refreshing. Conventional religions supported the idea that sense is acquired through the laws of thought and the result of reasoning and logic, but since Buddha-nature is beyond this, Zen tries to go beyond sense too, to non-logical sense. In Zen Buddhism, the individual is taken to the limits of thought, but not through dogmas, codes of ethics, or other such formulae. All the objects of the senses and emotions, philosophies and *isms* of any sort are overthrown and cast aside, so that the individual cannot be trapped in set patterns or be a slave to the kind of knowledge which is knowledge *about* – factual knowledge. Thoughts must be pushed, as it were, to the borders of a precipice and then beyond. Conventional thought and adherence to orthodox concepts only serve to prevent the intuitive understanding of the Buddha-nature within.

The master–pupil relationship

The master–pupil relationship is an important one in Zen, but since its abiding teaching is that humankind lacks only awakening, it is the pupil that is often expected to provide answers to the problem. Accordingly, the Zen master is not seen as some didactic teacher whose every word must be obeyed without question. He is necessary because the truth about life cannot adequately be conveyed by the written word, but is not the fount of all knowledge, and simply a spiritual guide that points the way to a truth that can only be realized by the pupil. Thomas Cleary notes that: "Offshoots of Korean and Japanese sects, not understanding the structure of the *koans*, have tended to make this aspect of Zen into a cult of secrecy, mystery, and/or simple mystification."[32] If this is so, then it is a misunderstanding that opens the door to further confusion, with the need for a master to unravel these supposed "mysteries" that are to the fore of practitioners' minds. Nor must we become attached to the master by virtue of the esteem in which s/he is held. Indeed, almost thirteen hundred years ago in China, Hui-neng raised the question of whether a teacher *is* necessary for every student.

Although there will always be a master–pupil relationship, in the strictest sense of the term the fulfilment of such a spiritual relationship will foster a realization of the emptiness of *both* parties. The role of the master has been likened to that of the helper who gives his arm in support of the novice swimmer. As soon as the pupil is an able swimmer, it is the master's *duty* to withdraw support, lest it becomes a crutch. No matter how skilled the driving instructor, and how inexperienced the pupil, once the pupil has passed the driving test, the skills of the instructor are superfluous, leaving the pupil free to continue to drive the road of experience. As surely as the raft is no longer required once the far shore is reached, the need for the master is impermanent.

A lay Buddhist, recently locked into a seemingly imponderable problem, reluctantly concluded after much deliberation that the realization of its solution was beyond his competence. He therefore determined to visit his abbot, a drive that took many hours. Although he was expected, the abbot seemed in no great hurry to see his pupil and could be seen occupying himself with apparently unimportant tasks for what seemed an eternity, while the pupil waited in anguish. At long last, he was summoned to the abbot, who listened patiently to the "insurmountable" problem. Having poured out his heart, the pupil waited expectantly for the words of wisdom that would ease his pain. He was prepared for a detailed analysis of the problem and its attendant solution, but as soon as he finished speaking was dumbfounded to find the abbot simply indicating the pupil's bench (a "bench" is what Soto Zen Buddhists call their meditation stool), and the abbot walked away. A thunderstruck pupil was left trying to cope with a flood of emotion, before reconciling himself to the fact that there was nothing he could do but heed the advice given, such as it was. The answer to his "insurmountable" problem came to him instantly!

When the Buddha Sakyamuni became dissatisfied with the instruction he had received from the celebrated forest hermits and teachers, he sought enlightenment without their help. Having, at last, realized this state, he overcame the (final) temptation to keep his own counsel, and resolved to offer other seekers of truth a prescription for their own transformation. It was this resolve that heralded the Buddhist tradition of spiritual guidance. In so far as the Buddha was not so much a teacher as a physician, the term "prescription" is entirely apposite. No responsible doctor would write the same prescription for every patient, and the teaching should always be appropriate to the level of consciousness of the audience; accordingly, contradictory teachings must have arisen.[33]

In some Buddhist traditions – Tantra is a case in point – the master's word carries absolute authority, and if the pupil does not understand what it is that the master advises (or, rather, *why* this advice is being given), it is because the practitioner's level of consciousness is deemed to be lower than that of the master. Absolute trust in the master finds manifestation in total devotion and obedience, for the *lamas* (Tibetan *gurus*) are the embodiment of emptiness. The Venerable Geshe Damcho Yonten, resident *lama* at Lam Rim Tibetan Buddhist Centre at Raglan, Monmouthshire, UK, made a salient point when he said, "Emptiness is not enlightenment, enlightenment is the all-knowing of everything." It is not without significance that the title "Dalai Lama" (the spiritual head of Tibetan Buddhism) means "Ocean" (of knowledge). Utter devotion to the master in Tantric Buddhism symbolizes the close relationship between the self (form) and the *lama* (emptiness). In attempts to overcome the self-imposed fetters of greed, anger and delusion (that comprise the ego), newcomers to Tantric Buddhism, who have admitted an aversion to meat or alcohol, have been instructed to partake of the same on a regular basis. Tantric Buddhists who have disobeyed their master have been asked to leave the order, since the master always knows best. *This is not the way of Zen.*[34]

Reverend Master Jiyu-Kennett distinguishes between absolute faith and perfect faith. Absolute faith, by definition, demands absolute obedience to the master. Perfect faith, on the other hand, invites a refreshing freedom of mind. Here, it is not a question of blind obedience to the master, but one of give and take, *with the master just as willing to learn as the pupil*. It is well to remember this. Some time ago Merv Fowler was speaking with a young student who happened to enquire what I enjoyed doing in my spare time. I explained that I love learning and that it is my sincere wish that I should be in a position to learn something even on the day that I die. "Oh, but you will be!" he assured me. Seeing my puzzled look, he added, "You will learn what's on the other side" ... the young student was eight years old!

> However humble a person may appear to be, if this desire (to save all living beings) has been awakened, he is already the teacher of all mankind: a little girl of seven even may be the teacher of the four classes of Buddhists and the mother of True Compassion to all living things.[35]

Ts'ao-tung (Jap. Soto) and the formula of the five ranks

The Soto Zen school (Chin. Ts'ao-tung/Caodong) is the oldest surviving school of the Zen tradition. Its emphasis is that all beings have the Buddha-nature, and that training and enlightenment are indivisible. The teaching operates within the framework of the Buddhist Precepts, not as an imposition, but for anyone wishing to participate of his or her own free will. With the House of Lin-chi/Linji (Jap. Rinzai), the House of Ts'ao-tung/Caodong remains today one of only two surviving Houses of Chinese Zen. The formula of the five ranks, though originating in this House, did not remain peculiar to it; both Chinese and Japanese Zen appropriated and employed it. This dialectical formula invites enquiry into the relationship between the Absolute and the relative, culminating in the final and fifth rank where there is total unity, often depicted by a black circle.

Generally, Zen accepts the non-duality of all things and thereby their total monistic identity. *Nirvana*, therefore, is *samsara* and all beings possess Buddhahood as the ultimate Reality and are equal to each other. It is a point beautifully illustrated when in Soto Zen initiation of lay people into the sect, the abbot bows to the lay person who is being initiated, symbolizing the inner equality between the two beings. In the lay ordination ceremony (Jap. *jukai*) the ordinand is given a *ketchimyaku*, a scroll depicting the unbroken line from Sakyamuni to the novitiate's own teacher, having his/her own name added. Having Buddhahood within means that one has to awaken to it – instantly in Rinzai Zen, gradually in Soto Zen – but both accept that each person is already a Buddha, as is every animate and inanimate object. Buddhahood means ultimately the interconnectedness of all within the cosmos, and that the cosmos itself is contained in each being and in every grain of dust.

One does not have to be a monk in order to become a Zen Buddhist. Monasteries are for those wishing to dedicate themselves to the spiritual life. The true monastery is the heart, and the monastic life is not mandatory for all Zen Buddhists since, in this light, the monastery is anywhere and everywhere; nor is there any suggestion that the monk – the Japanese term for which is *unsui*, "free as the clouds", so reminiscent of Chinese Taoism – is in some way superior to the lay Buddhist, nor that he or she has a deeper awareness of Buddha-nature. Some simply feel that practice within the monastic tradition is the right way for them while others do not. Both monastic and lay traditions have long and successful histories, and have proved good bedfellows.

The practice of *zazen*, or sitting meditation, is central to all forms of Zen, but in Soto Zen it is the most important factor. Appropriately, in the West the Soto Zen school is called Serene Reflection Meditation, advocating a meditative practice wherein the meditator simply *lets go* of any thoughts that arise without allowing them to develop. It's rather like a young man seeing girls go by and watching them as he would passing clouds. Settling down onto a *zafu* (round cushion), the practitioner places the left palm of the hand upon the right, with both thumbs touching. The practitioner next positions the tip of the tongue behind the top front teeth, inhaling and exhaling sharply, before returning to a normal breathing pattern. Each spring, the Tradition of Serene Reflection Meditation holds a retreat known as the Keeping of the Ten Precepts. Here, those becoming lay Buddhists formally take the Ten Precepts as outlined in Great Master Dogen's text, *Kyojukaimon* (*Giving and Receiving the Teaching of the Precepts*).[36]

Germane to these are the Three Pure Precepts, which are:

Cease from evil. By refraining from that which causes confusion and suffering, the Truth will shine of itself.

Do only good. Doing good arises naturally from ceasing to do evil.

Do good for others. To cease from evil is to devote one's life to the good of all living things.[37]

By practising *zazen*, and being aware of the Three Pure Precepts, the three grenades (defilements) of greed, anger and delusion diminish naturally. It is not a question of willpower or the rote learning of more rules. Doing only good, particularly for others, awakens the heart of compassion in ourselves. At the same time, it is necessary to examine what it is that we do that causes suffering and to cease from this. "Letting go" is fundamental to Zen Buddhism, and it finds echoes in the story of someone raking the gravel of a very simple, scarcely ornamented, Zen garden. It took three months to get it right, but on the day that person got it right, there was no need to do it again, insight had occurred. A Ph.D. student we once knew meticulously researched an area of Buddhism for five painstaking years. On completion of his doctoral dissertation, and when it was due for submission, he slowly walked to the bottom of his garden, gathered together some old newspapers, placed some kindling wood on them and, in the same meticulous manner . . . you don't need us to finish the story.

In Soto Zen, there are no frenetic interchanges with Zen Masters or meditating on *koans*, for it is simply *sitting*, termed *shikantaza*, which is the main practice. The Soto Zen method of meditation is perhaps the most natural of all forms of meditation, for there is no need to use *mantras* or to focus the attention on *mandalas*. The Buddhist simply sits on his or her chair or "bench", or on the floor, with a straight back and facing a blank wall. The eyes remain open but focused down, following the line of the nose to a point on the wall a foot or so above the floor. When thoughts arrive in the mind, they are simply brushed aside and passed away without allowing them to develop. So, as the sounds of the immediate environment filter into the mind, the mind does not react to them. Or, when the events of the day or previous day, or the concerns for the remainder of the day come to mind, the mind softly brushes them aside. The mind, then, is not allowed to think; thoughts are not allowed to develop. In this case, the mind is able to become tranquil and the Buddha-nature, which is beneath the ordinary levels of consciousness and mind processes, is allowed to surface.

Soto Zen is a simple, quiet and natural form of Buddhism, even when short periods of walking meditation or *kinhin* are interspersed with "sitting". Here, concentration is on walking in a slow, calm, yet aware manner – traits that foster a greater insight into how one should lead one's life. Soto Zen accepts that the experience of Buddhahood will gradually be awakened, for Buddhahood is already there in each being waiting to be experienced. None of the sudden and dramatic insight of Rinzai Zen is necessary here.

Yun-men/Yunmen (Jap. Ummon) and the "pass of a single word"

More dramatic was the enlightenment of Yun-men, among the most famous figures of the later T'ang/Tang period. Evicted from the monastery by a forceful master who broke Yun-men's leg in the process, Yun-men became enlightened at that very moment. For his part, Yun-men treated his disciples with the same ferocity, often striking them with his staff and shouting *kuan* at them when they were off-guard. Before he died in 949 Yun-men had gained the reputation of replying to profound spiritual questions with a single, apparently unrelated, word. Many examples are attested in Zen history. One will suffice:

> A monk asked Yun-men: "What is talk that goes beyond Buddhas and patriarchs?"
> Yun-men replied: "Cake!"

This type of innovative response became known in Zen as the "pass of a single word".

Fa-yen/Fayan (Jap. Hogen) and the inner unity of the six marks of being

The last of the Five Houses was equally ephemeral, though far more gentle than the aforementioned two. Well-versed in both Chinese classics and Buddhist literature, its founder, Fa-yen/Fayan (885–958) was a highly educated master, though his critics have questioned whether his erudition may have hampered his ability to teach in the true Zen spirit. His style, replete with sharp repartee and paradox, has been likened to the meeting of two arrow points, whereby the asking of a question is met head on, without explanation, by the repetition over and over again of an unrelated word or phrase. Totally steeped in the philosophy of Hua-yen/Huayan (Jap. Kegon), Fa-yen/Fayan was dedicated to the study of the *Avatamsaka Sutras*, particularly an understanding of the six marks of being: totality and differentiation, sameness-in-difference, becoming and disappearing – leading his disciples to a comprehension of their inner unity. The death of Fa-yen/Fayan saw the demise of the House, and within a generation his *Dharma* successor, T'ien-t'ai Te-shao/Diantai Deshao (891–971), had forsaken the teachings of his master and turned his attention to the science of the T'ien-t'ai/Tiantai (Jap. Tendai) school.

The Sung/Song period

Since the time of the Sung/Song, the path to enlightenment has been depicted in pictorial terms, along with associated interpretations, poems and commentaries. These are found in the parable of the Ox-herding Pictures – ten pictorial representations of the developing relationship between our Buddha-nature (the Ox) and ourselves (the Ox-herd). There are four well-known versions, some of which portray a darkened ox in the first picture (representing an ignorant, deluded mind), which lightens along its journey, as we gradually awaken to our own true (Buddha) nature. It is fitting that an animal so common in ancient China should be used in a parable that could be meaningful to the common man.[38]

The severe persecutions of Emperor Wu-tsung/Wuzong towards the end of the T'ang/Tang period left Buddhism in general in a state of decline. By the middle of the succeeding Sung/Song period (960–1279), but two of the original Five Houses of Ch'an survived, Lin-chi/Linji (Jap. Rinzai) and Ts'ao-tung/Caodong (Jap. Soto). Even the latter's future seemed insecure at that time, and it was to the Ch'an House of Lin-chi/Linji that Buddhism turned for survival. By the middle of the tenth century, Ch'an temples and monasteries of the House of Lin-chi/Linji alone were in profusion throughout Sung/Song China. Although riven with political instability, the Sung/Song period marks the high-water mark of Chinese culture, with Neo-Confucian philosophy, Ch'an art and the Ch'an way to enlightenment among its lasting contributions. Not that Ch'an Buddhism was without its critics, for the Neo-Confucian movement that began in the Sung/Song dynasty rejected it; indeed, Buddhists and Taoists alike were accused of turning their backs on Neo-Confucian ideals of humanity and righteousness.

These criticisms apart, the main threat to Ch'an Buddhism in China was the temptation to fuse (or confuse) Ch'an with the teachings of other schools of Buddhism. This was made all the easier by the fact that an ever-growing Ch'an *sangha* still had neither doctrine nor systematized practice to preserve its uniqueness. To Ch'an's (at least, initial) chagrin, the school found itself being associated with the highly philosophical doctrine of T'ien-t'ai/Tiantai (Jap.Tendai), as well as Amida (Pure Land) piety. Ch'an masters of the T'ang/Tang period had emphasized the superiority of enlightenment over study of the *sutras* and, under the fear of syncretism, it was not unknown in the Sung/Song era for scriptural study to be condemned. The aforementioned *Avatamsaka Sutras* posed little threat since they were intimately allied to Ch'an thought, but other *sutras* were castigated. The mystical enlightenment of Ch'an and the piety of Amidism were coming to be regarded as similar experiences, while the rhythmic chanting of the name of the Buddha of Pure Land (Chin. *nien-fo/nianfo*; Jap. *nembutsu*), and the Ch'an application of *koan* practice, were not seen to be too dissimilar.

The ancient chronicles of Japan record the appearance of Ch'an (attested as "Zen") in that country as early as 654, when the eminent Japanese Buddhist monk, Dosho, returned from China and demonstrated his conviction in Zen by constructing the first Zen hall in Japan. Chinese Ch'an masters soon returned the compliment and their visits to Japan were not without a following. Nevertheless, Zen was but one of several schools of Buddhism in Japan at the time, and by no means the most popular; meditation was forced to play second fiddle to the philosophical speculation and magical extravagance of Tendai and Shingon. Buddhism in general had fallen into decay and remained so for three centuries. By the end of the Heian period (794–1192) a decadent court had polluted not only the populace, but the Buddhist monasteries themselves.

It was from China that Japanese culture gained some of its now famous cultural and aesthetic artistic characteristics as in architecture, gardening, water-colour painting, literature and ceramics. The martial arts from China were attractive to the *Samurai* warriors of Japan, so much so that Rinzai Zen became the faith of the warrior. This was because it taught that the warrior could engage in warfare and still participate in the spiritual life because the two, in reality, one. The martial arts of judo, *kung fu*, *karate*, archery and fencing were engaged in from the Taoist point of view of *wu-wei*, action rooted in inaction, and from the point of intuitive knowledge, not simply the mastery of skills. In archery, for example, the aim was not to hit the target, but to bring the deeper intuitive knowledge into the action, to let the self disappear, and to "go with" the action.[39]

Confucian orderliness and properness may be seen behind the famous Tea Ceremony, which is a religious and ritualistic ceremony used at group meditations. Here, everything is prepared and carried out with the utmost concentration, silence, gracefulness and serenity, an act of meditation just to watch. One of the most beautiful expressions of Japanese Rinzai Zen is its Haiku poetry, another legacy from China.

Haiku poems, confined to a mere seventeen syllables, express the affinity of humankind with nature and have something of the Taoist touch about them in their utter simplicity and yet paradoxical depth. They express quietness and spontaneity, the "suchness" of things and an element of mystery. Curiously, this rich Chinese spiritual and cultural legacy has never been reciprocated, and it is generally recognized today that the Japanese Zen masters had little to offer that was new to the teachings and methods of Ch'an Buddhism.

Nevertheless, for Zen master Dogen, the practice of *zazen* ("sitting in meditation") and the realization of Buddhahood are synonymous, and Dogen's impact on *zazen* continues to this day. Indeed, more than any other person, Dogen, who introduced Soto Zen to Japan from China, may be described as "the master of *zazen*". Correct posture, characterized by the lotus position (Jpn., *zazen*; Chin., *tso-ch'an/zuochan*), and breathing are all important, and much has been written on these issues, both then and now.[40] Among all the Zen schools, each with its own ideas on spiritual training, meditation in the posture in which Sakyamuni "awakened" remains, to this day, the chief path to enlightenment (Jap. *satori*). This said, there are Zen *sanghas* today that acknowledge that the recognized meditative posture is not possible for everyone. Western Ch'an Buddhism, for example, advocates the so-called *chrysanthemum* position, wherein one adopts the most comfortable position, regardless of protocol.

Meditation

Since the words "Zen" and "meditation" are often used synonymously, it is fitting that we examine their relationship more closely. It is a common mistake to see meditation as some form of escapism, with the meditator staring at the wall – intentionally facing in that direction so as to turn the back on the world and all its problems. But there is nowhere to hide in meditation: one cannot hide from oneself. With extraneous thoughts not allowed to come to fruition, one comes face-to-face with oneself and all one's personality problems – a sobering thought indeed.

Zen is not isolated from life, it is life; it is working, eating, cooking, gardening as much as meditating or engaging in spiritual activity, and working meditation is an important dimension of both Rinzai and Soto Zen. Zen Buddhists are not to be found seated in meditation all day long. Most lay Buddhists in the West are in regular employment, and are engaged in the everyday aspects of life. Effort has to be put into these mundane tasks as much as into meditation in the monastery, but it is a natural effort, not a striving of the self to get rid of the self. The Taoist concept of *wu-wei* in Rinzai Zen means the acquisition of the goal of enlightenment without really aiming for it. There would therefore be no distinction between ordinary, secular existence and the sacred life of a monk. *Satori* can be gained as much through practical activity as through intensive meditation. One Soto Zen Buddhist said of his being assigned to the working meditation of cleaning the Priory during one of his stays at Throssel Hole, the Soto Zen Priory in Northumberland, England:

> In cleaning the temple I came to realize that you are not cleaning the temple, the temple is cleaning you. And ultimately the temple is pure, and so are you; neither needs cleaning, but I had to clean it to realize it. In such working meditation there is a formal cognitive commitment to the task after which comes an experience of the realization of things as they *really* are.[41]

It is true that Zen/Ch'an is normally translated "meditation" (Skt. *dhyana*), and Zen practice is certainly characterized by sitting meditation, but in the course of its development in China it became clear that meditation is the means and not the end – the aim of Zen is to realize *prajna* (intuitive knowledge and power), not *dhyana*. Undoubtedly, the practice of sitting meditation as a means of settling an agitated mind was universal among Buddhist monks, but they had no necessary affiliations to either a *dhyana* school in China itself, or to a Zen school in India, China, or anywhere else for that matter. Indeed, the presence of a *dhyana* school is unattested in Indian Buddhist literature, "the special instructors who supervised this practice were called *dhyana* masters, no matter what their school or sect. There were likewise *vinaya* masters, or instructors in monastic discipline, and *dharma* masters, or instructors in doctrine. Zen became a distinct school only as it promulgated a view of *dhyana* which differed sharply from the generally accepted practice."[42] In fact, as already seen, after its arrival in China from India, two centuries elapsed before the advent of a Ch'an school, with the subsequent founding of Ch'an monasteries.

So Indian Buddhist teaching was introduced to the Chinese mind. Its assimilation lost nothing of the Chinese feeling for life, yet conjoined Indian metaphysics with Taoist thought. Nor must we lose sight of the fact that the Chinese Ch'an or Japanese Zen masters never deviate from the frame of reference of Buddhist teaching. At no point does talk of destroying the Buddha, his Patriarchs, or his images (even when the last named *are* burned!) represent the reviling of Sakyamuni Buddha: "Once the intoxication of enthusiasm is over, the Zen monks assemble before the Buddha image for the ritualistic reading of the sutras."[43] These apparent vilifications are symbolic gestures, which emphasize that understanding is born of self-revelation, not the imparted teaching of another by means of the spoken or written word.

流行宗教

9 Popular Religion

What is popular religion?

Popular religion is the religion of ordinary folk, and it lies to some extent outside the realms of institutional, established beliefs and practices. While there was a long hiatus of praxis in twentieth-century China, in places such as south-east Asia, Singapore, Hong Kong and Taiwan, in Thailand, the Philippines and Indonesia – indeed, wherever Chinese communities have taken root, popular Chinese religion flourishes. Even in mainland China itself, it is struggling to be reintroduced and revived. Instead of being based on scriptures, like institutional religions, popular religion has emerged from admixtures of local customs, myths, legends, and is informal and heterogeneous on the one hand, yet can be universally Chinese on the other. It is, indeed, a *Chinese* phenomenon that has no particular name, and yet a good deal of history. We cannot even say that it was a rural or peasant phenomenon, because it was courted by the literati and nobility throughout Chinese history. Essentially, it is linked with lay belief, is expressed in localities, and affects the whole gamut of society extraneous to specifically clerical beliefs and practices, though sometimes these two overlap. It is so widespread in Chinese religion that it eclipses institutional religions in popularity.

Why, then, should such a phenomenon be necessary in Chinese society? The answer to such a question is as much apparent in the ordinary lives of human beings of any culture as it is in Chinese culture. We are all concerned with basic necessities of life – health, long life, economic, familial and social stability. And whether we are religious or not, our first words when something goes radically wrong are often "Oh

God"! In times of distress or ill health, the Chinese need for comfort is directed to deities that they feel are closest to them, rather than appeals to distant and more formal supernatural beings. Alvin Cohen lists six categories that underpin the values of Chinese popular religion. Summarized, the first four are pragmatic – protection of life and property; adjustment to, and harmony with, one's natural surroundings; peace and harmony at home; and success in life. The next two are more culturally religious – salvation after death and a good rebirth.[1] To these can be added another rationale, and that is the acquisition of merit. Chinese beliefs accept the notion of rewards for good deeds and punishment for evil ones not only in this life but in the life to come. Good or evil deeds affect the entire family, both living and deceased, so the ability to acquire good merit or gain appeasement for evil deeds needs to be instant and not remote. Chinese local deities provide the answers.

Given the nature of Chinese popular religion as localized, it is necessarily widely different from one locality to the next. What might be said, however, is that there is a good deal of commonality of beliefs at the *core* of much praxis, what has been called "disorganized unity".[2] It is a very apt description that might link popular religion *per se* and also popular religion with institutional religion. One common theme that stands out is the acceptance of the supernatural world that is beyond ordinary existence yet inextricably involved with it. The reciprocal needs of deities and ancestors on the one hand, and the basic needs of the living on the other, lie at the root of all Chinese popular religion. If the deities, ancestors, ghosts do not get their correct attention they can wreak havoc. But if they do get attention and still wreak havoc, their adherents will go elsewhere for assistance. This factor is one reason that makes popular religion so fluid, and it is also a factor that underpins much institutional religion. At the root of both is the acceptance of the *yin* and *yang* forces of existence that interact in every situation in life, the three realms of Heaven, Earth and humanity, the Five Agents, and the *I Ching/Yijing* with its trigrams and hexagrams. And humans, gods, ancestors, ghosts, Heaven and Earth all have their respective natures, roles, interactions and reciprocal responsibilities that are to the Chinese the norms of existence – the natural and harmonious order of things. Maintaining such harmony informs all Chinese religion whether institutional or popular.

Historically, popular religion could thrive alongside a state structure, occasionally accepting the basic philosophies and beliefs of the official framework while, at the same time, expressing itself at local levels in less orthodox but more meaningful ways. Then, too, popular religion was often courted by higher classes. Richard Smith makes the interesting point that: "Although many aspects of popular religion differed significantly from the religious rituals of the orthodox elite, many did not, or differed only in degree and particulars, not in kind. For all their alleged agnosticism, many elite families worshiped a variety of gods and employed a variety of religious agents."[3] It is the maintaining of harmony between the spirit and human world that provides the common denominator between institutionally orthodox, and popular religion. Confucianism pervaded the local level of life with its emphasis on the family, particularly filial piety, on morality, and on correct ritual for the wealth, health and success of the family and community through honour to the various levels of the supernatural world. However, while historically there are common factors underpinning both orthodox and popular religion it is the *diversity* in local praxis – especially in relation to the many deities – that provides layers of difference. And as we shall see below, many local deities and even deities more widely accepted in popular religion are often radically unorthodox. Nevertheless, the bottom line of all religious praxis was the avoidance of supernatural malevolence and the courting of its benevolence. In the words of Jack Potter: "The universe was essentially a stage on which human beings, impersonal supernatural power, and supernatural beings, interacted in a constant drama of life and death, success and failure. A person's fortunes were determined by how he fared in this complicated drama of life."[4]

In the complications and vicissitudes of life, then, members of a locality will be concerned with their own immediate welfare. Benevolent supernatural beings – deities, some spirits and one's ancestors – are lucky and bright, *yang* and helpful. It is they who are propitiated for help, power, prosperity, and for individual needs. Their malevolent counterparts are dark and unlucky. They are *yin* spirits and ghosts that often reside in the hells, and that plague human beings with all sorts of misfortunes. But these malevolent forces must be humoured, kept happy and comfortable, so that they will favour humans rather than torment them. If such harmonizing of the individual, of the family, the locality, and state with supernatural forces is the basis of most aspects of Chinese religion, whether in its Confucian, Buddhist, Taoist or popular aspects, there is a suggestion of an awareness of an underlying unity in Chinese religion despite the variation in praxis. Where localized differences occur, and they did so and do so widely, awareness of orthodox beliefs and practices still obtains.[5]

Despite similar bases, however, there are profound differences between orthodox and popular religion. Confucianism, Taoism and Buddhism have long histories during which the cults of certain deities and their associative rituals have been established, yet such cults may not by any means be incorporated into local practices. If we think of the pre-eminence of Lao-tzu/Laozi in the Taoist pantheon, for example, he is certainly not a prominent local deity. Then, too, orthodoxy tends to be restrictive to change in a way that local religion is not, and local, popular cults have the luxury of more fluidity and the acceptance of unorthodox characters as deities. Indeed, Arkush's analysis of twentieth-century Chinese peasant proverbs shows that "peasant acceptance of orthodox values and beliefs was limited, somewhat grudging, and mixed with feelings of cynicism about Confucian moralism".[6] It has been emphasized many times in the previous pages that Confucianism, Taoism and Buddhism borrowed ideas from each other. However, at least there were established canons of scripture to provide fundamental guidelines. Popular religion, lacking any scriptures, has been and is incredibly more eclectic, allowing a more informal development of its religious dimensions. We must turn now to examine those dimensions more finely by an analysis of some of the popular deities that pepper Chinese religion.

Deities of popular religion

Throughout the history of orthodox, institutional religion the hierarchy of deities normally reflected the earthly imperial bureaucratic hierarchy of China. There were the greatest, highest deities at the top of the hierarchy, and the lowly house gods at the bottom. In between were the various ranks of gods and ministers. But the hierarchy linked them all in the sense that each deity had his or her respective role to play in the whole scheme of supernatural things. It was a mirror image of what happened on Earth with royal officials, city magistrates and so on, reflected in the heavenly pantheon. Even in the hells, the bureaucratic paradigm was prevalent. Inevitably, there was some overlap in the acceptance of this bureaucratic image of deities by both orthodox and popular Chinese religion. However, as we shall see, many deities of popular religion do not fit into the bureaucratic theme at all. There were also exceptions to the bureaucratic image amongst the orthodox. The rather eccentric, often drunk, and at times rather naughty, Eight Immortals of Taoism exemplify this point well. Pragmatically, just as in the earthly sphere, officials could be bribed, and gifts were used to establish favourable relationships, it was believed that deities, too, could be bribed or given gifts in order to establish a favourable relationship with them. Confucians called this process *shu*, reciprocity. Just as in real life the dynamics of power *between* people and the power *of* people could facilitate advantageous or disadvantageous results in life, the same was thought of the deities, too. And the dynamics of power between humans was also reflected in the power struggles and changing faces of institutional deities, who might wax and wane according to the political powers of those on Earth who had promoted them.[7]

These are all ideas that have come to characterize Chinese polytheism, and that have informed beliefs in popular as much as orthodox religion. But there is a whole wealth of quite contrasting beliefs and praxis that obtains in popular religion. Instead of orthodoxy we find blatant unorthodoxy that flies in the face of the bureaucratic paradigm of a divine hierarchy. Writing of the 1980s in Taiwan, Robert Weller makes the following very interesting comment concerning popular deities in Taiwan:

> This entire set of unbureaucratic deities happily gave stock-market tips, illegal lottery advice, and help in the shadier sides of the capitalist market. From executed bank robbers to unidentified corpses to a monk who mocks his own (already unbureaucratic) discipline, this group stands out for its challenge to bureaucratic order. Most of them are eccentrically individualistic, and none of them has the associations with common morality that typify our images of most gods.[8]

Weller notes that alongside economic growth in Taiwan, "the fastest growing segment of popular religion involved spirits of bandits, drunkards, unknown corpses, and others who offered little to bureaucratic propriety".[9] How, then does such a band of renegade deities come about? The following story cited by Weller may give some idea.

Something like a century ago, a fishing boat containing seventeen corpses and a dog that was alive were washed up in Taiwan. Villagers buried the unknown seventeen corpses and the dog, who refused to be separated from the bodies. The villagers set up a small shrine for the Eighteen Lords (seventeen humans and a dog), and vague offerings were made at it for the decades to come. In the 1970s, the little mound that was the shrine was destined for destruction to make way for a nuclear power plant. But strange things happened at the shrine and the locals rose up to defend the site. Ultimately, the government had to build a new shrine at another spot in order to respect the customs of the local people. Weller takes up the story:

> Not only had the previously forgotten shrine brought the state itself to do its bidding, it had done so in front of an audience of workers from all over Taiwan. The newly built temple was larger and fancier than any other

ghost temple ever built in Taiwan, and within a few years it rivaled the island's most important god temples in popularity, attracting thousands of people every night and thoroughly tying up traffic on the coastal road for hours.[10]

Despite the new grand shrine, the old one was retained, not demolished for a power plant, and became the focus of much attention for its power in granting requests that "resembled contracts with mobsters more than the respectful petitions to proper gods".[11] Weller's point is that such spirits as the Eighteen Lords and other ghost shrines were more approachable for economic aid than the more orthodox gods: "These capricious deities matched the capricious nature of profit itself."[12]

The deities of popular religion, then, do not by any means always conform to the bureaucratic pattern. Nor are they orthodox, as the tale above indicates. They arise from all kinds of bizarre backgrounds – robbers, unmarried women, virgins, suicides, military expertise, reputable and disreputable characters, even gamblers and murderers, for example. Even as early as Han times, worthy people of the distant, and recent, past were exalted to divine status despite their being outside the official pantheon.[13] From early times there were obviously local deities that did not conform to Confucian expectations, though it would be a mistake to think that this was always the case: many deities, such as worthy people who later came to be honoured as deities, were so because they had conformed to the expected norms of social behaviour and excelled in them. Nevertheless, in local cults a great number of female deities are found. These can satisfy the needs of women in a way that the Confucian state religion, where women are subservient to men, do not. And in contradistinction to upright Confucians, local deities are more humorous, more fun-loving, often eccentric, younger, and military rather than the serious, aged and scholastic official deities. Worship of them is an outlet for women and for the young who, in the state scheme of things, are suppressed in favour of males and the old: it is a means of social defiance. Thus, like two sides of a coin, the official deities exist alongside popular ones, providing overlapping responses to the needs of the Chinese people.[14]

The media for the popularization of such unorthodox deities is quite diverse. Naturally, there were local folk tales and legends that were handed down, but cults were spread more widely by those whose trades took them far and wide. Stories about deities were repeated in written and musical forms and enacted in drama and puppetry. But since they were extra-scriptural in nature there is equally no established ritual for deities that is cast in tablets of stone. Their nature is, thus, more fluid, and it is easier for the cult of a new deity to arise, as Weller's account above shows. Many Buddhist deities are adopted in local cults where they provide a different, non-bureaucratic and unofficial focus for worship. Buddhism influenced the iconographic portrayal of deities, and certainly the elaborate character of the Chinese hells. There are about ten such hells, and they feature very strongly in popular belief and practices. Death is followed by passage through these hells over a very long period, in order to reap retribution for evil deeds. But once through the hells, the soul is ready for rebirth. With a vibrant belief in ancestors, and a knowledge of their inevitable fate in the hells, much ritual and worship is dedicated to assisting their paths – not only of known ancestors, but also of unknown ghosts, who may well visit earth with malevolent intent.

Let us turn now to some of the important deities that feature in Chinese popular religion. One highly important, official personage is the Jade Emperor, Yü-huang Shang-ti/Yühuang Shangdi, a colourful figure that is prolific in Chinese legends. He appears on the official scene rather late, at the beginning of the second millennium, though his cult had been developing for centuries before.[15] He is the present, supreme ruler of all Heaven and Earth, "the One, the axis, the mediator, and the centre toward which everything converges".[16] At a philosophical level, this is an apt comment, but pragmatically and anthropomorphically, his task is a difficult one, for he has to deal with all kinds of problems, and it is here that he features in popular legend. Very often he is unsuccessful, and is even ridiculed and cheated. One tale tells of his inviting all creatures to his birthday party. But few of them bothered to turn up – only twelve in fact. It was these animals that were rewarded by being the twelve animals of the Chinese calendar. All mortals, deities, spirits of the underworld, and even buddhas and *bodhisattvas*, are inferior to him. It is the Jade Emperor who presides over the Heavenly courts and to whom deities, ministers and officials of all kinds report on events in their jurisdiction, and on the misdemeanours of all others. While he is very much a bureaucratic, orthodox deity, there are many popular tales about him that defy orthodoxy, presenting him as an opportunist and even as an impostor.

As noted earlier, Lao-tzu/Laozi, surprisingly, is not a popular deity, though Livia Kohn points out that he has inspired the rise of many other deities who took on some of his functions. Nevertheless, he is always known as the author of the *Tao Te Ching/Daodejing*, and is revered through the work attributed to him.[17] Much more popular, and worshipped throughout China, are Kuang-kung/Guangong, Chen-wu/Zhenwu, Sun Wu-k'ung/Sun Wukong, Na-cha/Nazha, Kuan-yin/Guanyin, Ma-tsu/Mazu and the Eight Immortals. While some deities were also recognized by the state and had official temples, their popular cults were served by different temples. Meir Shahar cites the example of Mazu in Taiwan of late imperial China, where people flocked to the popular temple and virtually ignored the state temple to Mazu.[18]

Goddesses, who do not feature prominently in the official religion, are very popular locally. Of these, the two mentioned above, Kuan-yin/Guanyin and Ma-tsu/Mazu, are the most important popular female deities, especially the former. Kuan-yin/Guanyin is a Buddhist *bodhisattva*, an enlightened being that delays final *nirvana* in order to stay in the world and help others to salvation. Known outside China as the male *bodhisattva* Avalokitesvara, in China there is some significance in the fact that she is a woman, and readily champions the role of women and symbolizes compassion. Contrary to accepted societal norms, she did not marry and was executed, so she is a rather unconventional deity. Kuan-yin/Guanyin is a perfect motherly figure who aids all who need her. She grants sons to childless women, and heals illnesses. She is usually portrayed as covered in a white veil and holding a child in her arms. She sits on a lotus, the symbol of enlightenment. While she is rarely seen in temples, she is almost always to be found in the home.

Ma-tsu/Mazu or T'ien-shang Sheng-mu/Tianshang Shengmu, "Holy Mother in Heaven", whom we met in chapters 6 and 7, is the Empress or Queen of Heaven. She is a goddess that takes care of sailors, travellers, women and children. She is a particular favourite in Taiwan, and is a good example of a goddess that is both accepted in the official ranks as well as by popular religion. Unmarried virgins are believed to become harmful ghosts after they die and therefore create enough attention to warrant propitiatory shrines. Her unorthodox end, and the fact that she never married, make her rise to divine status equally unorthodox.

Hsi Wang-mu/Xiwangmu the "Queen Mother of the West" was first introduced in chapter 6. She is an interesting goddess because some of her characteristics are so terrible. While she is mainly an institutionalized goddess, again, her background demonstrates very well how the origins and nature of a deity can be very unorthodox indeed. Like her, Lady Linshui, or Ch'en Ching-ku/Chen Jinggu, a popular goddess in Fujian and Taiwan, has darker sides to her personality, with malevolent characteristics of a snake demon alongside her kinder aspects. It is the latter that make her a protector of women and children, though she can harm them if they neglect her. She, like other female deities of popular religion, never married and died a young virgin.[19] She is another example of a very popular goddess with unorthodox beginnings, and of a woman who defied the social norms of marriage and subservience to the male. Na-cha/Nazha and Miaoshan are also examples of deities that do not conform to the bureaucratic paradigm of official deities and that provide reversal of normal roles. Miaoshan, believed to be an incarnation of Kuan-yin/Guanyin, was killed by her father after refusing to marry. She thus refused to fulfil her role as a woman and daughter. The god Na-cha/Nazha is similar in that he refused to be the usual submissive son. These are popular figures that fly in the face of Confucian ethics.[20]

A very popular goddess is Wu-sheng Lao–mu or Wu-shen Sheng-mu, the Eternal Mother. She has eclectic appeal, being popular with Confucian sects in Taiwan, was associated with the secret Buddhist sect the White Lotus Society and with the Taoist personification of Tao. In Singapore she eclipses the Jade Emperor and Maitreya Buddha in importance, but while a popular goddess of salvation she does not champion women to the extent that she places them alongside men: women in her cults are inferior to males.[21]

Of male deities, the Three Rulers, Officers or Agents, *san-kuan/sanguan* are closely appropriate to the daily lives of ordinary folk. They have been venerated since early times, and featured in a Celestial Masters' rite by which people confessed their sins to the three. T'ien-kuan/Tianguan is the Agent of Heaven, and is responsible for the prosperity and good fortune of people. He is the Agent of happiness. Ti-kuan/Diguan is the Agent of Earth, and was especially concerned with absolving peoples' transgressions. Shui-kuan/Shuiguan is the Agent of Water, and is particularly associated with the overcoming of people's difficulties. He is the Agent that removes misfortune.

Even more revered popularly are the three stellar gods of longevity, health and blessing – happiness in general. They are Fu, Lu and Shou, mentioned in chapter 6, and are found in Chinese homes, on the roofs of temples, in the workplace, in Chinese restaurants, and even in some shops and garden centres in the West. They are three very characterful individuals. Shou is the one who appears most in Chinese art. He is the God of Longevity, and is easily recognized by his bald, highly-domed head. There is a bulge on the front of his head, accentuating the domed shape. It is indicative of the *ch'i/qi*, the pure vital energy, that he has transmuted. The same can be said about his bulging belly. In one hand he holds a peach of immortality, and in the other, a long, gnarled branch of a tree, often as a staff, and sometimes showing one or two gourds on it. He is the oldest of the three, has a long white beard, and is the strangest looking of them, though he is usually portrayed with a happy smile and rosy cheeks that belie his great age. When seated, he is on a crane, one of the many symbols of longevity. Lu, the God of Official Position or Dignitaries and, therefore, of wealth, happiness and honour, is dressed very regally. Fu, who has a kindly face, is the God of Blessings. He is often depicted carrying a child, for it is he who grants children, particularly sons.

Kuan-ti/Guandi (also known as Kuan-kung/Guangong),[22] the God of War and patron of military arts, is an important deity. Indeed, Shahar believes he is the most widely worshipped male deity in China.[23] He was a historical person, Kuan Yü/Guan Yu, a third-century general in the state of Shu. He was executed by his enemies in 220 despite his complete fidelity and honour, and became a great hero. As the God of War, he leads the armies of Heaven against evil, but he is also the defender of officials. These twin roles are depicted in his iconography, the former reflected in his image as a man of huge size, clad in the armour of war, with his horse at his side, and the latter in official dress without military trappings. He is expected to protect the country from invasion. In his less military role, he is a patron of literature and commerce and of loyalty and trustworthiness. He has a red face – a feature of his character in theatre performances – a magnificent beard and legendary eyebrows that look like silkworms. What is noticeable about him in relation to popular religion is that he stems from a martial tradition in contradistinction to the favoured literati of the Confucians.

The God of Wealth is an important one for those in business, as well as for ordinary families. He is Ts'ai-shen/Caishen. His form is to be found in many homes and even on bank statements. He is frequently to be found on Chinese calendars, especially since, at New Year, it is hoped that he will bless the family with financial gain in the year to come. He is dressed impressively as a high-status official and carries a scroll bearing his name. Naturally, he heads the Ministry of Wealth in the divine bureaucracy with many accompanying officials in his department. In Chinese homes he is usually found on the rear of the door leading out of the house.

Kenneth Dean cites the popularity of the god Kuo Ch'ung-fu/Guo Chongfu in Fujian. The god was a human who lived in the tenth century and died at the age of thirteen, thereafter appearing to villagers in dreams and visions. The nature of this god typifies well the custom of deifying those who were once mortals, but who had unusual deaths. As Dean states, the temple around which this cult centres is given the Buddhist term for a monastery, but the specialist rituals carried out there are Taoist and Confucian.[24] Popular custom sees no contradictions in beliefs and praxis by amalgamating the three religions.

Some of the other deities need only be mentioned here. A god of longevity and a god of immortality are often to be found on almanacs as symbols of good luck. They are perhaps not so much worshipped for longevity or immortality – the average person would be fully aware that neither would be his or her fate – but as "representations of an idea".[25] There are deities representing professions and trades, even gambling and prostitution! Lu Pan/Lu Ban is the god of carpenters, joiners, black-smiths and potters: each trade has its patron.[26] Hou-chi/Houji is the god of agriculture, and She-chi/Sheji the god of the land, the soil and grain. In Taiwan, multiple deities called Wang-yeh/Wangye are the patrons of the immigrants who fled from the island of Fukien to Taiwan after World War Two.[27] In the Taiwanese pantheon, too, is the "Great Emperor Who Preserves Life", Pao-sheng Ta-ti/Baosheng Dadi. He, like so many other deities, had once been human, a medical practitioner called Wu Chen-jen/Wu Zhenren.

Then, too, the Eight Immortals that we met in chapter 6 are partic-ularly popular, especially Lü Tung-pin/Lü Dongbin, the most colourful of the Eight. It is especially the miracles he wrought, and the unsavoury stories about him that are popular in folk religion. He is another example of a deity and Immortal that does not fit the estab-lished idea of what a god should be. Paul Katz aptly encapsulates the duality of character in Lü Tung-pin/Lü Dongbin in the very title of his article "Enlightened Alchemist or Immoral Immortal? The growth of Lü Dongbin's Cult in Late Imperial China."[28] He points out, too, that while there are many different representations of Lü Tung-pin/Lü Dongbin, they all have in common the factor that they do not fit the bureaucratic paradigm of deities.[29] Many tales of deities certainly chal-lenge the norms of morality. Shahar refers to a "vast gallery of clownish eccentrics" – renegades, criminals, beggars, bandits, morally degenerate and once human as many of them are – that can be found in the Chinese pantheon,[30] and this is exactly what makes them attrac-tive to ordinary people.

Deities of the earth, of locations, and of the home have always been important. The concept of earth deities is an ancient one in China, as explained in chapter 1. But it is now part of Chinese belief. Homage to the earth god in the form of the god of the home or the flat is the first action of the day. Just as in ancient times, when the earth god was notified before major events like harvesting, so in the home today the earth god is notified about activities in the home. The hierarchy of gods is evident at this level, too, for the house god is responsible to the local god, he to the district god, and the district god to the city god, and he to the god of the province – a bureaucratic model. But, again, many of the earth gods have been mortals who have died in tragic circumstances, females who have died as virgins, for example, or those who have committed suicide. It is as if their destiny were cut off, and they were held to the localities in which they lived by being prevented from moving on. Again, others are former local heroes, whose wisdom, bravery, sagacity or outstanding qualities make them good candidates for the status of localized earth gods.

The deities connected to cities have been termed in the past the gods of walls and ditches or wall-and-moat deities. These are terms that replaced the old one of "earth gods", though the latter term describes rather well their function today. Gods of walls and moats, *ch'eng-huang-shen/chenghuangshen*, or city gods, originated in T'ang/Tang times when walls and moats surrounded the cities, and their shrines or temples were therefore built on the perimeter of the city.[31] The city deity is responsible for the care of the city, protecting it from harmful flooding, disease or drought, so it has some function in providing rain. Each city deity has its special temple and is honoured on its particular festival day. Some of these city gods are famous, like the City God of Hsin-ch'u/Xinzchu in Taiwan.[32]

Deities specific to a locality, to small areas like a street, a district, hamlet, a plot of land, a bridge, a building, a temple, and also the home, are *t'u-ti/tudi*. It is these deities that are the closest to the inhabitants, and their relatively meagre-looking shrines belie their importance in daily life. It is to these deities that people turn in difficult times, when there are problems at home or in the locality, at work, or on farmland. The *t'u-ti/tudi* of these small areas are different from the *t'u-ti/tudi* of the home, the latter being even more intimately associated with the family. It is these deities that really know the woes and joys of the home they protect. The small images that represent these deities are placed on the ground, next to the earth near the altar, thus effectuating closer control of the space on which the home is built. In Taiwan, shrines to the district deities are prolific. Just how far such popular gods are removed from the official ones is exemplified well by Robert Weller, who encountered the Cloth-Bag Buddha – "the fat, jolly character with a big bag of goodies slung over his shoulder" – in a restaurant in Taiwan.

Weller describes him as a bit like Santa Claus, but with a burning cigarette hanging out of his mouth![33]

It is the deities associated with the home itself that are carefully respected. There are two door gods who stand either side of the entrance to a home, and one at the back door. Their function is to drive away evil spirits. They sometimes take the form of scrolls, but more often pictures of warriors in remembrance of warriors who guarded the entrance to an emperor's bedroom, preventing disturbing demons from harming him. After he saw they lacked sufficient sleep, he had portraits made of them instead. They are to be found either side of the entrance to temples. The Kitchen, Hearth or Stove God, is a colourful character. While being low in the hierarchy of earth gods, his role is such that he is usually given great respect. Situated in the kitchen, at the hearth of the home, he is strategically placed to pick up all the gossip, and to note all the little good and bad things done by the family. At the end of the year, he leaves the home to report all he has seen and heard to the Jade Emperor. He is represented by a picture on the kitchen wall, or sometimes by a piece of paper on which an invocation is written. This is burnt at the end of the year to send him on his way, and a new piece is put up to herald his return in the New Year. Since the fortune of the family in the coming year will depend on his report, before he leaves he may be sweetened up by sweet food, or he may be given a very glutinous rice to seal his mouth together so that he cannot report anything! Fireworks often herald his departure and his return is an occasion for ceremony and offerings. But at least the revelries of New Year can be enjoyed while he is away.

Although he is an official deity, popular religion has many different oral traditions about the Kitchen God in the same manner as the Jade Emperor. Official views of both may afford them the status they should warrant as deities, but popular religion often has tales that malign them. In the case of the Kitchen God, perhaps this is because he is a deity of two realms – the bureaucratic one that puts him as a spy in each home, and the personal god who resides in a home and should be fond of its inhabitants.[34] In popular legend, the Kitchen God is said to have once been a poor man who had to sell his wife in marriage to someone else. Years later, while he was begging in an area, he recognized her, felt ashamed, and hid himself in the stove, in which he was accidentally burned. While the Kitchen God is the key deity of the home, there are a number of others, like the Lady of the Toilet and Bathroom, an old deity who was formerly the Goddess of the Latrine-Ditch, and the Lord and Lady of the Bed.

Earth Gods are highly significant in the context of the vision we have of religious practice. While remote celestials hardly enter into daily life, these localized deities are the intimate mediums by which humans engage with divinity. Angela Zito makes the point that these gods are indicative of the way in which, in the past, people shaped their social world, "a world that combined the family, the imperial domain, and the cosmos into an interactive whole".[35] This connective tissue that links the heart of the home with the wider cosmic reality is no less evident in present-day belief. What takes place is, to borrow Zito's phrase, a "sacralization of place in the universe".[36] In a similar context are the festival troupes of southern Taiwan. These are the Chia-chiang/Jiajiang that sacralize space by representing divinity at festivals, accompanying deities in processions, dancing wildly and acting as exorcists. They are regarded by locals as minor gods, and their function is to bring harmony to the locality, though the deities they represent are not respectable official ones. They are, then, not confined to usual social norms, though they are cognizant of boundaries of ritual, and are a very popular local phenomenon.[37]

The position of the stars in the sky is felt to influence human life, particularly since the stars overlook Earth. The sun, moon and stars have their respective deities, and many groupings of stars have been connected with the Five Agents, along with major planets.[38] Ch'ang'o/Chango, Goddess of the Moon, is exquisitely beautiful, with long dark hair. She and her husband lost their divine status and had been banished to Earth. She became Goddess of the Moon by drinking an elixir of immortality that had been given to her husband by the Queen Mother of the West. He didn't take the elixir straight away, but hid it, intending for them both to take it a few days hence. There was only sufficient for both of them to have eternal life, but not enough for them to have immortality. However, Ch'ang'o/Chango found the elixir, and took the lot, so that she rose up immediately to the Heavens. But rather than rise to Heaven, where the gods might chide her for her actions, she decided instead to reside on the moon.

In addition to all the deities and good spirits, there are also demons, devils and evil spirits. They are pests that create havoc for deities and mortals, causing sickness, hardship, droughts, fires, and natural, elemental phenomena like typhoons. The demon and evil spirit world is swelled by those whose deaths have been particularly violent or unhappy, and by those who have no family to accept them as ancestors. These are "orphan souls", hungry ghosts. Some houses have "devil walls" a few feet from the door in order to keep out unwanted spirits.

The belief in such spirits has been a part of Chinese pre-history and history to the present day, and the old shamanic practices to get rid of them have evolved into all kinds of superstitious ritual.

The calendar

Religious events are mainly determined by the lunar rather than the solar calendar. A lunar month, the time it takes the moon to revolve around Earth, is about twenty-nine to thirty days. The first day of the month occurs at the new moon, and the middle of the month is the time of the full moon. Of course, this means that the New Year would never be fixed in terms of the seasons. To ensure that it was fixed, and to keep in line, too, with solar time, the time it takes Earth to revolve around the sun, extra months had to be added to the lunar year now and then. In the time of the legendary Yellow Emperor, in the year 2637 BCE, the Chinese calendar was begun, and time was mapped out in cycles of sixty years. Indeed, the sixty-year cycle is still important today, for one's sixtieth birthday is a time for special celebration.

Each cycle of sixty years is informed by the cycle of Five Agents, and since each Agent has a *yin* and *yang* nature, altogether these amount to "Ten Heavenly Stems". Additionally, the Ten Heavenly Stems are combined with "Twelve Earthly Branches",[39] and it is these that are associated with the twelve animals – Rat, Ox, Tiger, Hare, Dragon, Snake, Horse, Goat, Monkey, Rooster, Dog, Pig.[40] The year in which one is born will dictate the kind of personality one has, so horoscopes are taken seriously by the Chinese. Earlier, it was noted that, according to one legend, the twelve animals were the only ones to turn up at the Jade Emperor's birthday party. Another legend tells that the Jade Emperor, in order to create a calendar, invited all the animals to cross a wide, swiftly running river. The first to arrive would give its name to the first year, the second to the second, and so on. The machinations of the animals and how they crossed the river in the order shown above make a delightful story.[41]

The meticulous divisions of the calendar to reflect the Five Agents, *yin* and *yang*, the Stems and Branches, the position of the planets and stars, and the nature of change, permitted some forecast of the way things might be on a given day and, also, the way things *should* be on a given day. Maintaining harmony in one's daily life necessitates knowledge of each hour, day, and greater period of time. Here, the almanac provided in the past, as in the present, a forecast of what might be auspicious or inauspicious on a particular day. In late imperial China, the almanac was surely the most widely circulated book. It gave not only the nature of a particular day, but broke down the day into the best and worst times at which to do something, thus advising times for marriage, business arrangements, agriculture, visits, and so on. Indeed, the almanac was a veritable encyclopedia for daily life, even explaining dreams, the right charms to use as well as divination methods, and is very evident in many Chinese homes today.

Festivals

Festivals pepper the calendar year, providing times for communal cele-bration in localities and households. Some celebrations are universal; others, like the birthdays of village deities, are local. Generally, there is considerable variety in the ways in which festivals are celebrated from one community to another, for it is the laity that decides how things should be done according to local needs. The festivals celebrated today are too numerous to detail, and in what follows only a few can be mentioned, singling out about three of the most important. Festivals are part of the *yin* and *yang* pattern of creating harmony between the community and the cosmos, and of channelling the blessings of the gods into the community and the home. It is often a time when the specialist functions of priest – both Taoist and Buddhist – are called upon, as well as the mediums and diviners who provide supporting roles.

Chinese New Year occurs at the second new moon after the winter solstice. It is a highly auspicious time, for it heralds the time at which *yang* begins to rise again in the cosmos. While the winter solstice marks the solar New Year, the lunar New Year, which is the beginning of spring, is so much more important that preparations for it begin on the twenty-fourth day of the last lunar month. On this day, the household deities leave the home to report to the Jade Emperor on the good and evil deeds of the members of the family during the year. In particular, the Kitchen or Stove God is given a banquet and bribed with offerings of sweet foods before he leaves. Five is a key number for the festival and represents the Five Agents with five talismans, each dish of food being set out in five dishes, and so on.

New fire is important at the festivities. It represents new life, rather like the new fire that was started in the springtime in ancient times. Red, the colour of life, is the colour of the festival – red posters on the doors, red flowers in the women's hair, red envelopes containing money for the children. On the first day of the New Year, everyone bathes and dons new clothes before visiting the temple, relatives and friends, and exchanging presents. In each home there will be five kinds of sweets for visitors, symbolic of the Five Agents, and sweetened tea. It is a time for pleasant behaviour, pleasant words and lucky sayings. Everyone tries to laugh and be happy, and avoid fractious interchange. The whole tenor of New Year is a time for the neutralizing of evil forces so that the New Year can be started afresh.

The calendar year is divided into three unequal parts. The first part begins on the fifteenth of the first month and is the Period of the Heavenly Spirits, and lasts for six months. It is this day that marks the end of the New Year period. It is, therefore, the time to bid farewell to the spirits of ancestors who have been invited for the New Year festivities. This is done in the Lantern Festival, when lanterns of all kinds are hung up to light the souls' journey away from their families. The lanterns, too, represent the renewal of the *yang* energies in the cosmos. Another feature of this festival is the dragon-lantern processions, when an immensely long and grotesque-looking dragon is animated by many men (and sometimes women) underneath, who act as its feet.

Festivals for the birthdays of deities are particularly colourful affairs and are mainly lay occasions and may not involve the functions of priests. It will be around the major temple dedicated to the deity that the festival will take place, attracting people from far and wide, if the deity is a major one. The main part of the festivities is the processing of the deity on a palanquin or open truck around the town, accompanied by musicians, dancers and firecrackers. Some participants may have brought other deities to honour the celebrated god or goddess. This kind of festival is called a *tan/dan*. The most important deities, the Three Pure Ones, have their birthday celebrated on New Year's Day, but the prestigious Jade Emperor's birthday also falls within the New Year period. In the city of Peikang in Taiwan a special festival for Ma-tsu/Mazu occurred recently, when the city attracted thousands of visitors to her temple there. It was a particularly stunning and colourful festival, vividly described by Christian Jochim, with processions, spirit mediums inflicting themselves with wounds to show that the goddess was present, and rituals at the sacred brazier to renew the spiritual protection granted by the goddess – all culminating in her birthday celebrations with a procession of her image around the city accompanied by firecrackers.[42] The festival is a good example of localized celebrations as much for its lay participation as its special features.

Traditionally the third of the third month is the time of Ch'ing-ming/Qingming, "Bright and Clean". Despite the connotations of springtime in the name, the festival is a time for the cleaning of graves. Perhaps the two aspects were separated in the past. It is one of the major three festivals for the dead and, like the other two, was probably influenced by Buddhism. Cemeteries did not exist in China, and people set up their own graveyards outside the village or town and planted trees around the graves until the Communist regime ploughed many of the areas. The whole family – the living and deceased ancestors – joins together at the graveside for the cleaning ritual. This usually takes place early in the morning when the spirits are "at home" in their tombs after their rest through the night. After offering food as a sacrifice to the ancestors, the family combines the occasion with a picnic nearby.

At the beginning of autumn, on the first day of the seventh lunar month, the Gates of Hell are opened and souls are allowed to go free. Those who have no one to honour them roam listlessly from place to place for the whole month. It is a time when they can visit the living in ways that are not really welcome. So merit can be acquired through the offerings made to these lonely, orphaned and hungry souls while, at the same time, the offerings afford the souls some release from their plight, and a means of coaxing them not to plague and take revenge on the living. A strong Buddhist influence informs the beliefs here. In Taiwan, these lost souls are called "the good brothers", even though, or especially since, some of them are believed to be in Hell for crimes they have committed – all the more reason to placate them! It is the responsibility of the whole community to assist these lost souls for the safety and security of everyone. Rites to appease the hungry souls occur throughout the month.

The fifteenth of the month is particularly important. It is a time to appease but beware! And it is not a time when one would want to open a business, get married, move house or go to the dentist! On this day is the festival for Earth Spirits or Hungry Ghosts. It is a time in which forgiveness of sins is possible, especially for the souls in the hells. It is thus a major festival, dwarfed only by the New Year. It is a time when the souls, freed from the hells, are invited to a sumptuous communal banquet. Again, it is a concept thoroughly influenced by Buddhism's view of universal salvation. Such ritual is important enough to require the skills of the specialist priests, both Taoist and Buddhist. Lanterns and beacons are lit to attract the souls and then at the end of the festival, lanterns are also floated on the rivers to light the souls on their way to Heaven or back to Hell, before the Gates are closed once again.

Popular praxis

Temples

A significant feature of popular religious praxis is the considerable contribution and even control by the laity. Priests became increasingly marginalized in their localities, being called on only for the more prestigious ceremonies. By and large, there is little to distinguish between the organization and administration of Taoist and Buddhist temples, and many temples may have no specific connection with the institutional facets of either. No one needs to be a member of a specific religion to enter a temple. Local temples are the responsibility of the laity and are independent of each other. It is the laity that funds their building and maintenance, and each temple will act as a community meeting place, a chess club, a school, a playground, a business conference place, and so on. It would not be unusual for such temples to be devoid of any resident priest, for their affairs are run entirely by a lay committee, and it would be up to that committee to invite a priest for any special religious occasions. Thus, there is a limited role for Taoist priests of any kind in the local temples.

Since temples are the responsibility of the laity, and often funded by wealthier citizens, architecturally they are usually the most prestigious buildings in a locality. They are palaces of the deities, and are built so that the major deity within, and the main door, faces South, which is *yang*. The cosmology of Heaven and Earth and the energies between them underpin the careful design.[43] The whole design of the temple is based on the theories of *yin* and *yang* and the Five Agents.

Inside the temple the most important item is the incense burner or brazier, whose smoke symbolizes rising *ch'i/qi*, (vital energy), and is the means by which ritual is performed to the gods. Care of it is essential and often local families take the responsibility of such care for it in turn. Ashes from one burner will be used to begin a new temple. The worshipper also burns incense or *joss* sticks on the central brazier as part of his or her private ritual, for temples are always open, and individuals can present their pleas to a deity at any time. The most frequent images to be found inside are of the Three Pure Ones, the God of War, as well as city deities. Local temples will have their own central deity which, at special festivals, will be moved to the side to accommodate the Three Pure Ones, as well as other high-ranking deities.

Spirit mediums

If priests are at a premium in the lives of ordinary people, spirit mediums, mentioned in chapter 6, are very different phenomena, and are to be found in all localities. They are sometimes involved with the same rituals as the more orthodox priests, but it is as mediums for the deities that they are used. Mediums are possessed, and are used as oracles. In their trance states they are known to push skewers through their cheeks, arms and calves, or cut themselves in some way to illustrate their entranced imperviousness to pain. In Taiwan, they are often attached to small temples or shrines though, equally so, many are not. However, it is a temple area that usually provides the environment for their trances.

When special local celebrations take place, mediums are sent from other localities for the occasion. On a smaller scale, they are often used for private séances in which they may be used to contact the dead, for example. Such smaller-scale mediums may be women, and old or young. In fact there are many different kinds of mediums. Some use divination to convey their message – spirit writing, or the divining chair, for example – but it is always through the power of a deity particular to the medium that his or her skills are exercised. In Taiwan, such general mediums may have "offices" where they can be consulted in times of personal difficulty. Importantly, it is communication with the deities, the spirit world, or the world of the dead, that renders the mediums essential in the lives of individuals and communities. This is shamanistic practice in the present day.[44] Requests can range from cure of illness to advice on gambling and winning the lottery! It is interesting that many of the deities to which mediums are attached are unconventional to say the least. Jean DeBernardi comments that: "Ji Gong, the 'Mad Monk' or 'Dirty Buddha', for example, is a trickster who despite his Buddhist vows eats dog meat and drinks rather than fasting and abstaining . . . he will call for ale, and he jokes and teases his clients. His trance performances are at times serious, though in many cases his teachings were parodies of orthodoxy rather than solemn didactic events."[45]

Exorcists

Local people may also be involved with exorcists for the purification of homes, villages, or curing of illness. These exorcists are the *fa-shih/fashi*, the masters of method, and it is they who interpret the words or divination writing of the mediums who are attached to them, and who are masters of the mediums. They are Red-head Taoists, unlike the more orthodox Black-head Taoists, and like the shamans of old can travel to any part of the world, to the underworld, or to the heavens where they acquire their knowledge. The interaction between priest and medium and the colourful, dramatic and theatrical ritual adds to the otherwise solemn nature of such occasions. These magical rites are, in foundation, performed for the same reasons as those of the ancient shamans – anything from rain-making to healing. The exorcist is often like a magician, or sorcerer, who has acquired skill in the procuring of power from the gods and the ability to use it.

Divination

The early chapters of this book explained that divination was a prominent feature of ancient Chinese practice; it is still very popular today, albeit in wider format. The use of moon blocks, as they are called,[46] is reminiscent of the *yin* and *yang* negative or positive responses, and is underpinned by such. They are so called because they are shaped like a pair of quarter moons. They can be quite small when used in the home, but are larger when used in temples. The curved, outer sides of the blocks symbolize *yang* while the flat inner sides are *yin*. When a request is made to a deity, the petitioner casts the blocks onto the ground. If they land unevenly, and so one flat and one curved surface are seen, then the answer is favourable. If, however they both land flat sides down, or curved sides down, the answer of the gods is negative.[47] (Flat sides upward indicate that the god is laughing, and the inquirer should try again!). It is a form of divination that is very popular in Taiwan,[48] as well as Hong Kong. For more elaborate responses, divination slips are found at the larger temples. A slip of paper bearing a number is drawn at random and then matched with a bamboo slip on which is a short verse supplying the answer to a question or problem. Since the responses on the slips are difficult to understand, an interpreter is often at hand in the temple. Some questions are profound, others are mundane: "Why is our child doing poorly in school? Why is my husband always tired? What can be done about the pain in my left arm? Should we build a new wing on the east side of our house or the west side?"[49] Complementary or separate is *ch'ien/qian* divination with the use of bamboo sticks, individually numbered and held in a bamboo container. This is then shaken until one stick falls out, its number being matched to a printed response.[50]

Spirit writing

Spirit writing is another form of divination known from Sung/Song times.[51] One form of it is the use of divination chairs. These are small sedan chairs carried by two mediums holding its legs. A deity is invoked to sit in the chair and the mediums in trance reflect the animation of the deity by the jerking of the chair. From time to time the chair appears to write in Chinese characters in sand that has been placed on a platform or specially prepared table. It is this message from the god that is divined by the experts. Sometimes, the deity conveys its message by means of the medium writing in the sand with a willow or peach-tree stick, the traditional tool used for the divination. Illiteracy was once required of the mediums who engaged in such divinatory writing. Such spirit writing is not just a means to request advice of a deity; it is also a means of revelation of whole texts. Jordan and Overmyer note the importance and popularity of possession and divination in Taiwanese culture, where it is practised by all classes.[52]

Additionally, the calendar itself is an important medium of divination. For the position of the stars and planets, in conjunction with the time of one's conception, will be indicative of the ways in which changes in time and space in ever-flowing cycles are having an effect on the life of an individual at a given point in time. Since there are no set cosmic patterns, an individual's life can be adapted and changed in accordance with the tenor of the present pattern of events. Creating harmony and balance is the key here in understanding why divination is important. Divination is a way of putting oneself back on the cosmic track by making the right choices and changes. It can take many forms – the observation of the stars; the way in which the energies of the earth are presently aligned; the configuration of energies at a given moment; the reading of natural phenomena like the flight of birds; the configuration of clouds or mists; the reading of omens; the casting of *joss* sticks on which hexagrams are inscribed. However, the concept of regaining or maintaining harmony between Heaven and Earth, macrocosm and microcosm, lies at the root of all such divination. The ancient ideas of change according to the interplay of *yin* and *yang* and the interaction of the Five Agents inform the concept of divination as a means to ascertain the way in which events are moving. So requests of moon blocks, the use of divination chairs or slips are all attempts to interpret the pattern of events or, more pertinently, the way in which adverse events in personal life are out of line with cosmic change. Divination has been a Chinese phenomenon from ancient times, and is very much a part of folk custom.

Worship

Lighting candles and burning incense at the family altar and ancestor shrine in the home are central acts of worship. Maintaining harmony and acquiring merit are the immediate aims of ordinary people, who know that they are a long way from immortality. Yet there is, too, an idea of ultimately universal salvation, a concept for which the average individual has the influence of Buddhism to thank. But, apart from offerings to gods and ancestors, meditation, breathing exercises, the slow exercise of T'ai Chi Ch'üan/Taijiquan or the similar *ch'i-kung/qigong*, are practices that are adopted as part of the lay attitude to religious life. Keeping oneself healthy in body and mind is a facet of the religious quest. Harmony and merit are the requisite results of worship in the home. Jordan makes the point that possession of an image of a deity is tantamount to a contract between the two: the deity supplying welfare and blessings for the family, and the family supplying care for the deity.[53] While a number of deities might be worshipped, apparently it is not wise to have too many. If one deity out of many is requested for help it might well take the attitude that, since the worshipper usually worships "Old So-and-so", why should it bother to respond![54]

The absence of a priestly focus in the religion and the lack of institutionalization means that it is up to the individual to maintain any format of worship. However, it is usually the mother of the home that presents the offerings to the ancestors and deities, performing this function for her family twice a day at the long table containing the deities at one end and the ancestors' tablets at the other. Incense is an especially important offering with food offerings being more occasional. Despite such traditional praxis, the more industrial cultures like Hong Kong have abandoned the local, community earth god, though he is still to be found protecting the home in less urban areas. In Hong Kong, too, the economically dispersed families have resulted in a distinct lack of family unity in home worship.[55] In all, worship and religion are informal. A special problem might occasion a visit to a temple, or the employment of a Taoist or Buddhist specialist, but usually the family conducts its own worship without the need of an intermediary.

For more communal occasions, temple processions are beloved by festival participants.[56] The young men of the area display their skills in choreographed martial arts. Part of the ritual programme is the theatrical performances or puppet shows that are themselves entertainment, and offerings to the deities. Puppets, moreover, are believed to aid in dispelling evil forces by chanting and dancing. This is because they are supported by the deities who observe and enjoy their performance. There has always been a strong connection between temples and drama, but while religious ritual could be conducted in the temple, so too could religious drama or secular shows – the latter even "raucous and spectacular".[57]

While the main focus of family worship would be the deities, a smaller part of the family altar would be used for ancestors. The ritual involved here is aimed at ensuring that the dead are comfortable in their post-life abode. For those in living memory, the ritual is individualized. For those long passed into general ancestry, a collective ritual takes place at special festivals. The spirit of the deceased, if properly cared for, should be able to progress easier through the hells to a new rebirth. In return for such care, the deceased spirit watches over the family's interests. It is sons, and mainly the eldest, who have the responsibility of creating the ancestor tablet and of maintaining the offerings to the deceased. Not to do so would bring hostile fortune to the family through an unhappy ghost. If a man has no sons to undertake such a task, such is the importance of ritual for ancestors that a foster son may be acquired by adoption from a family who has several sons, or a daughter's husband or first son is adopted.[58]

One important aspect of ancestor ritual is the use of "spirit money" to aid the journey in the hereafter. Such is the belief that beings in the other world – whether gods or deceased souls – have the same kinds of needs as humans that artificial money is ritually burned to assist them. In Taiwan, deities are given gold paper money in this way, ancestors, silver-coloured money, and ghosts, copper coloured. The paper for the gods is yellowish-gold with a square of aluminium foil on which are depicted the three Gods of Happiness, Success and Longevity. Many temples provide braziers for the burning of such spirit money. Wads of it can be bought in the markets. Adler notes an interesting custom in Taiwan: "Every fifteen days business owners in Taiwan burn spirit money in red braziers and set out offering tables on the sidewalk for both gods and ghosts. . . . Some of the offering tables are quite elaborate; for example a restaurant may offer an entire meal, complete with beer or wine."[59] The point is that happy and pleased gods protect and bless people, angry ones cause havoc.

Another aspect of spirit money is the depositing of money in the Banks of Hell or the Celestial Treasury – money that is owed purely by living life.[60] The powerful Taoist priests called Black-head priests are able to transfer the money on behalf of someone by a writ. Red-head priests, however, use a medium, who will take the money to the appropriate bank while in trance. But spirit money is also used to bribe the officials of Hell, or to offset stolen or defective money; it is even sent as pocket money! At festivals for the dead the burning of such spirit money is very important. Such ritual of ceremonies is designed to bring comfort and deliverance from harm for both the living and the dead and to release the latter from suffering in Hell.

Finally, it would have to be said that a certain amount of magic and superstition has always pervaded popular Chinese belief. Today, for example, talismans are widely used. They are charms that provide protection from evil forces. They may be worn by an individual, placed in the home, or burned and their ashes mixed with water and ingested in order to cure an illness. While at the most mundane level talismans may be worn purely for good luck, they are also thought to bring about protection from a particular deity, or to protect people from evil forces at the time of death. In a culture that accepts the presence of unseen forces, there are all kinds of customs that surround life-cycle events such as birth and marriage. These are too intricate to detail here, but a few examples might suffice. Before birth, the foetus is looked after by a spirit called T'ai-shen/Taishen, who lives in a variety of places in the house, in the wardrobe, or under the bed, for example, and so it is imprudent to disturb the spirit by moving the furniture around or by cleaning out cupboards.[61] If the pregnant woman's in-laws cause her any problems, the spirit may become angry. It is a sensible arrangement for, with variations from culture to culture, the pregnant woman is protected from moving heavy objects herself, or from an accident by others doing so. In short, her duties are minimalized so that she and her baby are safe.

The security and blessing of the family, its cohesion and vision for the future, as well as its links to its past ancestral line, depended on the children who were born. However, in the past century, China's population growth has been colossal. A rigorous policy by the state has sought to limit families to just one child each. Even so, the population continues to expand. But, aside from the problems of economy with an enormous population, family life has been curtailed. Bearing a son is impossible should the first child be a daughter, and the old family ties and ancestral traditions have broken down. Such is so at least on the surface, and more so in the towns and cities, than in the countryside.[62]

While popular religion is fluid and often unorthodox, it is at the end of life that the individual turns to the recognized institutional and orthodox practice. The colourful events of life are over, and the deceased has to be dispatched with the utmost care and precision, and the living protected from exposure to the malign forces of death. It is fear of such

248   *Popular Religion*

a kind that provides one reason for the extensive rituals surrounding death. The other main reason for death rituals is concerned with the Confucian-influenced concept of filial respect. To neglect the correct rituals is a shameful thing to do and would bring a family into disgrace. David Johnson points out that both priests and exorcists are present at a funeral to respond to these two main needs: the priest performs the correct and respectful ritual, and the exorcist makes sure the deceased departs and does not hang around to pester the family.[63]

To ensure that the deceased person really does depart, a funeral rite known as *The Attack on Hell* is performed. Here, a paper and bamboo fortress is built and the family of the deceased crouch in a semi-circle round it. Each one puts a hand on it and shakes it now and then. It represents Hell, and the ritual is enacted to release the soul of the deceased from there. At the same time, it is the ritual at which the living really say farewell to the dead, so it is a cathartic and moving experience for the immediate family.[64] Ritual such as that found at funerals is ancient, and while there are always variations, it is usually detailed and protracted – a fact that emphasizes its immense importance.[65]

While funeral proceedings may seem laboriously long, they provide full expression for mourning, for assuring the living that the dead are well cared for, and assuring them, too, that blessings will be reaped for the living through their time and care. Lack of respect for such a goal by not performing ritual for the dead is tantamount to being ostracized by the family and community. At the same time there are fears of the "contagion" of death, and neighbours may put red paper or cloth over their front doors to act as protection. Red is a symbol of life, and serves to prevent any malign influence from the dead. The whole process is a vivid reminder of the closeness between the living and the dead in Chinese culture. The end product is the release of the soul after as short as possible a time in the hells and a raising of its status to Heaven. The bridge is crossed between the world of the living and the world of the dead and, finally, between the world of Hell and the world of Heaven. And those bridges can only be crossed by the interaction of the living with the dead – albeit at a safe distance for most of the time. It is interesting that authorities in China prevented such funerals from taking place and encouraged cremation. However, with the relaxing of the bans on religious praxis there, traditional funerals have become something of a status symbol.[66] It is this revival of religion in China after a long demise that will occupy some space in our concluding chapter.

当代中国宗教

10 Chinese Religions Today

Communist China

In the last centuries of imperial rule in China, religious life was pervasive, with a proliferation of temples, shrines, door gods and protective house deities. The beauty of the mountains boasted splendid monasteries and temples to which pilgrims flocked, and life-cycle rites and festivals peppered the lives of ordinary individuals. For such people, religious life was a mixture of Buddhist, Taoist, Confucian and local beliefs and practices. Neither Taoism nor Buddhism had much organizational influence, and Taoism had been only minimally an institutional facet of Chinese religion. But alongside the proliferation of religious beliefs came western influence in the nineteenth century, and a decline in the functions of both Taoist and Buddhist monasteries and temples.

Politically, the Ch'ing/Qing dynasty was crumbling. China was humiliated by her defeat at the hands of the Japanese in 1895 and, in the wake of the Boxer Rebellion of 1900, by the allied Japanese and western powers. Apart from famines and natural disasters, there was considerable public unrest, and a number of revolutionary groups sprang up. The last dynasty of China, the Ch'ing/Qing dynasty, ended in 1911 after a revolution led by Sun Yat-sen's Nationalist Party, and China became a Republic. The Emperor abdicated the following year. Sun Yat-sen died in 1925, a few years after the formation of the Communist Party in 1921. The successor to Sun Yat-sen was Chiang Kai-shek, who attempted to consolidate his power in the early new Republic. However, political disorder remained throughout the rule of the Nationalist government that he led. War with the Japanese from 1937 to 1945 brought further political disaster.

Changes in outlook in the urban towns and cities produced a new kind of Chinese intellectual, one not held so much by traditional values, but one who questioned economic, political and social balances, and who was ripe for radical change. Such intellectuals, many of whom had studied abroad, began to see China as underdeveloped in an otherwise modern world. Students objected to having their education dominated by the old classical language that restricted the use of modern concepts and prevented wider literacy for all people. Exposed to western ideas, they felt hampered by their cultural identities, and their attitudes to religion became indifferent. As people moved from country areas to the factories in the towns, seeking work, their old familial ties were broken, creating a vacuum that nothing seemed to fill.

All this changed under the leadership of the Communists. In 1949, Mao Tse-tung/Mao Zedong led a revolution against the Nationalist government, forcing it to retire to Taiwan, and instituted the People's Republic of China. Mao Tse-tung/Mao Zedong fostered not familial but nationalistic identity, and a more thorough rebuttal of traditional ideas. Initial thought was that, with modernization, old religious ideas would become obsolete and a move to atheism would be the natural path. When this did not occur, there was an overt attempt to eschew "superstitious practices". It was the Communist Red Guards who perpetrated the worst horrors against religious praxis – killing and maiming, forcing religious individuals into acts against their beliefs, invading their homes to destroy any vestiges of religion. In these turbulent years, what replaced religion was allegiance to Mao Tse-tung/Mao Zedong in what must be regarded as a deification of him. A doctrine of propaganda to make Chairman Mao the focus of every individual's attention was adopted. In homes, schools, the workplace, cinemas, parks, streets, there were posters of Chairman Mao, and quotations from his *Quotations from Chairman Mao* were ubiquitous. Lucy Jen Huang wrote:

> While the Communists attacked religion as the opiate of the people, Maoism seemed to have similar euphoric influence on the masses, chanting and reciting Mao's quotations at every important occasion and believing it could perform feats and miracles. The unification of the nation is more effectively achieved if the masses possess religious zeal and dauntless faith in Maoism. At the same time, through the worship of Mao, the insecure and the alienated find a sense of identity, belonging and esprit de corps in the common struggle and dedication of a common course.[1]

Under Mao, improvement in education, industry, health care, land distribution, new occupations and the vision of a vibrant future helped to foster the kind of Maoism found in the words above in some constructive ways. But Mao also wanted grass, flowers and pets eliminated.[2] Even today cats and dogs are rarely found in the cities. Inevitably, young people grew up with allegiance not to their family, but to the state. In the words of a popular song of the time: "Father is close, Mother is close, but neither is as close as Chairman Mao".[3] Young students had no objection to the destruction of religious objects during the Cultural Revolution from 1966 until Mao's death in 1976. It was a time of systematic destruction of temples, and local committees saw to it that ancestral tablets and altars in all homes were burned. Thousands of volumes of religious texts were destroyed – either burned or made into pulp at a paper factory. As soon as the old empire fell and China became a Republic, state support for temples ceased, and many monasteries and temples that remained fell into disrepair. When the Japanese armies invaded in 1937, such buildings had already been devastated. Under the Communists, monks and nuns were persecuted, forced from their monasteries, and put to work in labour gangs where many died. Religion was all but obliterated.

With the post-Mao years came changes in policy with regard to religion. After a few unsettled years, Teng Hsiao-p'ing/Deng Xiaoping took over the Communist leadership in 1979, and opened China to greater western influence and greater freedom of religion. Five religions were accepted as official – Buddhism, Taoism, Protestant Christianity, Roman Catholic Christianity and Islam, though Taoism is not now regarded as having any eminent position in China.[4] Confucianism came under great persecution in the twentieth century, and was blamed for the antiquated ideas of the Chinese more than other religions, so it is absent from the list. It is tolerated only as a subject for scholastic study. What is not tolerated is superstition and, therefore, popular religion continues to be regarded as illegal.

The revival of religions in China is permitted politically mainly because of the tourist attraction of the old temples and monasteries, so the state is investing in their rebuilding and refurbishment as prudent economy, despite underlying inhibition and much prohibition. Yet, there is a good deal of support from outside China to reinstate religious practices once again, and encouragement for the training of priests, monks and nuns. The number of priests in China is now increasing.

Limited tolerance of religion is giving support to the setting up of religious seminaries, some religious ceremonies, and salaried religious personnel. However, there is still careful control and monitoring of religious movements and bodies, and a Religious Affairs Bureau oversees practices. Local Buddhist, Taoist, Muslim and Christian Religious Associations control the practices in a locality, making sure that they are not out of line with state policies. Special permission is required to hold large-scale religious festivals, though celebration of festivals is now very much in evidence. Religious ritual in life-cycle rites is also more acceptable. Yet it has to be said that China's youth has grown up without any form of religion. It is difficult to see how socialist-orientated youths and, indeed, people of middle age, can adopt a religious culture outside of which they have grown up and matured. Some of these individuals continue to revere the long deceased Chairman Mao's portraits at Chinese New Year, and taxi drivers have been known to carry portraits of him to protect them from traffic accidents.[5] To be a member of the Communist Party itself, one *has* to be an atheist, a fact that suggests to the Chinese that religious belief is inferior.

Confucianism

Confucianism faired badly in the revival of religious institutions in China. Its conservatism and traditionalism were blamed for holding China back from emerging economic and social change despite having many forward thinkers in its midst. In China itself, it has been accepted as a phenomenon for study, particularly in the search to understand the foundations of Chinese thought and culture. However, there are many who find Confucianism very relevant to the modern age. While it would be necessary to eschew notions such as the subservience of women to men, for example, there is much that is socially humanistic. Scholars of Confucianism have written sympathetically of its relevance not only in the past, but of its possibilities for the future, though there are also *Confucian* scholars today who seek to revive the old traditions – some with the old conservatism, others with more relevance to the post-modern age. The centres for such thought are mainly outside China, like the Confucian Academy of New Asia in Hong Kong. Confucian scholars have contributed to what has become New Confucianism in the post-modern world, a disparate movement but one, nevertheless, that has gained ground not only in Hong Kong, but also in Taiwan, Europe, North America and south-east Asia. Most of these New Confucians claim that there need be no anomaly between Confucian values and modernization.

Yet in China itself, Confucianism has gained less ground. It cannot exist there in institutional form or with any focus in society. Its rituals are dead and, as Xinzhong Yao points out, it has little practical meaning for modern life. And yet, he makes the following rather interesting comment:

> The umbilical cord between the Confucian tradition and modern China cannot be easily severed. Elements of Confucian heritage have been transmitted to the present, either hidden in Nationalist and Communist doctrines, principles, ethics, public opinions and the system of a bureaucratic elite, etc., or implicitly underlying the whole structure of Chinese community (family, community, society and the state), in whatever forms it may take, either capitalist or socialist, Nationalist or Communist.[6]

This is a fascinating comment, which reflects the fact that so often submerged ideologies and cultural psyches remain evident at all kinds of subtle levels. It is impossible to annihilate centuries of thought that have dictated the way in which individuals think and behave just by a mere hiatus of half a century. And many of the moral ethics of Confucian humanism – inner virtue, trust, respect, humaneness, sincerity, a learning spirit, family stability, education, working for the common good, and so on – are no less needed in the post-modern world than in the distant and near past. Projected into social interactions, these are the kinds of ways in which New Confucians believe Confucianism can make a valid contribution as a world philosophy. A more proactive engagement between East and West is now more acceptable in most Confucian circles.

Confucian rituals are no longer extant in China, but in Hong Kong, the 28th of September is celebrated as the birthday of Confucius, with events taking place at his temple there. Confucius' birthday is celebrated in South Korea, and in Taiwan, too, where the day is marked by a national holiday. Since Confucius was a great teacher, his birthday in Taiwan is a day when all teachers are honoured. It is in Confucian temples in Taiwan that the old Confucian rituals are still carried out. Taiwan also has a Dragon Boat Festival to mark the death of the Confucian Ch'u Yüan/Chu Yuan who committed suicide in 299 BCE in order to emphasize the need for state reform. The old Confucian rituals are still performed in South Korean temples, and South Korea also boasts the Sung Kyun University, founded in 1398, which is still run on Confucian principles.

Taoism

Field studies in Fujian have revealed that Taoist rituals were again being performed in restored temples in the mid-1980s, and large-scale processions were evident there in the early 1990s, though restoration of practices is slower elsewhere.[7] However, the number of Taoist monks and nuns is far fewer than the personnel of the other four official religions.[8]

The two major Taoist sects to be found in China today are Celestial Master Taoism and the Cheng-i/Zhengyi, Complete Reality, monastic order. Taoism has survived, and perhaps has done so better than is thought, considering its amorphous nature that defies categorization.[9] In Pas' words, "the Chinese people are very tenacious and resilient; like the loyalists of early times, when the Tao prevails in the country, they come forward; when the Tao is in darkness, they go into hiding".[10] While a number of young men and women want to be trained to be Taoists and can, for example, take a one-year study course in Beijing, they are hardly likely to be commensurate with the early Taoists who undertook a lifetime of study. Those who train in the monasteries themselves do little better in terms of commitment and knowledge.

Any visitor to China today is unlikely to see a profusion of Taoist temples, with perhaps more tourists than pilgrims on the mountain slopes leading to the major temples and monasteries. But great temples like the White Cloud Monastery, the largest in North China, are now functional and training monks. Thus, Taoism is far from dead in China, as was once thought it would be. As Schipper poignantly remarks about culture in China, "one only has to scratch the surface in order to find living Taoism".[11]

From the field studies undertaken in recent years, it can certainly be claimed that Taoism is alive in China, particularly so in the coastal provinces of Fujian and Canton in the South.[12] The cult of Ma-tsu/Mazu is especially popular now in south-east China. Slowly, old texts that survived the purges are being copied, and vestments and temple hangings are being restored where possible. Any vestiges of shamanism, including *feng-shui* now popular in the West, as will be seen below, are strictly regarded as superstitious and, therefore, illegal. Such a policy excludes much that might be considered as Taoist praxis.

Elsewhere, Taoism has always been allowed to thrive outside China. Especially in Taiwan, its traditions have been relatively undisturbed. It also thrives in Hong Kong and Singapore and in Chinese communities in the United States and elsewhere where Chinese immigrants have settled. Although practised world wide, there are perhaps no more than thirty million Taoists today; religious belief is a tenacious phenomenon. Thompson aptly remarks that: "Religious forms, like certain plants, can remain dormant for a very long time, only to spring up again when the environment becomes favourable."[13]

Buddhism

We said in chapter 5 that a casual visitor to the study of contemporary Chinese religions might well be forgiven for concluding that in China today there is little place for Buddhism. But how has Buddhism fared on the Chinese mainland under a Communist regime? At first glance, there is the temptation to dismiss Buddhism in China as a thing of the past. The profusion of schools is nowhere to be seen, and some have disappeared altogether, though there are still monks in China today who have studied under the guidance of the T'ien-t'ai and Hua-yen lineages. Buddhism in China today is not generally considered to be a panacea to the problems of the twenty-first century, but it would be wrong to minimize its contribution to Chinese thought and culture. Buddhism's abiding legacy is to be seen in the architectural landscape, felt in the literary genres, and expressed in the ritual practices and religious beliefs of the nation.

The spread of Chinese Buddhism from its homeland is self-evident – an observation that is confirmed by the profusion of sects and temples extant in Japan, where there are frequent calls to revive Buddhism.[14] In Korea, too, the monastic discipline is well preserved. By 1983, the True Pure Land school, Jodo Shinshu, of which there are ten sects, the largest being the eastern and western Honganji, boasted a worldwide membership of over thirteen million, with forty thousand priests and twenty-one thousand temples. Today, it is reputedly the largest Buddhist sect in Japan. In the 1980s, the other major Pure Land School today, the Pure Land or Jodoshu, had an estimated seven thousand temples and nunneries throughout the world, and offered visible support in the secondary and university sectors of education, as well as to those socially dependent.

Popular religion

Popular religion is thriving in China! It is springing up wherever a loop-hole can be found for it to emerge. Research today demonstrates that it is in rural areas that it is most evident.[15] Apparently, many homes have reinstated their family altars and the old funeral rites have been revived with all the extravagance of the past. Even young people are fascinated enough with religion to go on pilgrimages to temples.[16] One researcher estimated that, in southern Szechuan/Sichuan in 1988, as many as eighty percent of homes had a traditional altar dedicated to Heaven first and then the country, as well as ancestors, the Kitchen God and the earth god. However, daily rituals seem to have been abandoned, and incense is only burned at the altars on festival days.[17] But door gods have returned to guard the entrances of homes, usually two at the front door and one at the rear. Julian Pas remarked on the "amazing and fasci-nating" variety of door gods that he saw in China decades ago in 1985.[18] Religious drama and marionette theatre have re-emerged also, in conjunction with the old priestly rites in the temples.

Influences of Chinese religions in the West

We live in a time of considerable excitement and interesting challenges on the one hand, and heightened stresses and conflict at so many levels on the other. More and more today, people are turning towards non-institutional spiritual pathways in order to ease the dis-ease of mind and body, and a diminished state of well-being that seems to plague our times. Such factors are surely behind the attraction of eastern concepts and practices. The *Tao Te Ching/Daodejing*, unknown to the vast majority of people half a century ago, is now often found in bookshops. Indeed, J. J. Clarke remarks that: "The long slow decline of Daoism in China is synchronous with its long slow rise in western conscious-ness."[19] Many westerners now believe in *karma* and reincarnation, and many seek alternative eastern therapies when they are ill or ill at ease. We were surprised recently to be sent for acupuncture treatment under the National Health Service, and to find that training for it is now possible for National Health staff. Those wanting alternative medical therapy do not have to search far to find it in their local area.

Chinese religion has now had some impact in the West. The cultural history, and relative proximity of the United States to the Mahayana strongholds of East Asia, ensured that Buddhism gained a foothold on the American mainland. Chinese labourers began arriving in the States for the Californian Gold Rush just after the middle of the nineteenth century, setting to work in the gold mines and on the railroads, and establishing first typically Chinese syncretistic temples and, later, centres that were purely Buddhist orientated. Hawaii became home to both Chinese and Japanese immigrants some time before it became a United States' possession, while the end of the Vietnam war saw some half a million settlers arriving in the States from south-east Asia. Buddhism today is even more popular in the United States than it is in Europe, and it is estimated that between three and five million Buddhists are to be found across a thousand Buddhist groups.

The spontaneous, simple and direct appeal of Zen was attractive indeed to post-war America, whose military personnel had gained personal experience of Zen in World War Two Japan. The writings of D. T. Suzuki, the anti-authoritarian appeal of Zen to the "Beat" movement of the 1950s and the "Hippy" generation of the 1960s, all increased the momentum, and large Zen centres were established in Los Angeles in 1956, San Francisco in 1959, and Rochester, New York in 1966. The Order of Buddhist Contemplatives has its headquarters in Shasta Abbey, California, founded in 1970 by the late Rev. Master Jiyu Kennett as the headquarters of the Zen Mission Society. Known in Britain as the Serene Reflection Meditation tradition, the Soto Zen school has Throssel Hole Priory in a quiet valley in Northumberland as its training monastery and retreat centre. Founded in 1972, the monastery has over thirty ordained men and women under the guidance of the incumbent Abbot, Rev. Master Daishin Morgan, a senior disciple of Rev. Master Jiyu-Kennett. The monastic order is celibate, though there are some thirty meditation groups affiliated to the monastery throughout the United Kingdom.

Most people today are familiar with the visual expression of T'ai Chi Ch'üan/Taijiquan,[20] or simply T'ai Chi/Taiji, as it is more familiarly known. It is a practice, in fact, that is multi-layered and multi-faceted, but that ultimately unifies all its elements into a wholeness that mirrors the unified fabric and rhythms of the universe. While we do not see groups of people practising T'ai Chi/Taiji in the parks and town or city squares of the West – a common sight in China – classes in T'ai Chi/Taiji are now very popular in leisure centres of the western world. In the busy and somewhat stressful lives that we seem to live in the West, even the *sight* of people practising T'ai Chi/Taiji offers an immediate contrast to abnormally tense lives that have come to see stress and hectic living as normal. Few people realize when watching or practising T'ai Chi/Taiji that there is a wealth of Chinese and Taoist culture and traditions that have contributed to its present expression. Paul Crompton makes the apt point that "the world of Tai Chi today is like an enormous warehouse in which the past has accumulated".[21] Multiple strands inform its practice, strands that reach back into the distant past of ideas and practices – alchemy, meditation, spiritual development and martial arts. It is concerned with the holistic evolution of body and mind, the evolution of the physical and the spiritual.

T'ai Chi/Taiji has been termed "China's cultural ambassador to the world" by Douglas Wile. He writes, too: "Touching the lives of more Westerners, and perhaps more deeply, than books, films, museums, or college courses, T'ai-chi Ch'üan is often the entrée to Chinese philosophy, medicine, meditation, and even language."[22] Those who know nothing of Chinese thought will almost certainly be familiar with the symbol of *yin* and *yang* and with the graceful movements of the T'ai Chi/Taiji *form*. Paul Crompton's words describe rather well what we now witness: "Moving slowly, under the trees, breathing, it seems, in time with a gentle breeze; merging with Nature itself in a healing rhythm. Head, shoulders, arms, trunk, legs and feet moving as one; continuously, smoothly and restfully; as if swimming into a new, all pervading element; a different time, a different space . . . "[23]

T'ai Chi/Taiji has its roots in many practices of the ancient past. Gymnastic exercises were popular, for example, in the time of Chuang-tzu/Zhuangzi, and there is evidence for their existence in chapter 15 of his text. It seems, too, that gymnastic exercises were widely used for therapy in the third and second centuries BCE.[24] Throughout the following centuries, many variations on these exercises, postures and movements developed. But we can go back even earlier than these gymnastic exercises, to the dances of the shamans. These dances were important to remedy lack of rain, illnesses, aberrations of climate and the like. The dances facilitated the flow of energy on earth as much as in the human body. Despeux writes: "The dances are therefore conceived of as a means of resolving the congestion and stagnation of vital energy, to ensure its healthy circulation within human beings, as much as they are used to help the flow of the rivers on the earth."[25] The idea of harmonizing energies, of creating the correct balances in nature and in the human self are clear from these words. So the idea of movement to create harmony is a very old one in Chinese culture.

Then, too, shamanic dances often imitated the movements of creatures, a feature that has also inspired some of the movements in T'ai

Chi/Taiji. The Han silk manuscripts found at Ma-wang-tui/Mawangdui, which date back to about the second century BCE, have drawings of people of all ages and both sexes engaged in physical exercises, rather like today's practices of T'ai Chi/Taiji. Today, it is seen as a holistic practice that combines meditation with movement, mind with body, the spiritual with the physical. The circulation of energy in the body is essential for sound health. But in T'ai Chi/Taiji as a martial art it is the awareness of that energy, and how it is about to be used in an opponent's body, which is at the root of each movement. Ultimately, the aim is to create the same kind of harmony that obtained at the beginning of the universe. Stuart Olson makes the pertinent point that in the West we treat our bodies like a car, not bothering with it too much until it breaks down, and then we see a mechanic. We wait until we get ill before we help our bodies. The Chinese, he says, treat the body more like a garden, weeding it, nourishing it, caring for it, and strengthening it against illness from the inside.[26]

Another facet of Chinese religion and culture that has found its way to the West is *geomancy*, or *feng-shui* (pronounced *fung-shway*), a practice that is at least three thousand years old. The art of divination, so long a facet of Chinese philosophy and practice, was extended also to the patterns of the earth itself. The Chinese term means "wind and water", and just as wind and water shape the contours of the earth, it refers to the vibrant and changing energies of the land itself. It perhaps stemmed originally from the idea that ancestors had to be comfortable in their graves. Later the idea was influenced by the concepts of the *I Ching/Yijing*, *yin* and *yang* and the Five Agents. By the early T'ang/Tang dynasty, there were many different schools of geomancy.[27]

Running through the whole of the earth is the power, the energy, of *ch'i/qi*, which is the creative force behind all the earth's patterns, and which comes from Heaven. It mingles with the *yin ch'i/qi* energy of Earth to form veins of energy in the land, often called "dragon vapours" or "dragon veins". Sometimes it twists and turns, rises and falls, creating mountains and valleys, or it suddenly surges upward causing volcanic reaction. All its formations can be negative or positive, *yin* or *yang*. Building a temple, monastery, home, grave, or any kind of building at places where there are negative forces can only serve to bring misfortune to the occupants, who will be affected by those energies. Quite the contrary is the case when buildings are placed where there are positive energies, for here, success, health and harmony will ensue from the beneficial forces that pervade the environment. But energy, like the cosmos itself, is constantly undergoing change and experts have always been needed in the past, as in the present, to determine the lie of the land's energies.

There are certain visual characteristics of the land that are more obvious markers of beneficial energies – softness of the landforms, for example. Conversely, sharpness and harshness of the land will produce negative energies. Eva Wong writes:

> Roads, rivers, and valleys are pathways along which energy flows. Energy that flows down steep roads, gorges, or slopes is destructive; energy that meanders is beneficial. The most undesirable places to build a house or erect a grave are at the end of a T-junction and in the fork of a Y-junction in a road. At a T-junction, energy rushes straight at the house, as waves crash against the shore. In a Y-junction, the dwelling is squeezed between two roads.[28]

Visually, too, a building that is exposed and not nestled with higher ground behind for protection is likely to be in a disadvantageous location. Yet the peaks of mountains are especially known to be places that emit an immense amount of vital energy, like massive power stations. Also emitting powerful positive energies are the many grottoes or caves on mountainsides, perhaps because they were attractive to the Taoist recluses, and were said to be the dwellings of deities and spirits. Old monasteries were, therefore, often built in places of natural perfection on a mountainside. Flowing water is a special medium for the carriage of energy, but if it is flowing away from a place it will take energy away with it, though it can bring it if it flows towards a place. Wind sweeps *ch'i/qi* away, so no home should be in a windswept place.[29] Straight lines are especially inauspicious, particularly if they point directly to the site of a home or garden. Where they occur, they are usually diverted or blocked, perhaps by a pool or pond, a cluster of trees, or some rounded and smooth boulders. Nature is happier running in curved lines rather than straight ones, and the best kind of *ch'i/qi* runs like the contours and twists of a dragon.

But, apart from these obvious visual determinants of the nature of the land's energies, there are far less obvious and far subtler aspects of the energy forces that only experts can understand. All in all, there should be three-fifths *yang* and two-fifths *yin* at site. Such calculations are for specialists, or *hsien-sheng/xiansheng*, to determine. And in Jack Potter's words: "Handling *fung shui* is like dealing with a high voltage electric current; the benefit one receives from its power is directly proportional to the technical skill employed."[30] The energy forces are sufficiently crucial, too, for the well-being of a whole village. Moreover, if a grave were to be placed in the wrong way – just, perhaps, a few inches amiss – the well-being of all the descendants of the deceased would be adversely affected.

Ch'i/qi has different kinds of energies, which are dependent on the direction from which it flows. The four cardinal points of the compass each has an animal to symbolize the character of its energy. South is the Red Phoenix, and when ch'i/qi comes from this direction it is a symbol of fame, and good fortune. It is the source of goodness and beauty. South is associated with the summertime, as is the yang Red Phoenix, and is a time of energy and invigorating strength. Having the front of one's home or business facing this direction will bring these qualities. This was the direction in which all monasteries and temples faced. The North is associated with the yin Black Tortoise, with long life and endurance. If ch'i/qi comes from this direction it is, like the tortoise, slow, sluggish and sleepy. The North and the Tortoise are connected with winter, so having one's home facing North is to invite tiredness and sluggish energy into the home. West is associated with the White Tiger, a yin and unpredictable animal that might snooze quietly one moment and bring roaring change the next. Having one's house facing in this direction invites adventure, disruption to routine, and surprise events from the ch'i/qi that flows to it. To the East is the Green/Blue/Azure Dragon, from which flows protective ch'i/qi and the kind of yang energy that promotes wisdom and educational enhancement, which is what the occupants of a home will acquire if the home faces East. East is associated with springtime and new growth. Richard Craze summarizes the best location for any home in the light of such data:

> Ideally you would have low hills to the west to lessen the power of the White Tiger and good sloping Dragon hills to the east to get as much wise Ch'i as possible flowing down towards the house. To the south there should be a flat open view, preferably with a stream, to encourage all that invigorating Ch'i. And to the north more hills – even mountains – to protect and nurture.[31]

The Dragon is the left-hand side when looking out of a home, not facing it. The Green Dragon should always be a little higher than, and predominant over, the White Tiger in order to keep it in check, so high hills, or forests to the East and low hills or treeless terrain to the West are important in maintaining the harmony of energies. Additionally, there can be good, auspicious ch'i/qi, which is called sheng ch'i/qi, or bad, inauspicious ch'i/qi, called shar ch'i/qi. The former is known as the dragon's cosmic breath, and the latter the dragon's killing breath. Simple devices such as wind chimes or a mirror surrounded by the *Pa-kua/Bagua* are used to deflect any adverse energies.

Kwok Man-ho and Joanne O'Brien note the interesting case of the building of the greatest banks in Hong Kong according to *feng-shui* praxis. When the Hong Kong and Shanghai Bank was built in Hong Kong, it faced North, was in a favourable position according to *feng-shui* experts, and was the tallest building in the city. The Bank of China also intended to build a bank nearby, but waited until the Hong Kong and Shanghai Bank was finished. Then, they built their bank taller and in such a way that adverse *feng-shui* would affect the business of the Hong Kong and Shanghai Bank. Kwok Man-ho and Joanne O'Brien take up the tale of rivalry in the following words:

> The construction of the bank also adversely affected the feng shui of other nearby businesses – the reflective windows of the Bank of China turned bad fortune back on to its neighbours and the sharp corners of the buildings acted like daggers, slicing through neighbouring businesses. To avert further bad luck, and to protect clients and staff, the managing directors of neighbouring office blocks hung ba-gua mirrors or small tridents on the outside walls of their offices to stave off the ill-effects of the sharp corners. A third office block, known as the Central Plaza, has been built on Honk Kong Island – it is the tallest building in the area, and has symbolic financial dominance over all the surrounding businesses.[32]

The machinations of the bankers illustrate rather well the interconnectedness of energies that underpins the theory of *feng-shui* – albeit that it was used here in the context of economic skulduggery.

Today, *feng-shui* is becoming popular in the West, where home designers ascertain the best lay-out of a room, the right situation for a study, a bedroom, a kitchen and so on, and also the best places in which to put furniture. The layout of a garden, especially, is becoming influenced by the principles of *feng-shui*. Michael Page writes sensitively of the traditional plan of a *feng-shui* home and garden:

> A house or a room is like a body, having its own metabolism. Its occupants are its organs, to be nourished by a healthy and balanced flow of ch'i. Traditional houses . . . were built around a central court: it was believed that, no matter how far from the country, the residents should never lose touch with the elemental universe. So they kept Nature just outside in the central courtyard, where there would be rocks, bonsai and water. The garden was seen as a reflection of the macrocosm, so that every opportunity was taken to encourage the interplay of yin and yang.[33]

At its heart, *feng-shui* seeks to align the individual self, the home, room, or garden with the energies of the land. It is underpinned by the belief of creating harmony with the environment, so that the individual's energies flow with those of the land and, hence, with cosmic changes. Even deeper, it harmonizes the microcosm of Earth, the macrocosm of Heaven, and humanity as the middle element between the two. Ultimately, *feng-shui* is concerned with the harmonious interrelation of, and concomitant changing interaction with, the ten thousand things in all existence. Where *ch'i/qi* runs freely just below the surface of the earth, nature responds well, with verdant grass, lush vegetation and large numbers of trees. When humankind destroys what is natural, the energy goes much deeper, deserting the surface of the earth, and leaving it a desert.

The contours of energies and rhythms that pulsate in the earth are reflected in Chinese landscape painting, as well as gardens. Jean Cooper points out that the energy of *ch'i/qi* pervades the end product of all the arts – music, painting, poetry or landscape gardening. All remain true to nature, she says: "In a well-designed garden", for example, "it should be difficult to distinguish between the work of man and Nature."[34] Chinese art, therefore, usually reflects the simplicity of nature and, especially, space. The Chinese were the inventors of watercolour painting, and watercolours are the best medium for achieving a fluidity that permits a certain unity in the painting. Chinese painting is concerned with capturing the energies of a scene – the *ch'i/qi* and the balances of *yin* and *yang*. Outward forms are less important; it is the *essence* of the subject matter that is the focus. The interrelation of all things in life means that a bird or butterfly in a painting is seen as part of the unity of the whole and not in isolation. Space is essential: it suggests infinity, and sets the subject matter against such a philosophical backdrop through intentional statement. Two-thirds of a Chinese painting is usually given over to space, while the remaining third contains the subject matter. The space is usually above the subject, suggesting the vastness of Heaven.

In gardens, too, the changing rhythms of light in the day, of the seasons, of the weather are reflected in the freedom and softness of space, simplicity and curves. The mind is moved forward into space and infinity by carefully positioned boulders, shrubs and trees. The features of the wider landscape – mountains, valleys, rivers, lakes – are portrayed in the microcosm of the garden. Mountains are represented by rocks surrounded by a lake or pool of water – the *yang* of Heaven surrounded by the *yin* of Earth. Water is particularly symbolic of the weakness and adaptability that overcomes the hard and the rigid.

The art of *feng-shui* is one that harmonizes human life into its environment – an aim that is perhaps all too exigent given today's concerns for the state of our planet. In Eva Wong's words: "By cultivating intuition and sensitivity to the environment, we can become aware of the energy that flows through the universe and catch a glimpse of the fleeting moments of transformations and the underlying reality of all things."[35] Whether or not we would want to adopt the practices of *feng-shui* into our personal lives, engendering deeper sensitivities to the environment on individual levels is surely the way forward to regaining respect for the planet on which each individual lives for such a very short period of time. Gill Hale reiterates:

> We have reached a stage where the human race has become capable of the most amazing feats on the one hand and the most amazing follies on the other. We have the capacity to cure hereditary diseases but also to let genetically-engineered organisms loose into the environment in the most dangerous form of warfare humankind has ever known. We send people into space to collect information never dreamed of half a century ago, yet at the same time we allow the planet we inhabit to become increasingly polluted and less able to sustain the life forms on which we depend for our survival.[36]

Balance and harmony are essential ingredients in the many dimensions of human existence. It is important to be sensitive to the interrelatedness in life's energies that makes one action, one thought, part of a wider matrix.

注 釋

Notes

Introduction

1　*Peoples Republic of China: Administrative Atlas* (Washington D.C.: Central Intelligence Agency, 1975), pp. 46–7.

1　Ancient China: The Three Dynasties

1　See Conrad Schirokauer, *A Brief History of Chinese Civilization* (San Diego, New York, Chicago, Austin, Washington, D.C., London, Sydney, Tokyo, Toronto: Harcourt Brace, 1991), p. 5.

2　Chang Kwang-chih, *Shang Civilization* (New Haven and London: Yale University Press, 1980), p. 349.

3　*Ibid.*, p. 361.

4　*Ibid.*, p. 339.

5　The material relating to the Shang is to be found in *Yin-pen-chi/Yinbenji*, an important chapter in the *Shih Chi/Shiji* of Ssu-ma Ch'ien/Sima Qian.

6　Joseph Needham, *Science and Civilisation in China, Vol. 1: Introductory orientations* (Cambridge, New York, New Rochelle, Melbourne, Sydney: Cambridge University Press, 1988 reprint of 1961 edn, first published 1954), p. 89.

7　*Ibid.*, p. 84.

8　For the full range of topics used, see David N. Keightley, "Shang Oracle-Bone Inscriptions" in Edward L. Shaughnessy (ed.), *New Sources of Early Chinese History: An introduction to the reading of inscriptions and manuscripts* (Berkeley, California: Society for the Study of Early China and The Institute of East Asian Studies, University of California, 1997), pp. 30–41.

9　Sarah Allan, *The Shape of the Turtle: Myth, art and cosmos in early China* (Albany, New York: State University of New York Press, 1991), p. 113.

10　David N. Keightley, "Late Shang Divination: The Magico-Religious Legacy" in Henry Rosemont Jr. (ed.), *Explorations in Early Chinese*

Cosmology. Journal of the American Academy of Religion Studies vol. 50, no. 2 (Chicago, California: Scholars Press 1984), pp. 13–14.
11 *Ibid.*, p. 20.
12 Richard J. Smith, *Fortune-Tellers and Philosophers: Divination in traditional Chinese society* (Boulder, San Francisco, Oxford: Westview Press, 1991), p. 14.
13 Keightley, "Shang Oracle-Bone Inscriptions", p. 53.
14 Keightley, "Late Shang Divination", p. 22.
15 *Ibid.*, p. 16.
16 Allan, *The Shape of the Turtle*, p. 46.
17 Donald Bishop, "Chinese Thought before Confucius" in Donald H. Bishop (ed.), *Chinese Thought: An introduction* (Delhi: Motilal Banarsidass, 2001), first published 1985), p. 7.
18 See Allan, *The Shape of the Turtle*, p. 20.
19 Henri Maspero, *Taoism and Chinese Religion*, translated by Frank A. Kierman, Jr. (Amherst: University of Massachusetts Press, 1981, first published in 1971 as *Le Taoisme et les religions chinoises*), p. 4.
20 Henri Maspero, *China in Antiquity*, translated by Frank A. Kierman, Jr. (Folkestone, Kent: Dawson, 1978, first published in 1927 as *La Chine Antique*), p. 162.
21 Martin Palmer, *The Elements of Taoism* (Shaftesbury, Dorset and Rockport, Massachusetts: Element, 1991), p. 14.
22 The word "shaman" may have some connection with the Sanskrit word *sramana*, a word that is associated with ascetic wanderers, and with the Chinese term *hsien-men/xianmen*. See Joseph Needham, *Science and Civilisation in China, Vol. 2: History of scientific thought* (Cambridge: Cambridge University Press, 1956), p. 133.
23 The synonymy between shamans and sorcerers is variously asserted and denied. Eva Wong considers them to be separate because the shaman invites a spirit to enter his or her body at will, whereas sorcerers are possessed by the spirit. Eva Wong, *The Shambhala Guide to Taoism* (Boston and London: Shambhala, 1997), pp. 14–15.
24 Julia Ching, *Chinese Religions* (Basingstoke, Hampshire and London: The Macmillan Press, 1993), p. 49.
25 Maspero, *China in Antiquity*, p. 132.
26 *Ibid.*, p. 133.
27 Peter Hessler, "The New Story of China's Ancient Past" in *National Geographic* (Washington D.C.: National Geographic Society, July, 2003), p. 64.
28 *Ibid.*, p. 71.
29 See Keightley, "Late Shang Divination", p. 13.
30 *Ibid.*, p. 26.
31 Edward L. Shaugnessy, "Western Zhou Bronze Inscriptions" in Shaughnessy (ed.), *New Sources of Early Chinese History*, p. 84.
32 Gilbert L. Mattos, "Eastern Zhou Bronze Inscriptions" in Shaughnessy

(ed.), *New Sources of Early Chinese History*, *ibid.*, p. 86.

33 *Ibid.*, p. 88.

34 Named after the chronicle of these years, the *Spring and Autumn Annals*.

35 Needham, *Science and Civilisation in China, Vol. 1*, p. 96.

36 Maspero, *Taoism and Chinese Religion*, p. 16.

37 John S. Major, "Shang-ti" in Mircea Eliade (ed.), *Encyclopedia of Religion* (hereafter *ER*, New York and London: Macmillan Publishing Company, 1987), vol. 13, p. 223.

38 *Ibid.*, pp. 223–4.

39 *Shu*: Kao Tsung 3, translator D. Howard Smith, *Chinese Religions* (New York, Chicago, San Francisco: Holt, Rhinehart and Winston, 1970 reprint of 1968 edn), p. 19. It is easy to see from words such as these how a later Buddhist doctrine of *karma* could be incorporated into the Chinese psyche.

40 The prevalence of an ongoing belief in demons, for example, is reflected in more recent fears. When Mildred Cable and Francesca French were preparing for an expedition into the Gobi Desert in the early part of the last century, the local people of then Kiayükwan were terrified of the demons of the desert. "They call out", said one young man of the desert demons, "just as a man would shout if he wanted help, but those who turn away from the track to answer them never find anyone, and the next call is always a little farther from the path, for those voices will lead a man on, but they will never call him back to the right way." Mildred Cable with Francesca French, *The Gobi Desert* (London: Landsborough Publications, 1958, first published 1943), p. 12.

41 Female *wu* were still prevalent in the second century when they were employed in the performance of ancestral sacrifices. By the end of the T'ang/Tang dynasty, however, they no longer featured in state praxis and became a persecuted, though persistent, sector of social and religious life, branching out into all sorts of practices.

42 Smith, *Fortune-Tellers and Philosophers*, pp. 17–18.

43 *Ibid.*, p. 18.

44 The year was based on the cycles of the moon, with the addition of an extra lunar period from time to time in order to harmonize with the solar year.

45 Maspero, *China in Antiquity*, p. 107.

46 Matthias Eder, *Chinese Religion*, Asian Folklore Studies Mongraph no. 6 (Tokyo: The Society for Asian Folklore, 1973), p. 19.

47 Derk Bodde, *Essays on Chinese Civilization*, edited and introduced by Charles Le Blanc and Dorothy Borei (Princeton, New Jersey and Guilford, Surrey: Princeton University Press, 1981), p. 133.

48 Bodde, "Dominant Ideas in the Formation of the Chinese Culture" in Bodde, *Essays on Chinese Civilization*, p. 132.

49 Keightley, "Late Shang Divination", p. 25.

50 Bishop, "Introduction" in Bishop (ed.), *Chinese Thought*, p. 174.

51 Bodde, "Dominant Ideas in the Formation of Chinese Culture", p. 133.

52 Eder, *Chinese Religion*, p. 37.

2 Rhythms of the Universe

1 Carl Jung, *Foreword* in Richard Wilhelm, translator, *I Ching or Book of Changes*, translated into English by Cary F. Baynes (London: Penguin, Arkana, 1989 third edn, first published 1950).

2 Richard J. Smith, *Fortune-tellers and Philosphers: Divination in traditional Chinese society* (Boulder, San Francisco, Oxford: Westview Press, 1991), p. 15.

3 Richard Rutt, *The Book of Changes (Zhouyi): A Bronze Age document translated with introduction and notes.* Durham East-Asia Series no. 1 (London: RoutledgeCurzon, 2002 reprint of 1996 edn), pp. 30–1.

4 In other words he took some ideas from his own body and others from things extraneous to his body.

5 *Ta-chuan /Dazhuan* 2:1, translator Wilhelm, *I Ching or Book of Changes*, p. 328.

6 Henri Maspero, *Taoism and Chinese Religion*, translated from French by Frank A. Kierman, Jr. (Amherst: The University of Massachusetts Press, 1981, first published in 1971 as *Le Taoïsme et les religions chinoises*), p. 59.

7 Rutt, *The Book of Changes (Zhouyi)*, p. 29.

8 *Ibid.*, pp. 97–8.

9 See Xinzhong Yao and Helene McMurtrie, "History and Wisdom of the Book of Changes: New Scholarship and Richard Rutt's Translation", *Journal of Contemporary Religion*, 14 (1999), p. 135.

10 Rutt, *The Book of Changes (Zhouyi)*, p. 122.

11 Stephen Karcher, *Total I Ching: Myths for change* (London: Time Warner Books, 2003), p. ix.

12 In 1973, a silk manuscript of the *I Ching/Yijing*, dating to second century Han times, came to light at Ma-wang-tui/Mawangdui. In this text the hexagrams were in a different order.

13 The second, third and fourth lines from the bottom, and the third, fourth and fifth lines from the bottom.

14 For a full account of how this method is done, see Rutt, *The Book of Changes (Zhouyi)*, pp. 158–66.

15 In pre-revolution China, Chinese coins were round, representing Heaven with a square hole in the centre, representing Earth. One side was inscribed and was considered to be *yin*, the uninscribed side being *yang*. With coins outside China it is often difficult to ascertain which should be the inscribed side. Perhaps the side giving its value should be regarded as inscribed. But most regard the head side as *yang* and the reverse side as *yin*.

16 6 = moving *yin*; 7 = *yang*; 8 = *yin*; 9 = moving *yang*.

17 Joseph Needham, *Science and Civilisation in China, Vol. 2: History of scientific thought* (Cambridge: Cambridge University Press, 1956), p. 337.

18 *Ibid.*, p. 336.

19 Laurence G. Thompson, *Chinese Religion: An introduction* (Belmont, California: Wadsworth Publishing Company, 1989 reprint of 1979 edn), p. 3.

20 Sarah Allan, *The Shape of the Turtle: Myth, art, and cosmos in early China* (Albany, New York: State University of New York Press, 1991), p. 17.

21 *Ibid.*, p. 73.

22 *Ibid.*, p. 176.

23 See Fung Yu-lan, *A History of Chinese Philosophy, Vol. 2: The period of classical learning (from the second century BC to the twentieth century AD)*, translated by Derk Bodde (Princeton, New Jersey: Princeton University Press, 1983 reprint, first published in English in 1953. First published in Chinese in 1934), p. 9.

24 Translator Fung Yu-lan, *A History of Chinese Philosophy, Vol. 1: The period of the philosophers (from the beginnings to circa 100 BC.)*, translated by Derk Bodde (Princeton, New Jersey: Princeton University Press, 1983 reprint of second English edn 1952), p. 160.

25 Jean C. Cooper, *Taoism: The Way of the mystic*, Wellingborough, Northamptonshire: Crucible, 1990 revised and expanded edn, first published 1972), p. 40.

26 From Liu I-ming/Liu Yiming, *Eight Elements of the Spiritual House*, translator Thomas Cleary, *The Taoist I Ching* (Boston, Massachusetts and London: Shambhala, 1986), p. 20.

27 From Huang Yüan-ch'i/Huang Yuanqi, *Annals of the Hall of Blissful Development*, translator Cleary, *ibid.*, pp. 15–16.

28 From Liu I-ming/Liu Yiming, *Eight Elements of the Spiritual House*, translator Cleary, *ibid.*, p. 20.

29 A term favoured by Vitaly A. Rubin, "The Concepts of *Wu-Hsing* and *Yin-Yang*", *Journal of Chinese Philosophy*, 17 (1982), p. 141.

30 *Tao Te Ching/Daodejing* 2.

31 Chung-Ying Cheng, "Chinese Metaphysics as Non-metaphysics: Confucian and Taoist Insights into the Nature of Reality", in Robert Allinson (ed.), *Understanding the Chinese Mind: The philosophical roots* (Oxford, New York and Hong Kong: Oxford University Press, 1989), p. 177.

32 Translator Fung Yu-lan, *A Short History of Chinese Philosophy* (London: Collier Macmillan and New York: The Free Press, 1948), p. 134.

33 Fritjof Capra, *The Tao of Physics: An exploration of the parallels between modern physics and eastern mysticism* (London: Flamingo, 1990 impression of 1983 edn, first published 1975), p. 157.

34 *Tao Te Ching/Daodejing* 36.

35 Jean Cooper, *Yin and Yang: The Taoist harmony of opposites* (Wellingborough, Northamptonshire: The Aquarian Press, 1981), p. 17.

36 *Tao Te Ching/Daodejing* 22.

37 See A. C. Graham, *Yin-Yang and the Nature of Correlative Thinking*. Occasional Paper and Monograph Series no. 6 (Singapore: The Institute of East Asian Philosophies, 1989 reprint of 1986 edn), pp. 27–8.

38 See Thompson, *Chinese Religion*, p. 32. Numerically, *yang* numbers are always odd, because they have undivided lines. The symbol is one of

strength. Conversely, *yin* lines are weak, having no middle. They are always even numbers and thought of as "unlucky". The first odd number (other than one, unity) is three, and is assigned to *yang*. Nine, or three *yang* lines, are the optimum *yang*, the optimum light, and are indicative of Heaven, the *Ch'ien/Qian* trigram.

39 Derk Bodde, *Essays on Chinese Civilization*, edited and translated by Charles Le Blanc and Dorothy Borei (Princeton, New Jersey: Princeton University Press, 1981), p. 279.

40 *Ibid.*, p. 280.

41 See R. H. Mathews, *Mathew's Chinese–English Dictionary* (Cambridge, Massachusetts: Harvard University Press, Revised American Version 2000, first published 1931), pp. 409–10.

42 See Graham, *Yin-Yang and the Nature of Correlative Thinking*, p. 47.

43 *Ibid.*, p. 74.

44 Some, however, much prefer the translation "Elements". See, for example, Rubin, "The Concepts of *Wu-Hsing* and *Yin-Yang*", p. 132.

45 Smith, *Fortune-tellers and Philosophers*, p. 15.

46 Translator Fung Yu-lan, *A History of Chinese Philosophy, Vol. 1*, p. 163.

47 See Rubin, "The Concepts of *Wu-Hsing* and *Yin–Yang*", p. 151.

48 Graham, *Yin-Yang and the Nature of Correlative Thinking*, p. 52.

49 The *Monthly Commands*, indeed, reflects such a separation.

50 Allan, *The Shape of the Turtle*, p. 102.

51 *Ibid.*, p. 101.

52 Not all were enamoured by the extensive theories applied to the Five Agents. Wang Ch'ung/Wang Chong in the first century was one who applied rationalism to the theories of his day. In his essay *Wu-shih/Wushi The Nature of Things*, he pointed out that there were many anomalies in the Five Agents correlates. Animals associated with the Agents did not have the same characteristic power to overcome. Thus Water, for example, may overcome Fire, but the rat, which is associated with Water, cannot chase away a horse associated with Fire. Nature, he showed, does not in fact support the Five Agents theory. Then, too, Chia K'uei/Jia Kui, also in the first century, pointed out that irregularity and not harmony characterized the heavens, and that the future could not be predicted by aligning oneself to the unbalanced macrocosm. A little later, Ch'ang Heng/Chang Heng suggested that the earth was round and not square, and that natural disasters were more to do with earthly irregularities than imbalances between Earth and Heaven. So one must not think that the Five Agents theory was unchallenged. Yet it passed into Chinese belief and practice.

53 Cheng Xinnong (ed.), *Chinese Acupuncture and Moxibustion* (Beijing: Foreign Languages Press, 1999 revised edn, first published 1987), p. 24.

54 Angus C. Graham, *Disputers of the Tao: Philosophical argument in ancient China* (La Salle, Illinois: Open Court, 1991 reprint of 1989 edn), p. 350.

55 *Ibid*, p. 355.

56 Conrad Schirokauer, *A Brief History of Chinese Civilization* (San Diego,

New York, Chicago, Austin, Waschington D.C., London, Sydney, Tokyo, Toronto: Harcourt Brace, 1991), p. 73.

3 Confucianism

1 Benjamin Schwartz, "Some Polarities in Confucian Thought" in Arthur F. Wright, *Confucianism and Chinese Civilization* (Stanford, California: Stanford University Press, 1975, first published 1959), p. 4.

2 Wm. Theodore de Bary, *The Trouble with Confucianism* (Cambridge, Massachusetts, London: Harvard University Press, 1996, first published 1991), p. xi.

3 Jacques Gernet, *A History of Chinese Civilisation Vol. 1*, translated by J. R. Foster and Charles Hartman (London: The Folio Society, 2002), p. 80. This two-volume work was first published in French as a single volume entitled *Le Monde chinois* (Paris: Librairie Armand Colin, 1972).

4 Robert Eno, *The Confucian Creation of Heaven: Philosophy and the defense of ritual mastery* (Albany: State University of New York), pp. 2–3.

5 Wm. Theodore de Bary and Irene Bloom (eds), *Sources of Chinese Tradition Volume 1: From earliest times to 1600* (New York: Columbia University Press, second revised edn 1999, first published 1960), p. 41.

6 Xinzhong Yao, *An Introduction to Confucianism* (Cambridge, New York, Melbourne, Madrid, Capetown: Cambridge University Press, fourth, 2005, printing of first 2000 publication), p. 21.

7 *Ibid.*

8 *Ibid.*

9 Wm Theodore de Bary, Wing-tzit Chan and Burton Watson (eds), *Sources of Chinese Tradition Vol. 1* (New York: Columbia University Press, 1960), p. 15.

10 Fung Yu-Lan, *A Short History of Chinese Philosophy* (New York: Macmillan, 1966), p. 38 footnote, reminds us that: "The word 'Tzu' or 'Master' is a polite suffix added to names of most philosophers of the Chou Dynasty, such as Chuang Tzu, Hsün Tzu, etc., and meaning 'Master Chuang,' 'Master Hsün,' etc."

11 Julia Ching, *Chinese Religions* (London: Macmillan, 1993), p. 54.

12 de Bary, *The Trouble with Confucianism*, p. ix *et passim*.

13 Herrlee G. Creel, *Chinese Thought: From Confucius to Mao Tsê-tung* (London: Methuen, 1962, first published 1954), p. 52.

14 Vergilius Ture Anselm Ferm (ed.), *An Encyclopedia of Religion* (Westport, CT: Greenwood Press, 1976), p. 150.

15 Fung Yu-Lan, *A Short History of Chinese Philosophy*, p. 3.

16 Gernet, *A History of Chinese Civilisation*, Vol. 11, p. 538.

17 de Bary, *The Trouble with Confucianism*, pp. ix–xiv.

18 Yao, *An Introduction to Confucianism*, p. 42.

19 Ninian Smart, *The World's Religions* (Cambridge University Press, 1992, first published 1989), pp. 10–21.

20 de Bary, *The Trouble with Confucianism*, p. 35.

21 Daniel Goleman, *Emotional Intelligence: Why it can matter more than IQ* (London: Bloomsbury, 1996).

22 Goleman, *ibid.,* p. 311 note 4, acknowledges his debt to Paul Ekman's key essay, "An Argument for Basic Emotions", *Cognition and Emotion*, 6, 1992, pp. 169–200.

23 See de Bary, *The Trouble with Confucianism*, p. 17.

24 Robert E. Allinson, "An Overview of the Chinese Mind" in R. E. Allinson (ed.), *Understanding the Chinese Mind: The philosophical roots* (Oxford: Oxford University Press, 1989), p. 15. See also note 6, p. 25.

25 Kenneth Dean, *Lord of the Three in One: The spread of a cult in southeast China* (Princeton, New Jersey; Chichester, West Sussex: Princeton University Press, 1998).

26 Yao, *An Introduction to Confucianism*, p. 44.

27 *Ibid.* See further, Xinzhong Yao, *Confucianism and Christianity: A comparative study of jen and agape* (Brighton, Sussex and Portland, Oregon: Sussex Academic Press, 1996), *passim.*

28 Martin Palmer, *The Elements of Taoism* (Shaftsbury, Dorset: and Rockport, Massachusetts: Element, 1991), p. 71.

29 Yao, *An Introduction to Confucianism,* p. 29.

30 Confucius, *Analects* 16:9 translated by Deborah Sommer (ed.), *Chinese Religion: An anthology of sources* (New York and Oxford: Oxford University Press, 1995), p. 43.

31 *Ibid.*, 14:29, translated by Sommer, p. 43.

32 *Ibid.*, 15:20, translated by Sommer, p. 44.

33 de Bary, *The Trouble with Confucianism*, p. 28.

34 *Ibid.*, p. 20.

35 Howard D. Smith, *Chinese Religions* (New York: Holt, Rinehart and Winston, 1970 reprint of 1968 edn), p. 33.

36 Translated by de Bary and Bloom, *Sources of Chinese Tradition Volume 1*, p. 46.

37 Creel, *Chinese Thought,* p. 43.

38 de Bary, *The Trouble with Confucianism*, p. 35.

39 Arthur F. Wright (ed.), *Confucianism and Chinese Civilization*, p. ix.

40 Schwartz, "Some Polarities in Confucian Thought", p. 5.

41 Translated by de Bary and Bloom, *Sources of Chinese Tradition*, p. 59.

42 A view taken by Confucius' outstanding pupil, Tseng-tzu/Zengzi.

43 Smith, *Chinese Religions*, p. 42.

44 Julia Ching, "Confucius" in *Encyclopedia of Religion* (16 vols) edited by Mircea Eliade (New York: Macmillan, 1987), vol. 4, p. 41.

45 Yao, *An Introduction to Confucianism*, p. 47.

46 de Bary, *The Trouble with Confucianism*, p. xi.

47 Yao, *An Introduction to Confucianism*, pp. 4–9.

48 Schwartz, "Some Polarities in Confucian Thought", p. 3.

49 Translated by Deborah Sommer (ed.), *Chinese Religion: An anthology of sources*, p. 58.

50 Schwartz, "Some Polarities in Confucian thought", p. 9.
51 Fung Yu-Lan, *A Short History of Chinese Philosophy*, p. 207.
52 A sentiment not dissimilar to the twentieth century theory of Daniel Goleman. See notes 21 and 22 above.
53 Yao, *An Introduction to Confucianism*, p. 8.

4 Classical Taoism

1 Various paradigms are offered by modern scholarship on how to divide Taoism. The bifurcation suggested here is the simplest one. Some add folk Taoism as a third division, or even new Taoism. More specialized divisions have been put forward by Russell Kirkland and Livia Kohn, see Livia Kohn (ed.), *Daoism Handbook* (Leiden, Boston, Köln: Brill, 2000), pp. xxix–xxx.
2 Ssu-ma T'an/Sima Tan, translated by Wu Yao-yü, and cited in *The Taoist Tradition in Chinese Thought*, translated by Laurence G. Thompson, edited by Gary Seaman. *San Chiao Li Ts'e, Part 1* (Los Angeles: Ethnographics Press, University of Southern California, 1991), pp. 1–2.
3 Robert E. Allinson, "An Overview of the Chinese Mind" in Robert E. Allinson (ed.), *Understanding the Chinese Mind: The philosophical roots* (Oxford, New York and Hong Kong: Oxford University Press, 1989), p. 15.
4 Toshihiko Izutsu, *Sufism and Taoism: A comparative study of key philosophical concepts* (Berkeley, Los Angeles, London: University of California Press, 1983), p. 372.
5 Benjamin Schwartz, "The Thought of the *Tao Te Ching*" in Livia Kohn and Michael LaFargue (eds), *Lao-tzu and the* Tao-te-ching" (Albany, New York: State University of New York Press, 1998), p. 190.
6 See Angus C. Graham, *Disputers of the Tao: Philosophical argument in ancient China* (La Salle, Illinois: Open Court, 1991 reprint of 1989 edn), p. 204.
7 Harold D. Roth, "The *Laozi* in the Context of Early Daoist Mystical Praxis" in Mark Csikszentmihalyi and Philip J. Ivanhoe (eds), *Religious and Philosophical Aspects of the* Laozi (Albany, New York: State University of New York Press, 1999), p. 60.
8 Mark Csikszentmihalyi, "Mysticism and Apophatic Discourse in the *Laozi*" in Csikszentmihalyi and Ivanhoe (eds), *Religious and Philosophical Aspects of the* Laozi, p. 53.
9 Graham, *Disputers of the Tao*, p. 218.
10 See Michael LaFargue and Julian Pas, "On Translating the *Tao-te-ching*" in Kohn and LaFargue (eds), *Lao-tzu and the* Tao-te-ching, pp. 277–301.
11 See R. Peerenboom, "Cosmogony: The Taoist Way", *Journal of Chinese Philosophy* 17 (1990), pp. 158–60.
12 Robert G. Henricks, "Re-exploring the Analogy of the Dao and the Field" in Csiksentmihalyi and Ivanhoe (eds), *Religious and Philosophical Aspects of the* Laozi, pp. 161–2.
13 Michael LaFargue, *Tao and method: A reasoned approach to the Tao Te Ching* (Albany, New York: State University of New York Press, 1994), p. 127.

14 The Kuo-tien/Guodian text was discovered in 1993. Its contents are parallel to parts of the first sixty-six chapters of the traditional text.

15 For a summary of the authorship and dating of the *Tao Te Ching/Daodejing* see Alan Chan, "The *Daodejing* and its Tradition" in Kohn (ed.), *Daoist Handbook*, pp. 4–6, and for the textual recension pp. 9–17.

16 *Lao Tzu Tao Te Ching: The book of meaning and life*, translation and commentary by Richard Wilhelm, translated into English by H. G. Ostwald (London, New York, Ontario, Toronto, Auckland: Arkana,1990 reprint of 1985 edn), p. 98.

17 Burton Watson in the *Foreword* to Victor H. Mair (ed.), *Experimental Essays on Chuang-tzu*. Centre for Asian and Pacific Studies (University of Hawaii: University of Hawaii Press, 1983).

18 Martin Palmer, translator, with Elizabeth Breuilly, Chang Wai Ming and Jay Ramsay, *The Book of Chuang Tzu* (London, New York, Ontario, Toronto, Auckland: Penguin, Arkana, 1996), p. xv.

19 For a more detailed account of authorship, see Harold Roth, "Who Compiled the *Chuang Tzu*" in Henry Rosemont Jr. (ed.), *Chinese Texts and Philosophical Contexts: Essays dedicated to Angus C. Graham* (La Salle, Illinois: Open Court, 1991), pp. 80–128.

20 Such was Angus Graham's division of the text, though there are others. There is some evidence of a longer version of the text – some 52 chapters – that existed before Kuo Hsiang/Guo Xiang edited the text and reduced the chapters to 33. See Angus Graham, *Chuang-Tzu: The Inner Chapters* (London, Boston, Sydney, New Zealand: Unwin Paperbacks, 1989, first published 1981), p. 27.

21 Palmer, *The Book of Chuang Tzu*, pp. xix–xx.

22 Sam Hamill and J. P. Seaton, translators and eds, *The Essential Chuang Tzu* (Boston, Massachusetts: Shambhala, 1998), p. xix.

23 Robert E. Allinson, *Chuang-Tzu for Spiritual Transformation: An analysis of the inner chapters* (Albany, New York: State University of New York Press, 1989), p. 7.

24 *Ibid.*, p. 11.

25 He may even have been the author, see Russell Kirkland, "The History of Taoism: A New Outline: Research Note", *Journal of Chinese Religions* 30 (2002), p. 179.

26 Alan Watts, *Tao: The watercourse Way* (London, New York, Victoria, Ontario, Auckland: Penguin, 1975), p. 39. Watts likened the movement to going (*yang*) and pausing (*yin*).

27 R. H. Mathews, *Mathews' Chinese–English Dictionary* (Cambridge, Massachusetts: Harvard University Press, revised American edn 2000, first published 1931), p. 884.

28 *Ibid.*, p. 882.

29 In this chapter the Chinese term *Tao* will be retained rather than its translation of "Way". We also want to avoid the tendency to project the concept of *Tao* to a transcendent Absolute in any sense of an indescribable *divine*

entity. Certainly, there will be evidence later that such a move has taken place in the meanderings of Taoist evolution. It is important to avoid the link here because we do not think there is much evidence for it in the books attributed to the Old Masters. Thereby the concept of *Tao* is kept as open and fluid as possible at this juncture. Dropping the definite article from *the Tao* aids in pulling the concept away from the embraces of a divine ultimate that so many wish it to have. It will be for the reader to draw his or her own conclusions as to the ultimate nature or non-nature of *Tao*.

30 The word *tao* occurs three times in the first line, and in the second case is normally translated as "told", "spoken of", "expressed".

31 *Chuang-Tzu/Zhuangzi* chapter 2, translator Graham, *Chuang-tzu.*

32 *Chuang-tzu/Zhuangzi*, chapter 6, translator Palmer, *The Book of Chuang-tzu.*

33 LaFargue, *Tao and Method*, p. 177.

34 *Ibid.*, p. 257.

35 For an analysis of Wang Pi/Wang Bi's commentary on the *Tao Te Ching/Daodejing*, see Alan K. L. Chan, "A Tale of Two Commentaries: Ho-shang-kung and Wang Pi on the *Lao-tzu*" in Kohn and LaFargue (eds), *Lao-tzu and the* Tao-te-ching, pp. 100–17.

36 Chad Hansen, *A Daoist Theory of Chinese Thought: A philosophical interpretation* (Oxford: Oxford University Press, 1992), p. 268.

37 See Norman J. Girardot, *Myth and Meaning in Early Taoism: The theme of chaos (hun-tun)* (Berkeley, Los Angeles, London: University of California Press, 1988 reprint of 1983 edn), p. 55.

38 Graham, *Chuang-Tzu*, p. 18.

39 In the Neo-Taoism of the third century CE, *Tao* and the One were merged by Wang Pi/Wang Bi, in particular, who saw the world as emerging from the One as *Tao*. Here, the One becomes the Supreme Ultimate, *T'ai Chi/Taiji*, the cause and essence of all. While *Tao* retains much of its original mystery, it moves closer to the realm of form in Wang Pi/Wang Bi's view of it. It becomes One as opposed to two, or One as opposed to many – a dualism of Non-Being and Being. Such deleting of the principle *Tao produced the One* was, thus, responsible for a radical change in the concept of *Tao* from the third century on. However, Girardot is suspicious about the *Tao Te Ching/Daodejing*'s statement of "*Tao* produced the One", since he thinks elsewhere in the text (chapters 10, 14, 22, 39) that *Tao* is identified as the One. What is more, the *Huai-nan-tzu/Huainanzi* omits the line. Girardot, in fact, prefers to accept the One as *Tao* in its pre-creative chaotic state. See Girardot, *Myth and Meaning in Early Taoism*, pp. 57–8.

40 Nevertheless, we have to reckon with the fact that reference to *yin* and *yang* occurs only once in the *Tao Te Ching/Daodejing*, and that other interpretations of the two may be possible.

41 See Livia Kohn, *Early Chinese Mysticism: Philosophy and soteriology in the Taoist tradition* (Princeton, New Jersey: Princeton University Press, 1992), p. 47, and Terry F. Kleeman, "Daoism and the Quest for Order", in Norman

J. Girardot, James Miller and Liu Xiaogan (eds), *Daoism and Ecology: Ways within a cosmic landscape* (Cambridge, Massachusetts: Harvard University Press, 2001), p. 62.

42 Girardot, *Myth and Meaning in Early Taoism*, p. 59.

43 *Ibid.*, p. 62.

44 Julian Pas has noted the awkwardness of *yin* and *yang* blending with *t'ai chi/taiji* to produce the three, see "Yin–Yang Polarity: A binocular vision", *Asian Thought and Society* 8 (1983), p. 195.

45 Isabelle Robinet, "The Diverse Interpretations of the *Laozi*" in Csikszentmihalyi and Ivanhoe (eds), *Religious and Philosophical Aspects of the* Laozi, p. 145.

46 In later times there were many other variations of pre-Taoist cosmology. See, for example, the outline of Han cosmology from the *Huai-nan-tzu/Huainanzi* given by Julian F. Pas in cooperation with Man Kam Leung, *Historical Dictionary of Taoism* (Lanham, Middlesex and London: The Scarecrow Press, 1998), pp. 168–70. The account here is essentially the view of the *Tao Te Ching/Daodejing* and the *Chuang-tzu/Zhuangzi*.

47 Kohn, *Early Chinese Mysticism*, p. 163. This, we would have to accept, is a mystical description of returning. LaFargue, however, would disagree. He thinks that "return", "turning back" is a process of self-cultivation to the still mind, not a return to a metaphysical cosmic source of *Tao*. In his view, returning is a reversal of the mind that is involved in the myriad events of life to an original stillness of mind, see *Tao and Method*, pp. 227–8. As we have seen, he sees *Tao* as a convenient term to explain the inner experiences of the "self-cultivated". As such, it would be synonymous with *feelings* of stillness, oneness, equilibrium and the like.

48 Hansen, however, opposes any sense of unity in the classical literature positing not one but many different *taos* that are specific to different contexts. See *A Daoist Theory of Chinese Thought*, pp. 269, 285, 292–303 *passim*.

49 *Chuang-tzu/Zhuangzi* chapter 2:3, translator Thomas Merton, *The Way of Chuang Tzu* (New York: New Directions, 1965), p. 42.

50 Jonathan Star, *Lao Tzu Tao Te Ching: The definitive edition* (New York: Jeremy P. Tarcher, 2001), p. 260.

51 Arthur Waley, *The Way and Its Power: The Tao Tê Ching and its place in Chinese Thought* (London, Sydney and Wellington: Unwin Paperbacks, 1987 reissue of 1977 edn, first published 1934), pp. 31–2.

52 Wilhelm, *Lao Tzu Tao Te Ching*, p. 84.

53 Harold H. Oshima, "A Metaphysical Analysis of the Concept of Mind in the *Chuang-tzu*" in Victor Mair (ed.), *Experimental Essays on Chuang-tzu*, Asian Studies at Hawaii no. 29 (Honolulu: University of Hawaii Press, 1983), p. 69.

54 Roger T. Ames, "The Local and the Focal in Realizing a Daoist World" in Girardot, Miller and Xiaogan (eds), *Daoism and Ecology*, p. 278.

55 Mathews, *Mathews' Chinese–English Dictionary*, p. 1048.

56 Paul Carus, translator, *The Teachings of Lao-tzu: The Tao Te Ching* (London, Sydney, Aukland, Johannesburg: Rider, 1999 revised edn, first published 1913), p. 22.

57 Liu Xiaogan, "Non-Action and the Environment Today" in Girardot, Miller and Xiaogan (eds), *Daoism and Ecology*, p. 334.

58 As a modern example of the unnatural path, consider the following: "One of the main reasons for the continued rain forest conflagration in Indonesia is 'industrialized burning' set by plantation owners and subcontractors, which has devoured at least two million hectares of the world's second-largest region of rain forest. For every hectare of burned land, one hundred hectares is engulfed in smoke stretching from Thailand to the Philippines to New Guinea and the northern coast of Australia. Smoke has affected people's health right across the region. An estimated forty thousand Indonesians have suffered respiratory problems, and up to one million have suffered eye irritations. Smoke has been blamed for ship and air crashes that killed about three hundred people." Liu Xiaogan, *ibid.*, p. 318.

59 Liu Xiaogan, "Naturalness (*Tzu-jan*), the Core Value in Taoism: Its Ancient Meaning and its Significance Today" in Kohn and LaFargue (eds), *Lao-tzu and the* Tao-te-ching, p. 211.

60 *Ibid.*, pp. 217–18.

61 *Chuang-Tzu/Zhuangzi* chapter 2, translator Graham, *Chuang-Tzu*, p. 59.

62 *Lieh-tzu/Liezi* chapter 4, translator Angus C. Graham, *The Book of Lieh-tzu: A classic of the Tao* (New York: Columbia University Press, 1990 reprint, first published 1981), p. 90.

63 *Tao Te Ching/Daodejing* 28, translators Gia-fu Feng and Jane English, *Lao Tsu Tao Te Ching* (New York: Vintage books, 1989, first published 1972).

64 Girardot, *Myth and Meaning in Early Taoism*, p. 75.

65 Philip J. Ivanhoe, "The Concept of *de* ("Virtue") in the *Laozi*" in Csikszentmihalyi and Ivanhoe (eds), *Religious and Philosophical Aspects of the* Laozi, p. 242.

5 Buddhism

1 Henri Maspero, *Taoism and Chinese Religion*, translated from French by Frank A. Kierman Jr. (Amhurst: The University of Massachusetts Press, 1981, first published in 1971 as *Le Taoïsme et les religions chinoises*), p. 38.

2 *Ibid.*, p. 39.

3 *Ibid.*, p. 258.

4 Tenshin Fletcher and David Scott, *Way of Zen* (London: Vega, 2001), p. 37.

5 Isabelle Robinet, *Taoism: Growth of a religion*, translated by Phyllis Brooks (Stanford, California: Stanford University Press, 1997, first published in 1992 as *Histoire du Taoïsme des origins au XIV siècle*), p. 188.

6 Maspero, *Taoism and Chinese Religion*, p. 252.

7 Burton Watson (translator), *The Lotus Sutra* (New York: Columbia University Press, 1993), p. xvi.

8 Daisaku Ikeda, *Buddhism: The first millennium*, translated by Burton Watson (Tokyo, New York, London: Kodansha International, 1977), p. 126.

9 W. E. Soothill, *The Lotus of the Wonderful Law* (London: Curzon Press, 1987), pp. 3–4.

10 Susan Mattis, "Chih-hi and the Subtle Dharma of the Lotus Sutra: Emptiness or Buddha Nature?" in Gene Reeves (ed.), *A Buddhist Kaleidoscope: Essays on the Lotus Sutra* (Tokyo: Kosei, 2002), p. 247. Although if the term "Buddha-nature" is not mentioned in the *Lotus Sutra*, the *nature of the Buddha* is, and that nature is said in the *Lotus* to be the same in all things, that is to say, tantamount to Buddha-nature.

11 *Ibid.*

12 *The Art of Living: An Introduction to Nichiren Shoshu Buddhism. UK Express*, no. 180 (Richmond: NSUK), p. 24. See also D. Bloomfield, "Ichinen" *UK Express* no. 319, January 1998), p. 6.

13 Stephan Schuhmacher and Gert Woerner (eds), *The Rider Encyclopedia of Eastern Philosophy and Religion* (London: Rider, 1989), p. 373.

14 Richard H. Robinson and Willard L. Johnson, *The Buddhist Religion: An historical introduction* (London, New York: Wadsworth, fourth edn 1997, first published 1970), p. 190.

15 Kenneth Ch'en, *Buddhism in China: A historical survey* (Princeton, New Jersey: Princeton University Press, 1973, first published 1964), p. 320.

16 Erik Zurcher, "Amitabha" in *Encyclopedia of Religion* (16 vols) edited by Mircea Eliade (New York: Macmillan, 1987, hereafter, ER), vol 1, p. 235.

17 Charles S. Prebish, *Historical Dictionary of Buddhism* (London: Scarecrow, 1993), pp. 168 and 220.

18 Sangharakshita, *A Survey of Buddhism* (London: Tharpa, 1987), p. 356.

19 Zurcher, "Amitabha", p. 235

20 Hisao Inagaki, *The Three Pure Land Sutras: A study and translation from Chinese* (Kyoto: Nagata Bunshodo, second revised edn 1995, first published 1994), Larger Sutra 7 (18), p. 243.

21 See Burton Watson, *The Lotus Sutra*, pp. 107–16.

22 *The Smaller Sukhavati-vyuha Sutra* 10, translated by F. Max Muller in *Sacred Books of the East*, vol. 49 (Oxford: Oxford University Press, 1886, reprinted by Motilal Banarsidass: Delhi, 1981).

23 Zurcher, "Amitabha", p. 235.

24 See Alfred Bloom, *Strategies for Modern Living: A commentary with the text of the Tannisho* (Berkeley: Numata Center for Buddhist Translation and Research, 1992). See also entry "Tanni Sho" in *A Dictionary of Buddhist Terms and Concepts* (Tokyo: Nichiren Shoshu International Center, 1983), p. 417.

25 See Hisao Inagaki, *The Way of Nembutsu-Faith: A commentary on Shinran's Shoshinge* (Kyoto: Nagata Bunshodo, 1996), *passim.*

26 An observation made to me by Jim Pym of the Pure Land Buddhist Fellowship. For a record of Ippen, see Fujiyoshi Jikai, "Jodoshu", in *ER*, vol. 8, p.106. More particularly, see Dennis Hirota, *No Abode: The record*

of *Ippen* (Honolulu: University of Hawai'i Press, revised edn 1997, first published 1986), *passim*.

27 Deisetz Taitaro Suzuki, *Buddha of Infinite Light* (London: Shambala, 1997; completely revised edn of Suzuki's *Shin Buddhism*, first published by Harper and Row in 1970 from a talk given by the author in 1958 at the American Buddhist Academy in New York City), p. 61.

28 Fujita Kotatsu, "Pure and Impure Lands", in *ER*, vol. 12, p. 90.

29 See Suzuki, *Buddha of Infinite Light*, pp. 55–67.

30 Hase Shoto, "Jodo Shinshu", in *ER*, vol. 8, p. 102.

31 "Own-power", it should be noted, is not the same as "self-effort", which is a misunderstanding of Jodo Shinshu; see Joren Macdonald, "The Importance of Self Effort" in *Pure Land Notes*, New Series no. 10 (Oxford: Pure Land Buddhist Fellowship, September 1997), pp. 2–3.

32 H. Byron Earhart, *Japanese Religion* (Belmont: Wadsworth, 3rd edn 1982), p. 94. More particularly, see Bloom, *Strategies for Modern Living*, pp. 4–5.

33 Inagaki, *The Way of Nembutsu-Faith*, p. 37.

34 Daisetz Taitaro Suzuki, "Rennyo's Letters", in *Mysticism Christian and Buddhist* (London: Unwin, 1979, reprint of 1957 edn), pp. 119–24. See also Suzuki, *Buddha of Infinite light*, p. 39.

35 Philip Kapleau, in Thich Nhat Hanh, *Zen Keys* (London: Doubleday, 1995, first English edn, New York: Anchor: Doubleday, 1974), p. 8.

36 John Crook, "Awareness in Everyday Life", in *Western Ch'an Forum* (Lancs: The Western Ch'an Fellowship, Autumn 1995), pp. 14–15.

37 George Gatenby and John Paraskevopoulos, *A Primer of Shin Buddhism* (Neutral Bay, NSW: Honganji Buddhist Mission, Australia, 1995), p. 12.

38 Zurcher, "Amitabha", p. 236.

39 Kotatsu, "Pure and Impure Lands", p. 90.

6 Religious Taoism

1 It was Ch'in Shih Huang-ti/Qinshi Huangdi, who gave his name to China, who had the Great Wall of China built, and the famous "terracotta army" constructed.

2 The Han dynasty was divided into the Former or Western Han (206 BCE–9CE), and the Later or Eastern Han (9–23 CE).

3 See Donald Harper, "Warring States, Qin and Han Manuscripts Related to Natural Philosophy and the Occult" in Edward L. Shaughnessy (ed.), *New Sources of Early Chinese History: An introduction to the reading of inscriptions and manuscripts* (Berkeley, California: Society for the Study of Early China, and The Institute of East Asian Studies, University of California, 1997), p. 224.

4 Kenneth J. DeWoskin, *Doctors, Diviners, and Magicians of Ancient China: Biographies of Fang-shih* (New York: Columbia University Press, 1983), p. 10.

5 For a general overview of religious trends in the Han, see Mark Csikszentmihalyi, "Han Cosmology and Mantic Practices" in Livia Kohn

(ed.), *Daoism Handbook* (Leiden, Boston, Köln: Brill, 2000), pp. 53–73.

6 *Ibid.*, p. 57.

7 Chang Chüeh/Zhang Jue, Chang Liang/Zhang Liang and Chang Pao/Zhang Bao.

8 Tsuchiya Masaaki, "Confession of Sins and Awareness of Self in the *Taiping jing*" in Livia Kohn and Harold D. Roth (eds), *Daoist Identity: History, lineage, and ritual* (Honolulu: University of Hawaii Press, 2002), p. 54.

9 For the content of the *Scripture*, see Barbara Hendrischke, "Early Daoist Movements" in Kohn (ed.), *Daoist Handbook*, pp. 147–52.

10 Julian F. Pas in cooperation with Man Kam Leung, *Historical Dictionary of Taoism* (Lanham, Middlesex and London: The Scarecrow Press, 1998), p. 143.

11 For a full description of talismans and registers see Catherine Despeux, "Talismans and Sacred Diagrams" in Kohn (ed.), *Daoist Handbook*, pp. 498–540. Despeux writes of talismans and diagrams: "Formed by the spontaneous coagulation of cosmic energies and transmitted by the gods, all these sacred documents are contracts that give their holders power over divine troops and ensure the authenticity of scriptural transmission to human society . . ." (p. 498).

12 Joseph Needham, *Science and Civilisation in China, Vol. 2: History of scientific thought* (Cambridge: Cambridge University Press, 1956), p. 437.

13 Isabelle Robinet, "Shangqing – Highest Clarity" in Kohn (ed.), *Daoist Handbook*, p. 210.

14 Fabrizio Pregadio, "Elixirs and Alchemy" in Kohn *ibid.*, p. 168.

15 Robinet, "Shangqing – Highest Clarity", pp. 196–7.

16 John Lagerway, "The Taoist Religious Community" in Mircea Eliade (ed.), *The Encyclopedia of Religion* (hereafter *ER*, New York and London: Macmillan Publishing Company and Collier Macmillan Publishers, 1987), 14: p. 309.

17 However, the T'ang/Tang should not be seen as a totally clear success for Taoism. Kohn and Kirkland point out that gaps in priestly lineages such as at the Taoist centre at Mao Shan suggest leaner times of success. Livia Kohn and Russell Kirkland, "Daoism in the Tang (618–907)" in Kohn (ed.), *Daoist Handbook*, p. 349.

18 Lowell Skar, "Ritual Movements, Deity Cults, and the Transformation of Daoism in Song and Yuan Times" in Kohn (ed.), *ibid.*, p. 413.

19 For a succinct summary of Taoist movements from the twelfth century to the present, see Russell Kirkland, "The History of Taoism: A new outline" *Journal of Chinese Religions* 30 (2002), pp. 187–92.

20 Pregadio, "Elixirs and Alchemy", pp. 165–91.

21 Tu Wei-ming, "Soul: Chinese Concepts" in *ER*, 13: p. 448.

22 Isabelle Robinet, *Taoism: Growth of a religion*, translated by Phyllis Brooks (Stanford, California: Stanford University Press, 1997, first published in Paris in 1992 as *Histoire du Taoïsme des origines au XIVe siècle*), p. 14.

23 Cinnabar is the oxide of mercury.

24 Livia Kohn (ed.), *The Taoist Experience: An anthology* (Albany, New York: State University of New York Press, 1993), p. 133.

25 Michael Page, *The Power of Ch'i: An introduction to Chinese mysticism and philosophy* (Wellingborough, Northamptonshire: The Aquarian Press, 1988), p. 11.

26 Chang Po-tuan/Zhang Boduan, *Understanding Reality* 1:1, translator Thomas Cleary, *The Taoist Classics: The collected translations of Thomas Cleary, Vol. 2* (Boston, Massachusetts: Shambhala, 2003, first published 1986), p. 35.

27 Isabelle Robinet, "Original Contributions of *Neidan* to Taoism and Chinese Thought" in Livia Kohn (ed.) in cooperation with Yoshinobu Sakade, *Taoist Meditation and Longevity Techniques*. Michigan Monographs in Chinese Studies, vol. 61 (Ann Arbour: Centre for Chinese Studies, The University of Michigan, 1989), p. 322.

28 Needless to say, this was not a reciprocal, two-way process: only one of the two could benefit, the woman preventing orgasm but receiving male semen, or – and more frequently – the male preventing ejaculation (achieved by applying pressure to a point in the perineal region in order to block the urethra) and receiving energy from the woman's orgasm. Love, passion and desire do not enter into the contract, for if they do energy is lost, not gained. The aim is purely pragmatic in generating *ching/jing*, and considerable training has to be undergone in order to make the sexual act free of ego and desire. The more partners one has, the greater the acquisition of energy gained. The younger and healthier the partner, the better the quality of energy. As Wile comments on this point: "Partners are chosen then on the criteria of looks, feel, freshness, and taste – like fruit in the marketplace" (Douglas Wile, *Art of the Bedchamber: The Chinese Yoga Classics including women's solo meditation texts* (Albany, New York: State University of New York Press, 1992), p. 7.

29 For a detailed description of such processes, see Joseph Needham, *Science and Civilisation in China, Vol. 5, Chemistry and Chemical Technology Part 5: Spagyrical Discovery and Invention: Physiological alchemy* (Cambridge: Cambridge University Press, 1983), pp. 52–67.

30 For a very concise and clear description of these changes see Eva Wong, translator, *Cultivating Stillness: A Taoist manual for transforming body and mind* (Boston, Massachusetts and London: Shambhala, 1992), p. 133–4.

31 *Li* and *K'an/Kan* are the products of the union of *Ch'ien/Qian* and *K'un/Kun*. That union causes the middle lines of the trigrams *Li* and *K'an/Kan*. The *yin* in the middle of the trigram *Li* is called "True Lead", and is descending. The *yang* in the middle of *K'an/Kan* is "True Mercury" and is rising. They are dynamic representations of the original, primal *yin* and *yang* in the pure trigrams of Heaven and Earth. Ordinarily, the *yang* has the tendency to rise towards Heaven, or the head in the human body, and the *yin* is striving to descend to pure Earth and to the lowest cinnabar field of the body. Bringing the two together in a central place of the body is the goal.

In the alchemical process, the *yang* in the Water is used to settle the *yin* in Fire: the Water rises and the Fire descends, inverting their normal functions.

32 Titus Burckhardt, *Alchemy* (Shaftesbury, Dorset: Element Books, 1987 impression of 1986 edn, first published 1960), p. 123.

33 Laurence G. Thompson, *Chinese Religion: An introduction* (Belmont, California: Wadsworth Publishing Company, 1989 fourth edn, first published 1979), p. 36.

34 We have used the term "veneration" to avoid the pitfalls that the more frequently used expression "worshipped" suggests. For in fact, while ancestors of the great emperors frequently found themselves deified and ritually approached as such, in the wider context of family life, ancestors were respected and venerated, but hardly worshipped, though reciprocal aid might be expected between the living and the dead. Such a concept was the foundation of much Chinese belief and practice from ancient times, and remained so throughout its long history.

35 Stephen F. Teiser, "Introduction" in Donald S. Lopez, Jr. (ed.), *Religions of China in Practice* (Princeton, New Jersey: Princeton University Press, 1996), pp. 26–7.

36 Martin Palmer and Zhao Xiaomin, *Essential Chinese Mythology: Stories that change the world* (London: Thorsons, 1997), p. 30.

37 See Henri Maspero, *Taoism and Chinese Religion* translated by Frank A. Kierman, Jr. (Amherst: The University of Massachusetts Press, 1981, first published in 1971 as *Le Taoïsme et les Religions Chinoises*), pp. 86–7.

38 Sarah Allen, *The Shape of the Turtle: Myth, Art, and Cosmos in Early China* (Albany, New York: State University of New York Press, 1991), p. 64.

39 Livia Kohn (ed.), *The Taoist Experience: An anthology* (Albany, New York: State University of New York Press, 1993), pp. 351–2.

40 Anna Seidel, "Huang-ti", in *ER*, 6, p. 485.

41 The Celestial Venerable of the Primordial Beginning, also called the Celestial Venerable of Jade Clarity (Yü-ching/Yujing), and Tao of Majestic Vacuity, heads the triad. His name, Yüan-shih T'ien-tsun/Yuanshi Tianzun has survived from T'ang/Tang times. The Celestial Venerable of the Numinous Treasure, or Magic Jewel, is also called the Mysterious Majesty of the Jade Aurora, the Eminent Saint of Supreme Purity. His name is Ling-pao T'ien-tsun/Lingbao Tianzun, though he is sometimes referred to as T'ai-shang Tao-chün/Taishang Daozun "Supreme Lord of Tao". As the second of the Three Pure Ones, he rules over the Heavens of Supreme Purity, Shang-ch'ing/Shangqing. The third of the Three Pure Ones is Celestial Venerable of *Tao* and *Te*, Tao-te T'ien-tsun/Daode Tianzun. In T'ang/Tang times he was known as T'ai-shang Lao-chün/Taishang Laojun, "Supreme Lord Lao-tzu/Laozi". Thus, he was the deified Lao-tzu/Laozi.

42 See the *Jinque dijun sanyuan zhenyi jing* "*The Scripture of the Three Primordial Realized Ones by the Lord of the Golden Tower*" in Kohn, *The Taoist Experience*, p. 204. There are, however other deities representing the same triad. Palmer warns: "This triad has taken many different shapes and

forms over the centuries, and to this day is capable of different sets of deities." Martin Palmer, *The Elements of Taoism* (Shaftesbury, Dorset and Rockport, Massachusetts: Element, 1991), p. 114.

43 T'ien-kuan/Tianguan is the Agent of Heaven, and is responsible for the prosperity and good fortune of people. Ti-kuan/Diguan is the Agent of Earth, and is especially concerned with absolving peoples' transgressions. Shui-kuan/Shuiguan is the Agent of Water, and is particularly associated with the overcoming of people's difficulties.

44 Livia Kohn, "The Lao-tzu Myth" in Livia Kohn and Michael LaFargue (eds), *Lao-tzu and the Tao-te-ching"* (Albany, New York: State University of New York Press, 1998), pp. 41–50.

45 See Charles Benn, "Religious Aspects of Emperor Hsüan-tsung's Taoist Ideology" in David W. Chappell (ed.), *Buddhist and Taoist Practice in Medieval Chinese Society: Buddhist and Taoist studies II* (Asian Studies at Hawaii no. 34, University of Hawaii: University of Hawaii Press, 1987), p. 130.

46 See Livia Kohn, *God of the Dao: Lord Lao in history and myth* (Ann Arbor: Center for Chinese Studies, The University of Michigan, 1998), p. 35.

47 *Ibid.*, p. 51.

48 See Suzanne E. Cahill, *Transcendence & Divine Passion: The Queen Mother of the West in medieval China* (Stanford, California: Stanford University Press, 1993), p. 3.

49 Particularly in the lengthy account of Tu Kuang-t'ing/Du Guangting in his *Yung-ch'eng Chi-hsien lu/Yongcheng Jixianlu*, "Records of the Assembled Transcendents of the Fortified Walled City", as well as in a number of poems.

50 But see Cahill, *Transcendence and Divine Passion*, p. 13.

51 *Ibid.*, pp. 13–14.

52 There have been many that have seen this more colourful and religious aspect of Taoism as a degenerate form of the earlier mystical philosophy so well expressed in the texts of the *Tao Te Ching/Daodejing* and the *Chuang-tzu/Zhuangzi*. The view, however, is a myopic one; for religious Taoism does not depart radically from some of the foundational ideas of philosophical Taoism; it is just that it is more social, more communal, more group-orientated than the latter. It supplies, in fact, the emotional and spiritual expressions of religion that permit the warmth of theistic belief, thus catering for the ordinary human being as opposed to the mystic recluse. It makes more sense, therefore, to view philosophical and religious Taoism as complementary rather than disparate, both supplying different needs within the same conceptual framework of creating harmony and balance between the self, the community of those alive and those dead, and *Tao*. For a sound paradigm of the periods of Taoism see Kohn, *God of the Dao*, pp. 163–7.

53 Asano Haruji, "Offerings in Daoist Ritual" in Kohn and Roth (eds), *Daoist Identity*, *passim*.

54 Maspero, *Taoism and Chinese Religion*, pp. 78–9.

55 Also known as Complete Realization, Complete Perfection, Realization of Truth or Perfect Truth Taoism.
56 Monica Esposito, "Daoism in the Qing" in Kohn (ed.), *Daoism Handbook*, p. 628.
57 John Blofeld, *Taoism: The quest for immortality* (London, Boston, Sydney, Wellington: Mandala, Unwin Paperbacks), pp. 98–9.
58 There are a number of excellent contemporary case studies of the *chiao/jiao* in south-east Asia particularly. See, for example, Kenneth Dean's work, *Taoist Ritual and Popular Cults of South-east Asia* (Princeton, New Jersey: Princeton University Press, 1993) and the descriptions of a *chiao/jiao* on the occasion of the birthday of a god, chapter 2, pp. 61–98. See also Michael Saso's work, *Taoism and the Rite of Cosmic Renewal* (Pullman, Washington: Washington State University Press, 1990 reprint of 1989 edn) *passim*. For a very vivid and warm account, that captures the atmosphere more than other works, see John Lagerwey, *Taoist Ritual in Chinese Society and History* (New York: Macmillan Publishing Company and London: Collier Macmillan, 1987), chapter 4. For celebration in Hong Kong, see Tanaka Issei, "The Jaio Festival in Hong Kong and the New Territories" in Julian F. Pas (ed.), *The Turning of the Tide: Religion in China Today* (Oxford, Hong Kong, New York: Hong Kong Branch Royal Asiatic Society in association with Oxford University Press, 1989), pp. 271–98.
59 For a succinct historical development of the concept of immortality see Benjamin Penny, "Immortality and transcendence" in Kohn (ed.), *Daoist Handbook*, pp. 119–22.
60 Robinet, *Taoism*, pp. 37–8.
61 Kristofer Schipper, *The Taoist Body*, translated by Karen C. Duval (Berkeley, Los Angeles, London: University of California Press, 1993, first published in 1982 as *Le corps taoïste*), p. 164.
62 For the full tale, see Kwok Man Ho and Joanne O'Brien (translators and eds), *The Eight Immortals of Taoism: Legends and fables of popular Taoism* (London, Sydney, Auckland, Johannesburg: Rider, 1990), pp. 61–3.
63 A term, according to Benn, that had many characteristics similar to those of deities, "Religious Aspects of Emperor Hsüan-tsung's Taoist Ideology", p. 130.
64 Strictly speaking the word "being" should be translated as "man". We have avoided genderized language where possible, but it needs to be remembered that the sage was almost invariably male, as is evident in what follows.
65 For distinction between the different terms, see Isabelle Robinet, *Taoist Meditation: The Mao-Shan Tradition of Great Purity*, translated by Julian F. Pas and Norman J. Girardot (Albany, New York: State University of New York Press, 1993, first published in French in 1979 as *Méditation taoïste*), pp. 42–8.
66 See Kohn, *The Taoist Experience*, pp. 280–1.
67 Hellmut Wilhelm, *Heaven, Earth, and Man in the Book of Changes: Seven Eranos Lectures* (Seattle and London: University of Washington Press, 1977), p. 179.

68 Livia Kohn, *Taoist Mystical Philosophy: The Scripture of Western Ascension* (Albany, New York: State University of New York Press, 1991), p. 142.

7 Neo-Confucianism

1 Douglas Wile, *Art of the Bedchamber: The Chinese sexual yoga classics including women's solo meditation texts* (New York: State University of New York Press, 1992), p. 191.
2 Kenneth Dean, *Lord of the Three in One: The spread of a cult in southeast China* (Princeton, New Jersey; Chichester, West Sussex: Princeton University Press, 1998).
3 Robert E. Allinson, "An Overview of the Chinese Mind" in Robert E. Allinson (ed.), *Understanding the Chinese Mind: The philosophical roots* (Oxford: Oxford University Press, 1989), p. 15. See also note 6, p. 25, in the same source.
4 See John H. Nagai and Evelyn Berthrong, *Confucianism* (Oxford: Oneworld, 2000), p. 91.
5 Benjamin Schwartz, "Some Polarities in Confucian Thought" in Arthur F. Wright (ed.), *Confucianism and Chinese Civilization* (Stanford, California: Stanford University Press, 1975, first published 1959), p. 3.
6 Wing-Tsit Chan, "Confucian Thought: Neo-Confucianism" in *Encyclopedia of Religion* (16 vols) edited by Mircea Eliade (New York: Macmillan, 1987, hereafter, *ER*), vol. 4, p. 24.
7 Jian Zang, "Women and the Transmission of Confucian Culture in Song China" in Dorothy Ko, Jahyun Kim Haboush, and Joan R. Piggott (eds), *Women and Confucian Cultures in Premodern China, Korea, and Japan* (Berkeley, Los Angeles, London: University of California Press, 2003), p. 129.
8 *Ibid.*
9 *Ibid.*, p. 124.
10 *Ibid.*, p. 138.
11 Dorothy and Thomas Hoobler, *Confucianism* (New York: Facts on File, second edn 2004, first published 1999), p. 48.
12 Xinzhong Yao, *An Introduction to Confucianism* (Cambridge, New York, Melbourne, Madrid, Capetown: Cambridge University Press, 2000), p. 99.
13 Angus Graham, *Two Chinese Philosophers: The Metaphysics of the Brothers Ch'eng* (La Salle, Illinois: Open Court, 1992, first published 1958), p. xxi.
14 Wing-tsit Chan, "Confucian Thought", p. 24.
15 Yao, *An Introduction to Confucianism*, p. 106.
16 See Wm Theodore de Bary and Irene Bloom (eds), *Sources of Chinese Tradition: Vol. 1 From Earliest Times to 1600* (New York: Columbia University Press, second edn 1999), pp. 698–9.
17 Arthur F. Wright, *Confucianism and Chinese Civilization*, p. xiv.
18 See chapter 3, *Confucianism*.
19 Robert Cummings Neville, "Orientation, Self and Ecological Posture" in Mary Evelyn Tucker and John Berthrong (eds), *Confucianism and Ecology*

(Cambridge, Massachusetts: Harvard University Press, 1998), p. 268.

20 *Chuanxilu*, in *Wang Yangming quanshu (SBBY)* 2:4b-5a-*WTC*, translators de Barry and Bloom, *Sources of Chinese Tradition*, p. 849.

21 Hoobler and Hoobler, *Confucianism*, p. 58.

22 Yao, *An Introduction to Confucianism*, p. 117.

23 *Ibid.*, p. 128.

24 *Ibid.*, p. 126.

25 Jacques Gernet, *A History of Chinese Civilisation* vol. 2, translated by J. R. Foster and Charles Hartman (London: The Folio Society, 2002. This two-volume work was first published in French as a single volume entitled *Le Monde chinois*, Paris: Librairie Armand Colin, 1972), see plates following p. 692.

26 Fangqin Du and Susan Mann, "Competing Claims on Womanly Virtue in Late Imperial China" in Dorothy Ko, Jahyun Kim Haboush and Joan R. Piggott (eds), *Women and Confucian Cultures in Premodern China, Korea, and Japan* (Berkeley, Los Angeles, London: University of California Press, 2003), p. 242.

27 Chung-ying Cheng, "Recent Trends in Chinese Philosophy in China and the West" in Chung-ying Cheng and Nicholas Bunnin (eds), *Contemporary Chinese Philosophy* (Oxford: Blackwell, 2002), p. 353.

28 *Ibid.*, p. 354.

29 Yao, *An Introduction to Confucianism*, p. 252.

30 Jiyuan Yu, "Xiong Shili's Metaphysics of Virtue" in Chung-Ying Cheng and Bunnin (eds), *Contemporary Chinese Philosophy* (Oxford: Blackwell, 2002), pp. 127–46.

31 Yanming An, "Liang Shuming: Eastern and Western Cultures and Confucianism", in Chung-Ying Cheng and Bunnin (eds), *Contemporary Chinese Philosophy, ibid.*, pp. 147–64.

32 Lauren Pfister, "Feng Youlan's New Principle Learning and his Histories of Chinese Philosophy" in Chung-Ying Cheng and Bunnin (eds), *Contemporary Chinese Philosophy, ibid.*, pp. 165–87.

33 Jiwei Ci, "He Lin's Sinification of Idealism" in Chung-Ying Cheng and Bunnin (eds), *Contemporary Chinese Philosophy, ibid.*, p. 188.

34 Wing-tsit Chan, "Confucian Thought", p. 35.

35 For a full treatment of the contribution made to Chinese philosophy by such scholars, see Chung-ying Cheng, "Recent Trends in Chinese Philosophy in China and the West" in Chung-Ying Cheng and Bunnin, *Contemporary Chinese Philosophy*, pp. 349–64.

36 Wm Theodore de Bary, *The Trouble with Confucianism* (Cambridge, Massachusetts, London: Harvard University Press, 1996, first published 1991), pp. 87–112.

37 Joseph R. Levenson, *Confucian China and its Modern Fate*, 3 vols (London: Routledge and Kegan Paul, 1958–65), *passim. Cf* Yao, *An Introduction to Confucianism*, p. 274 and Rodney L. Taylor, *The Religious Dimensions of Confucianism* (New York: State University of New York, 1990), pp. 137–47.

38 Berthrong and Berthrong, *Confucianism*, p. 185.
39 John Berthrong, "Motifs for a New Confucian Ecological Vision" in Mary Evelyn Tucker and John Berthrong (eds), *Confucianism and Ecology*, p. 237.
40 Yao, *An Introduction to Confucianism*, p. 277.

8 Ch'an Buddhism

1 An interesting discussion of the word "Zen" is to be found in Andy Furguson, *Zen's Chinese Heritage* (Boston: Wisdom, 2000), p.1. The author notes that: "In China, from the sixth century onward, the word *Zen* . . . gained additional meaning and color."
2 Of the three credible texts from an early period that help to throw possible light on the historicity of Bodhidharma, the two main sources are in disagreement concerning the place where Bodhidharma first set foot on Chinese soil. See Heinrich Dumoulin, *Zen Buddhism: A History. Volume 1, India and China* (London, New York: Macmillan, 1988), p. 90.
3 See Sangharakshita, *The Essence of Zen* (Glasgow: Windhorse, 1992), p. 25.
4 Dumoulin, *Zen Buddhism*, p. 85.
5 Venerable Myoko-ni, "Zen – Tradition and History", in *The Middle Way*, vol. 73, no.1 (London: The Buddhist Society, May 1998), p. 14.
6 Ruth Fuller Sasaki, in Yanagida Seizan, *Chugoku zenshushi* (History of the Zen School in China), Volume 3 of *Zen no rekishi* (History of Zen), Suzuki and K. Nishitani (eds) (Tokyo, 1974), p. 8 following.
7 Dumoulin, *Zen Buddhism*, pp. 89–90.
8 *Ibid.*, p. 86.
9 Katsuki Sekida (translator, with commentaries) *Two Zen Classics: Mumonkan and Hekiganroku*, edited by A. V. Grimstone (New York: Weatherhill, 1977), Case 41, Bodhidharma's Mind Pacifying.
10 Kenneth Ch'en, *Buddhism in China: A Historical Survey* (Princeton, New Jersey: Princeton University Press, 1974), p. 353.
11 Dumoulin, *Zen Buddhism*, p. 111. For further discussion, see note 22.
12 Fung Yu-lan, *A History of Chinese Philosophy Volume 2*, translated by Derk Bodde (Princeton, New Jersey: Princeton University Press, 1952), p. 388.
13 *Ibid.*
14 Ch'en, *Buddhism in China*, p. 354.
15 Robert E. Buswell, Jr., *The Zen Monastic Experience: Buddhist practice in contemporary Korea* (Princeton, New Jersey: Princeton University Press, 1992), p. 220.
16 A concise biography of Hui-neng is found in Dumoulin, *Zen Buddhism*, pp. 129–37.
17 Dumoulin, *A History of Zen Buddhism* (London: Faber and Faber, 1963), p. 104.
18 Isabelle Robinet, *Taoism: Growth of a religion*. Translated from French by Phyllis Brooks, (Stanford, California: Stanford University Press, 1997, first published in 1992 as *Histoire du Taoïsme des origines au XIVe siècle*), p. 187.
19 Dumoulin, *Zen Buddhism*, p. 179.

20 Tenshin Fletcher and David Scott, *Way of Zen* (London: Vega, 2001), p. 58.

21 *Ching-te ch'uan-teng-lu*, vol. VI.

22 *Ibid.*

23 Katsuki Sekida, *Two Zen Classics*. Case 14. Nansen Cuts the Cat in Two.

24 *Ibid.*, Case 28. Ryutan Blows out the Candle.

25 I am indebted to Rupert Gethin for this stark observation.

26 Buswell, *The Zen Monastic Experience*, p. 4.

27 Deisetz Taitaro Suzuki, *The Training of the Zen Buddhist Monk* (Boston: Charles Tuttle, 1994, first published Kyoto: The Eastern Buddhist Society, 1934), p. xi.

28 Thomas Cleary, *The Five Houses of Zen* (Boston: Shambala, 1997), pp. vii–xvii.

29 Robert E. Allinson, *Chuang-Tzu for Spiritual Transformation* (New York: State University of New York, 1989), p. 9.

30 Isshu Miura and Ruth Fuller Sasaki, *The Zen Koan: Its History and Use in Rinzai Zen* (New York: Harcourt, Brace and World, 1965), pp. xi–xii.

31 Charles S. Prebish, *Historical Dictionary of Buddhism* (Metuchen, New Jersey and London: Scarecrow, 1993), p. 233.

32 Thomas Cleary, *Kensho: The Heart of Zen* (London: Shambala, 1997), p. xi.

33 A point made long ago by Candrakirti (flourished between 600 and 650 CE).

34 Although it was drawn to my attention recently that there are, "one or two Japanese monks" who might dispute this. See, Venerable Sochu, review of Merv Fowler, *Zen Buddhism: Beliefs and practices* (Brighton and Portland, Oregon, 2005) in *The Middle Way*, vol. 81. no. 3, November 2006, p. 180.

35 Great Master Dogen, "Shushogi. What is Truly Meant by Training and Enlightenment", reprinted in *An Introduction to the Tradition of Serene Reflection Meditation* (Mount Shasta, CA: Shasta Abbey Press, 1997, first published 1986), p. 13.

36 Reprinted in *An Introduction to the Tradition of Serene Reflection Meditation*, pp. 32–6.

37 *Serene Reflection Meditation Pamphlet* (no date), p. 2.

38 The Ox-herding sequence is described pictorially and in words in Merv Fowler, *Zen Buddhism: Beliefs and practices* (Brighton and Portland, Oregon: Sussex Academic Press, 1975), pp. 13–24.

39. A point well made by E. Herrigel, *Zen in the Art of Archery* (London: Routledge and Kegan Paul, 1982, first published 1953), *passim*.

40 See, recently, Merv Fowler, *Zen Buddhism: Beliefs and practices* (Brighton and Portland, Oregon: Sussex Academic Press, 2005), especially the last chapter entitled, "Holding the Mind".

41 Brian Gay, a lay minister of the Order of Buddhist Contemplatives in conversation with the authors.

42 Alan Watts, *The Way of Zen* (London: Arkana, 1990, first published 1957), p. 105.

43 Dumoulin, *A History of Zen Buddhism*, p. 195.

9 Popular Religion

1 Alvin P. Cohen, "Chinese Religion: Popular Religion" in Mircea Eliade (ed.), *The Encyclopedia of Religion* (hereafter *ER*, New York and London: Macmillan Publishing Company, 1987), 11: p. 290.

2 Meir Shahar and Robert P. Weller (eds), "Introduction: Gods and Society in China" in Meir Shahar and Robert P. Weller (eds), *Unruly Gods: Divinity and society in China* (Honolulu: University of Hawaii Press, 1996), p. 31.

3 Richard J. Smith, "Ritual in Ch'ing Culture" in Kwang-Ching Liu (ed.), *Orthodoxy in Late Imperial China* (Berkeley, Los Angeles, Oxford: University of California Press, 1990), p. 308.

4 Jack Potter, "Wind, Water, Bones and Souls: The Religious World of the Cantonese Peasant", *Journal of Oriental Studies* VIII, 1 (1970), cited in Laurence G. Thompson, *The Chinese Way in Religion* (Belmont, California: Wadsworth Publishing Company, 1973), p. 220.

5 See Shahar and Weller, "Introduction: Gods and Society in China", p. 22.

6 R. David Arkush, "Orthodoxy and Heterodoxy in Twentieth-Century Chinese Peasant Proverbs" in Kwang-Ching Liu (ed.), *Orthodoxy in Late Imperial China*, p. 331.

7 Shahar and Weller, "Introduction: Gods and Society in China", pp. 4–5.

8 Robert P. Weller, "Matricidal Magistrates and Gambling Gods: Weak States and Strong Spirits in China" in Shahar and Weller (eds), *Unruly Gods*, p. 261.

9 *Ibid.*, pp. 257–8.

10 *Ibid.*, p. 258.

11 *Ibid.*, p. 260.

12 *Ibid.*, p. 262.

13 Ellen Neskar, "Shrines to Local Former Worthies" in Donald S. Lopez, Jr. (ed.), *Religions of China in Practice* (Princeton, New Jersey: Princeton University Press, 1996), p. 293.

14 A point made by Shahar and Weller: "The bureaucratic image coexists with social deviance within the images of the gods themselves." Shahar and Weller, "Introduction: Gods and Society in China", p. 12.

15 See Anna Seidel, "Yü-huang" in *ER*, 15, p. 541.

16 Kristofer Schipper, *The Taoist Body* translated by Karen C. Duval (Berkeley, Los Angeles, London: University of California Press, 1993, first published in 1982 as *Le corps taoïste*), p. 87.

17 Livia Kohn, *God of the Dao: Lord Lao in History and Myth* (Ann Arbor, Michigan: Center for Chinese Studies, The University of Michigan, 1998), p. 139.

18 Meir Shahar, "Vernacular Fiction and the Transmission of Gods' Cults in Late Imperial China" in Shahar and Weller (eds), *Unruly Gods*, p. 185.

19 For the history of her cult and details about this goddess, see Brigitte Baptandier, "The Lady Linshui: How a Woman Became a Goddess" in Shahar and Weller *ibid.*, pp. 105–49.

20 See P. Steven Sangren, "Myths, Gods and Family Relations" in Shahar and Weller, *ibid.*, pp. 150–84.

21 Julia Ching, *Chinese Religions* (Basingstoke and London: Macmillan, 1993), p. 219.

22 He has a number of other names, too: Kuan-sheng Ti-chün/Guansheng Dijun, "Holy Emperor Lord Kuan/Guan" is perhaps the main one, but he is also called Wen-heng Ti-chün/Wenhen Dijun, Fu-mo Ta-ti/Fumo Dadi, Hsieh-t'ien Ta-ti/Xietian Dadi and En-chu kung/Enzhu Gong.

23 Shahar, "Vernacular Fiction and the Transmission of Gods' Cults in Late Imperial China", p. 199.

24 Kenneth Dean, "Daoist Ritual in Contemporary Southeast China" in Donald S. Lopez (ed.), *Religions of China in Practice* (Princeton, New Jersey: Princeton University Press, 1996), pp. 306–7.

25 Kwok Man Ho and Joanne O'Brien, translators and eds, *The Eight Immortals of Taoism: Legends and fables of popular Taoism* (London, Sydney, Auckland, Johannesburg: Rider, 1990), pp. 22–3.

26 For a full account of these see Henri Maspero, *Taoism and Chinese Religion* translated by Frank A. Kierman, Jr. (Amherst: The University of Massachusetts Press, 1981, first published in 1971 as *Histoire du Taoïsme des origins au XIVe siècle* in 1992), pp. 147–9.

27 Laurence G. Thompson, *Chinese Religion: An introduction* Belmont, California: Wadsworth Publishing Company, 1989 fourth edn, first published 1979), p. 63.

28 Paul R. Katz, "Enlightened Alchemist or Immoral Immortal? The growth of Lü Dongbin's Cult in Late Imperial China" in Shahar and Weller, *Unruly Gods*, pp. 70–104.

29 *Ibid.*, pp. 98–9.

30 Shahar, "Vernacular Fiction and the Transmission of Gods' Cults in Late Imperial China", p. 184.

31 Valerie Hansen, "Gods on Walls: A Case of Indian Influence on Chinese Lay Religion" in Patricia Buckley Ebrey and Peter Gregory (eds), *Religion and Society in T'ang and Sung China* (Honolulu: University of Hawaii Press, 1993), pp. 75–6.

32 See Angela Zito, "City Gods and their Magistrates" in Lopez (ed.), *Religions of China in Practice*, pp. 74–6 for a detailed discussion of this god, and the story surrounding his investiture.

33 Weller, "Matricidal Magistrates and Gambling Gods", pp. 260–1.

34 See Robert Hymes, "Personal Relations and Bureaucratic Hierarchy in Chinese Religion: Evidence from the Song Dynasty" in Shahar and Weller, *Unruly Gods*, pp. 66–7.

35 Zito, "City Gods and their Magistrates", p. 72.

36 *Ibid.*

37 Donald S. Sutton, "Transmission in Popular Religion: The Jiajiang Festival Troupe of Southern Taiwan", in Shahar and Weller, *Unruly Gods*, p. 239. See also *passim*, pp. 212–49.

38 See Julian F. Pas in cooperation with Man Kam Leung, *Historical Dictionary of Taoism* (Lanham, Middlesex and London: The Scarecrow Press, Inc., 1998), pp. 292–4.

39 These seem to have been current in ancient times, see Donald Harper, "Warring States, Qin, and Han Manuscripts Related to Natural Philosophy and the Occult" in Edward L. Shaughnessy (ed.), *New Sources of Early Chinese History: An introduction to the reading of inscriptions and manuscripts* (Berkeley, California: Society for the Study of Early China, and The Institute of East Asian Studies, University of California, 1997), pp. 233–4. According to Kwang-chih Chang, as early as Shang times, all the names of kings contained one or another of the Ten Stems, *Shang Civilization* (New Haven and London: Yale University Press, 1980), p. 5. The Shang also used the Ten Stems as a unit of time – ten days.

40 These are sometimes given different names: the Rat is sometimes the Mouse; the Ox, Bull or Buffalo; the Hare, a Rabbit; the Goat, a Sheep or Ram; the Rooster, Chicken or Fowl; the Pig, Boar.

41 See Yin-lien C. Chin, Yetta S. Center and Mildred Ross, *Chinese Folktales: An anthology* (Armonk, New York and London: North Castle Books, 1996), pp. 157–67.

42 See Christian Jochim, *Chinese Religions* (Upper Saddle River, New Jersey: Prentice Hall, 1986), pp. 152–6.

43 For a full description see Schipper, *The Taoist Body* pp. 20–3, and Thompson, *Chinese Religion*, pp. 68–74.

44 For a detailed account of traditional Chinese spirit divination see Richard J. Smith, *Fortune-tellers and Philosophers: Divination in traditional Chinese Society* (Boulder, San Francisco, Oxford: Westview Press, 1991), chapter 6, pp. 221–57.

45 Jean DeBernardi, "Teachings of a Spirit Medium" in Lopez (ed.), *Religions of China in Practice*, p. 230.

46 Called *chiao/jiao, pei/bei, pei-chiao/beijiao* or *chiao-kua/jiaogua*, see Smith, *Fortune-tellers and Philosophers* pp. 234 and 234–5 for a full description of their use.

47 See Wei Yi-min and Suzanne Coutanceau, *Wine for the Gods: An account of the religious traditions and beliefs of Taiwan* (Taiwan: Ch'eng Wen Publishing Company, 1976), pp. 26–7.

48 See David K. Jordan, *Gods, Ghosts, and Ancestors: The folk religion of a Taiwanese village* (Berkeley, Los Angeles, and London: University of California Press, 1972), pp. 6–2.

49 David K. Jordan and Daniel L. Overmyer, *The Flying Phoenix: Aspects of Chinese sectarianism in Taiwan* (Princeton, New Jersey: Princeton University Press, 1986), p. 125.

50 Smith gives a colourful account of such practice in Hong Kong, *Fortune-tellers and Philosophers*, pp. 1–3.

51 For an interesting account of the *daotan* religious spirit-writing organization in Hong Kong, see Shiga Ichiko, "Manifestations of Lüzu in Modern

Guangdong and Hong Kong: The Rise and Growth of Spirit-Writing Cults" in Livia Kohn and Harold D. Roth (eds), *Daoist Identity: History, Lineage, and Ritual* (Honolulu: University of Hawaii Press, 2002), pp. 185–209.

52 Jordan and Overmyer, *The Flying* Phoenix, pp. 13 and 36.

53 Jordan, *Gods, Ghosts, and Ancestors*, p. 104.

54 *Ibid.*, p. 103.

55 See David Faure, "Folk Religion in Hong Kong and the New Territories Today" in Julian F. Pas (ed.), *The Turning of the Tide: Religion in China today* (Oxford, Hong Kong, New York: Hong Kong Branch Royal Asiatic Society in association with Oxford University Press, 1989), p. 259.

56 For an account of these in Taiwan, see Avron A. Boretz, "Righteous Brothers and Demon Slayers: Subjectivities and Collective Identities in Taiwanese Temple Processions", in Paul R. Katz and Murray A. Rubinstein (eds), *Religion and the Formation of Taiwanese Identities* (New York and Basingstoke: Palgrave Macmillan, 2003), pp. 219–52.

57 Stephen H. West, "Drama" in William H. Nieuhauser, Jr. (ed. and compiler), *The Indiana Companion to Traditional Chinese Literature* (Bloomington: Indiana University Press, 1986), p. 14.

58 See Jordan, *Gods, Ghosts, and Ancestors*, p. 91. For a full account of ancestor offerings and ritual at special times, see Michael Saso, *Blue Dragon White Tiger: Taoist rites of passage* (Washington DC.: The Taoist Center, 1990), pp. 153–6.

59 Joseph A. Adler, *Chinese Religions* (London and New York: Routledge, 2002), p. 117.

60 See Anna Seidel, "Buying One's Way to Heaven: The Celestial Treasury in Chinese Religions", *History of Religions*, 17 (1978), p. 421.

61 See Saso, *Blue Dragon White Tiger* pp. 121–39 for detailed descriptions of life-cycle rites in Taoism.

62 Conrad Schirokauer, *A Brief History of Chinese Civilization* (San Diego, New York, Chicago, Austin, Washington D.C., London, Sydney, Tokyo, Toronto: Harcourt Brace & Company, 1991), p. 371.

63 David Johnson, "Popular Beliefs and Values" in William Theodore de Bary and Richard Lufrano (compilers and eds.), *Sources of Chinese Tradition: Vol. 2 from 1600 through the twentieth century* (New York: Columbia University Press, second edn 2000), pp. 85–6.

64 See Johnson, *ibid.*, and John Lagerwey, *Taoist Ritual in Chinese Society and History* (New York: Macmillan Publishing Company and London: Collier Macmillan, 1987), pp. 216–37.

65 For a full account see Thompson, *The Chinese Way in Religion*, pp. 140–53.

66 Donald E. MacInnis, *Religion in China Today: Policy and practice* (Maryknoll, New York: Orbis Books, 1989), p. 370.

10 Chinese Religions Today

1 Lucy Jen Huang, "The role of Religion in Communist Chinese Society" in

Laurence G. Thompson, *The Chinese Way in Religion* (Belmont, California: Wadsworth Publishing Company, 1973), p. 241.

2 See the biography of Jung Chang cited in Deborah Summer (ed.), *Chinese Religion: An anthology of sources* (New York and Oxford: Oxford University Press, 1995), p. 315.

3 *Ibid.*, p. 313.

4 1982 Policy Paper on religion cited in Julian F. Pas, "Introduction: Chinese Religion in Transition" in Julian F. Pas (ed.), *The Turning of the Tide: Religion in China today* (Oxford, New York and Hong Kong: Hong Kong Branch Royal Asiatic Society in association with Oxford University Press, 1989), p. 11.

5 Julia Ching, *Chinese Religions* (Basingstoke, Hampshire: Macmillan, 1993), pp. 211–12.

6 Xinzhong Yao, *An Introduction to Confucianism* (Cambridge, New York, Melbourne, Madrid, Capetown: Cambridge University Press, 2005 reprint of 2000 edn), p. 275.

7 Kenneth Dean, "Daoist Ritual in Contemporary South-east China", in Donald S. Lopez (ed.), *Religions of China in Practice* (Princeton, New Jersey: Princeton University Press, 1996), p. 310.

8 For these statistics, see Pas, "Introduction: Chinese Religion in Transition", pp. 8–9.

9 Restoration of temples, for example, has to be with official sanction, but there is some evidence to suggest that local people build temples anyway, and flout state requirements where they can. See Thomas A. Hahn, "New Developments Concerning Buddhist and Taoist Monasteries" in Pas, *The Turning of the Tide*, p. 88.

10 Pas, "Introduction: Chinese Religion in Transition", p. 20.

11 Kristofer Schipper, *The Taoist Body* translated by Karen C. Duval (Berkeley, Los Angeles and London: University of California Press, 1993, first published in 1982 as *Le corps taoïste*), p. 19.

12 For detail of today's Taoist practices in Fujian, see Kenneth Dean, "Revival of Religious Practices in Fujian: A Case Study" in Pas, *The Turning of the Tide*, pp. 51–78 and, also Dean, *Daoist Ritual and Popular Cults of South-east China* (Princeton, New Jersey: Princeton University Press, 1993), *passim*.

13 Laurence G. Thompson, *Chinese Religion: An introduction* (Belmont, California: Wadsworth Publishing Company, 1989 reprint of 1979 edn), p. 145.

14 See George Tanabe, Jr., "The Death and Rebirth of Buddhism in Contemporary Japan", in *Buddhist Studies Review*, vol. 23.2 (London: Equinox, 2006), pp. 249-58.

15 See Donald E. MacInnis, *Religion in China Today: Policy and practice* (Maryknoll, New York: Orbis Books, 1989), pp. 367–8.

16 See the excerpt from Helen F. Siu's *Reforming Tradition: Politics and popular rituals in contemporary China*, in MacInnis, *ibid.*, pp. 368–72.

17 Stevan Harrell in a private letter to Donald MacInnis, *ibid.*, p. 373.
18 Julian F. Pas, "Revival of Temple Worship and Popular Religious Traditions" in Pas, *The Turning of the Tide*, pp. 176–7.
19 J. J. Clarke, *The Tao of the West: Western transformations of Taoist thought* (London and New York: Routledge, 2000), p. 37.
20 For a comprehensive study of T'ai Chi Ch'üan/Taijiquan see Jeaneane Fowler and Shifu Keith Ewers, *T'ai Chi Ch'üan: Harmonizing Taoist belief and practice* (Brighton: Sussex Academic Press, 2005).
21 Paul Crompton, *Tai Chi: An introductory guide to the Chinese art of movement* (Shaftesbury, Dorset and Boston, Massachusetts: Element, 2000, first published in different format in 1990), p. 119.
22 Douglas Wile, *Lost T'ai-chi Classics from the Late Ch'ing Dynasty* (Albany, New York: State University of New York Press, 1996), p. xv.
23 Paul Crompton, *Tai Chi: An introductory guide to the Chinese art of movement* (Shaftesbury, Dorset, Boston, Massachusetts and Melbourne, Victoria: Element, 2000, first published in different format in 1990 as *The Elements of Tai Chi* also by Element), p. 7.
24 Catherine Despeux, "Gymnastics: The Ancient Tradition" in Livia Kohn (ed.) in cooperation with Yoshinobu Sakade, *Taoist Meditation and Longevity Techniques*. Michigan Monographs in Chinese Studies, vol. 61 (Michigan: Center for Chinese Studies, The University of Michigan 1989), p. 241.
25 *Ibid.*, p. 239.
26 Stuart Alve Olson, *T'ai Chi According to the I Ching: Embodying the principles of the Book of Changes* (Rochester, Vermont: Inner Traditions, 2001), pp. 11–12.
27 Patricia Buckley Ebrey, "The Response of the Sung State to Popular Funeral Practices" in Patricia Buckley Ebrey and Peter N. Gregory (eds), *Religion and Society in T'ang and Sung China* (Honolulu: University of Hawaii Press, 1993), p. 215.
28 Eva Wong, *The Shambhala Guide to Taoism* (Boston, Massachusetts and London: Shambhala, 1997), p. 138.
29 With limited knowledge of *feng-shui* when we bought our home twenty-five years ago, we now find it to be in a perfect spot! It is protected from high winds by hills behind it in the north. It is a place where a stream meanders slowly, and it nestles in the embrace of hills that provide protection, rather like an armchair, with a sloping view to the south. See Michael Page, *The Power of Ch'i: An introduction to Chinese Mysticism and Philosophy* (Wellingborough, Northamptonshire: The Aquarian Press, 1988), p. 80.
30 Jack Potter, "Wind, Water, Bones and Souls: The Religious World of the Cantonese Peasant", *Journal of Oriental Studies* 8 (1970), cited in Laurence G. Thompson, *The Chinese Way in Religion* (Belmont, California: Wadsworth Publishing Company, 1973), p. 221. Potter's research was based on his study of the village of Ping Shan in the New Territories of Hong Kong in 1961–3. It makes interesting reading, particularly concerning the lengths

to which the villagers go to adopt the principles of *feng-shui* – even to the extent of growing a moustache to change the energies in one's face! See pp. 218–30 in the same source.

31 Richard Craze, *Practical Feng Shui: The Chinese art of living in harmony with your surroundings* (London, New York, Sydney, Bath: Lorenz Books, 1997), p. 15.
32 Kwok Man-ho with Joanne O'Brien, *Feng Shui: An introductory guide to the Chinese way to harmony* (Shaftesbury, Dorset, Boston, Massachusetts and Melbourne, Victoria: Element, 1999, first published in different format in 1991), pp. 11–12.
33 Page, *The Power of Ch'i*, p. 78.
34 Jean Cooper, *Yin and Yang: The Taoist harmony of opposites* (Wellingborough, Northamptonshire: The Aquarian Press, 1981), p. 43.
35 Eva Wong, *Feng-shui: The ancient wisdom of harmonious living for modern times* (Boston, Massachusetts and London: Shambhala, 1996), p. 255.
36 Gill Hale, *The Practical Encyclopedia of Feng Shui* (London: Hermes House, 2001, first published 1999), p. 7.

词汇表

Glossary of Chinese Names and Terms

Amida/Amitabha	the Buddha of the Western Paradise in Devotional Buddhism.
Analects	(Chin. *Lun-yü/lunyu*) conversations recollected as having taken place between Confucius and his disciples or between Confucius and the rulers of various feudal states that he visited.
Avalokitesvara	the Buddhist *Bodhisattva of Compassion*, also found in female form as the goddess Kuan-Yin/Guanyin (Jap. Kwannon) "Regarder of the Cries of the World".
Bodhidharma	the Indian monk credited with personally introducing to China the form of Buddhism known as Ch'an (Jap. Zen).
Chang Chüeh/Zhang Jue	one of the three Chang/Zhang brothers who founded Way of Great Peace Taoism, and led the Yellow Turbans against the Han in 184.
Chang Liang/Zhang Liang	one of the three Chang/Zhang brothers who founded Way of Great Peace Taoism, and led the Yellow Turbans against the Han in 184.
Chang Lu/Zhang Lu	grandson of the founder of Five Bushels of Rice and Celestial Masters Taoism, who consolidated his grandfather's work.
Chang Pao/Zhang Bao	one of the three Chang/Zhang brothers who founded Way of Great Peace Taoism, and led the Yellow Turbans against the Han in 184.
Chang Po-tuan/Zhang Boduan	tenth to eleventh century Taoist and inner alchemist; traditional founder of the Southern branch of inner alchemy.

Chang San-feng/Zhang Sanfeng	the traditional founder of T'ai Chi Ch'üan/Taijiquan.
Chang Tao-ling/Zhang Daoling	founder of Five Bushels of Rice and Celestial Masters Taoism in the early second century.
Chang Tsai/Zhang Zai	one of the Five Neo-Confucian Masters of the early Sung/Song period.
Ch'eng Hao/Cheng Hao	one of the Five Neo-Confucian Masters of the early Sung/Song period.
Ch'eng I/Cheng Yi	one of the Five Neo-Confucian Masters of the early Sung/Song period.
Cheng-i Meng-wei Tao/ Zhengyi Mengweidao	Way of Orthodox Unity Taoism (Celestial Masters).
cheng-ming/zhengming	the doctrine of social and moral order known as the "rectification of names", the so-called Five Relationships of Confucianism.
*chen-jen/zhenren*a	Taoist term for "perfected, true, real, being".
ch'i/qi	energies within and surrounding all things; vitality.
chiao/jiao	pure sacrifice, ceremonial offerings.
Chih-i/Zhiyi	the first great systematic architect of the T'ien-t'ai/Tiantai school of Buddhism, also known by the name of the school.
chih-jen/zhiren	"perfect being".
ching/jing	essence; the liquid element of the body, including saliva, sweat, semen and gastric juices.
Ch'in Shih Huang-ti/ Qinshi Huangdi	the first Emperor of China.
Chou I/Zhouyi	*The Changes of the Chou/Zhou*, the early name for the *I Ching/Yijing*.
Chou Tun-i/Zhou Dunyi	one of the Five Neo-Confucian Masters of the early Sung/Song period.
Ch'üan-chen/Quanzhen	Complete Reality school of Taoism.
Chuang-tzu/Zhuangzi	a Taoist classic, said to have been written by Chuang-tzu/Zhuangzi.
Chuang-tzu/Zhuangzi	an early sage, traditional author of the *Chuang-tzu/Zhuangzi.*
Chuan-hsü/Zhuanxu	one of the mythical Five August Emperors.
Chu Hsi /Zhu Xi	a Neo-Confucian master whose influence was second only to that of Confucius himself.
chün-tzu/junzi	the central focus of the *Analects* and the Confucian term for "noble man", "son of the ruler", "superior man" or "gentleman".
Confucius	the Latinized form of K'ung Fu-tzu/Kong Fuzi, a reverend title for K'ung-ch'iu/Kong Qiu or K'ung Chung-ni/Kong Zhongni.

dokusan and *sanzen*	the formal, private meeting between master and pupil in Zen Buddhism, especially Rinzai. Today, both technical terms are virtually synonymous.
fang-shih/fangshi	an early diverse group of people who practised divination, magic, medicine, and the like, and who promoted ideas of immortality.
fa-shih/fashi	Red-head Taoist priests.
Fa-tsang/Fazang	the first great architect of the Hua-yen/Huayan (Flower Garland) school of Buddhism.
Fa-yen/Fayan	one of the Five Houses of Zen.
feng-shui	"earth magic", geomancy.
Fu Hsi/Fu Xi	mythical Emperor, the founder of hunting and animal husbandry; reputed founder of the eight trigrams.
hsien/xian	an immortal.
hsing/xing	human nature.
hsin/xin	the heart/mind.
Hsi Wang-mu/Xiwangmu	the goddess Queen Mother of the West.
Hsüan-hsüeh/Xuanxue	"Mystery Learning" metaphysical, eclectic school of Taoism.
Hsüan-tsung/Xuanzong	eighth century Emperor of the T'ang/Tang dynasty.
Hsüan-yüan chaio/Xuanyuan jiao	recently founded "Yellow Emperor Religion" in Taiwan.
Hsü Hui/Xu Hui and Hsü Mi/ Xu Mi	two persons to whom the Shang-ch'ing/Shang-qing scriptures were revealed.
Hsün-tzu/Xunzi	an outstanding pupil of Confucius, passionate in his loyalty to the teachings of the master.
Huai-nan-tzu/Huainanzi	second century text.
Huang-po Hsi-yün/Huangbo Xiyun	one of four dominant figures in the Zen Buddhist movement after Hui-neng.
Huang-ti/Huangdi	the Yellow Emperor.
Huang-ti Nei-ching/Huangdi Neijing	the *Yellow Emperor's Classic of Internal Medicine.*
Hua-yen/Huayan	the Buddhist Flower Garland school, the second of the great multi-system schools.
Hui-k'o/Huike	(formerly Shen-kuang), Bodhidharma's successor.
Hui-neng	the sixth patriarch of Ch'an Buddhism.
Hui-ssu/Huisi	said to be the founder of the T'ien-t'ai/Tiantai school of Buddhism.

hun	the spirit that survives the body at death and that transforms into a *shen*.
Hung-jen/Hongren	the fifth patriarch of Ch'an Buddhism.
i/yi	"righteousness", "right intention".
I Ching/Yijing	*Book of Changes*, the ancient Chinese *Classic* concerning change and transformation in the universe.
I-nien san-ch'ien / yinian sanqian	(Jap. *ichinen sanzen*) an immense philosophical system put forward by T'ien-t'ai/Tiantai as an explanation of the unity and interconnectedness of the universe.
jen/ren	"love", "humaneness".
ju/ru	an ancient Chinese tradition. Confucius is credited with being an outstanding *ju/ru* of his day.
karma	a Sanskrit term literally meaning action, but used in the sense of action and reaction (cause and effect).
Ko Ch'ao-fu/Ge Chaofu	founder of the Ling-pao/Lingbao tradition of Taoism.
Ko Hung/Ge Hong	fourth-century naturalist and alchemist, author of the *Pao-p'u-tzu/Baopuzi*.
K'ou Ch'ien-chih/Kou Qianzhi	reformer of the Celestial Masters school.
Kuan-ti/Guandi	God of War
kuei/gui	physical forms or ghosts after death.
Kuei-yang/Guiyang	one of the Five Houses of Zen. The others are Lin-chi/Linji (Jap.Rinzai), Yun-men/Yunmen, Ts'ao-tung/Caodong (Jap. Soto) and Fa-yen/Fayan.
kung-an	(Jap. *koan*) short, apparently paradoxical riddles, or slightly longer stories posed by Zen Buddhist masters.
kyosaku	"encouragement stick" used in some forms of Rinzai Zen Buddhism to return the mind wandering while meditating.
Lao-tzu/Laozi	early sage, traditionally the founder of Taoism and author of the *Tao Te Ching/Daodejing*.
li	propriety; reason; principle; the norms of correct social behaviour.
Li Chi/Liji	*Book of Rites* or *Rituals* from the Chou/Zhou dynasty.

Lieh-tzu/Liezi	early Taoist sage, traditional author of the text that bears his name.
Lin Chao-en/Lin Zhao'en	a cult figure widely worshipped today throughout south-east China and south-east Asia.
Lin-chi/Linji	(Jap. Rinzai) one of the Five Houses of Zen.
Lin-chi I-hsüan/Linji Yixun	one of four dominant figures in the Zen movement after Hui-neng.
Lin-chi-Lu/Linjilu	(Jap. *Rinzairoku*) a record of the sayings of the founder of the Lin-chi/Linji (Jap. Rinzai) school. Considered by some to be the ultimate in Zen literature.
ling	power.
Ling-pao/Lingbao Taoism	influential school of Taoism in the Six Dynasties period.
Liu P'ang/Liu Pang	the leading revolutionary who founded the Han dynasty in 206 BCE. He later became Emperor Kao-tsung/Gaozong.
Lotus Sutra	one of the most important of the Mahayana *sutras.*
Lu Hsiu-ching/Lu Xiujing	compiler of the first collection of Taoist scriptures in the fifth century, and founder of a splinter group of Celestial Masters Taoism in the South of China.
Lu	the small East China state where Confucius was born in 551 BCE.
Lü-shih Ch'un-ch'iu/Lüshi Chunqiu	*Annals of Spring and Autumn from the state of Lu* dated to Chou/Zhou dynasty times.
Lü Tung-pin/Lü Dongbin	one of the Eight Taoist Immortals.
Lü Yen/Lü Yan	Ancestor Lü, reputed forerunner of the Complete Reality school of Taoism and one of the Eight Taoist Immortals, also known as Lü Tung-pin/Lü Dongbin.
Mahavairocana	the central Buddha of Shingon Buddhism.
Ma-tsu/Mazu	a common rural woman who became a goddess, "Empress or Queen of Heaven", also called T'ien-shang Sheng-mu/Tianshang Shengmu.
Ma-tsu/Mazu	one of four dominant figures in the Zen movement after Hui-neng.
Meng-tzu/Mengzi	(Lat. Mencius) an outstanding pupil of Confucius.
mo-fa	(Jap. *mappo*) "the final phase of the Doctrine", the widely-held view in currency throughout

	East Asia at the beginning of the common era that, due to humanity's decadence, the downfall of the world was not only inevitable but imminent.
mondo	the "question and answer" method of instruction between master and pupil that became characteristic of Rinzai Zen (Chin. Lin-chi/Linji).
Nei-p'ien/Neipian	the esoteric chapters of Ko Hung/Ge Hong's *Pao-p'u-tzu/Baopuzi* dealing with Taoism.
nei-tan/neidan	inner or internal alchemy, the alchemy of the body.
nien-fo	(Jap. *nembutsu*) the repetition, either silently or chanted, of the name, or formula containing the name, of a Buddha or *bodhisattva* e.g, "I pay homage to (or take refuge in) Amida/Amitabha Buddha".
Nü-kua/Nügua	one of the Three August Ones, a mythical ancestor credited with the creation of humans.
Pai-chang	one of four dominant figures in the Zen movement after Hui-neng.
Pa-kua/Bagua	the basic eight trigrams of the *I Ching/Yijing* arranged in a circular system.
P'an-ku/Pangu	a mythical ancestor and source of the world according to one legend; also one of the Three August Ones.
Pao-p'u-tzu/Baopuzi	literally, "the Master that embraces simplicity", the literary name of the fourth century naturalist and alchemist Ko Hung/Ge Hong, and the name of a text that he wrote.
p'o/po	the physical *yin* spirit that survives after death and returns to the earth.
Sakyamuni	literally "the sage of the Sakyas" (tribe). The Buddha of early Indian Buddhism, Siddhartha Gautama.
samsara	a Sanskrit term taken into Chinese. It means "aimless wandering", a reference to the repeated cycle of redeath and rebirth.
Shang-ch'ing/Shangqing Taoism	influential school of Taoism in the Six Dynasties period.
Shang-ti/Shangdi	"Lord on High", the major deity of the Shang dynasty.

Shao Yung/Shao Yong	one of the Five Masters of the early Sung/Song period.
shen	spirit; the spiritual essence of the body.
sheng-jen/shengren	"sage", "saint".
shen-jen/shenren	"divine" or "spirit" beings.
Shen-nung/Shennong	ox-headed, mythical Emperor who founded agriculture and medicine.
shen spirits	*yang* spirits that rise from the body at death and that are capable of rebirth.
shih	phenomenon.
Shih Chi/Shiji	*Records of the Grand Historian* composed by Ssu-ma Ch'ien/Sima Qian in the second to first centuries BCE.
Shih Ching/Shijing	*Book of Poetry* or *Songs* from the Chou/Zhou dynasty.
Shu Ching/Shujing	*Book of Documents* from the Chou/Zhou dynasty.
Shun	one of the mythical Five August Emperors.
sunyata (*shunyata*)	a Sanskrit term taken into Chinese. It means "emptiness" (of inherent existence).
Ssu-ma Ch'ien/Sima Qian	second to first-century historian, author of the *Records of the Grand Historian*, the *Shih Chi/Shiji*.
Sukhavati	the best-known and one of many Pure Lands pivotal to Devotional Buddhism.
T'ai-i/Taiyi	"Supreme One/Changer/Transformer", the major deity of the Three Pure Ones.
T'ai-ping Ching/Taipingjing	*Scripture of Great Peace.*
T'ai-tsung/Taizong	a ruler of the T'ang/Tang dynasty in China who decided that Confucianism needed a material religious dimension, and subsequently ordered the establishment of Confucian temples throughout the realm in 630.
T'an-luan/Tanluan	the founder of Pure Land Buddhism in China.
tan-t'ien/dantian	a term in inner alchemy for three "cauldrons", three important areas of the body – upper middle and lower – which are important in the circulation and transmutation of energy in internal alchemy.
Tao	the non-manifest and manifest essence of the universe.
Tao-chia/Daojia	philosophical and mystical Taoism.
Tao-chiao/Daojiao	religious Taoism.

Tao-hsüeh/Daoxue	also *Li-hsüeh/Lixue* "The Learning of the Way" and "The Learning of the Principle" respectively in Neo Confucianism.
T'ao Hung-ching/ Tao Hongjing	founder of the Shang-ch'ing/Shangqing school of Taoism.
tao-jen/daoren	"being" or "person" of *Tao*.
tao-shih/daoshi	"specialists of Tao", or Black-head priests.
Tao Te Ching/Daodejing	text of eighty-one short chapters attributed to Lao-tzu/Laozi.
Tao-tsang/Daozang	the Taoist canon.
Te/De	the spontaneous, natural and rhythmic expression of *Tao* in the universe.
ti/di	ancestors and personal gods.
T'ien/Tian	Heaven.
T'ien-i/Tianyi	"Heavenly One", one deity of the Three Pure Ones.
T'ien-t'ai/Tiantai	a sixth-century Chinese Buddhist school.
Ti I/Tiyi	"Earthly One", one deity of the Three Ones.
Ts'ao-tung/Caodong	(Jap. Soto) one of the Five Houses of Zen.
Tsou Yen/Zou Yan	founder of the combined school of *Yi –Yang* and the Five Agents.
Tung Chung-shu/ Dong Zhongshu	an eminent Confucian scholar.
tzu-jan/ziran	naturalness, spontaneity.
Wai-p'ien/Waipian	the exoteric chapters of Ko Hung/Ge Hong's *Pao-p'u-tzu/Baopuzi*.
wai-tan/waidan	outer or external alchemy, the alchemy of the laboratory.
Wang Yang-ming	(also known as Wang Shouren) a highly influential Neo-Confucian of the Idealistic school of Lu Chiu-yüan/Lu Jiuyuan (Xiangshan), also castigated and blamed for the fall of the Ming dynasty.
wu	(Jap. *satori*) instant realization.
wu-hsing/wuxing	the Five Agents, Phases or Elements.
Wu-men-kuan	(Jap. *Mumonkan*) "The Gateless Gate", a famous Buddhist text by Wu-men Hui K'ai containing a collection of *koans*.
wu-wei	non-action. The concept of *wu-wei* in Rinzai Zen means the acquisition of the goal of enlightenment.
Yang Hsi/Yang Xi	fourth-century revealer of the scriptures of

	the Shang-ch'ing/Shangqing school of Taoism.
Yao	one of the mythical Five August Emperors.
yin and *yang*	the two complementary forces in all existence.
Yü/Yu	mythical founder of the Hsia/Xia dynasty according to some traditions, and one of the Five August Emperors; also known as K'ao-hsin/Kaoxin.
Yü-huang Shang-ti/Yuhuang Shangdi	the Jade Emperor.
Yun-men/Yunmen	one of the Five Houses of Zen.
zazen	the practice of sitting meditation central to all forms of Zen, but the most important factor in Soto Zen.

深层阅读

Further Reading

For **primary source** material on Chinese religions in general, two sources are invaluable – the detailed text of William Theodore de Bary and Irene Bloom (compilers, with the collaboration of Wing-tsit Chan), *Sources of Chinese Tradition Vol. 1: From earliest times to 1600* (New York: Columbia University Press, 1999 revised, second edition, first published in 1960), and the more succinct text by Deborah Sommer (ed.), *Chinese Religion: An anthology of sources* (New York and Oxford: Oxford University Press, 1995). As to **secondary sources**, a sound historical survey of Chinese history can be found in Conrad Schirokauer's *A Brief History of Chinese Civilization* (San Diego, New York, Chicago, Austin, Washington D.C., London, Sydney, Tokyo, Toronto: Harcourt Brace Gap College, 1991). An easy reader is Joseph A. Adler's *Chinese Religions* (London and New York: Routledge, 2002), as well as Christian Jochim's *Chinese Religions: A cultural perspective* (Upper Saddle River, New Jersey: Prentice-Hall, 1986). The sixteen-volume *Encyclopedia of Religion*, currently under revision and edited by Mircea Eliade (New York: Macmillan, 1987), is an excellent source for all aspects covered in this book.

For **secondary sources** on Confucianism, an excellent recent work is that of Xinzhong Yao, *An Introduction to Confucianism* (Cambridge, New York, Port Melbourne, Madrid, Capetown: Cambridge University Press, 2005 reprint of 2000 edn). The title of Rodney L. Taylor's work, *The Religious Dimensions of Confucianism* (Albany: State University of New York, 1990) speaks for itself, while William Theodore de Bary's, *The Trouble with Confucianism* (Cambridge, Massachusetts, London: Harvard University Press, 1991), raises some interesting questions.

There is a legion of translations of the short *Tao Te Ching/Daodejing* as a **primary source** of Taoism, and, since translations vary considerably, the serious reader is advised to consult a variety of them for comparison. The same may be said for the *I Ching/Yijing*, though here, Richard Rutt's *The Book of Changes (Zhouyi): A Bronze Age document translated with introduction and notes* (Durham East-Asia Series no. 1, London and New York: Routledge Curzon,

2002) provides an excellent account of the historical development of the *I Ching/Yijing*. Also, Edward Shaughnessy has translated the *I Ching/Yijing* from the second-century BCE Mawangdui texts in his *I Ching: The Classic of Changes* (New York: Ballantine Books, 1996). As to the *Chuang-tzu*, Angus Graham's *Chuang-Tzu: The Inner Chapters* (London, Boston, Sydney, New Zealand: Unwin Paperbacks, 1989) is excellent, as is Graham's *The Book of Lieh-tzu: A classic of the Tao* (New York: Columbia University Press, 1990, first published 1960). Another excellent translation of the *Chuang-tzu/Zhuangzi* is *The Book of Chuang Tzu* by Martin Palmer with Elizabeth Breuilly (London, New York, Victoria, Ontario, Auckland: Penguin, Arkana, 1996). For an anthology of Taoist texts, *The Taoist Experience: An anthology*, edited by Livia Kohn (Albany, New York: State University of New York Press, 1993) is an outstanding work.

A comprehensive **secondary source** introduction to Taoism can be found in Jeaneane Fowler's *Pathways to Immortality: An introduction to the philosophy and religion of Taoism* (Brighton, Sussex and Portland, Oregon: Sussex Academic Press, 2005). This book covers such aspects as the early period of China, Chinese cosmogony, classical and religious Taoism, and alchemy in greater depth than in the present book. A very expensive book, though with excellent entries, is that edited by Livia Kohn, *Daoist Handbook* (Leiden, Brill, 2000). A critical view of Taoism is to be found in *Taoism: The enduring tradition* by Russell Kirkland (New York and London: Routledge, 2004). A more mystical analysis of Taoism is the approach taken by Isabelle Robinet in her *Taoism: Growth of a religion* (Stanford, California: Stanford University Press, 1997). The book was first published in French in 1992 as *Histoire du Taoïsme des origins au XIVe siècle* and has been translated into English by Phyllis Brooks. Two excellent secondary sources devoted to the *Tao Te Ching/Daodejing* are Livia Kohn and Michael LaFargue (eds), *Lao-tzu and the Tao Te Ching* (Albany, New York: State University of New York Press, 1998), and Mark Csikszentmihalyi and Philip J. Ivanhoe (eds), *Religious and Philosophical Aspects of the Laozi* (Albany, New York: State University of New York Press, 1999).

Primary sources for the study of Pure Land Buddhism include *The Three Pure Land Sutras: A study and translation*, by Hisao Inagaki (Kyoto: Nagata Bunshodu, 1995), and *Strategies for Modern Living: A commentary with the text of the Tannisho*, by Alfred Bloom (Berkeley, California: Numata Center for Buddhist Translation and Research, 1992). A commentary on Shinran's *Shoshinge* is to be found in *The Way of Nembutsu-Faith* by Hisao Inagaki (Kyoto: Nagata Bunshodo, 1996). **Secondary sources** include the excellent introductory booklet by George Gatenby and John Paraskevopoulos, *A Primer of Shin Buddhism* (Neutral Bay, New South Wales: Hongwanji Buddhist Mission of Australia, 1995). A more complete introduction to the Pure Land tradition of Shin Buddhism is Taitetsu Unno, *River of Fire, River of Water* (New York: Doubleday, 1998). Engaged Buddhism in the Jodo Shinshu school is addressed in *Engaged Pure Land Buddhism: The challenges facing Jodo Shinshu* *in the contemporary world. Essays in honor of Professor Alfred Bloom*, edited by Kenneth K.Tanaka and Eisho Nasu (Berkeley, California: Wisdom Ocean, 1998).

Primary sources that record the poignant sayings of Zen masters include *Zen's Chinese Heritage: The Masters and their Teachings* by Andy Ferguson (Boston; Wisdom, 2000), and *The Old Zen Master: inspirations for awakening* by Trevor Leggett (Totnes: Buddhist Publishing Group. 2000). Similar works include *Two Zen Classics: Mumonkan and Hekiganroku*, translated by Katsuki Sekida (New York: Weatherhill, 1996, first published 1977), *Moon in a Dewdrop: Writings of Zen Master* Dogen, edited by Kasuaki Tanahashi (San Francisco: North Point Press, 1985), and *Zen Flesh, Zen Bones: A Collection of Zen and Pre-Zen Writings* by Paul Reps (Garden City, New York: Anchor Press, 1961).

For **secondary sources** on Zen Buddhism, we must look to Heinrich Dumoulin's two-volume work for the definitive word on the history of Zen Buddhism, *Zen Buddhism, A History: Volume 1, India and China* (London, New York: Macmillan, 1988), and *Zen Buddhism, A History: Volume 2, Japan* (London and New York: Macmillan, 1990). The Five Houses of Zen, which arose in China during the Golden Age of Zen, are the subject of Thomas Cleary's work, *The Five Houses of Zen* (Boston, Massachusetts: Shambhala, 1997). The history of Rinzai Zen Buddhism is detailed in Martin Colcutt's *Five Mountains: the Rinzai Zen Monastic Institution in Medieval Japan* (Cambridge, Massachusetts: Harvard University Press, 1981). Among the many introductions to Zen Buddhism are to be found *Zen Keys: A guide to Zen practice* by Thich Nhat Hanh (Berkeley, California: Parallax Press, 1995), and, more recently, Merv Fowler's *Zen Buddhism: Beliefs and practices* (Brighton, Sussex and Portland, Oregon: Sussex Academic Press, 2005).

There have been a number of field studies related to religious praxis in China and places like Taiwan and Hong Kong. Among the best are Kenneth Dean's *Taoist Ritual and Popular Cults of South-east China* (Princeton: Princeton University Press, 1995 reprint of 1993 edn), and David K. Jordan, *Gods, Ghosts and Ancestors: The folk religion of a Taiwanese village* (Berkeley, Los Angeles and London: University of California Press, 1972). Jordan has also collaborated with Daniel L. Obermyer to produce *The Flying Phoenix: Aspects of Chinese sectarianism in Taiwan* (Princeton, New Jersey: Princeton University Press, 1986). John Lagerwey writes very vividly on ritual in *Taoist Ritual in Chinese Society and History* (New York: Macmillan Publishing Company and London: Collier Macmillan, 1987). Julian Pas also deals with ritual and religion in China in *The Turning of the Tide: Religion in China today* (Oxford, Hong Kong, New York: Hong Kong Branch Royal Asiatic Society in association with Oxford University Press, 1989). Those interested in T'ai Chi Ch'üan/Taijiquan – either for its academic background and setting within a Taoist framework, or for its practical outcome in the Yang Style Simplified 24-Step Form, can find both in Jeaneane Fowler and Shifu Keith Ewers, *T'ai Chi Ch'üan: Harmonizing Taoist belief and practice* (Brighton, Sussex and Portland, Oregon: Sussex Academic Press, 2005).

索引

Index

Absolute, the 94, 215
acupuncture 39, 63
afterlife 34, 76, 152, 160 *see also* death and
 the dead
alchemy 53, 116, 140, 142, **144–52**, 155,
 157, 169, 259; inner 11, 143, 145,
 146–52, 156, 161 *see also nei-
 tan/neidan*; external/outer 143, 145
 see also wai-tan/waidan; sexual
 149, 282 n. 28
almanac 234, 238–9
anger 133, 136
altars 15, 33, 247, 252, 257
Amida/Amitabha/Amitayus 7, 127, 128,
 129, **129–30**, 131–2, 133, **135–8**, 219,
 220, 297
Amitayurdhana Sutra 130, 132
Analects 65, 69, 72, 73, 74, **75–80**, 85,
 178, 179, 186, 297
Ananda 117, 131, 132, 197
ancestors 16, 18, 19, 20, 21, 22, 23, 24, 26,
 27, 28, 29, 30, 31, 32, 33, 34, 35, 36–7,
 76, 114, 143, 152, 153, 154, 155, 225,
 226, 230, 237, 241, 246, 247, 248, 260;
 veneration of 4, 15, 16, 20, 26, 27,
 34, 36–7, 70, 78, 146, **152–4**, 246, 252,
 283 n. 34
ancient China **14–38**
Annals of Spring and Autumn (*Lü-shih
 Ch'un-ch'iu/Lüshi Chunqiu*) 5, 28,
 57, 58, 83, 89, 90
anthropomorphism 94, 154, 156, 163
Anti-Confucius Campaign 68

aristocracy/nobility 16, 20, 21, 25–6, 32,
 34, 66, 67, 81, 186, 187
astrology 32, 33, 140
astronomy 32, 33, 53, 140
atman 121, 138
Avalokitesvara 128, 131, 133, 231, 297
Avatamsaka Sutra 125, 218, 220

balance 1, 21, 27, 34, 48, 52, 53, 54, 59,
 62, 63, 72, 78, 82, 88, 103, 110, 150,
 152, 159, 166, 245, 259, 265
Big Dipper 157, 159
birth 109, 123
Bodhidharma 8, **196–201**, 211, 297
bodhisattva(s) 116, 117, 118, 121, 124,
 128, 129, 131, 132, 133, 135, 160, 164,
 205
body 23, 39, 50, 63, 109, 122, 126, 141,
 142, 143, 144–5, 146, 146–7, 148–9,
 150, 151, 152, 157, 246, 259, 260, 282
 n. 31; gates of 147, 149, 151
Book of Changes 175 *see also I
 Ching/Yijing*
Book of Documents/History (*Shu
 Ching/Shujing*) 6, 28, 58, **82**, 88, 90
Book of Mencius 177, 178, 179, 180
Book of Music 82, 89
Book of Poetry, Songs or *Odes* (*Shih
 Ching/Shijing*) 28, 30, **71**, 80, **82**, 90
Book of Rites/Rituals (*Li Chi/Liji*) 28,
 70, **83**, 178, 179
breath/breathing 145, 147, 148, 149, 150,
 246

Index **317**

Index   **319**

Personal Notes

Personal Notes

Personal Notes

Personal Notes